COMMUNICATION NETWORKS

COMMUNICATION NETWORKS

Toward a New Paradigm for Research

Everett M. Rogers
and
D. Lawrence Kincaid

 THE FREE PRESS
A Division of Macmillan Publishing Co., Inc.
NEW YORK

Collier Macmillan Publishers
LONDON

The Free Press
A Division of Macmillan Publishing Co., Inc.
866 Third Avenue, New York, N.Y. 10022

Collier Macmillan Canada, Ltd.

Library of Congress Catalog Card Number: 80–65202

Printed in the United States of America

printing number

1 2 3 4 5 6 7 8 9 10

Library of Congress Cataloging in Publication Data

Rogers, Everett M.
  Communication networks.

  Bibliography: p.
  Includes index.
  1. Communication—Network analysis.
2. Communications research. I. Kincaid,
D. Lawrence   joint author. II. Title.
P96.N48R6   1980   001.51   80-65202
ISBN 0-02-926740-4

CONTENTS

70518

PREFACE

The purpose of this book is to present what is currently known about communication networks and to illustrate methods of network analysis. *Communication network analysis* is a method of research for identifying the communication structure in a system, in which relational data about communication flows are analyzed by using some type of interpersonal relationship as the unit of analysis. This distinctive emphasis of network analysis upon communication links, rather than on isolated individuals, as the units of analysis, enables the researcher to explore the influence of other individuals on human behavior. Network analysis focuses upon the communication structure that people live within, making it visible, understandable, and manageable as a variable under study.

We shall argue, in chapter 2, that communication research in the past has almost entirely followed a linear, "components" model of the human communication act. Such research mainly investigated the effects of communication messages from a source to a receiver, in a one-way, persuasive-type paradigm that is not consistent with our basic conception of the communication process as mutual information-exchange, as sharing meanings, as convergence. Unfortunately, the dependence on individuals as the sole units of analysis in past communication research has severely constrained our capacity to study human communication as *a process of mutual information-exchange*

Network analysis is one promising step toward using the relationships of information-exchange as the units of analysis, and toward bringing the operations of communication research more closely in line with our theoretical conceptions of the nature of the communication process. Our work here is guided by a convergence model of communication based on a cybernetic explanation of human behavior from a systems perspective.

The investigation of communication networks is interdisciplinary in nature, involving sociologists, mathematicians, social psychologists, anthropologists, and several other social scientists, as well as communication scholars. *The central aspect captured in network analyses, however, is human communication.* That is why this book was written by two communication scientists, from a communication point of view, and why it stresses communication as the essential quality of all network relationships.

The study of networks is represented by a tremendous literature, begun by such social science forefathers as Georg Simmel and Jacob Moreno. But much of the interest in networks is of very recent vintage. For example, a comprehensive bibliography on social networks by Freeman (1976) lists over sixteen hundred publications, of which about 600 were added in the last year of the twenty-five years that were covered. Pitts' (1979) bibliography on network analysis included 481 items that were published in the 1970s.

Unfortunately, most of this network literature is (1) overmathematized, (2) confusing in terminology and concepts, and (3) devoid of much application that would aid the understanding of human behavior. Network analysis has been dominated in the past by tool-makers rather than tool-users. The field has been characterized by sophisticated methodologies looking for theoretical problems to answer. We know of one scholar who posted a sign on his office wall: "Network analysis is the answer, but what was the question?" The typical journal article about communication networks consists of a few paragraphs of prose, followed by five pages of formulae. Much of network methodology has been so highly quantitative that most social scientists, who might profitably use such analytical techniques, cannot understand them. Few of the elegant computer algorithms are widely available; several of the most sophisticated are "up" only on the computer of the scholar who developed them. Most of the tool-makers do not know the data they use to illustrate their methods; often the data are hypothetical, or else borrowed from another scholar's work. In the past, much of network analysis has amounted to an elaborate scaffold, without a building inside.

Further, the field of network analysis is a hopeless thicket of confusing concepts and measures of network dimensions: (1) the same network concept is used for different meanings, (2) the same dimension is called by different conceptual labels, and (3) different operational formulae are used by two scholars to measure the same concept (even when it is defined similarly). Almost every network researcher has his own pet concepts: density, connectedness, centrality, distance, proximity, integration, betweenness, and so on.

Unfortunately, there have been few convincing illustrations of how network analysis has improved our understanding of human behavior *over what could be achieved without considering network variables* (this issue is one of the main themes of the present book, especially in our chapters 5, 6, and 7).

Herein we seek to overcome these three main limitations (just cited) of past network literature.

1. We emphasize a communication network *philosophy*, rather than just analysis *techniques*. Most of our book is essentially nonmathematical,

with no more competence required than freshman college algebra. We advocate a convergence model of communication that stresses the mutual exchange of information in order to reach common meanings.

2. We follow a standard terminology in our network concepts and methods, one that is as consistent as possible with past communication research on networks.

3. We focus heavily (although not exclusively) on one set of empirical data to illustrate our approach to communication networks. These data come from an evaluation of a highly successful development program in the Republic of Korea, which is based on a strategy of mobilizing interpersonal networks through 28,000 mothers' clubs enrolling 750,000 members.

This evaluation, sponsored by the Asia Foundation and conducted with colleagues at Seoul National University, was specifically designed as a communication network analysis (unlike many other investigations in which network analysis techniques are imposed on data gathered with other purposes primarily in mind). We personally interviewed (1) 1,003 married, fertile-aged women living in a national sample of 24 Korean villages with mothers' clubs, and (2) the 69 women living in Oryu Li, a village with an unusually successful mothers' club that we analyze in chapter 1. Our purpose in using illustrations from the Korean data throughout this book is to provide a reality-based, common foundation for our theoretical framework as an aid to its understanding.

Many other network scholars have collaborated in producing the present book. Most important are Dr. Hyung Jong Park and Professor Kyung-Kyoon Chung of the School of Public Health, Seoul National University, who took the main responsibility for gathering the Korean data and making the first analyses. They were assisted by Dr. Dal Sun Han and Dr. Sea-Baick Lee at Seoul National University; Dr. Lee's doctoral dissertation at the University of Michigan dealing with network effects of the adoption of family planning is featured in chapter 5. Dr. Il-Chul Kim, Professor of Sociology at Seoul National University, collaborated on the study of village leadership and communication networks that we summarize in chapter 6.

Two graduate students from the East–West Communication Institute in Honolulu, Dr. June Ock Yum and Dr. Chin-Chuan Lee, helped conduct the case study of Oryu Li (Dr. Lee is now Assistant Professor of Communication at the Chinese University of Hong Kong). William S. Puppa and Brenda A. Doe, then research assistants at the University of Michigan, helped carry out the network analysis of villages "A" and "B," featured in chapters 4 and 6. We particularly utilize one computer-based method of data-analysis in this book, NEGOPY, developed by Dr. William D. Richards, Jr., at Michigan State University and at Stanford

University (Richards is presently Assistant Professor of Communications at Simon Fraser University). Professor Richards' comments on our draft chapters were especially useful.

In addition, we thank Dr. Lytton Guimarães, Dean, School of Communication, University of Brazilia, who pioneered a matrix multiplication computer program while we were colleagues at Michigan State University. We used this program for part of the network analysis in chapter 6. We also acknowledge Dr. Nan Lin, Professor of Sociology, State University of New York at Albany, for his network analysis research during our Michigan State days, and since.

The East–West Communication Institute sponsored part of the Korean research reported here and a series of annual workshops on communication network analysis. Four of our colleagues at Stanford University's Institute for Communication Research played an important role in the present book: Dr. David M. Dozier, whose doctoral dissertation on thresholds in the adoption of family planning is summarized in chapter 5; Joung-Im Kim, whose network analysis of Oryu Li appears in chapter 1; Katherine Strehl, who carried out the analysis of network variables and mothers' club performance (chapter 6); and Dora Schael, who assisted in the final editing and rewriting of the manuscript. The constructive comments of Ronald Rice were especially useful.

We began the Korean venture as what we thought was just another problem of applied research on communication and development. Because we attempted to collect data about communication networks, and because we listened very closely to the women of one village telling their own story of development, we began to make a sharp turn in our thinking, toward communication as a process of convergence. This change is presented in the present monograph as the first steps toward a new paradigm for communication theory and research. This book, it should be emphasized, is but a report of work in process, work that we expect will continue in the years ahead. We hope that communication network analysis will be taken up by our colleagues in this field, and improved over the humble illustrations that we offer herein.

EVERETT M. ROGERS
Institute for Communication Research
Stanford University

D. LAWRENCE KINCAID
East–West Communication Institute
Honolulu, Hawaii

1 THE MIRACLE OF ORYU LI

The sun will never rise when the hen crows.

Village elder in Oryu Li

*The Traditional rule that woman is inferior by nature, for example,
worked well so long as she was given no opportunities for trying
alternatives to her assigned sex- and work-roles.*

Daniel Lerner (1958, p. 399)

A man with an ax is no match for a woman with a needle.

Traditional Korean proverb

The village of Oryu Li lies about four hours' drive south of Seoul, first
along a superhighway to the provincial capital of Jeonju City, then forty
minutes more on a narrow paved road to the county seat town of Imsil,
and the final five miles on a dirt lane. In July of 1973 when our research
team first traveled to Oryu Li, this dirt lane was being bulldozed into a
gravel road (an activity that we later realized was symbolic of the miracle
of Oryu Li).

We had first learned of the self-development accomplishments of the
village of Oryu Li from personnel in the Seoul headquarters of the
Planned Parenthood Federation of Korea (PPFK), the agency responsible for family planning communication in the nation. They told us of a
poor village whose womenfolk had banded together to achieve a remarkable record of family planning adoption, community development,
and financial progress. The PPFK official who told us about Oryu Li, a
respected veteran of community development in Korea, Mr. Duck Chun
Yoo, had not visited Oryu Li, and indicated that he would like to
accompany us.

We were engaged in research on communication networks in the
diffusion of family planning methods in Korean villages, and especially in

Previous analyses of the case of Oryu Li by Kincaid and others (1975) and Kincaid
and Yum (1976) differ somewhat from the present account, especially because we
have here included data on later events in the village. Parts of the present chapter
are adapted with permission from D. Lawrence Kincaid and June Ock Yum (1976),
"The Needle and the Ax: Communication and Development in a Korean Village,"
in Wilbur Schramm and Daniel Lerner (eds.), *Communication and Change: The
Last Ten Years—and the Next*, Honolulu, East–West Center Book, copyright © 1976
by the University Press of Hawaii.

1

the role of mothers' clubs in such diffusion. Oryu Li sounded like a success story worth investigating, a case study from which we could gain insight into our more quantitative data (obtained from a sample of 1,003 women in 24 other villages). So we set off for Oryu Li.

"We" in this case consisted of a team of investigators composed of Dr. Hyung Jong Park, Dean of the School of Public Health at Seoul National University; Professor Kyung-Kyoon Chung of his faculty; four experienced female interviewers from the staff of our network research project (Miss Kim, Miss Chi, and two Miss Lees); Dr. D. Lawrence Kincaid from the East–West Communication Institute in Honolulu; Chin-Chuan Lee, a graduate student at the Institute; and Dr. Everett M. Rogers, then from the University of Michigan and now at Stanford University.

As is protocol in Korea, we had paid a courtesy visit to the provincial governor in Jeonju City, prior to driving to the village of Oryu Li. The governor told us we would be impressed by the wonders worked by "woman power" in the village we planned to study. Enroute there, we stopped to explain our visit to the chief of Imsil County. So it was not until midafternoon on a hot day in July, 1973, that our team arrived in the village.

At first glance, Oryu Li did not impress us. The 103 homes are cramped between the tracks of a railroad and the steep foothills of a mountain range along the edge of a narrow valley (Figure 1-1). The flatland was dark green with the postage plots of healthy growing rice, but the village homes looked small and poor. The roofing was only straw thatch. No TV aerials; not even a school. In fact, before the women of Oryu Li began their self-development activities in 1971, Oryu Li was one of the poorest villages in one of the poorest counties in one of the poorest provinces in the Republic of Korea. Its acreage in riceland per family was only half that of surrounding areas. Here in a nutshell were exemplified the major problems of rural Korea: overpopulation, poverty, lack of cooperative trust, underdevelopment. Certainly the village had little to commend it from the hundreds of thousands of other hamlets in Asian countries, caught in their dusty circle of poverty.

How Oryu Li escaped this vicious cycle is the story of this chapter, the introduction to our book, an illustration of how communication networks function. If you like success stories, you'll like the "miracle" of Oryu Li. For it is well on its way to becoming one of the richer villages in Korea. Certainly it is one of the most famous today, featured in film, television, and the print media. Oryu Li represents what is possible for other peasant villages to achieve, regardless of their economic resources, through strong leadership, local organization for self-development, and adequate government support.

Figure 1–1.   Map of the Village of Oryu Li:

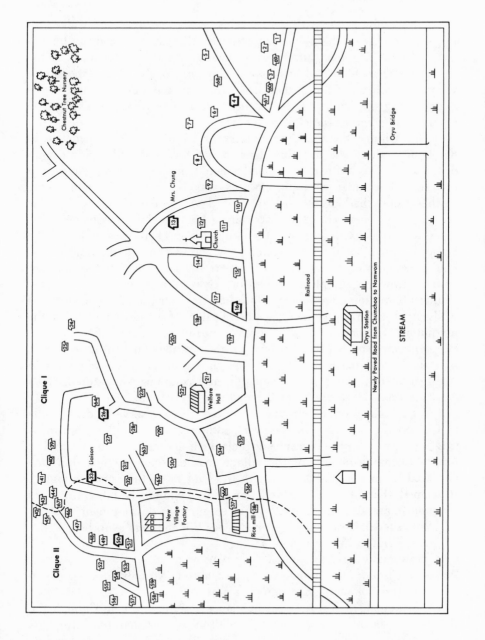

Chestnut Tree Nursery

Mrs. Chung

Clique I

Church

Clique II

Liaison

New Village Factory

Welfare Hall

Rice mill

Oryu Station

Newly Paved Road from Chumchoo to Namwom

Railroad

STREAM

Oryu Bridge

Note: The heavy dotted line shows the boundary between cliques I and II, identified by network analysis techniques.

GETTING ACQUAINTED WITH ORYU LI

On arriving at Oryu Li we parked below the village and walked up toward the cluster of small homes, bisected by trails too narrow for our automobiles. The four interviewers, young women experienced in the ways of village folk, had arrived the day previously. Under the supervision of Professor Chung, they had explained our purposes and begun interviewing the leader of the mothers' club in Oryu Li, Mrs. Moon Ja Chung, and some of the club members.

Mrs. Chung, the four interviewers, and Professor Chung met us at her home, where she introduced us to her husband and children with deep bows. The mothers' club leader acted modest and respectful, but one sensed a quiet strength. So this was the village woman whose mothers' club had accomplished such development progress that the governor had been moved to tears during his visit the previous year. We sat in her home, with a view out a sliding door. There were other village homes below, a small church tower on which was mounted a pair of new loudspeakers, and, below that, a huge tree (under which the mothers' club usually met in pleasant weather, we were to learn later). Mrs. Chung's home served as a sort of headquarters for the mothers' club; the walls held several plaques and certificates of achievement, and the ubiquitous performance chart with the number of family planning adopters per month (IUDs in red on the graph, oral contraceptives in blue, and condoms in black). In one corner of the main room was a small cabinet in which supplies of pills and condoms were stored, along with the financial accounts of the mothers' club "bank."

We sat, shoes off, on straw mats where we were served a drink made of Chinese quince. Our interviewers, although respectfully subdued as was appropriate in the presence of their dean, indicated their enthusiasm for the accomplishments of the village mothers' club (which they had garnered in an informal session with the leaders on the previous night). It seemed that Mrs. Chung and her club members had literally been "moving mountains" in their efforts at community development.

We asked: "How many members does this mothers' club have?"

Mrs. Chung: "We are now 53."

"How many have adopted family planning?"

Mrs. Chung: "Every member is an adopter. No baby has been born in this village for more than one year now."

We exchanged surprised silent glances. While walking through the village, the usual crowd of small children had trailed us, little girls carrying their smaller brothers and sisters. But, unlike the usual public scene in Korea, there were no very small babies! The national rate of adoption of family planning was about 36 percent; Oryu Li had achieved 100 percent adoption by its mothers' club members. And we knew of the demographic rule-of-thumb in rural Korea, that about 60 percent of all households would contain a married woman of reproductive age. So almost all such fertile-aged women in Oryu Li were club members.

"How many *won* does your mothers' club fund now have?"

Mrs. Chung answered with evident pride, "We have almost 600,000 *won* [about $1,500 U.S.]. This is in addition to the 2,000 chestnut trees we are growing up there on the mountainside." The club leader gestured to the steep slopes above the village. "And we own a cooperative grocery store down there." She pointed to a small building near the church tower. "It was once the village wineshop."

Our Korean colleagues seemed to shift slightly as if to say, *Hmmm, now, closing down the men's winehouse.* This was an unusual act when carried out by village women. Or perhaps they were impressed by the 600,000 *won*, a huge sum by village standards.

Then we recalled the words of the governor that morning. He had personally visited over one thousand villages in his province during the past year, and he considered Oryu Li the most impressive that he had seen because of the accomplishments of Mrs. Chung's mothers' club. He had said, "I have noticed many fantastic accomplishments by women's clubs. Their cooperation is great, and they work very hard . . . even in heavy men's work, women can be effective. Mrs. Chung's target [for her club's 'bank'] for the year 1973 is two million *won*; in my eyes, she's just crazy!" He finished our interview by saying, "We have student power in Korea, which has become universal over the last few years. I think I am one of the few government officials, however, who recognizes that *women power* is so strong."

Mrs. Chung invited us to accompany her on a tour of Oryu Li's development projects, prior to the mothers' club meeting to be held that afternoon. As we left her home, four or five club members arrived to donate their weekly savings of rice to the club "bank." Each housewife saved about a spoonful of rice from the bowl of each family member at every meal. This seemed like a rather petty matter, until we multiplied three meals per day times five individuals per household times 53 club members times 365 days . . . almost 300,000 spoonfuls of rice! Perhaps 3,000 pounds per year.

We saw the new village bathhouse, the food storage stands (both built by the club members), and the coop store. Three blows on the mammoth village gong called the mothers' club members to their late afternoon meeting place under the big tree on the edge of the village. They sat on the ground in irregular rows, curious dark button eyes fixed on their guests, each woman wearing the club uniform of a white shirt, black skirt, and green baseball cap with the three-leafed symbol of the New Village Movement. Most of the 53 members were noticeably present. None had babies slung on their backs.

We tape-recorded the meeting, and listening to the cassette today, several years later, brings back the scene, with the sun almost setting at the far end of the valley. The club leader gave a financial report of the current club savings in their "credit union," or bank, fund. There was a brief discussion of future money-making plans, undoubtedly cut short by the presence of visitors. Mrs. Chung led the women in group singing of the national folk song of Korea, "Arirang" (something equivalent, perhaps to "The Battle Hymn of the Republic" at a Farm Bureau meeting in Iowa), with special words she had composed for the club:

1. The umbrella is ours for rainy days
   The credit union is ours for future life.

   Stars twinkling in the dark sky
   Bright hope in the Oryu Li credit union.

   (Chorus) Arirang, arirang, arirang
   Hand in hand let's climb the hill of hope.

2. Let's put our savings in the credit union
   and use them when we really need them,
   When dust accumulates, it forms a mountain.

   Diligent work, honest conduct.
   God helps those who help themselves.

   (Chorus) Arirang, arirang, arirang
   Hand in hand let's climb the hill of hope.

We were introduced as "university professors" who had traveled far to see the accomplishments of Oryu Li and its mothers' club. Instead of a speech, as perhaps was expected of professors, we asked questions of the group. Could we see a show of hands of the original ten members who organized the club in 1968? How many women had five children or more? Two or fewer? (Some dozen of the members, mostly younger women, indicated they followed the government's admonition to "stop at two," but polite giggling suggested this might be a sensitive topic.)

After adjournment, we accompanied the members to the mountainside above the village, to chop weeds among their chestnut trees. Soon it was really getting dark. With more deep bows and promises to return the next morning, we left Oryu Li for a hotel in Jeonju City (the four interviewers remained as guests of the village, enough of an imposition on Mrs. Chung's hospitality).

We were to return many times to the village in 1973, and at least one of us would come back each year to gather data monitoring Oryu

Li's further development. Our reports on the "miracle" of Oryu Li, which led to some of the mass media recognition given the village, were, in fact, to contribute to its further development. Perhaps that July day in 1973 we had "joined" the mothers' club, at least in becoming indirect partners in its progress. Actually, whatever we have given to Oryu Li was small in comparison to the lessons that it taught us about self-development, village leadership, and communication networks.

Following is our account of these lessons.

BACKGROUND OF DEVELOPMENT IN KOREA

To understand the case of Oryu Li requires some knowledge of its specific historical and socio-economic context. In many respects Korean culture was traditionally more Confucian than that of China. Before contact with Western cultures in the late nineteenth century, woman's place in society was accurately described by the Korean word for housewife: "inside person." It was strictly improper for women to take the initiative in activities outside their own homes. For instance, they could not attend the "men-only" village-wide meetings. Women existed without status until they produced sons for their husbands. Woman's role was always subordinate, first to her father, then to her husband, and finally to her eldest son.

Change began slowly after contact with Western culture in the late nineteenth century, increasing greatly in scope during the Japanese annexation from 1910 to 1945, the disruption caused by the Korean War from 1950 to 1953, and the American influence during the reconstruction era. "When the whales fight, the shrimp suffers," is an old Korean proverb that rather concisely describes that nation's traditional relationship with the large superpowers in Asia that surround it. This pattern worked to the Koreans' advantage in the 1960s, however, when the dramatic economic growth of Japan and the stability in the relationships of China, Russia, and the United States created a favorable environment for their own economic growth.

From 1960 to 1970, the average rate of growth in Korea's gross domestic product was 8.9 percent, one of the highest among developing nations. Per capita income reached $261 by 1971, although it was not very equally distributed between urban and rural sectors. The rapid rate of industrialization during the 1960s was accompanied by such rapid urban migration that almost 50 percent of the Republic of Korea's 35 million people lived in urban areas by 1974. The changes were so great that one of the world's most densely populated countries suffered from a labor shortage in the rural sector in the early 1970s. This shortage pulled women into the labor market, contributing to their emancipation.

To restore their country's rural–urban equilibrium and improve the rural standard of living, the government launched the national Saemaul Undong, or New Village Movement, in 1970, to mobilize the human and material resources of the villages for their own development.

THE STORY OF ORYU LI

. Oryu Li was poor in 1973. Over five hundred people lived in the 103 households. In 1968, each family had barely one-half hectare (about one acre) of land, whereas the average for the rest of the province was almost twice that. Because of their poverty, most villagers could not afford to send their children to middle school or high school. Over the past decade most of the young men and women from Oryu Li were forced to leave for the city to find jobs as factory workers or housekeepers, about the only occupations available for young Koreans with only a primary school education.

The village social structure has been dominated by one family clan. Of the 103 households, 80 are members of the Kang clan. There are 11 Yoo clan households, three from the Kim clan, and so forth.

This clan system meant that if anyone suggested a change perceived as threatening by the dominant clan, they would be criticized severely and treated harshly by clan members. A very serious mistake during the 1950 war with North Korea undoubtedly undermined community cohesion. During the occupation by North Korean troops, a village leader became a member of the Communist Party. The North Koreans told him to enroll all the Kang family members in the Party. When the area was later reconquered by South Korean forces, many villagers were killed, and the police and soldiers have closely watched the village since. Consequently, many of the Kang leaders have been afraid to hold any kind of meeting in the village. This background made it especially difficult to organize the Mothers' Club in 1968.

MOTHERS' CLUBS IN KOREA

The national family planning program in Korea was launched in the early 1960s to cope with a burgeoning rate of population growth. Until 1968 this program mainly emphasized the IUD as a family planning method, which was promoted to rural housewives by a corps of 1,467 township-level family planning field workers. Each such employee was typically responsible for about 1,500 eligible couples (married and with the wife in the reproductive age range of 15 to 45), living in perhaps 30 to 50 villages over a scattered geographical area. Because the field worker is usually a young, unmarried woman, she found it embarrassing and socially difficult to discuss family planning, a relatively taboo topic, with older females. She could hardly make home visits to all 1,500 of her client families on any regular basis.

Further, a plateau in the rate of adoption of the IUD was reached in 1968. The Korean government wished to introduce oral contraceptives as one part of the national program, but there was no effective means for delivering the monthly cycles of pills to village women.

It was in light of this situation that mothers' clubs were launched by the Korean government in 1968. They were originally conceived as village-level organizations established to encourage family planning practice among married women of childbearing age, and to serve as a channel for family planning information and supplies.[1] Korea is the only nation in the world in which so much effort has been given to organizing small groups of women as a means of promoting the community-level diffusion of family planning methods. And once begun, the clubs' activities ranged far beyond family planning into community development, money-making, and female equality.

The typical mothers' club is a small discussion and action group, composed of about 25 members or so. Such small groups are an ideal means for changing individuals' attitudes and behavior, especially if there is a channel by which new ideas can come into the group from external sources. The township family planning field worker is one such channel. The mothers' club helps extend the field worker's influence, through the club members, into many of the interpersonal communication networks in the village.

LAUNCHING THE MOTHERS' CLUB IN ORYU LI

The mothers' club in Oryu Li was initiated in 1968 by a visit of the township family planning field worker, who asked the village chief to organize the club. He promptly appointed his wife, Mrs. Yang Soon Choi, as the club leader, and she found nine other women who were interested. All of these founders were "good wives," meaning they were respectful to their husbands. None were thought by Mrs. Choi to be "leading figures of the village." In fact, the richer wives (the village elites) scoffed at the idea of joining a mothers' club. "What could it do?" they said.

The relative ease of "organizing" a mothers' club in Oryu Li (a matter quite different from its effective operation, as later events showed)

---

[1] Throughout the present volume we follow the usual convention by referring to these groups as "mothers' clubs," while acknowledging that the Korean terminology of "omoni whoe" might be more literally translated as "mothers' gathering."

was matched by the experience in 12,000 other Korean villages, which also established mothers' clubs in 1968 (the total number increased to 28,000 by 1976). One reason for the rapid founding of mothers' clubs may lie in their similarity to *kaes*, which are rotating credit associations,[2] particularly popular among village women in Korea. In such an informal savings group, each member pays a small fee into a common fund, which is awarded to one member at each monthly meeting. There are usually 12 or 24 members, and the monthly "winner" is rotated through a full cycle. Although Korean women were traditionally barred from attendance at village assemblies, and from participaton in other formal organizations, they were allowed to have their *kaes*, a form of penny capitalism. And the *kae experience* was good training for the skills needed to operate a mothers' club: trust of fellow members, leadership, and the ability to handle financial records.

As in most other Korean villages, the women of Oryu Li had a number of *kaes* in operation in 1968: a rice *kae* (in which the monthly contribution was made in rice), a wedding *kae* (to pay for wedding expenses, a friendship *kae* (to provide its members with a reason for monthly social get-togethers), and a sixtieth anniversary *kae* (which paid off when a member reached 60 years of age, the so-called *whangap*).

The new mothers' club in Oryu Li at first began to operate much like a *kae:* Mrs. Choi and the nine other members began a Mothers' Club "credit union," funded by each individual's savings of rice from her family's table (the government of Korea was then promoting a national rice-saving campaign in order to encourage thrift). Naturally, the mothers' club in Oryu Li also sought to enlighten its members about family planning, and Mrs. Choi was given a small supply of pills and condoms by PPFK, for sale at a special price to villagers.

But the club had to overcome many obstacles. In the beginning, the members' husbands had very traditional attitudes about women, and most of them disapproved of the use of contraceptives. Because of the village's problems with the Communists during the war, many village elders were still wary of public meetings. The men criticized the mothers' club activities. Parents-in-law did not understand the purpose of the club, so that many club members experienced very difficult situations in their homes. Ashamed of attending public meetings, they met secretly because of fear that their families would object to their participation in the club.

To overcome these problems, Mrs. Choi encouraged the members to show *extra respect* to their elders, their in-laws, and their husbands.

[2] There is a considerable anthropological literature on rotating credit associations in a variety of Asian, African, and Caribbean cultures: Geertz (1962), Raum (1969), and Light (1972).

They even agreed to prepare and serve especially delicious foods to please their husbands and in-laws twice every month (on the first and fifteenth). They made sure that this new behavior was recognized as one of the activities of the mothers' club. As a member explained: "In the past our husbands mistook the mothers' club for 'women's liberation.' But now they understand it . . . we persuaded them by serving them various delicious foods and by making a special effort to please them."

While the members discussed family planning among themselves, they also began concentrating on their credit fund, as a means of establishing their own cooperative store to sell small household goods toward the more ultimate goal of providing a better education for their children. Soon the village elders realized that their daughters-in-law were "behaving" even better than before, and they gradually began encouraging them to become more active in mothers' club projects. Eventually, meetings were held openly under the traditional village meeting tree once every month (under a full moon until the village obtained electricity).

THE FAMILY PLANNING PIG

Early in 1971, the PPFK office in Jeonju City gave a piglet as a prize to one mothers' club in each of the 13 counties of the province, in order to stimulate the most promising clubs to undertake joint livestock projects to increase their income. When Oryu Li was given a piglet, the mothers' club was faced with an immediate problem: Who would feed and take care of it? Who would benefit from it? They held meetings every day to discuss the problem until they finally worked out a plan to care for the piglet, and later to breed it. Of the 13 piglets given to mothers' clubs only theirs and one other survived (or was not sold immediately).

While a success from the standpoint of encouraging cooperation among the club's members, the pig did miserably. Her first litter had only two female piglets, followed by just two male piglets in the second litter. Since most pigs produce much larger litters (from four to seven piglets), the club's pig soon became renowned throughout the area as the "family planning pig of Oryu Li." Since the pig belonged to the mothers' club, it was accused of taking PPFK's national slogan too seriously: "Girl or boy, stop at two and raise them well." They kept the pig in spite of her early record of subpar fertility, and she eventually produced a normal litter. Perhaps the joke about the "mothers' club pig" made it easier for the members to talk about family planning, in that the humor removed some of the tabooness of the topic.

THE CLUB'S NEW LEADER

While the mothers' club was being organized in Oryu Li, Mrs. Moon Ja Chung (who hosted our 1973 visit to Oryu Li) and her husband lived in the mountains a few miles above the village, striving to establish a small livestock operation. They were financially overextended and when some of their 50 cows died of an uncontrollable disease, they were forced into bankruptcy. They moved into the village of Oryu Li. Since the train station was in Oryu Li, they had often stopped there on their trips to Jeonju City. Mrs. Chung had become good friends with Mrs. Choi, the mothers' club leader. The two frequently discussed the problems of the club, and since Mrs. Chung was a high school graduate, her advice and suggestions about the organization were often accepted by Mrs. Choi.

When Mrs. Chung and her husband moved to Oryu Li in April, 1971, Mrs. Choi asked her to become the formal leader of their club, finally persuading her to accept by agreeing to be the club's vice-leader. As an outsider, Mrs. Chung was met initially with mistrust, resistance, criticism, and some open hostility from members of the dominant family clan. For example, they blamed her for an unfavorable newspaper article about their village's earlier involvement with the Communists. She finally convinced them that the reporter had not interviewed her. Then she was accused of reporting some of the villagers' illegal connections to a nearby electric power line. She denied it, and when they finally learned that she had been falsely accused, they became sympathetic and began to cooperate. Mrs. Choi's support was crucial, since her husband was the village chief and a member of the dominant Kang clan.[3]

Under Mrs. Chung's competent leadership, the rate of Oryu Li's development began to take off. She completely reoriented the club after becoming its leader. At her first meeting (with 30 members and potential members present) she proposed five basic goals: (1) family planning, (2) village improvement, (3) love for Korea, (4) love for neighbors, and (5) love for God. After a general consensus was reached, they decided to begin by founding a mothers' club "bank," a general fund (separate from their individual savings and from their credit union) that could be used for village development projects, and ultimately for their children's education.

Mrs. Chung first heard about this idea on a weekly radio program, "Let There Be No Despair," a half-hour documentary on the government station. The program was about a village like Oryu Li that learned to

---

[3] According to Korean naming customs, this woman is called "Mrs. Choi" rather than "Mrs. Kang" because her maiden name of Choi is not changed at marriage; nevertheless, she is considered to be a member of her husband's clan.

overcome its fatalism and eventually prospered by starting a cooperative village fund. She told other club members this story in order to convince them to start their own fund. Meanwhile, she visited the five most stubborn village elders, and persuaded them to become consultants to the club. They accepted, and in fact became helpful to the club.

In the summer of 1971, the club members pooled their savings to buy cloth from which they made uniforms to sell nearby middle-school children for their school's annual sports competition. The combined profit of this project was 6,000 *won* (U.S. $15), half of which the club donated to the school for the sports event. The rest was used to start the club's mutual fund. Although this was a small start, through it the club members earned considerable respect from the school officials, from surrounding villages, and from resistant individuals in their own village. It convinced the mothers' club members they could create ways to earn money for their mutual fund.

Just before the annual harvest, Mrs. Chung proposed that they formally open an account for their fund with the government agricultural cooperative bank, and learn the procedures for deposits, withdrawals, and bookkeeping. Each member was given a bankbook with her share of the mothers' club fund, so that she would realize that the funds belonged to her. At first, some club members wanted to use the fund like a traditional *kae*, in a monthly rotation of payoffs, but Mrs. Chung urged against this. At one meeting she said, "You women who just want to make money for your individual benefit, you go somewhere else and start a *kae*. Our mothers' club will raise money, but only for the development of our village, especially our children's education." The club members hoped to break the hold of the village money-lenders, who often charged 6 percent interest *per month*. In order to provide an alternative credit source, the club would have to amass a considerable fund, and they would have to own and operate a village store (for the money-lenders often managed credit at the time of villagers' purchases of food or dry goods).

Mrs. Chung also rallied the womenfolk against the local wineshop, where many of their husbands drank and gambled. Just like the poolhall in "River City," the Oryu Li winehouse was a symbolic object of much female concern. Wives felt their husbands were throwing away their earnings, which could be better spent for food, clothes, and other essentials.

So the leader challenged her club members to greater heights of sacrifice and saving by appealing to their felt needs regarding the money-lenders and the wineshop. She proposed a substantial increase in the scale of their club's savings operations. She recommended that each member begin saving 100 *won* (U.S. $.25) and increase her rice savings to about one liter every month. And she proposed that they expand the membership of the club, as the larger base of members would increase their fund more rapidly.

The original ten members of the club balked at this idea, claiming that the 9,900 *won* they had already saved belonged only to them, and should not be shared with the new members. Finally, Mrs. Chung just said, "Okay, you take all of your money out of the fund, and I'll lend the fund 10,000 *won* of my own money to get it started again." This remark made quite an impression. According to one member, "All the members were greatly moved by her unselfish act, and they contributed their money voluntarily." The club soon grew to 41 members. They began working together in their free time, harvesting rice on neighboring farms at 200 *won* per woman per day. They often had to leave their homes before dawn for such labor and many of their regular household duties had to be sacrificed. Often they sang while they worked and the time passed quickly. And they accumulated almost 120,000 *won* (U.S. $300) by the end of the next harvest, enough to gain control of the village winehouse, and make their dream of a cooperative store a reality.

DEATH OF THE WINEHOUSE

The mothers' club in Oryu Li, in its first era of early successes, largely had concentrated on rather small-scale projects that did not directly threaten to change traditional norms on the role of women. For instance, the village elders were coopted by the club's emphasis on female obedience and respect. But when the temperance drive was launched in Oryu Li, the mothers' club sought to change not just their members' behavior, but that of their husbands. The wineshop, a rather low-class tavern in a tiny building served *makulee* (rice wine) and *sojoo* (a vodka-like rice liquor). The fondness of the village males for their wineshop can be well imagined. It was a place of comradeship and relaxation after a hard day of planting rice. "Chopstick girls" were employed in this "sparrow-house," so-called because they keep time to their singing (for the enjoyment of the patrons) by tapping with chopsticks. Perhaps these waitresses increased the potential for male pleasure (and their wives' displeasure). The expense of drinking, and the gambling which usually accompanies it, was also one of the main sources of village disharmony and family conflict.

The first step in the temperance drive was for the mothers' club to fix a 100 *won* fine on each club member whose husband was seen drinking (in contrast, a fine of only 30 *won* was charged for a members' absence from a club meeting). Next, the club offered to buy the wineshop, whose owner was now more willing to sell, due to the recent decline in sales. The mothers' club then converted the former winehouse into a cooperative grocery store. Needless to say, the co-op did not sell alcoholic spirits.

When we first visited Oryu Li in 1973, the cooperative store was stocked with items like soap, salt, and socks made by the club members. The wineshop was dead, gambling and drinking had declined (although a few husbands were said to occasionally slip off to the wineshop in a nearby village for a quick cup). Some of the club members' husbands, in our interviews with them, indicated being vexed at the loss of their social center. But most male attitudes were typified by the comment of one husband who indicated pride, and considerable wonderment, in what the village's "little women" had accomplished.

The death of the wineshop was a turning point, we see now, in the process of Oryu Li's self-development. The women gained a strong sense of solidarity and collective efficacy, a feeling they could control their future, rather than depending on how their fate was defined for them (usually by male society). They would not thereafter return to being quiescent "inside persons."

THE COLLECTIVE DECISION FOR FAMILY PLANNING

Before the mothers' club was organized in 1968, a few women used contraceptives secretly, out of fear their husbands would beat them. The first family planning field worker who visited Oryu Li was severely criticized by some of the village men (and in a nearby village, the first field worker was spanked by a village elder and forced to leave). She had to work secretly when she visited Oryu Li. There were unexplained side effects from the contraceptives. The mothers' club members provided some of the reluctant village women with enough confidence to try the IUD or pills, but in the beginning it was often difficult to distinguish those who accepted from those who opposed family planning, because everyone was afraid to talk about it.

Between 1968 and 1970, several women in Oryu Li began using oral contraceptives. Then one of the first women to use the pill became seriously ill and almost died. When others heard about this, 13 other women who were taking the pill decided to discontinue. During 1971, when Mrs. Chung became the club leader, 12 unwanted babies were born in Oryu Li. To restore members' faith in family planning, she invited a university health lecturer, whom she met during a leaders' training program in Jeonju City, to visit the village and explain how family planning could facilitate village development. After this lecture, Mrs. Chung told the club that anyone who did not want to adopt the pill should come with her to the county clinic to have an IUD inserted. She asked for a show of hands at the meeting. Eighteen women volunteered, and marched off to the clinic with Mrs. Chung the next day (unfortunately, six of the women were not at the correct time in their menstrual cycle to have an IUD inserted).

Of the 12 members who had "loops" (IUDs) inserted, one of them was not completely convinced that loops were really safe. She soon suffered severe side effects and her fear increased. Mrs. Chung wrote her a letter every day from Seoul, where she was attending a training program for new club leaders, but when she returned to Oryu Li, she realized she should take the member back to the clinic to have the loop removed. Later she apologized to the whole club for trying to persuade someone to accept an IUD against her will. Fortunately, there were no serious problems with the other mothers who had volunteered.

Oryu Li's experience with family planning is unique for several reasons. The mothers' club provided, for the first time, an open forum in which family planning and other sensitive and personal problems could be freely discussed. Second, this example suggests that the adoption of family planning was more readily accomplished by a collective decision, rather than by an individual decison. This collectivistic spirit is very strong in Korean villages (and in many other Asian nations). Such villagers are accustomed to making group decisions, even regarding matters that in other cultures (like the United States) would be settled by individual choice. A Korean proverb illustrates the importance of such group influence: "One follows his friends to a far-off place even when there is no purpose in doing so." Naturally, this collectivistic spirit is a great boon to the efforts of mothers' clubs in promoting family planning in Korea.[4]

Finally, this example reveals that an important contribution to a family planning program is provided by personal follow-up and support for those who are risking the use of contraceptives for the first time. It is impossible for doctors, clinic nurses, or field workers to provide the close, personal support that Mrs. Chung gave to her anxious neighbor in Oryu Li. The mothers' club made this task a specific responsibility of the leader and other members, and the club meetings gave them the place and time to do so.

SELF-DEVELOPMENT PROJECTS

During the several years following 1971, the Oryu Li mothers' club initiated an extraordinary series of self-development, income-earning

[4] Park and others (1974) estimated that about one-third of all family planning adopters in rural Korea (about 180,000 adopters) are recruited by mothers' club leaders, thus extending the family planning field workers' efforts. Club leaders average 39 years of age, 12 years older than the typical field worker; this maturity, along with the fact that the club leaders are married and the field workers are usually single, contributes to the higher credibility of the club leaders about family planning.

projects. The government was launching a new integrated rural development program, the *Saemaul Undong* (New Village Movement), during this same period. The mothers' club readily accepted its expanded role in the New Village Movement, as the members were well prepared for its three basic means of village improvement: cooperation, self-reliance, and diligence.

To improve their food storage, the club members built concrete stands for their *kim chee* (pickled vegetables) jars; then they decided to modernize their kitchens by rebuilding their cooking stands and stoves with concrete bricks. Since they needed $250 for the kitchens of all 41 members, Mrs. Chung suggested that everyone lend the club her gold wedding ring. These would be pawned, and when they had enough money from other projects, they would buy their rings back. Some members were afraid of what their husbands would say if they found out, so she asked them, "What good does it do to wear gold rings when our village is so dirty and needs to be improved?" Moved once again by their leader's logic, and following her lead as the first to contribute her ring, the women donated their gold rings, and the club obtained the money to buy materials. Nevertheless, they decided to keep this a club secret until they were able to redeem their rings.

Once they had purchased the cement for brick-making, they divided themselves into eight work teams of five members each. The first set of bricks froze and broke apart. It was too cold and the material was poorly mixed. So they invited men in the village who were more skilled at brick-making to work with each team, under an agreement that the men would be exempt from other New Village Movement duties. Since the women had given some *kim chee* to the soldiers stationed at the train depot the year before, they were able to ask the soldiers to help with the brick-making by hauling in some sand from a nearby river bank. The women also used the concrete to build a public bathhouse for the village, which everyone agreed was needed.

Early in 1972, Mrs. Chung heard that the government was promoting reforestation by providing chestnut seedlings to village development councils. She told the county chief that Oryu Li had very little land for rice cultivation, but that the villagers could use the surrounding hillsides to grow chestnut trees. He was skeptical at first because the ground was still frozen, and he doubted whether *women* could dig holes 60 centimeters (about two feet) deep, which the seedlings required. But Mrs. Chung was persistent, and he finally promised them 2,000 chestnut seedlings.

The club members were overjoyed to hear the good news. In their enthusiasm they dug each hole 100 centimeters deep in the still-frozen hillside, even though 60 centimeters would have been enough. They expected that the planting of 2,000 trees would require at least sixteen days, but they were so eager that they finished in half the time, a remarkable achievement. People in surrounding villages could not believe such a feat was possible. They charged that the soldiers from the nearby station had dug the holes at night. The women were unperturbed, aware that this rumor stemmed from the soldiers' previous help with the sand.

After the seedlings were planted, the women decided to grow their own chestnut seedlings in a nursery. For this project, they organized the village men under 30 years old into a young men's club. Together they planted 16,000 seeds, of which 10,000 seedlings grew. They planned to donate $500 of profits from this project to the village fund, and to divide the rest among the members of the young men's club and the mothers' club.

According to one of the club members, "These chestnut trees have become our greatest hope for the future . . . and for better education for our children. We take care of our chestnut trees as if they were our own children." The meaning of the chestnut trees to members of the mothers' club is more than just a long-term economic investment to gain increased income. They have become a symbol of the new consciousness of the mothers' club members: they represent the growing belief that "we can do it ourselves." This message did not go unheeded by the men of Oryu Li.[5] The sign of the mothers' club was placed directly in front of the chestnut tree nursery by the main road into the village. The chestnut tree is a traditional symbol of endurance and prosperity, especially during the cold winter days when chestnuts are roasted at home, or sold in the streets of the cities. The chestnut trees represented a permanent commitment to the struggle for a better life in Oryu Li.

After the trees were planted, the club members turned to the spring planting of rice and barley. They cleared the rocks and heavy stones from some vacant land next to the river. Then they convinced the soldiers to transport ten truckloads of topsoil to improve this new plot. They planted their barley crop too late, however, so only half a normal yield was obtained. The heavy rain in July and August also harmed the yield. Then the grain was rejected by the government purchasing agency as not dry enough to store properly. The women returned to Oryu Li (1) to inform the other villagers about the fixed price offered by the government, (2) to dry their barley more thoroughly, and (3) to carry the barley a second time to the government buying agency. Although they eventually had to sell their grain at a loss, they had learned much about barley growing, and were prepared for their 1973 crop.

[5] As Mrs. Chung told us in a 1974 interview: "Women's power has grown very much. . . . At first the members of the mothers' club did all the work, but the other village people began to depend on us too much. Even something like clearing the roads right in front of their houses, which the village men should do, they expected us to do for them. So we tried to change this. We clear at the back of the houses and let the men do the front. . . . It is not easy though, to make a change like that."

So not all of the club's projects were successful, at least immediately. They felt a need for yet more land. They turned to the right-of-way along the railroad tracks, where they planted castor-oil seeds for about four kilometers, added fertilizer, and toiled very hard to cultivate their plants. Then, as part of a railroad beautification campaign, all of their castor-oil plants were uprooted before their pleas to the governor could be heard.

THE GOVERNOR'S SURPRISE VISIT

Late in 1972, the provincial governor made an unexpected visit to Oryu Li while visiting New Village Movement projects nearby. The governor's advance man arrived first, and told Mrs. Chung to gather all the women for a meeting because the governor wanted to talk to them. She objected, "The women are working in the field, not dressed for a meeting. . . . Why don't we get the fertilizer and have them putting it on the chestnut trees when the governor arrives?" The governor was very impressed to see the women working so hard. He went to Mrs. Chung's house and for over two hours she told him of all of the problems and activities of the club during its first four years.

Her exposition was so intensely emotional that the governor was actually moved to tears. As he explained later, it was the first time he had wept in 40 years, but it was from a feeling of gladness over what the club members had been able to accomplish with so little. This visit confirmed his belief that the New Village Movement was being spearheaded by the women in his province, rather than by the men. Before leaving, he donated 300 sacks of cement to the Oryu Li mother's club, and he agreed to electrify the village and improve the road to the village ahead of schedule. Later, one could see that the governor's visit marked the beginning of wide recognition for Oryu Li. At the time it led to serious problems.

Some days later, Mrs. Chung was asked by several village men to come to one of their houses. Inside were many of the husbands of the women who were not members of the mothers' club. They claimed that the governor's gift of cement was for the whole village, *not* just for the members of the mothers' club. According to Mrs. Chung, the whole future of the club was at stake:

> I didn't know what to do. The members were really counting on the cement to finish their kitchens. I had to refuse. . . . Finally, I just told them that even President Park would say that the cement should go to those who work, *not* the ones who do nothing. Then I had a good idea. I offered to share the cement with all members of the mothers' club, even those who joined *after* the cement was donated. They had no choice but

to accept this generous offer. Only their stubbornness would prevent their wives from joining the club and sharing the cement.

This confrontation helped Mrs. Chung realize that not all the women in the village were yet able to participate in the club, even if they wanted to. Some had to stay home to care for their young children, rather than to participate in the projects of the mothers' club. With the active members, she immediately began preparations for a special feast for the whole village: (1) to honor their own husbands' sacrifices, and (2) to dramatize the benefit that their club's activities were having for the whole village. Afterwards, the club membership grew from 41 to 53 mothers. Now there were few opponents of the club in Oryu Li.

Mrs. Chung's successful confrontation over the distribution of the cement was based on her estimate of the club's power. It included the village chief's wife as vice-leader. Mrs. Chung's husband's support before and during her response was also a critical factor. The achievements of the club were obvious to everyone in the village, and to government officials, a fact that her opponents could not have overlooked when she invoked the President's name in her reply. To have acceded to the men's demands would have seriously undermined the future efforts of the club. *How* Mrs. Chung resisted was most important of all: with compromise, deescalation of the conflict, and an offer to share the rewards with anyone willing to join and work with the club.

A FACTORY FOR ORYU LI

In the fall of 1973, some months after our initial visit, Mrs. Chung began searching for some way to prevent young girls from having to leave the village and to bring back some who were already working in factories or as housemaids in the city. A village factory would give these girls work to earn money for their future marriage. She visited a factory in a nearby city that produced traditional silk belts (*obizime*) for export to Japan. After returning to the factory four times, she at last obtained some raw materials for weaving the belts in the village. At first most village girls objected, saying that the wages were too low, but a few volunteered to try weaving the belts. Mrs. Chung returned to the factory with examples of their work and pleaded with the company president to build a factory for the young people in her village. When he asked if they had a building for his looms, she was forced to lie, saying they already had one.

Oryu Li was finally given ten new *obizime* hand-operated looms in October, 1973, which Mrs. Chung installed in her own house. Ten of Oryu Li's most skillful girls were selected, and an expert from Japan taught them the techniques of weaving. The first belts were of poor quality, but improvement occurred after Mrs. Chung told the girls their work would symbolize the quality of Korean craftsmanship when the products were sold in Japan.

Similar weaving machines were installed in four other villages, but the work done in Oryu Li was superior. The company agreed to construct a factory building in their village, where the machines from Mrs. Chung's house and from the other four villages were installed. In early 1974 an official ceremony was held to honor the factory's completion. Forty-eight young girls, who had been forced to leave the village to work in the city, returned to learn how to weave and thus to earn a living in Oryu Li. Since the mothers' club was deeply concerned with providing for children's education, Mrs. Chung immediately began special courses for the girls. Since they were too tired to study at night, they used the time from 8:00 to 9:00 A.M. for a middle-school correspondence course, and worked from 9:00 A.M. until 7:00 P.M., with one hour for lunch and another hour for recreation in the afternoon. With skill, each girl earned about U.S. $1.00 per day, about twice as much as their mothers were making harvesting rice on neighboring farms.

NEW LAND FOR THE VILLAGE

During the winter of 1973–1974, the villagers of Oryu Li heard that the government planned to sell the land the mothers' club had reclaimed along the river, the land that they had cleared to grow barley. They had obtained official permission to use this land, and they had been paying taxes on it each year. Mrs. Chung, her husband, and the New Village Movement leader in Oryu Li spent over two months in the procedures for purchasing the land from the county government. Then the provincial government intervened to prevent the county officials from handling the matter, claiming that the land near the river belonged to the province.

Most of the county and provincial officials had grown accustomed to dealing directly with Mrs. Chung, rather than with the village chief, when they wished to initiate village action. It was thus easier, through the club, to gather the villagers for meetings, and to obtain their cooperation. Furthermore, word of the success of the Oryu Li mothers' club had spread throughout Korea. By the time their land was threatened, Mrs. Chung was giving regular lectures at the New Village Movement's national training institute at Suwon (near Seoul). She knew that villages in Korea where high government officials were born, or had relatives, could easily get support for their projects, whereas villages like Oryu Li had only themselves to rely on for support. So they had to make their needs and efforts known.

Mrs. Chung went to the provincial government and argued with the head of the planning department for a whole day. The mothers' club of Oryu Li had become "famous enough that they had to hear our claims." Finally, the government yielded to the club's demands for the land.

All of the available money in the village was needed to purchase the land. The *Kang* clan fund provided over one hundred sacks of rice. But if it had not been for the mothers' club general fund, which had now grown to over 1 million *won* ($2,500), the village would not have been able to obtain the land. The purchase more than doubled the cropland in Oryu Li.

Ironically, it was *land*, the oldest and most traditional value in Korea, which led to the final integration of the mothers' club with the traditional family clan in Oryu Li.

THE BRIDGE AT ORYU LI

The crowning event in the four-year "miracle" of Oryu Li occurred during 1975. Like many of the previous accomplishments of the mothers' club, it fed on these prior successes and built upon them.

For over two hundred years, the citizens of Oryu Li had desired a bridge over the river that divided their homes from their fields. A system of stepping-stones provided a poor substitute for the dreamed-of bridge. Even during the dry season, the slippery stones were hazardous. Farmers could not drive their carts to their fields with fertilizer at planting time, nor could they bring out their harvest (except on A-frame "carrying boards" strapped to their backs). Farm mechanization was blocked by the river. The school children walked to their classes with wet feet on days when the river's level rose. It almost seemed as if the river mocked Oryu Li's progress. A neighboring, downstream village that Oryu Li regarded as its traditional competitor had spanned the river with a bridge (and, worse, the residents of Oryu Li often had to use *this* bridge, via a roundabout route, when the river was at flood level).

Much of the land purchased from the provincial government in 1974 lay across the river from the homes of Oryu Li's residents. So even this latest success of buying the farmland, had not only drained the village coffers, but also emphasized the need for a bridge at Oryu Li.

How could the millions of *won* to build the bridge be obtained? An answer came in an unexpected way.

In January, 1975, Mrs. Chung was notified that she was to receive a national award for being the outstanding leader of the year in the New Village Movement.

The club leader traveled to the Blue House in Seoul, where the award was presented by the late President Park himself. The honor was accompanied by a cash prize of 1 million *won* ($2,000 U.S. at then-current rates of exchange), from the President's personal fund. On her return from Seoul, Mrs. Chung announced that these funds would be committed toward construction of the bridge. This immediately set off a public controversy about the bridge project. Many villagers were cowed by the huge cost, estimated at about 5 million *won*. In fact, engineers from the county government actually discouraged construction. The engineers feared that Oryu Li would get the bridge project almost completed, but still lacking a million *won* or so, they would petition the county government for the needed money.

But Mrs. Chung argued that the presidential prize required that they use it to carry out a dramatic activity. The bridge, symbolically located at the entrance to the village, would fit the bill as being dramatic. After three months of debate over the bridge controversy, it was decided to start construction.

With the considerable cash impetus of the presidential prize, the villagers were inspired to "above and beyond" efforts at bridge-building. Each household head was assigned a quota of 20 work days (many villagers contributed even more), or a cash contribution of 30,000 *won*. The goal of 5 million *won* was finally approached with the help of a contribution from a rich businessman who had grown up nearby, and who heard a lecture by Mrs. Chung at a national training course. Finally, the provincial governor gave 1 million *won* to put the money-raising campaign over the top.

Construction began on April 7, 1975, and in two months the bridge at Oryu Li was completed, a solid concrete structure amid the rice fields, adequate for a jeep or automobile. Symbolically, the bridge represented a pinnacle of progress for the mothers' club and Mrs. Chung, for the New Village Movement in Oryu Li, and for every adult and child in the hamlet. It was a daily reminder of what the villagers' efficacy could accomplish, and what community action could do.

Originally, Mrs. Chung's husband had proposed that the name sign on the bridge should read "The Oryu Li Mothers' Club Bridge." But it was argued that the *entire* village had been involved in the construction, and so today the nameplate is shortened to "The Oryu Li Bridge."

"Li" means "village" in Korean (making our frequent use in the present account of the expression "the village of Oryu Li" redundant). "Oryu" is the Chinese character for "willow," indicating that the village was named in some distant and now-forgotten time for the stand of trees still growing along the river. Perhaps this namesake is especially appropriate, in terms of the strength and suppleness of the willow. Chestnuts and willows. Endurance and prosperity. Strong and flexible. Like the women of Oryu Li.

ORYU LI AND MRS. CHUNG TODAY

During the period from 1973 until our latest contact with Oryu Li, we note a great deal of change in the village, but much less on the part of the club leader.

One now approaches Oryu Li on a new paved ribbon that crosses the bridge (sporting its modest nameplate); the concrete is not to carry visitors and tourists to Oryu Li (although the guest book that we signed in 1973 now has many hundreds of entries, since the dramatized television series, "Pearl of the Soil," about Oryu Li, and the media coverage of Mrs. Chung's presidential award). Rather, the pavement is to transport officials to a New Village Movement training center and model village, located a few miles past Oryu Li. The taxi from Jeonju City to Oryu Li now costs only 3,000 *won*, thanks to the improvement of the previously bumpy lane that we first traveled in 1973.

Oryu Li today is not the same village that we visited in 1973. There are tile roofs on every home, and 15 of the houses boast TV aerials; the second, that was installed in 1974, is on Mrs. Chung's home (one wonders if she and her friends watched the 27-part series of "Pearl of the Soil"). No new homes have been constructed, but Mrs. Chung's house has been remodeled. A new mothers' club hall has been built (although the members usually prefer to sit and talk just outside the door, instead of gathering inside), with the cooperative store on one end (having been relocated from its site as the former wineshop). A new Presbyterian church of handsome brick attests to the villagers' newfound wealth and to their religious devotion.

Village leaders in Oryu Li are still not satisfied with their quality of life. Mrs. Chung's husband said in 1975, upon the completion of the bridge, that Oryu Li still needed two more projects in order to become a "perfect village": (1) piped water to every household, and (2) a methane gas plant to supply low-cost energy for heating and cooking. And, in fact, plans are afoot for launching both of these projects in Oryu Li.

But the real changes in Oryu Li are not the physical manifestations. They lie within, in feelings of efficacy, a sense of community solidarity, a capacity to mobilize human resources to meet future problems, and pride of past accomplishments.

Has success spoiled Mrs. Chung? She still seems much like the modest but strong leader we met in 1973. Her dress is standard village wear, even when we met her last in the coffeeshop of the New Korea Hotel in Seoul, where we had arranged an interview while she was in the city to address a women's convention (her speech was essentially the story of Oryu Li, as she understood it). When we asked her about the village mothers' club, she replied:

The members are doing very well, even when I am away. Recently, I have had to leave the village very often. . . . When Mrs. Park was assassinated, I was in Seoul. I returned a day earlier than I had planned, and found that the mothers' club members and the rest of the village were having a meeting in memory of her. The next day, 20 women volunteered to go to the provincial government office in white dress to offer prayers for Mrs. Park. The village people first heard the news on the radio, but since my house and one other house have TV, we watched the funeral on television together.

Mrs. Chung is now the leader of her township and county associations of mothers' club leaders, and in this capacity visits other villages as a consultant about mothers' club activities. Her own club members support her visits to these sites, and learn new ideas from her reports of other villages. She persuaded the other leaders of township and county associations in Korea to meet in each of their villages, rather than in government offices. Mrs. Chung maintains that if these meetings were in offices, the mothers' club leaders could not learn as much of each other's club activities, and the leaders would soon be considered an "inconvenience" and ignored by government officials. By meeting in villages, the officials are curious about what is happening and hence are more eager to participate.

It seems that Mrs. Chung continues to follow the shrewd strategies that earlier had enabled her to co-opt the village elders in Oryu Li, and to overcome other obstacles.

Mrs. Chung's head, it seemed, had not been turned by the extensive media coverage accorded the miracle of Oryu Li. These film, TV, and newspaper stories were initially set off by an article in the leading newsmagazine of Korea, based upon an interview with Dean Park on our return from the village in 1973. We had started calling Oryu Li a "miracle" at first in a manner only partly serious, but the name stuck after the newsmagazine titled their article about Oryu Li "A Miracle Village."

Perhaps the experience of Oryu Li implies that development is easy. It isn't. We feel that the real miracle of the "miracle" of Oryu Li lies in the similar success stories now underway in hundreds of other Korean villages. For example, women in many other villages are now organizing to remove their local winehouse. As part of the New Village Movement, hundreds of thousands of the straw-thatched roofs of village homes have been replaced with colored tile. Irrigation projects. New roads. Small groups of village men or women working together in the fields, when only five years ago such work was an individual task. Almost every month, the President of Korea gives a national award to some outstanding village for its self-development accomplishments. Sometimes these awards go to mothers' clubs; almost always the organized women are involved in their village's achievements. A survey (Kim, 1977) showed that women have gained access to village assemblies in about three-fourths of Korea's 37,000 villages, with most of this new equality occurring during the 1970s (mostly as a consequence of the mothers' club program and the New Village Movement).

A basic reevaluation is underway in Korea about what women can do for themselves, for their villages, and for the development of Korea, once they have seen the vision of their own power.

LESSONS FROM THE MIRACLE OF ORYU LI

We conclude our story of the miracle of Oryu Li with this brief postscript about what we learned. Mrs. Chung and her village taught us that:

1. Each successful self-development event can be reinforcing of the next step in this process, as those who participate learn a sense of personal efficacy through gaining power and control over their enviroment.

2. Local people, even women in a culture where they are regarded as unequal to men, can make a difference in the process of development if they are well organized and adequately led, and provided with external assistance in the form of information and other resources.[6]

3. The development of Oryu Li was not a linear process, or simply a direct response to the inputs of external assistance, but rather a series of events over time (from the organization of the mothers' club to the construction of the village bridge) which involved a search for improved solutions to mutual problems.

4. Along with each problem-solving event came positive changes in the village's networks of communication, decision making, and leadership, which accelerated the village's rate of growth and improved its capacity for self-development.

5. The traditional structure of communication and decision makng which controls the socio-economic development of a system can be re-structured from *within* through the efforts of a charismatic leader, organized group action, and effective strategies of change, so that a new communication structure emerges.

6. The capacity to develop and manage communication networks is an important prerequisite for self-sustaining socio-economic development over time.

[6] If the poorest of the poor in the world were to be identified, the majority would certainly be women. They constitute one-half of the world population and one-third of the official labor force, perform nearly two-thirds of the hours worked, and receive only one-tenth of the world income and own less than one-hundredth of world property. Out of 800 million people enumerated as illiterate in the world, two-thirds are women.

7. The role of communication in the develoment of Oryu Li was not a one-way flow of information and influence from government to the villagers, or even one of linear persuasion by a village leader of her followers, but rather a convergence process in which the villagers created and shaped information with one another to reach mutual understandings for collective action.

8. Self-development relies more heavily on the process of interpersonal communication through networks than on mass media communication, with the media's role mainly that of reporting the exemplary performance of "model" villages for others to emulate.

Taken as a whole, these eight lessons from the study of Oryu Li suggest that for purposes of development, communication should be studied within the context of interpersonal communication networks, and how such networks relate to decision making and leadership, external assistance, and mass communication. Furthermore, the case of Oryu Li suggests that models of human communication must be developed that are capable of representing communication as a process of mutual information-sharing within a system. How such a convergence communication model relates to network analysis is the subject of chapter 2.

COMMUNICATION NETWORKS IN ORYU LI

Until this point, we have based our reporting of the miracle of Oryu Li entirely on a qualitative analysis of the events that occurred there in the mid-1970s.

Another type of data-analysis is also available to help us understand the process of communication and development in Oryu Li: communication network analysis of the linkages among the 69 women in the village.

We gathered these data in early 1977, after much of the development process described in this chapter had already occurred (ideally, we wish we had also obtained sociometric data in July, 1973, on our first visit to the village). In personal interviews with the respondents, we asked: "Of the women living in this village, who do you talk with most about family planning?" Their answers were processed by the NEGOPY computer program (Richards, 1975) and Lingoes' Smallest-Space Analysis I, which will be described in chapter 4. The results are shown in Figure 1–2.

At first glance, the sociogram [7] in Figure 1–2 appears to be a con-

[7] A *sociogram* is a graphic means for displaying the patterns of communication or social choice in a system.

Figure 1–2. Sociogram of the Communication Network for the Diffusion of Family Planning for 69 Women in Oryu Li.

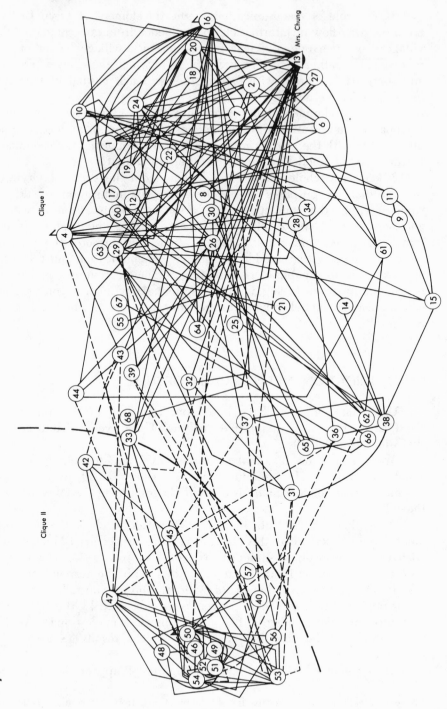

See bottom of page 29 for descriptive note and source for this figure.

fusing mass of individuals and links, illustrating the problem of information overload for an observer.[8] Even with the help of this sociogram,
produced by the use of the two network analysis computer programs,
the reader is overloaded with too much data about the network. Later
chapters will demonstrate how other aspects of network analysis can
help enable us to overcome this problem.

But careful inspection of Figure 1–2 allows us to detect certain
aspects of communication structure which provide further insights into
the development process in Oryu Li.

1. Compared to the other 24 Korean villages' networks that we
analyze in this book, Oryu Li is much more connected in a communication sense. Although there are two cliques, many dyadic links span the
boundaries of these two subgroups. Clearly the communication structure
of Oryu Li is connected in a way that would facilitate the collaboration
of these women in self-development activites.

2. Mrs. Chung (#13 in the sociogram) is the most central individual; 27 of the 68 other women (40 percent) say they talked with Mrs.
Chung about family planning. Further, Mrs. Chung's links connect her,
and thus clique I, to clique II. She plays a key communication role as a
"bridge"[9] in providing connectedness to the network. If she were removed, cliques I and II would not be so connected, and they would be
less able to cooperate in carrying out the various self-development
activities that made Oryu Li a miracle. Thus we see that network analysis can show more than just how much direct influence a leader has;
how this influence is patterned or distributed can also be understood.

3. Two of the three subleaders of the mothers' club are members of
clique I (individuals #4 and #26), and the other subleader (#50) is
a key communicator in clique II. Mrs. Chung was sagacious in identify-

---

[8] *Information overload* is the state of an individual or a system in which excessive
communication inputs cannot be processed and utilized, leading to breakdown.
[9] A *bridge* is an individual who links two or more cliques in a system from his or
her position as a member of one of the cliques.

Note: Mrs. Chung, the mother's club leader, is individual #13; #4, #26, and #50
are subleaders of the club; individual #33 is a liaison linking cliques I and II; individual #16 is the former club leader. Six isolates (#3, #5, #23, #41, #58, and
#59) plus #35 and #69 are not included in this sociogram. The smallest-space
analysis location of the individuals in the sociogram above corresponds closely to the
map of the village (Figure1–1), suggesting the importance of space in determining who
interacts with whom (chapter 7).

Source: All married women of reproductive age in Oryu Li were interviewed in 1977;
these data were analyzed by Richard's NEGOPY computer program and the results
were checked by Lingoes' Smallest-Space Analysis I, which printed out the above
sociogram in two-dimensional space (Kim, 1977b).

ing these three subleaders as a means of involving both cliques in mothers' club activities. The connectedness of the two cliques is also built through individual #33, a liaison linking the two cliques.

4. Clique II is almost entirely composed of women whose homes are located in the "upper village" (Figure 1-1), while clique I women live in the "lower village." Geographical location is a very important determinant of clique membership in Oryu Li (Kim, 1977b). Figures 1-1 and 1-2 show that individual #33, the liaison, lives midway between the upper and lower villages. Geographically, as well as socially, she links the two subgroups.

Our network analysis, briefly presented here to suggest the richness that such inquiry can bring to communication research, also answered the following questions.

1. What role does mothers' club membership play in each of the two cliques? That is, are the club members mostly in clique I (thus suggesting an overlapping of the mothers' club with clique I), or are they located throughout the village network?

2. How are the 27 individuals who directly contact Mrs. Chung different from the 41 individuals who do not have direct contact? Are mothers' club members more likely to have communication links wth Mrs. Chung? Has involvement in the self-development activities of the village been more characteristic of Mrs. Chung's contactees?

3. How are the six isolates, and the four semi-isolates, different from the 59 nonisolates?

4. Is clan membership the basis for the cliques in Oryu Li? For example, are the clique I individuals mostly members of the dominant Kang clan, while the other women are of the other clans?

The answers to these research questions, along with other analyses of the Oryu Li network data, will appear in future chapters.

2 THE CONVERGENCE MODEL OF COMMUNICATION AND NETWORK ANALYSIS

Learning nets and societies do not grow best by simplifying or rigidly supporting their parts or members, but rather with the complexity and freedom of these members, so long as they succeed in maintaining or increasing mutual communication.

Karl W. Deutsch (1968, p. 399)

Development in the Korean village of Oryu Li illustrated many important principles of social change. It underscored the importance of communication, especially interpersonal communication, in the process of change. However, we are struck by how poorly the existing models of communication apply to the case of Oryu Li. They simply do not usefully explain much that happened. Most such models describe one-way, linear communication and feature source-message-channel-receiver components. When communication is viewed in its full context, any particular "act" of communication can only be understood in terms of what was said before, or in terms of the communication that follows. In other words, in real-life, natural settings, communication can be understood better if it is not broken up into a sequence of source–message–channel–receiver acts, but rather examined as complete cycles of communication in which two or more participants mutually share information with one another in order to achieve some common purpose, like mutual understanding and/or collective action.

In this chapter we shall be frankly critical of linear models of communication, which have almost completely dominated communication research in the past. In their stead, we propose a convergence model of communication, in which we depart from the linear approach of past models. We argue that network analysis is an appropriate paradigm for theory and research, if one carries the implications of the convergence model of communication into the operations of communication research. We feel that the convergence model and network analysis should begin to replace the dominant approach in previous research which concentrated on linear models of communication effects among individual receivers.

This chapter is based upon Kincaid with Schramm (1975) and is adapted with permission from D. Lawrence Kincaid (1979), "The Convergence Model of Communication," Paper no. 18, Honolulu: East-West Communication Institute, copyright © 1979.

In the study of human communication, we feel that emphasis should be placed upon information-exchange relationships, rather than on individuals as the units of analysis. The important stumbling block in the field of communication research is how this should be done. The intellectual paradigm [1] consisting of the convergence model of communication and network analysis is our best answer to how to shift to studying information-exchange relationships as the basic unit of human communication. Other viable alternatives may also emerge in the future.

LINEAR MODELS OF COMMUNICATION

What kind of model would best represent the process of communication that we previously described in Oryu Li? Now we are no longer interested just in the particular case of Oryu Li, but rather in a communication model of behavioral change in social systems. A *model* is a representation of real-world phenomena in more abstract terms which can be applied to other cases at other times.

Probably the earliest communication model was proposed by Aristotle, who specified the speaker, the speech, and the audience as the constituent elements of the communication act. Communication as it is conceived by most scholars and practitioners today has been greatly influenced by the models proposed in the late 1940s by Harold Lasswell, and by Claude E. Shannon and Warren Weaver. Lasswell's (1948) basic model consisted of "*Who* says *what*, in what *channel*, to *whom*, and with what *effect?*" The addition of the channel as a specific element was a response to the growth in new communication media, such as print, the telegraph, and radio. The inclusion of effects was an important break with past models which mainly served descriptive purposes. The study of effects initiated a new field: the communication approach to human behavioral change.

The academic field of communication "took off" when Shannon and Weaver (1949) set forth their model in *The Mathematical Theory of Communication*. They defined communication as "all the procedures by which one mind may affect another," but the model itself (Figure 2–1)

---

[1] A *paradigm* is a scientific approach to some phenomena that provides model problems and solutions to a community of scholars. An "invisible college" is the collectivity of scholars that form around a revolutionary paradigm, seeking to investigate it further and thus to improve its ability to explain some type of behavior (Kuhn, 1970). Network analysts currently constitute one example of an invisible college. One function of an invisible college is to provide a temporary sense of order and a type of intellectual reinforcement in the face of the considerable uncertainty encountered by the scientist in seeking to cope with the unknown in his or her discipline. A paradigm provides a starting place for empirical investigation to the members of an invisible college.

Figure 2–1.   Shannon and Weaver's Linear Model of Communication.

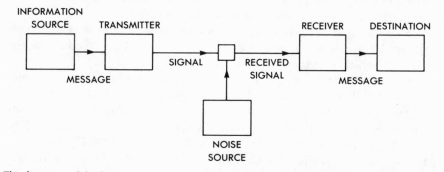

This linear model of communication helped set off the field of communication research, which followed a components approach to investigating the effects of communication. This linear model, and various later versions based upon it, thus represented the dominant paradigm for communication research until the present, when it was realized that the linear models may represent apt descriptions of the communication *act,* but that they do not accurately describe the complexities of communication as a *process.*

Source: Shannon and Weaver (1949), *The Mathematical Theory of Communication* (Urbana: University of Illinois Press), p. 34. Used with permission.

was designed for purposes of electronic engineering.[2] It is essentially a linear, left-to-right, one-way model of communication. It led to technical improvements in message transmission, and it served to bring together scholars from several disciplines to the scientific study of communication. The effort which it stimulated to create a unified model of human communication failed because the theory did not consider the semantic or the pragmatic levels of communication.[3]

Electronic communication usually is linear. But when the Shannon/ Weaver model was utilized by human communication researchers, they did not pay enough attention to feedback and noise as components in

[2] Looking backward to 1948–1949 from the advantageous viewpoint of today, one wonders why the Shannon and Weaver (1949) book had such a much greater impact on the scientific study of human communication than did Norbert Weiner's (1948) *Cybernetics,* a book which appeared at about the same time. Evidently a linear model of communication better fit the needs of the then-emerging field of communication than did a cybernetic model. Professor Wilbur Schramm was especially influential in the 1950s in facilitating use of linear models, and later led the move to relational models in the 1970s. "The most dramatic change in general communication theory during the last 40 years has been the gradual abandonment of the idea of a passive audience, and its replacement by the concept of a highly active, highly selective audience, manipulating rather than being manipulated by a message— a full partner in the communication process" (Schramm, 1971, p. 8).

[3] Although Shannon and Weaver (1949) did discuss the semantic problem of "the interpretation of meaning by the receiver, as compared with the intended meaning of the sender."

the communication process. Further, they tended to underestimate the subjectivity of communication, that a message usually means something quite different to a receiver than it did to the source.

Shannon and Weaver's most important contribution was their concept of information (a construct discussed in a later section of this chapter), which provided a central focus to the new field of communication research. It became the main conceptual variable around which the new intellectual approach began to grow.

During the thirty-one years since the informaton theory of communication appeared, other communication models were proposed by Osgood and others (1957), Westley and MacLean (1957), and Berlo (1960). These models are basically similar to the Shannon–Weaver conceptualization (Table 2-1). All specify a series of components in the model, most imply a linear sequence in the communication act, and these models generally imply an active source seeking to effect a passive receiver.[4] Most of these models state that communication, more or less, is a "process" by which an idea is transferred from a source to a receiver with the intent to change behavior.

The linear communication models of the 1950s and 1960s (like the S–M–C–R model of Berlo [1960], one of the most widely known) were useful for purposes of designing laboratory experiments which assumed one-way causality of the components of the model on communication effects. Such an assumption may have been justified in the study of propaganda and persuasion, especially when such messages were transmitted by the mass media. These models described a simple communication act, but not the *process* of communcation. Many important aspects of human communication do not fit linear models, and tended to be ignored by communication research based on linear models.

Most communication research has been conducted in light of these linear models. The usual approach has been to gather data from a sample of receivers about the effects of communication on their knowledge, attitudes, or overt behavior. Source variables, message variables, channel variables, and/or receiver variables are manipulated by the researchers as independent variables, in order to relate them to the dependent variables of communication effects. Usually the individual receiver is the unit of analysis, as well as the unit of response.

---

[4] Although Berlo's (1960) model of communication is essentially a linear model (source, message, channel, receiver), he warned that "it is dangerous to assume that one [of these elements] comes first, one last, or that they are independent of each other. This denies the concept of process, and communication is a process." Berlo (p. 106) stated: "The behaviors of the source do not occur independently of the behaviors of the receiver or vice versa. *In any communication situation, the source and the receiver are interdependent*" (emphasis of the original author).

TABLE 2–1.   Models of Communication.

Sources	Type of Model	Main Components of the Model	Definitions of Communication
1. Claude Shannon and Warren Weaver (1949)	Linear	source encoder message decoder destination noise feedback	All the procedures by which one mind may affect another.
2. Charles Osgood and others (1957)	Linear	message decoder interpreter encoder message decoder	One system, a source, influences another, the destination, by manipulation of alternative signals which can be transmitted over the channel connecting them.

3. Bruce Westley and Malcolm MacLean (1957), based on Newcomb (1953)	Linear	messages
		sources
		  (advocacy roles)
		gatekeepers
		  (channel roles)
		receivers
		  (behavioral
		  system roles)
		feedback
			Person A transmits messages about an object X to person B through gatekeeper C.

4. David Berlo (1960)	Linear	source message channel receiver feedback	A process by which a source intentionally changes the behavior of a receiver.
5. Wilbur Schramm (1973)	Relational	informational signs relationship among participants active receivers	A set of communication acts focused on a set of informational signs within a particular relationship.

6. D. Lawrence Kincaid (1979)	Convergence	information
		uncertainty
		convergence
		mutual
		  understanding
		mutual agreement
		collective action
		networks of
		  relationships
			A process of convergence in which information is shared by participants in order to reach a mutual understanding.

"Source Credibility and Persuasion: An Experiment Based on the Linear Model"

A core illustration of research on communication effects, following the linear model, is Hovland and others' (1953, pp. 27-31) well known laboratory experiment on source credibility. This study isolated one communication variable, source credibility,* while attempting to control other variables. Its mechanistic, atomistic design sought to reproduce the human reception of mass media messages in a laboratory setting.

The general procedures which were used in this study became a model for many subsequent communication experiments. Identical communication messages were presented to two groups of randomly assigned subjects. For one group, however, the source of the message which was identified had high credibility; for the other group the source had low credibility. This procedure was followed for four different topics, each with high-credibility and low-credibility versions. The subjects (college students) received the messages in the form of booklets containing written articles on each topic, with the name of the source given at the end of each article. The four topics were (1) antihistamine drugs, (2) atomic submarines, (3) the steel shortage, and (4) the future of movie theaters. The high-credibility sources were (1) the *New England Journal of Biology and Medicine* (2) J. Robert Oppenheimer (a famous atomic scientist), (3) the *Bulletin of National Resources Planning Board,* and (4) *Fortune* magazine, respectively. The low-credibility sources were given as (1) a mass circulation monthly pictorial magazine, (2) *Pravda* (the Russian newspaper), (3) an anti-labor, anti–New Deal, "rightist" newspaper columnist, and (4) a woman movie gossip columnist. Attitude questionnaires were administered to each experimental group before, immediately after, and a month after the communication treatment.

The results showed that immediately after the communication took place, there was more attitude change as a result of the high-credibility sources, except for the topic on the future of movie theaters, where the low-credibility group showed more attitude change. Four weeks after the booklets, however, the differences in attitude between the high-credibility group and the low-credibility group disappeared. The study concluded that the effect of source credibility is maximal at the time of communication, but fades with the passage of time.

This experiment is perhaps the best known of the Yale University communication experiments. It formed the model research design for many hundreds of persuasion experiments in the years that followed. It attempted to isolate one communication variable, a characteristic of the source, while experimentally controlling the effect of all other variables. Thus, it followed the basic linear (source–message–channel–receiver) model of the communication process in an

---

* *Credibility* was defined as the degree to which a communication source is perceived by a receiver as trustworthy and competent.

attempt to simulate the main elements of mass communication and persuasion. No interpersonal communication was allowed among the subjects in each experimental group. Even in later experiments where face-to-face, interpersonal communication was used, the most common context was the lecture, still following the one-way, linear model of communication.

Thus we see how the components approach to communication research, based on a linear model, was atomistic and mechanistic. The student subjects were not allowed to ask questions or to discuss the meaning of the print messages among themselves. The source credibility variable was not allowed to vary in its effects through interaction with other components of the linear model like receiver characteristics (for instance, *Pravda* may have been a credible source about atomic submarines for some respondents).

The artificial unreality of this experiment aided the control of extraneous variables. Unfortunately, this unreality also limited the generalization of the experiment's results to actual situations in which individuals do talk to one another.

Criticism of the Linear Models

Writing seventeen years after his original statement of the S–M–C–R model, Berlo (1977, p. 12) accepted the criticism of his linear S–M–C–R model that "our view of research [focusing on communication effects] and our view of communication [as a process] have been contradictory" (Smith, 1972). Berlo (p. 12) stated: "It could be argued that S–M–C–R was not intended as a 'model' of communication, that it met none of the tests of theoretic modeling, and that it was developed as *an audio-visual aid to stimulate recall of the components of a communication relationship*." [5] Berlo blamed the "limited fertility of the research tradition" in which he was trained (mainly a psychological approach to experimental research on one-way communication).

Berlo (p. 12) still claimed that linear models of "do-it-to-others" processes like persuasion are appropriate for much of human communication, although not for some of the most important communication: "I did not recognize that the assumptions underlying linear causal determinism may account for the major proportion of communication events, but not account for the portion that makes a significant difference in our lives." Berlo concluded that our interests in communication are changing, mainly from directional persuasion where linear models may have been more satisfactory, to "communication-as-exchange."

Bauer (1964, p. 319) pointed out the limitation of one-way models in mass communication research: "The model which *ought* to be inferred from the data of research . . . is of communication as a trans-

[5] Emphasis added by the present authors.

actional process in which two parties each expect to give and take from the deal approximately equal values." Writing almost a decade later, this author (Bauer, 1973, p. 142), reemphasized that communicators are, and should be, influenced by their audiences: "In other words, the audience would have influenced what he said before the audience ever heard or read what he had to say." In spite of numerous attempts to establish a transactional model over the past seventeen years, there has been "little effective impact on the organized research or systematic writing that is done" (Bauer, 1973, p. 143).

The limitations of linear models became apparent in their application to the study of mass communication (Klapper, 1960; Katz and Lazarsfeld, 1955), and the diffusion of innovations (Rogers, 1962 and 1976a). But the simple, linear model was appended, rather than replaced. The two-step flow hypothesis was proposed to explain why the mass media did not achieve their expected effects in political behavior (Lazarsfeld and others, 1948; Katz and Lazarsfeld, 1955, p. 132; Katz, 1957), which soon gave way to the idea of multistep flows (Schramm, 1973).

The main problem with the linear models of communication stemmed from their basic metatheoretical or epistemological assumptions about the nature of information, how it is transmitted, and what we do with it. In our daily experience there is a tendency to treat information as if it could be carried from a source to a receiver like "a bucket carries water" (Diaz Bordenave, 1972), like a dumptruck carrying sand across a city, like a hypodermic needle injecting a vaccine, or like a "bullet" shot at a target (Schramm, 1973). All of these analogies were created to criticize the treatment of information as if it were entirely a physical entity which could be moved around like other material objects. There is a physical aspect to information and so this assumption "works" in many situations. But this supposition about the nature of information is in part responsible for another theoretic error: that the individual mind is an isolated entity, separate from the body, separate from other minds, and separate from the environment in which it exists (Bateson, 1972). The context of human communication was thus ignored.

These assumptions (1) that information is only a physical substance and (2) that individual minds are separate, led to seven biases that we identify in past communication theory and research (Kincaid, 1979).

1. A view of communication as a linear, one-way act (usually vertical), rather than a cyclical, two-way process over time.
2. A source bias based on dependency, rather than focusing on the relationship of those who communicate and their fundamental interdependency.
3. A tendency to focus on the objects of communication as simple,

isolated physical objects, at the expense of the context in which they exist.

4. A tendency to focus on the messages per se at the expense of silence, and the punctuation and timing of messages.

5. A tendency to consider the primary function of communication to be persuasion, rather than mutual understanding, consensus, and collective action.

6. A tendency to concentrate on the psychological effects of communication on separate individuals, rather than on the social effects and the relationships among individuals within networks.

7. A belief in one-way mechanistic causation, rather than mutual causation which characterizes human information systems that are fundamentally cybernetic.

These seven biases are interrelated and cumulative. Each tends to support the others and to create a rather coherent image of communication behavior in spite of the limitations and problems that this image produces. When communication is perceived as one-way and vertical, and when one takes the point of view of sources as subjects who use communication to produce a change in receivers as objects (Freire, 1973), biases toward psychological effects and mechanistic causation are created. The last two biases may be especially serious, and we shall now explore them in some detail, as they can be overcome by the network/convergence paradigm that we propose in the present book.

The Psychological Bias

The psychological bias [6] in communication stems (1) from its overwhelming focus on the individual as the "object" or unit of analysis, and (2) from the researchers' acceptance of how social problems are usually defined in terms of individual-blame (Rogers, 1977). As a result, the relational nature of human communication is lost. Using random sampling of individuals, the survey is a "sociological meat-grinder," tearing the respondent from his or her social context and guaranteeing that no one in the sample interacts with any other respondent. "It is a little like a biologist putting his or her experimental animals through a hamburger machine and looking at every hundredth cell through a microscope; anatomy and physiology get lost; structure and function disappear and one is left with cell biology" (Barton, 1968). "By its very nature, the

---

[6] By no means are we the first critics of the psychological bias in communication research. For instance, Watzlawick and others (1967, pp. 21–22) criticized communication research for studying the individual out of his/her "communication nexus." Dr. Watzlawick is a leading member of the interactionist or Palo Alto School (Wilder, 1979).

survey technique threatened to atomize sociology . . . instead of viewing the human collectivity as a whole" (Lazarsfeld, 1970, p. 72).

Only recently and rarely has the main focus in communication research shifted to the dyad, clique, network, or system of individuals; to the communication relationships *between* individuals, rather than on the individuals themselves. Encouraging attempts to overcome the individual, psychological bias in communication research are provided by the coorientation model (McLeod and Chaffee, 1973), by relational analysis, by the general systems approach (Rogers and Agarwala-Rogers, 1976a), by studies of group transformation for development (Chu, 1976), and by network analysis.

These conceptual–methodological approaches suggest that even when the individual is the unit of response, the communication *relationship* (even though *it* can't "speak") can be the unit of analysis via some type of sociometric measurement. Sampling and data-analysis procedures for network analysis are being worked out, but until communication scholars begin to think in network terms, there will not be much network analysis of human behavior. In this sense, network analysis is a philosophy and a way of thinking, as well as a body of useful methodological tools.

A second reason for the artificially "destructured" psychological bias in communication research is the frequent acceptance of a person-blame causal-attribution definition of the social problems that are investigated. *Individual-blame* is the tendency to hold an individual responsible for his or her problems, rather than society. Obviously, what is done about a social problem, including research, depends upon how it is defined.

Many illustrations of individual-blame can be cited in various types of behavioral research. Caplan and Nelson (1973) find a high degree of individual-blame in psychological research on such social problems as highway safety and race relations.[7] Person-blame rather than system-blame permeates most definitions of social problems; seldom are the definers able to change the system, so they accept it. Such acceptance encourages a focus on psychological variables in social science research. Often, the problem definer's individual-level cause becomes the researcher's main variable.

[7] These authors provide an example of individual-blame from an analysis of a training program for inner-city Black men in Detroit. The training course stressed the importance of punctuality in holding a job, but within a few months after completing the training and being employed in the auto industry, many of the trainees lost their jobs for being tardy. Directors of the training course blamed the low-income men for their laziness (an example of individual-blame), but Caplan and Nelson concluded from their evaluation that the failure was caused by the system, not by the individual trainees: the men had no alarm clocks to awaken them in the morning, and they did not own cars, so they had to depend on unreliable public transportation to get to work. Often they were late as a consequence. The evaluators recommended that the federally-sponsored training program buy alarm clocks for the men, a system-blame suggestion that was rejected by the training agency.

How can the person-blame bias be overcome? By keeping an open mind about the presumed causes of a social problem, at least until exploratory data are gathered; by involving the participants in the definition of the problem, rather than just those persons who are seeking amelioration of the social problem; by considering structural variables, as well as intraindividual variables, in communication research.

Research on the diffusion of innovations was originally (and for many years) as guilty as other types of behavioral research in following a psychological, individual-blame approach. For example, Ryan and Gross (1943) did not gather sociometric data about the interpersonal diffusion of the innovation of hybrid corn within their two Iowa communities of study even though (1) they found that interpersonal communication from the farmers' neighbors was essential in clinching individuals' adoption decisions, and (2) their sampling design of a complete census of farmers in the two communities was ideal for gathering relational data for the purpose of network analysis.

A similar individual-blame, psychological viewpoint influenced national development and family planning programs in developing countries during the 1960s and 1970s. Government officals wanted to lower their national population growth rate, and urged their citizens to have fewer children, usually two or three. But the typical village parents wanted four or five children, including at least two sons, to provide them with sufficient farm and household labor, economic support and care in their old age, and a kind of religious immortality after death. Rather than developing programs to overcome these structural constraints, and thus perceiving a system-blame for large families, government officials continued to blame individual parents for not adopting contraceptives and for having "too many" children. Consequently, communication programs were designed to change individuals' fertility behavior (Rogers, 1973). In the past, most scholars of family planning behavior too readily accepted an individual-blame definition of the problem of overpopulation.

The Bias of Mechanistic Causation

The fundamental idea of causation is learned in early childhood from the experience of willfully moving one physical object (say a ball) with the force of another physical object (our hand, or another ball) (deCharms, 1968). From this early action in the "real" world, we develop an abstract conception of causation, described by such expressions as "this produces that" and "if this, then that." These early ideas of mechanistic causation are usually reliable: "The ball may not go where I want it to go, but if I hit it, it always goes."

Communication and information appear to work the same way at times. A child learns that if he cries loud enough, his mother will pay attention. But an important difference is readily apparent. The mother's reaction is not as immediate as that of a physical object's recoil from the impact of another object. Sometimes the mother does not come, no matter how loud the child's cry. Sometimes when she does come, she does not do what the child wants because cries vary a great deal and it may be difficult for the mother to interpret what a certain cry means.

Producing changes by mechanical effort in the child's physical world is more predictable and certain than using information to change the social world of his relationships with other human beings.

As the child grows up, he learns that science has developed ways to predict and control the movement of physical objects and energy with amazing accuracy and reliability. The concept and language of causality which the layman takes from science are based on the notion that all of the other influences (variables) in a situation can be held constant except the two that are causally related. In order to discover a simple causal relation, the experimental scientist attempts to hold constant all other factors which he suspects may influence the causal relationship that he is studying, or else he assumes that "other things are equal." An illustration is provided by the Hovland and others (1953) experiment on source credibility and persuasion; by randomly assigning the Yale sophomores to the two experimental groups, the investigators controlled all other variables than the treatment variable of source credibility.

This analytical method of experimentation has been extremely successful in the physical sciences. But it has also created an exaggerated and misleading conception of physical causality when applied to human behavior. The mechanistic assumptions underlying deterministic explanation are too often overlooked: that the effects of observation and measurement on the objects studied are negligible, and that other factors (like friction) can be considered equal or constant. For example, if a physicist knows the mass, position, and velocity of a billiard ball at one time, he can predict its position at a later time.

The greatest difference between the explanation of physical phenomena and human communication, however, is that the "objects" of communication (unlike billiard balls) have purposes of their own. Human beings do not always use information in the way that it is intended by its "source," nor in the way that it is necessarily interpreted by the observer/researcher. These factors are explicitly taken into account in the convergence model of communication.

As stated previously, most past communication research followed a components approach in which a source, message, channel, or receiver variable is varied in order to determine the consequences of this manipulation in the effects of communication. Changes in the source, message, channel, or receiver here constitute the independent variables, and the resulting communication effects are the dependent variable.

In order for the independent variable X to be the cause of dependent variable Y: (1) X must precede Y in time-order, (2) they must be associated or covary together, and (3) X must have a "forcing quality" on Y. Much past communication research has only been concerned with determining whether X and Y are associated through correlational analysis of data from one-shot surveys. Other researchers have also determined the time-order of X and Y through use of an experimental design. Forcing quality, the way in which X acts on Y, is a theoretical rather than an empirical matter, and rests on the inherent nature of the X and Y variables. Systems theory implies that X and Y are probably interdependent, and so search for forcing quality may be futile. Both X and Y may be the "cause" and "effect" of each other. Mechanistic, one-way causation is replaced by mutual causation.

A main theme in Western science has been reductionism: chopping things up and studying the parts. The method was thus atomistic and mechanistic; ambiguities were reduced by isolating one or a few elements in a total process, and then examining each piece separately. This atomistic–mechanistic approach to science seemed to work fairly well in physics, chemistry, and other physical sciences.[8] But it was found wanting in the biological sciences and the social sciences.

In living systems, where the parts are highly interdependent, the mechanistic atomism that had functioned so effectively in physics could not cope with the interaction among the parts. During the 1960s, a different approach to scientific thinking arose to fill this gap in the biological and social sciences: general systems theory. The central credo of systems theory is the statement that the whole is more than the sum of its parts. Systems theory is holistic, concentrating on wholes, the relationships between parts, interactions of the system with its environment, and with control or self-regulation of direction.

Systems theory is one of the main theoretical influences on our convergence model of communication.

THE CONVERGENCE MODEL OF COMMUNICATION

In this section we shall (1) trace the background of the convergence model, (2) define communication as a process in which participants create and share information with one another to reach a mutual under-

---

[8] Bertalanffy (1975, pp. 13–14) gave a clear picture of this major change in scientific approach from the atomistic–mechanistic method born of classical physics in the nineteenth century to a systems approach: "This scheme of isolatable units acting in one-way causality has proved insufficient . . . we must think in terms of systems of elements in mutual interaction."

standing, and (3) relate cybernetic explanations to the convergence model.

Theoretical Roots of the Convergence Model

The basic idea of the convergence model of communication was first articulated almost a century ago by the philosopher Charles Sanders Peirce. His inquiry into the nature of signs and meaning led him to realize the inherent vagueness of language as it is actually used in everyday life. According to Peirce, a sign is objectively vague if it requires some further sign or further experience to delimit its meaning. He reached the conclusion that "*no* concept, not even those of mathematics, is absolutely precise [because] . . . no man's interpretation of words is based on exactly the same experience as any other man's" (in Gallie, 1966, p. 175). Every symbol, word, sentence, or scientific formula must be given meaning if it is to communicate intelligent thought.

The interpretation of a sign is accomplished in terms of, or by means of, "some further sign, which may confirm, amplify, qualify, or correct the original sign [and] *develop* it" (in Gallie, p. 46). The meaning of any utterance is revealed by the reply that it evokes, which in turn needs a return reply to interpret it, and so on, in a potentially endless sequence. Recognition of this sequential aspect of communication means that the competent use and understanding of any sign is always a matter of degree. Peirce's insights capture the two basic principles underlying the convergence model: that information is inherently imprecise and uncertain, and that communication is a dynamic process of development over time.

Two students of Peirce's work, Charles W. Morris and George Herbert Mead, later developed major contributions to the theory of signs, language behavior, and symbolic interaction, which we credit (in a later section) as influences on our present paradigm. Peirce is also acknowledged as one of the founders of semiotics, the science of signs.

In 1922 Georg Simmel (1964) introduced the phrase "intersection of social circles," to indicate that each individual is unique, in that his pattern of "group-affiliations" is never exactly the same as that of any other individual. Although the translation of Simmel's book, *The Web of Group-Affiliations*,[9] emphasizes group affiliations, the "web" of the affiliations has been generalized to mean the personal network composed of other individuals with whom one interacts, whether they belong to identifiable "groups" or not. Hence, each individual is unique in his pattern of interpersonal communication.

[9] Simmel's book was translated from German to English forty-two years later (Simmel, 1964).

The uniqueness of an individual's personal network is responsible for the uniqueness of his meanings. In other words, the codes and concepts available to interpret information are based on each individual's past experiences which may be similar, but never identical, to another individual's. As an individual's patterns of interaction with others become similar (overlapping) to those of another individual's, so do their codes and concepts for interpreting and understanding reality.

Simmel demonstrated the dynamics of personal networks with examples from two important social movements of his time: the labor movement and the women's movement. Through the process of social organization the collective concept of "laborer" evolved from such concepts as weavers, mechanics, miners, and so forth. Through their common experience with other tradesmen, the members of each trade gradually developed a collective consciousness as wage laborers, at a higher level of abstracton. Such a change in meaning represented a convergence toward a more mutual understanding of the laborers' common predicament resulting from increased information-exchange and the formation of labor unions.

At about this same time, the anthropologist Edward Sapir (1935, p. 78) argued against the concept of society as if it were a static structure defined by tradition: "It is, in the more intimate sense, nothing of the kind, but a highly intricate network of partial or complete understandings *between* the members of organizational units . . . reanimated or creatively affirmed by particular acts of a communicative nature which obtain among the individuals participating in it" (emphasis added by the present authors). Sapir's approach to communication emphasized both the dynamic and the relatonal aspects of communication. From this point of view, the focus of communication research should be on the development of mutual understanding that emerges over time between those who share information with one another.

Karl Mannheim (1946, p. 28) was an early critic of the individual, psychological approach to the study of human behavior. His sociological approach was meant to "end the fiction of the detachment of the individual from the group, within the matrix of which the individual thinks and experiences." Accordingly, the capacity of abstract thought grows to the extent that individuals and groups are part of heterogeneous collectivities and organizations. The individual that engages in this type of thought "is rather a subject which is ever more inclusive, and which neutralizes the earlier particular and concrete points of view" (Mannheim, 1946, p. 302).

The work cited thus far in the present section was authored prior to the development of information theory (Shannon and Weaver, 1949) and cybernetics (Weiner, 1948). With the availability of these conceptual tools, Gregory Bateson (1972) challenged the prevailing concept of a separate, isolated mind which could be differentiated from the body and from the individual's environment. Each "individual" exists only as part of a cybernetic (information) system, in which his/her behavior is determined by behavior at a previous time. There is not a mind, but rather an ecology of the mind, for the *"mental characteristics of the system are immanent, not in some part, but in the system as a whole"* (Bateson, 1972). The mind exists only because of the network of closed circuits within the human system, brain plus body, and man plus environment. It is not possible to draw a fine line between that part of the human system which "thinks" and that part which does "not think," because thinking itself is made possible and occurs only within the network of closed circuits composed of man and his environment (which for an individual consists of all other individuals that are part of his information network). The unit which processes information (and thinks, decides, and acts) is a system whose boundaries do not coincide with one person's body, mind, or consciousness. From Bateson's point of view, communication, whether an utterance or an action, does not occur "in" the context of this ecological subsystem of ideas, but rather as a part of this subsystem. Communication is not a product or effect of what remains of the context after the piece we want to explain has been "cut out from it."

The rejection of the idea that the individual is an isolated entity, separate from his environment and other individuals, is consistent with the basic principle of general systems theory. General systems theory, the "science of 'wholeness'" (Bertalanffy, 1967, p. 37), has been an influential intellectual movement of the past three decades, especially in the behavioral sciences. Key figures in the development of systems theory reflect its interdisciplinary nature: the biologist and philosopher Ludwig von Bertalanffy, the mathematician Anatol Rapoport, the philosopher–economist Kenneth Boulding, and the sociologist Talcott Parsons.

A *system* is a set of interrelated parts coordinated to accomplish a set of goals (Churchman, 1968, p. 29). The systems approach achieved a following in each of the social sciences because it represented an alternative to the mechanistic atomism common in most previous research on human behavior. Systems theory is holistic: it assumes that the complex interactions among the parts of a given system would be destroyed by the dissection of the system through atomistic research procedures. Systems should be studied as a total unit, not as separated parts.

General systems theory emphasized interaction among the parts of a system, a viewpoint that recognized the importance of communication. Not surprisingly, many communication scholars embraced systems theory with great enthusiasm. Concepts like "feedback," "input–output," and "open systems" crept into the vocabulary of most communication scientists. But unfortunately, most communication scholars (as well as other social scientists) continued to utilize their existing research techniques: personal interviews with individuals, data about individual variables punched on IBM cards, and then analyzed with statistical tools like analysis of variance and multiple correlation. This business-as-usual approach failed to effectuate the potential of systems theory in the operations of behavioral research.

After a thorough review of the impact to date of systems theory in biology, cybernetics, communication, and economics, Lilienfield (1978) concluded that "systems theory is an ideology rather than a set of techniques" and urged a more becoming modesty in its missonary claims. A basic reason for the unfulfilled potential of systems theory has been the lack of appropriate methods of research. One cannot achieve holistic research objectives by using atomistic–mechanistic methodologies.

Exactly what would it mean to take a systems approach in communication research? To many, it means taking a broader view of communication, looking at all possible relationships in the system of study. This intent has often been translated by communication scholars into highly elaborate multivariate research strategies: asking more questions, measuring more variables, using sophisticated statistical methods of data-analysis (like multiple correlation, path analysis, or multidimensional scaling techniques). But these procedures are just extensions of atomistic–mechanistic approaches; they are not really systems approaches (Richards, 1976, p. 16).

There have been two main obstacles to adoption of the systems approach in the study of human communication: (1) the lack of a model of communication which could adequately represent the interdependent relationships among parts, and (2) the lack of suitable research methods to study the communication relationships. The convergence model and the methods of network analysis are designed to overcome these limitations.

Network analysis is distinctive as a research approach because it fits so well with systems theory. Just how well it fits will be explained in later sections and in the following chapters of this book.

In the present intellectual history of linear and convergence models of communication, we deal mainly with scholars in the field of mass communication theory and research. This historical development is in part paralleled by two invisible colleges, symbolic interaction and small groups, research, composed of sociologists and social psychologists. The central premises of symbolic interactionists like George Herbert Mead (1934) at the University of Chicago and Herbert Blumer (1969) at the University of Chicago and later at the University of California at Berkeley were (1) that individuals derive meanings from their interaction with others, and (2) that such meanings are the basis for human action. The invisible college of small group theorists was founded by Kurt Lewin (1951), and carried forward by Robert F. Bales (1950), Dorwin Cartwright and Alvin Zander (1962), and Leon Festinger and others (1950). Mullins with Mullins (1973, pp. 75-93 and 105–128) presented a kind of network analysis and history of these two invisible colleges.

The theoretical formulations and research activities of these two sets of scholars of interpersonal communication were generally consistent with our present paradigm of network analysis and convergence. Unfortunately, both invisible colleges, after a period of intellectual growth and promise, passed away in the 1960s (Mullins with Mullins, 1973). But both are a direct influence on our present thinking.

The Concept of Information

The fundamental element of communication in our convergence model is information. It is difficult to describe communication without some reference to information, or at least to one of its synonyms. In fact, both (1) the concept of network, and (2) the principle of convergence, derive from information. Information has become the fundamental concept for the study of all living systems.

What is information? And what makes it so important for the study of human communication? *Information* is a difference in matter–energy which affects uncertainty in a situation where a choice exists among a set of alternatives. This definition is conventional in the field of communication, but we feel that it is somewhat incomplete, as it does not do full justice to the richness of the concept or to its relationship to other important concepts that provide understanding of the same phenomenon. The emphasis of others on the "reduction" of uncertainty obscured the creative aspects of information-processing.

Information, and its convergence function in human communication, will be discussed in reference to four interrelated terms: (1) form, (2) difference, (3) invariance, and (4) uncertainty. The meaning of each of these terms is dependent upon their opposites: (1) substance, (2) similarity, (3) variance, and (4) certainty. It is the differences between each of these opposing terms which help give meaning to the concept of information in human communication.

It is, of course, no accident that the word "inform" is composed of "form" plus the prefix "in." The Latin word, *forma*, means contour, figure, shape, model, or pattern. *Form* is the shape or structure of something, as distinguished from the materal of which it is composed. Form is the arrangement of matter and energy. Although form can be distinguished from physical substance, it is made possible by the arrangement of that substance. Substance literally "stands under" form at a lower level of abstraction. Substance underlies form, the outward manifestation of change.[10]

The perception of form depends upon difference, the distinctive arrangement of matter. A particular form is just one of the many different modes of manifestation of the same substance. Thus variety is a prerequisite for form, order, or structure. A certain form is relative to other forms that could have occurred. To perceive a certain form, it must be different enough from other possible forms to be recognized. Information is "a difference which makes a difference," and communication is the transformation of such a difference through an information circuit (Bateson, 1972).

It is more accurate to say that we scan an object to search for its form, rather than that we "receive" form in a passive sense as if *it* came to *us*. As a transitive verb, "form" means to give something a particular shape, to shape it into a certain state. The observer of an object has a variety of forms in his mind which he actively projects onto the object to see how well each fits. So the coding or categorizing of form is an active role that the individual brings to the perception of an object.

The form of an object must be invariant over time and distance for us to perceive it efficiently. A mirror is a more invariant medium for reflecting the form of one's face than is the surface of a pond. A physical substance which varies too rapidly over time or space makes the perception of form difficult, if not impossible.

Some examples help show the relationship between difference and information, and demonstrate the related concepts of approximation, tolerance, and convention. In Set A of Figure 2–2 (see page 50) we have created information by giving a certain distinctive form to the page with our pen out of a variety of other possible forms.

Our drawing (Figure 2–2) shows that a rectangular shape does not have to be exactly the same, or very precisely drawn, in order to meet the conventional standards of most individuals. The form can approximate a rectangle within some degree of tolerance. Approximation and tolerance are important to information-processing and human communication. Our notion of the degree of tolerance places information-processing within the context of two or more persons rather than just one. The form of "rectangle" is applied by convention, according to the standards or rules of the group that create rectangles and use the word to refer to it. The degree of approximation and tolerance may vary from group to group according to their purposes for using rectangles. An architectual draftsman who draws a blueprint of a building with precision instruments may be less tolerant than an artist who makes a freehand sketch.

[10] In most other communication models, substance is the medium of exchange, commonly described (quite metaphorically) as if it "carries" or "conveys" information like a truck carries sand (as mentioned previously).

Figure 2–2. Information as Form, Difference, and Invariance.

Set A:

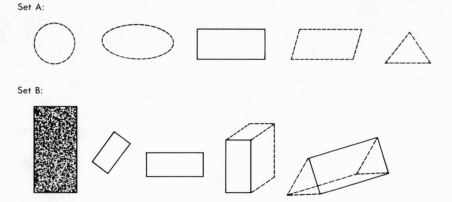

Set B:

Set C:

ka og informadon ov cvews. Glood One must recognize
Chuang Tzu brings out is precisely the point that there are

Set D:

form of information or views. One must recognize
Chuang Tzu brings out is precisely the point that there are

Note: Information is a difference in matter—energy which affects uncertainty in a situation where a choice exists among a set of alternatives. The importance of "difference"
in this definition is illustrated above; for example, in set A "rectangle" must be different enough from the other four figures so that it can be discriminated from them. This
figure must also possess some distinguishable quality in common with all other
"rectangles," with a certain range of tolerance, to be recognized as such.

Source: Kincaid (1979).

The eye is especially sensitive to contrast between two adjacent
regions of different light intensity or color. This perceived difference is
fundamental to the concept of information. Although we may see the
boundary "line" between two adjacent regions on a piece of paper, in
one space there is only a single region with two different levels of light
intensity, density, shade, or color. If the contrast in these two levels is
great enough, we can see a boundary line distinguishing two separate
regions. The difference itself—the information—cannot be exactly localized. It is not on one side or the other, nor in the space between them
(Bateson, 1972). The difference is at a higher level of abstraction: the
perceived relationship between one side and the other.

The perception of form requires the discrimination of difference (a boundary) and the recognition of similarity (invariance). To perceive a rectangle as a rectangle it must be recognized throughout numerous transformations of size, shade, and orientation. The basic "rectangleness" of the five figures in Set B of Figure 2–2, for example, must be invariant across the other variations which occur. To read the handwriting in Set C, the shape of the letters must be sufficiently invariant with respect to their conventional form, or else their recognition is impossible. Set D has sufficient invariance, while Set C does not.

Another example is a caricature line drawing of a man's face. It usually has very little resemblance to the actual face in terms of size, color, shading, depth, and so forth. Yet it may be quickly recognized as a portrait of its subject because the most important similarity is present, a similarity which makes the most difference in the recognition of the man's face. This similarity is based upon a relationship among parts: the relative proportion among its components (ears, nose, eyes, etc.). The understanding or meaning of symbolic language also depends upon this same principle of the relationship of parts to other parts, and the relationship of parts to the whole context in which they are imbedded. Proportion is dependent upon parts, but it is a characteristic of whole structures and exists in the mind of the observer at a higher level of abstraction than just the perception of the parts.

To be interpreted as a rectangle, a geometrical shape must have the length of its sides and the angles of intersection in the proper proportion, that is, in approximately the same proportions as the ideal standard (the code) which the viewer projects onto it.

What has been said thus far about visually processed information applies to other senses. The sounds of language, for example, do not acquire meaning because of some essential inner quality, but by means of a series of functional distinctions from other sounds. "Dog" can be pronounced in various ways (and approximated within some range of tolerance) as long as enough difference is maintained between it and "dag," "gog," and so forth. When it is heard, it must be similar enough to the conventional code or ideal sound for "dog" that a member of that language system can interpret it correctly. The verbal sounds that we make have no significance by themselves; they become elements of a language only by virtue of the systematic differences among them (Culler, 1977, p. 99).

The Meaning of Meaning

The cognitive processing of information is based upon the concept of information as defined previously, but it also requires the principles of uncertainty, decision, meaning, and convergence.

To create information with the letters of a word, for example, first requires that some physical substance (like ink on paper) be modified such that the desired form can be distinguished from other possible forms, and from the background or context of the medium itself (a blank page, for example). This difference-creating process requires expenditure of energy or, in other words, action. The geometrical pattern formed by the letters of a word must approximate the conventional form within the requisite range of tolerance if it is to be shared with others and understood. This creation of information that we just described is at the physical level of reality.

The occurrence of each letter in a word can be expressed as a probability depending upon the previous letter or surrounding letters. Similarly, the probability of a word occurring in a sentence is affected by which words precede and follow it. We can guess some of the handwritten words and letters in Set C of Figure 2–2. Our uncertainty, in the psychological sense, is reduced by comparing the similarity of the perceived pattern to some conventional word pattern from our memory, and then deciding whether or not this code applies.

The creation of information as a difference in matter–energy, or as a difference in a sequence of events, takes place at the physical level of reality. The awareness of differences in physical reality through one's senses is a perceptual process. The recognition of similarity, the projection of a standard form onto a perceived pattern, is an interpretive process of pattern recognition which can also be performed by a computer.

Most past discussions of communication have not stressed: (1) that the creation of information occurs at a physical level of reality, (2) that interpretation occurs at the psychological level of reality, and (3) that perception bridges the physical and psychological levels of reality.

The semantic understanding of a word takes place at a yet higher level of psychological abstraction; it is not as simple as deciding which remembered word pattern most closely resembles a perceived physical pattern. A particular word often has a wide variety of meanings. The semantic meaning of a word is thus another potential source of uncertainty. This meaning is determined, within some range of tolerance, by interpreting a word pattern in terms of its relationship to other relevant concepts in a particular context.

We use words to identify and to share concepts, but a word is not the same as a concept. We may think with words, but the conceptual meaning of a word is much greater than the word itself. For instance, some concepts require more than one word for their expression. "Kickoff return" is greater than the straightforward sum of its two constituent words. A "kickoff" and a "return" do not mean the same thing as a "kickoff return." There is not a one-to-one ratio of conceptual meaning and word (Terwilliger, 1968), nor is there identity between word and object (Quine, 1960).

Our convergence model of communication uses a contextual approach to meaning, rather than a referential approach.[11] Even in those cases where a word may have an obvious physical referent, such referent falls far short of our full meaning for the word. The word "table," for example, has little meaning by itself, independent of its relationship to chair, sitting, writing, and so forth. The word is given meaning by its specific context. The only way to account for the initially metaphoric use of "table" as a transitive verb in the sentence, "Let's table the motion until the next session," is due to its meaning in this particular context: the other words in which it is embedded, and the social situation in which it is used.

Bertrand Russell once said that "it would be absolutely fatal if people meant the same thing by their words." [12] Variety of meaning is a necessary aspect of human communication. Perhaps if everyone had the same meanings (that is, an identical understanding), communication would not be necessary. Communication reduces this difference in meaning for some particular purpose to some level of tolerance over some interval of time. If collective action among several people is to be sustained, continual communication over time is necessary to maintain a requisite level of convergence of meaning.

The meaning of a word changes when it is used in different ways, in new contexts, or in association with different words. The word used to understand any action, object, or situation will affect how we act toward the action, object, or situation. For example, in jurisprudence, the formal definition of a legal concept is a necessary starting point, but always insufficient. The legal significance of a term develops progressively over the "succession of new situations in which the concept has been applied, and the manner in which this changing application has reflected back on its original significance" (Toulmin, 1973, p. 167). Similarly, a new slang expression is given a common meaning successively. So concepts acquire meaning by serving relevant human purposes in actual, practical cases.

Belief and Action

The uncertainty of meaning and its potential for change lead to the question of truth. The truth value of any word is determined by its projection from a medium of interpersonal exchange onto an external domain, the world of action and events. The issue of truth arises when words are used in propositions, such as "Carter is a Democrat." The

---

[11] The contextual approach received its greatest impetus from the philosophical work of Wittgenstein (1958), while the work of Ogden and Richards (1927) is representative of the referential approach, especially their symbol–thought–referent "triangle of reference."

[12] And Hacking (1975, p. 173) remarked, somewhat facetiously, that "communication gets along because we do not mean the same things by our words!"

truth value of this proposition cannot be adequately determined by two or more individuals until they reach some appropriate level of mutual understanding of its meaning.

Meaning and truth are bound to one another through the application of concepts and codes to actual cases in empirical reality. Each such application occurs in a specified situation under certain conditions. Statements which explain the conditions in which a concept or proposition may be validly applied are metastatements, statements about statements. A particular concept can only refer indirectly to the "real world" because its meaning—and therefore its valid application—is always bound by its relationship to other concepts with which it is used.[13]

How we understand what someone says and how much we believe it to be true subsequently influences how we will act, alone and in concert with others. Talking, writing, smiling, driving, arriving late for a date, and so forth are all overt actions in the physical world, and hence available as information for oneself and others to perceive. Only through some form of overt action can the results of perceiving, interpreting, understanding, and believing be known to others. Some action in the form of transformation of matter and energy is required to create information. In this sense, action is information and all information is the result of action. Thus, we see the unity of action and information.

Action creates a difference capable of interpretation within the context of other differences which could have occurred. Thus, information is based on the potential for choice among a set of alternative patterns, each of which has some probability of occurrence greater than zero. Uncertainty is reduced when a decision is made, when one alternative is chosen out of the context of others. *Information* was defined previously as a difference in matter–energy which affects uncertainty in a situation where a choice exists among a set of alternatives. At the psychological level, a choice is made by the application of concepts. The greater the number and variety of concepts available in an individual's cognitive system, the greater the individual's ability to perceive differences in the environment (Kelly, 1955).

The reduction of uncertainty at the physical level of human information processing, however, has little to do with meaning, which occurs at a higher level of abstraction.[14] The distinction between the physical and the semantic levels of information-processing means that a reduction, and an increase, in uncertainty can occur simultaneously, but at different

[13] Wittgenstein (1958) emphasized this point when he spoke of Newtonian mechanics as "imposing a unified form on our description of the world rather than 'asserting anything about' the world, (adding that) 'the laws of physics do still speak, however indirectly, about the objects of the world'" (in Toulmin, 1972, p. 173).
[14] Confusion about this distinction between processing information and giving meaning is common in most past discussions of information theory.

levels of information-processing. Thus, interpreting a particular pattern that one perceives as the word for "Democrat," for example, may reduce one's uncertainty about which word has occurred (the physical level of reality), but at the same time may create uncertainty about the meaning of that particular use of the word "Democrat" (at the psychological level of reality).

A Summary of the Basic Components of the Convergence Model

Figure 2–3 shows the relationship among the basic components of the communication process. The unity of information and action is indicated by the three bold lines. All information is a consequence (or physical trace) of action, and through the various stages of human information-processing, action may become the consequence of information. A similar unity underlies the relationships among all of the basic components of the convergence model. The communication process has no

Figure 2–3. Basic Components of the Convergence Model of Communication.

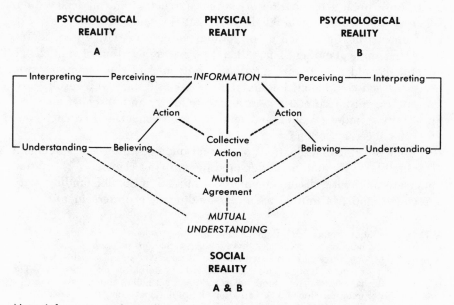

Note: Information and mutual understanding are the dominant components of the convergence model of communication. Information shared by two or more participants in the communication process may lead to collective action, mutual agreement, and mutual understanding.

Source: Kincaid (1979).

beginning and no end, only the mutually defining relationship among the parts which give meaning to the whole.

Information and mutual understanding are the dominant components of our convergence model of communication. Information-processing at the individual level involves perceiving, interpreting, understanding, believing, and action, which creates—potentially, at least—new information for further processing. When information is *shared* by two or more participants, information-processing may lead to mutual understanding, mutual agreement, and collective action. The components of the convergence model are organized in Figure 2–3 at three levels of "reality," or levels of abstraction: (1) the physical level, (2) the psychological level, and (3) the social level.[15]

Once the interpretation and understanding of information is raised to the level of shared interpretations and mutual understanding, what once could be considered as individual information-processing becomes human communication among two or more persons who hold the common purpose (if only for a brief moment) of understanding one another. Whether or not the participants actually do converge (or diverge) to reach a mutual understanding is a question for empirical research. Collective action requires the actions of two or more individuals, built upon a foundation of mutual agreement and understanding. When two or more individuals believe that the same statement is valid, it becomes true by consensus or mutual agreement with some degree of mutual understanding. The rather positive implication of our choice of terms should not obscure alternative outcomes of the communication process. Each component implies that its opposite may also result: misconception, misinterpretation, misunderstanding, and disbelief may reduce mutual understanding, and lead to disagreement and conflict (one type of collective action).

Four possible combinations of mutual understanding and agreement are possible: (1) mutual understanding with agreement, (2) mutual understanding with disagreement, (3) mutual misunderstanding with agreement, and (4) mutual misunderstanding with disagreement.[16]

---

[15] Human emotion, somewhat of an enigma for social science, is considered in the convergence model as an internal, physiological action or reaction to information which, above some threshold level of difference, is perceived and accessible for interpretation like any other type of information of either external or internal origin. The physiological characteristics of emotional reactions are similar, and their differentiation and interpretation depends greatly on the situational context in which they occur, according to the general principles of meaning discussed previously. Much of the mystery of emotion is due to its unpredictability, and the difficulty of interpreting and controlling it.

[16] McLeod and Chaffee's (1973) coorientation measurement model distinguishes between agreement, understanding, and accuracy. Their concept of accuracy (as the extent to which one's estimate of another's cognitions matches what the other person actually thinks) is equivalent to mutual understanding in our convergence model.

Like most other diagrams of communication, Figure 2–3 can only imply the dynamic nature of the process. The model becomes dynamic once two important factors are considered: (1) the inherent uncertainty of information-processing, and (2) mutual understanding as the basic purpose of communication. Information circuits (that is, networks), uncertainty, and purpose are the key elements of cybernetic explanation. The components of the convergence model become dynamic with the addition of the basic principles of cybernetic explanation (a topic to which we shall return in a later section).

"How Le Monde and The New York Times Created a Disaster in Africa"

Much of our present discussion of the convergence model of communication might seem to imply that reaching a common meaning through information-exchange only happens through interpersonal communication in face-to-face situations. On the contrary, convergence can typify any type of communication, including that occurring via the mass media to a national public or even to a world audience.

Here we consider an example of convergence that occurred on the part of two of the world's prestige newspapers (one on each side of the Atlantic Ocean), international relief agencies, and the publics of the United States and France. The issue is the severe drought in the six Sahel countries of West Africa in the early 1970s. This five-year disaster killed more than 100,000 people and starved millions of cattle and other livestock, leaving the Sahel's natural environment in a state that cannot again support its former human population for many years.

Despite the fact that this drought began in about 1969, it was not publicly *defined* as a disaster until March, 1973, four years later. During this time, the people simply died, the cattle slowly starved at parched waterholes, and the Sahara Desert marched southward through the Sahel at the rate of several miles a month. Very little was done to provide relief supplies by the six Sahel governments or by international agencies. As we shall see, until the local and the international press began interpreting the drought and its results as a "disaster," a "catastrophe," or a "famine," it was not adequately understood by those who were in a position to take appropriate action. The disaster just did not exist, at least in the minds of those individuals who might have provided relief.

There was no shortage of information. During the 1969–1973 period, a considerable body of information about the drought was available to any inquiring news reporter: reports about the advancing drought were filed regularly

---

Measurement of understanding/misunderstanding and agreement/disagreement may be possible with direct magnitude estimates of conceptual differences and metric multidimensional scaling (Woelfel and Danes, 1980).

by local government officials and by employees of FAO (the United Nations' Food and Agriculture Organization) and the U.S. AID (the U.S. Agency for International Development). Over 250 foreign experts resided in the six nations. Local newspapers and magazines regularly carried articles about the drought. Although President Moussa Traore of Mali spoke of the drought in November, 1972, at a national anniversary, most of the Sahel governments tried to suppress news of the drought, perhaps out of concern for the effect of such bad news on tourism. Both France and the United States began disaster-relief activities in late 1972. But "the silence of the United States and France about their relief efforts in the fall of 1972 was complete" (Morentz, 1979). When relief agencies issued press releases about the Sahel situation, the mass media often did not use them.

Then, near the end of 1972, the Sahel drought began to rise in the agenda of world "news"; the event was gradually being defined as a disaster. Analysis of this process of agenda-setting by the mass media provides a fascinating illustration of the convergence model of communication.

Three key journalists played a major role in this agenda-setting process, two Frenchmen and one American. Jeane Pierre Sereni's article, "La Famine Aux Portes?" (Famine at the Door?) appeared in December 23, 1972, issue of the weekly news review, Jeune Afrique. Sereni first became aware of the Sahel drought in November at a meeting of agricultural development experts in Paris; he immediately launched an investigation, and his articles a few weeks later drew together information from FAO press releases, wire service news, and other sources. Importantly, Sereni drew this information together in a fashion which put the threat of catastrophe clearly before the reader: "A plague of another age, famine, menaces men and beasts." The photographs in his article helped depict the drought as a human tragedy. The six Sahel nations are former French colonies, and so one might expect considerable interest in Sereni's piece in France.

But the December 23, 1972, Jeune Afrique article by Sereni did not lead directly to widespread reaction by other media. It was read, however, by Andre Fontaine, editor-in-chief of La Monde, one of the world's great newspapers. Fontaine traveled to West Africa a few months later, alerted to investigate the drought: "I did not go to cover the drought, but my attention was called to it . . . because of [the article] . . . I had seen in Jeune Afrique perhaps three months before" (personal interview reported by Morentz, 1976). At Fontaine's first stop in Africa, a layover at the Dakar airport, he noticed that "something was going on in Africa, the extent of which we did not know. Right in the airport was a huge poster calling for solidarity to help the victims of the drought" (personal interview reported by Morentz, 1976).

After returning to his office in Paris, the editor of Le Monde was convinced that "the drought was the important event [in West Africa]. . . . I knew that only one [article in a series of reports] would be on the front page, and the drought should be on page one" (personal interview reported by Morentz,

1976). But an election campaign was under way in France, and so Fontaine's article waited two weeks before being printed, on March 7, 1973. In "La Pire des Secheresses," Fontaine vividly described the carcasses of dead cattle piled up on roads, and stated that the drought was the worst in sixty years. That evening, French television broadcast a special program on the drought. It had been filmed two months before, but had not been considered important. Fontaine's front-page article made it clear that La Monde considered the drought a major event. Predictably, the newspaper began to publish many articles about the drought: 8 in March, 3 in April, 9 in May, 31 in June, and 17 in July (Morentz, 1979).

Suddenly, the Sahel drought emerged from being a "nonissue" to become a world news item that received front-page treatment. Other mass media in France now picked up the drought as an important topic. The French foreign assistance agency began to issue press releases about the shiploads of relief supplies that it was sending to Dakar.

Meanwhile, independent of Fontaine's agenda-setting, an American journalist, Thomas Johnson of The New York Times, discovered the drought. In November, 1972, Johnson traveled to Upper Volta to cover the state visit of French President Pompidou. Peace Corps volunteers and AID officials told Johnson that he was missing the biggest story in Africa by following the French president around; he had not previously heard of the drought, but he immediately began to investigate, interviewing informants and refugees in Niger. His article, "Famine Feared in African Area" appeared on December 3, 1972, in The New York Times, and was the first drought coverage by a major newspaper in the United States or France.

But The Times editors did not define the drought as major news. The December 3 article was placed on page 24. Johnson was assigned to cover a story in East Africa. The matter of the Sahel drought was dropped.

Until May 13, 1973. On that date, The New York Times carried an article captioned, "Aid Sought to Combat Drought in West Africa," that was based on an FAO press release (which in turn may have been triggered by the press attention being given by Le Monde to the Sahel situation; nevertheless, there is no evidence of a direct imitation by The Times of Le Monde). The Times article spoke of "famine," of "death" or "malnutrition" on the part of one-third of the 30 million population of the Sahel, and of "millions of cattle killed in past weeks."

A week later, a well orchestrated inspection trip by an FAO official to Africa helped catapult the disaster to a high position on The Times' agenda. A news-making pseudoevent that centered around a press conference by the FAO representative on his return from Africa, quickly led to several articles in The New York Times. The issue began to escalate in The Times: 5 articles in May, 1973; 8 in June, 3 in July, and 8 in August. Thomas Johnson was assigned to West Africa to continue covering the drought.

Public concern with the Sahel disaster began to build in the United States.

AID, previously silent about its relief aid in Africa, suddenly found its voice and began issuing press releases entitled: "West Africa: Famine Threatens," "Livestock Decimated," and "Shortfall." Other relief began to flow from the American Friends Service Committee, Operation PUSH (People United to Save Humanity), RAINS (Relief for Africans in Need in the Sahel), and others. The U.S. Congress held hearings on the Sahel disaster, and allocated an emergency aid package of $30 million in 1973, equal to the previous five years of aid to the Sahel (Morentz, 1979). Mass media coverage of the disaster continued to be strong through 1973 and 1974 (Rogers and Sood, 1979).

What does this case of disaster in the Sahel tell us about agenda-setting in the mass media? First, we showed that a body of relevant information existed about the drought prior to its mass media coverage. During these years, the Sahel drought existed as an objective reality, but it was effectively hidden from public view (Morentz, 1979). For example, a veteran *La Monde* reporter stationed in Dakar was aware of the disastrous effects of the drought, but he did not report his findings to Paris. *The New York Times'* editors placed Thomas Johnson's December 3, 1972, article on page 24, and dropped the issue for the next five months! Clearly, these two newspapers' inherent definition of news did not fit the drought, an event that occurred in incremental stages over a four-year period, and in a place far away from their readers.

Only when *La Monde's* editor came face to face with the Sahel drought did the disaster begin to become world news. Thereafter, other mass media institutions joined the bandwagon as they shared, with *La Monde,* a definition of the Sahel drought as a major event.

What created the disaster in West Africa in 1973? Not overpopulation and overgrazing. Not the long-term changes in climate and rainfall, or the encroaching Sahara Desert. Climate only created the drought. *Le Monde* and *The New York Times* created the disaster.

Cybernetic Explanation and Convergence

In the twentieth century the most dramatic improvements in the prediction and control of objects and events came not from the atomistic–mechanistic approach of physics, but rather from the newer sciences of information, cybernetics, and general systems theory (Krippendorf, 1979; Littlejohn, 1978). The most successful applications of the cybernetics paradigm thus far have been in the design of new information technology (such as computers and cruise missiles) rather than for improving understanding of human communication.[17]

[17] Even though Weiner's (1948) work on cybernetics and Shannon and Weaver's (1949) work on information theory both appeared at about the same time, communication scholars were much more influenced by the latter, probably because of their fascination with uncertainty reduction and the convenience of the linear model of communication in studying communication effects.

Initial attempts to apply cybernetics to human communication have not been very successful because of an over-reliance upon man–machine, man–nature, or machine–machine analogies and illustrations. Cybernetics has unfortunately come to imply communication between people and machines (Fisher, 1978, p. 285). Most discussions of cybernetics begin with self-regulating, thermostat-furnace systems (Boulding 1956), thermostats, automatic pilots, bicycle riders (Ashby, 1956; 1968, p. 298), or an individual driving a nail with a hammer (Miller and others, 1960 and 1968; Miller, 1978). Bateson (1972) made the most successful application of cybernetic explanations to human systems, but he also uses man–environment systems to illustrate the basic principles of information. The man–environment system of interaction is extremely important today, but it should be kept in mind that an individual's interaction with his environment is mediated by symbols and concepts of his own creation. As Rapoport (1974) points out, individuals live mostly in a "symbolic environment" that they create. It is obvious, for example, that the physical effects of an earthquake cannot be ignored. But we are more interested in what happens among people when they perceive and interpret information about an earthquake, or when they take (or refuse to take) action when someone shares information warning them about an earthquake.

As defined previously, a *system* is a set of interrelated parts coordinated to accomplish a set of goals (Churchman, 1968, p. 29). Human systems are connected and coordinated, not by mechanical means or by the force of matter and energy, but rather by the exchange of information (Watzlawick and others, 1967).

The most important characteristic of the information-sharing process is the communication circuit, or network of circuits, by which individuals within a system are interconnected. A circuit is not a one-way link; it is a circular loop, with the capacity for a continuous two-way exchange of information. The two-way exchange of information is a prerequisite for feedback. No human system can function properly—that is, be coordinated to accomplish a set of goals—without feedback. Feedback "produces action in response to an input of information and includes the results of its own action in the new information by which it modifies its subsequent behavior" (Deutsch, 1963, p. 390).

In everyday vocabulary, the concept of feedback has been taken more simply to mean "knowledge of results." It is most commonly used as if only two steps are required: information out, information back. These two steps are the necessary requirement for feedback, but one such cycle is usually insufficient for most human systems to function properly. When feedback is considered only at this minimal, one-cycle level, it is natural to think of it as an object or noun—knowledge of results—rather than as a *process* over time. When several cycles of information-exchange are considered, and the information is observed as changing over time, then feedback must be conceptualized as a process, and not as knowledge held at one point in time. To avoid the confusion that currently exists regarding this distinction, we must use the concepts of convergence and divergence.

When the process of feedback is observed over more than one cycle and when it is effective, the result may be described as "a series of diminishing mistakes—a dwindling series of under-and-over corrections converging on the goal" (Deutsch, 1963, p. 390). Thus, an effective feedback process may be described as a process of convergence. When feedback is not adequate to its task, "the mistakes may become greater; the network may be 'hunting' over a cyclical or widening range of tentative and 'incorrect' responses ending in a breakdown" (p. 390). Thus, an ineffective feedback process may be described as a process of divergence.

Technically speaking, the term "feedback" need only refer to one-half of the cycle of information-exchange. Thus, it was relatively easy to add feedback to the linear, one-way models of communication described previously. When the concept of feedback was added to these linear models of communication, it was a useful but incomplete step toward converting them into a convergence model of communication. Feedback was usually conceptualized as a second-phase linear communication event in which a message about the effectiveness of the original communication act was sent from the receiver back to the source. Even with the addition of the feedback element, the linear models of communication were still not interactive in a cyclical process (Kim, 1975); the one-way conception of communication simply became two-way. But it was still linear (Fisher, 1978, p. 286).

An adequate understanding of human communication as a process requires analysis of a series of such cycles of information-exchange over time. Convergence and divergence are the most useful terms to describe what actually occurs during this process.[18] *Convergence* is the tendency for two or more individuals to move toward one point, or for one individual to move toward another, and to unite in a common interest or focus. *Divergence* is the tendency for two or more individuals to move away or apart.

The most important feaure of convergence is that it implies that a purpose or goal already exists once the network or circuit of information-exchange has physically come into existence (Deutsch, 1963, p. 391). Communication cannot be adequately studied without reference to the purpose of a social system.

Unlike man–machine and machine–machine systems, however, most

---

[18] It is also possible that human communication can result in no movement or change (Kim, 1975).

of the goals of human systems are not given, externally imposed, or built into the mechanism. In fact, one of the more time-consuming activities of human systems is the search for, and creation of, personal and collective purposes. Communication is used for this search. The process of convergence implies that a goal already exists at the time of a communication event. What is the primary purpose that already exists when the information is exchanged? *The primary purpose of human communication is to define and to understand reality so that other human purposes can be achieved.* The primary purpose of communication as mutual understanding is crucial: the success of all other human endeavors depends upon it.

The Convergence Model of Communication

Communication is defined as a process in which the participants create and share information with one another in order to reach a mutual understanding.[19] A model of communication is incomplete if it only suggests the analysis of a single participant's understanding of a message. Communication is always a joint occurrence, a mutual process of information-sharing between two or more persons. In other words, communication always implies relationship. *Communication networks* consist of interconnected individuals who are linked by patterned flows of information. Such information-sharing over time leads the individuals to converge or diverge from each other in their mutual understanding of reality. By "reality" we do not mean physical reality itself, to which individuals may have no direct access, but rather information about physical reality. An individual's interaction with his environment is mediated by information, much of which refers not to physical reality but to other sets of information. An adequate, mutual understanding and agreement about symbolic information which is created and shared is a prerequisite for any other social and collective activity.

Although mutual understanding is the purpose or primary function of communication, it is never reached in any absolute sense due to the inherent uncertainty of information-exchange. Several cycles of information-sharing about a topic may increase mutual understanding, but not complete it. Fortunately, for most purposes, perfect mutual understanding is not required. Generally, communication ceases when a sufficient level of mutual understanding has been reached for the task at hand. The amount of mutual understanding that results can be depicted as a set of two or more overlapping circles which represent each participant's estimate of the other's meaning as it overlaps with the other's actual meaning.

[19] This definition of communication as convergence is more in line (than the definitions implied by Shannon and Weaver, and in other linear models) with the Latin root *communico,* meaning "share" (Cherry, 1978, p. 2).

Figure 2–4.   Communication as Convergence Toward Mutual Understanding.

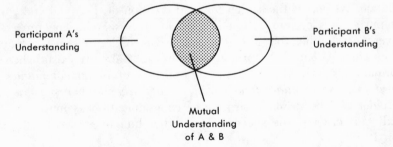

Participant A's Understanding   Participant B's Understanding

Mutual
Understanding
of A & B

Note: Communication is a process in which participants create and share information with one another in order to reach a mutual understanding, shown here as the overlap in understanding of two individuals.

Source: Kincaid with Schramm (1975).

The overlap, or mutual understanding, is indicated by the shaded area in Figure 2–4. The convergence of each participant's understanding with the other's is never complete, never perfect. The codes and concepts that one has available for understanding are learned through experience. Therefore, the conceptual systems that participants use for understanding can only approximate one another within some limit of error or uncertainty.

Mutual understanding is a joint decision process based on uncertainty. Uncertainty always involves the possibility of error (for example, "Is this what A really means?"). Unfortunately, "error" and "uncertainty" have negative connotations. Bronowski (1973) suggested that we use the term *tolerance,* the amount of variation allowed from some standard of accuracy.

By means of several iterations or cycles of information-exchange, two or more participants in a communication process may converge toward a more mutual understanding of each other's meaning, obtain greater accuracy, and come within the limits of tolerance required for the purpose at hand. Two demolition experts, for example, have a very narrow range of tolerance when they are working together to defuse a live bomb. They must understand one another at a very high level of approximation. On the other hand, when someone is trying to explain that it is just a "rather beautiful" day outside, we can tolerate a rather wide range of error in mutual understanding. The possible consequences of the latter situation do not warrant the same high standards of accuracy as in the former.

One can only know how well someone else understands a situation if the other person also shares information, and vice versa. After several

Figure 2–5.   A Convergence Model of Communication.

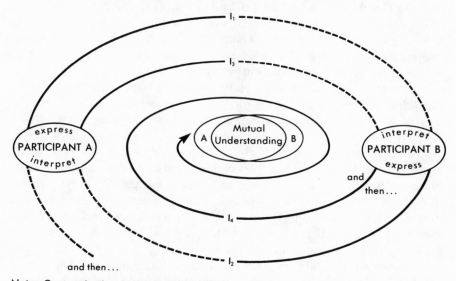

Note: *Communication* is a process in which participants create and share information with one another in order to reach a mutual understanding. This cyclical process involves giving meaning to information that is exchanged between two or more individuals as they move toward convergence. *Convergence* is the tendency for two or more individuals to move toward one point, or for one individual to move toward another, and to unite in a common interest or focus.

Source: Kincaid with Schramm (1975) and Kincaid (1979).

cycles of information-exchange, the participants may shift to a new topic of discussion. The model of the communication process shown in Figure 2–5 reflects the convergent nature of mutual understanding, and the cyclical nature of information-exchange.

The communication process always begins with "and then . . ." to remind us that something has occurred before we begin to observe the process. Participant A may or may not consider this past before he shares information (I_1) with Participant B. This individual must perceive and then interpret the information which A creates to express his/her thought, and then B may respond by creating information (I_2) to share with A. Individual A interprets this new information and then may express himself again with more information (I_3) about the same topic. Individual B interprets this information, and they continue this process (I_4 . . . I_n) until one or both become satisfied that they have reached a sufficient mutual understanding of one another about the topic for the purpose at hand. Each participant also interprets his own information, to understand himself better, and to find improved ways of expressing himself. Thus there are no arrowheads "to and from" each unit of information. The information is shared by both participants.

As the model suggests, mutual understanding is never perfect. The meaning of language is never complete. Some element of uncertainty and error always remains, as language undergoes continual development, through the process of communication in action.

The term "convergence" is not a static concept. One of the main obstacles to improving existing models of communication has been the lack of vocabulary capable of capturing its dynamic, processual nature. Convergence is dynamic: it always implies movement and goal orientation or purpose. It requires study of the direction and rate of change, and study of the networks of two or more persons who exchange information. Movement in one direction, toward one point, always implies movement away from other points (divergence). Convergence and divergence are two aspects of the same process. As mentioned previously, communication always has the potential for creating misunderstanding, disagreement, and divergence.

Convergence is always *between* two or more persons. The model compels us to study relationships, differences, similarities, and changes in these relationships over time. The minimal unit of analysis is the dyad, whose members are linked in some manner through the exchange of information. From dyads, the researcher can extend his analysis to the participant's personal networks and to cliques and to large, intact networks.

How does communication lead to the formation of cliques? How does communication contribute to the formation of divergent factions within a network? What types of communication (and other events) are capable of reversing a trend toward divergence, or vice versa? These questions are generated at the interface between the convergence model of communication and the network approach to communication research.

"The Strength of Weak Ties in Finding a Job"

Previously in this chapter, we illustrated how the linear model of communication was utilized in Hovland and others' (1953) experiment on source credibility and attitude persuasion. Here, in contrast, is an example of a network investigation based intuitively upon the convergence-network analysis paradigm of communication research. The difference in these two researches is instructive for illustrating the differences in communication researches that result when they are based upon contrasting paradigms.

For contrast we have chosen Dr. Mark S. Granovetter's (1970 and 1974) study of how people find and obtain jobs, which also formed the basis for his classic article on "The Strength of Weak Ties" (Granovetter, 1973), discussed in chapters 3 and 5. He knew that information-acquisition about new jobs was not a linear process involving the mass media. If everyone found his or her job through *The New York Times,* the topic would be of little sociological interest (Granovetter, 1974, p. 4). Instead, most prior research indicated that the main sources/channels of information about new jobs were "friends and neighbors." Unfortunately, previous investigations did not go further to determine exactly *which* friends and *which* acquaintances were most important. Therefore, Granovetter designed his study to trace the flow of job information through interpersonal networks.

Faced with very limited financial resources, Granovetter (1974, p. 6) decided to concentrate on a sample of individuals who had recently obtained a professional, technical, or managerial position. Many such workers resided in Newton, Massachusetts, a Boston suburb of about 100,000 population. The researcher first compared two consecutive telephone directories in order to identify the individuals who had installed phones within the past year. Then he telephoned each of these individuals to determine if they met his selection criteria: (1) of having found their occupational position within the past five years, and (2) of being a professional, technical, or managerial worker. He then conducted 100 personal interviews and obtained 182 mailed questionnaires from his respondents. In essence, the investigator's research strategy was to identify a sample of individuals who had recently obtained a job, and then to trace out the nature of communication behavior leading to this event.

Granovetter (1974, p. 11) found that interpersonal communication channels were more frequently cited by his respondents than mass media advertisements (which were reported by only about 10 percent of his respondents), or direct job applications (19 percent) as channels for finding their job. Most of the person-to-person chains for job information were quite short; none were of four links, and 39 percent were of zero length (that is, the respondent had direct contact with an employer). Surprisingly, it was the "weak ties" between acquaintances (rather than between close friends) that were informationally "strong" in the job-seeking process (this theory is detailed in our chapters 3 and 5). It seemed that close friends seldom possessed job information that the job-seeker did not already know.

Here are four case studies of job-seeking, from Granovetter's (1974, p. 49, 153–156) interviews:

Case # 5: George C. was employed as a technician for an electrical firm at an annual salary of about $8,000, and with little chance for advancement. While courting his future bride, he met her downstairs neighbor, who managed a candy shop, a concession leased from a national chain. After his marriage, George C. continued to see the downstairs neighbor when visiting his wife's family. This neighbor finally convinced him to apply for a trainee position with the candy chain, and arranged an interview. Within three years, George C. was earning nearly $30,000 in this position. He considered his occupational success to be remarkable, telling Granovetter, "Every morning I pinch myself to see if it's still true!"

Case # 7: Gerald F. was a salesman for a liquor distributor. A doctor friend asked him if he would be interested in managing a nursing home. On his resumé he listed as a reference his wife's cousin, owner of a fashionable antique shop. The nursing home job did not come through, but his wife's cousin, now alerted that Gerald F. was considering a job change, offered him a position as business manager of his antique shop. Gerald F. accepted.

Case # 23: Frederick Y. was out of college and had only part-time work. To pacify his family he agreed to have lunch one day with his brother and his brother's friend, who ran an employment agency. This friend took Frederick Y. back to his office and called a Boston newspaper that needed an assistant credit manager. He was interviewed and accepted the job.

Case # 30: Kevin C. was a midwestern magazine editor who came to Boston on a "busman's holiday" to look at various magazine operations that he knew only by reputation. On one such visit, he fell into a long discussion with another magazine editor. Their philosophies were congruent, and Kevin C. was offered a job. Although he had not come looking for a new job, the offer was attractive and he accepted it.

In these cases the network contacts were more or less accidental, yet the information obtained by the job-seeker was much more detailed than could be culled from an advertisement, from applying for the job, or even from the usual brief job interview (Granovetter, 1974, p. 156). Information-exchange through interpersonal ties was reported by Granovetter's (1973, p. 13) respondents to be of higher quality; often the job-seekers were told whether their prospective workmates were congenial, whether the boss was neurotic, and if the company was growing or stagnant. The informality of the interpersonal exchanges made the information more relevant and more valuable.

The four cases just described show that information was being exchanged in each of the dyadic links. This information-exchange was of a convergence nature, as the participants gave meaning to the occupational positions that were available. Finding a job is not so much an advertisement followed by application and hiring, as it is a process of mutual exchanges, often through seemingly distant intermediaries, until both employer and applicant reach a sufficient mutual understanding of one another to make a decision. Job information does not just flow in one direction, Granovetter's (1974) study indicates. It is a two-way, sequential exchange in which shared meaning is created. In short, it is a convergence process which takes place in the context of interpersonal communication networks.

Dr. Granovetter's investigation of the strength of weak ties was a bargain-basement buy in these days of high-budget research. His total funding was less than $900; his expenses included about 75 automobile trips from Cambridge to Newton, duplicating his research instruments, and the typing of his report. Plus the cost of two telephone directories.

All the personal interviewing was conducted by Professor Granovetter, and he was thus better able to understand the meaning of his respondents' job-searching experiences. "Many [principal investigators] not only never see their respondents (or their locale) but never even see those who *elicit* the survey results from them" (Granovetter, 1974, p. 141). The direct data-gathering approach utilized by Dr. Granovetter in his personal interviews also illustrates the convergence nature of communication, as he and his respondents interacted to reach a more accurate understanding, a shared meaning of the job-searching experiences. We should not forget that data-gathering itself is a communication process. Too often research is also treated as a linear act, rather than as a process of communication. Had Professor Granovetter organized his data-gathering like the militaristic hierarchy that is followed by many big researchers, with a corps of mercenary interviewers as the front-line troops, using a highly structured interview questionnaire, he might not have gained the insights that allowed him to formulate his theory of the strength of weak ties.

IMPLICATIONS OF THE CONVERGENCE MODEL FOR COMMUNICATION RESEARCH

The convergence model represents human communication as a dynamic, cyclical process over time, characterized by (1) mutual causation rather than one-way mechanistic causation, and emphasizing (2) the interdependent relationship of the participants, rather than a bias toward either the "source" or the "receiver" of "messages." Mutual understanding and mutual agreement are the primary goals of the communication process. They are the points toward which the participants either converge or diverge over time. The immediate purpose for which information is shared by individuals is to reach mutual understanding, a prerequisite for the successful achievement of other human purposes.

The convergence model of communication leads to a relational perspective of human communication because of the shift to *information* as opposed to *messages* as the content that is created and shared by participants. *Information* was defined previously as a difference in matter–energy which affects uncertainty in a situation where a choice exists among a set of alternatives. Information is about objects and events in the environment and about relationships in the environment, interpreted through the application of available codes and concepts. Once the interpretation and understanding of information is raised to the level of shared interpretations and mutual understanding, what was considered as individual information-processing becomes human communication among two or more persons who hold the common purpose (if only for a brief moment) of understanding one another. The participants may converge or diverge, that is, reach a mutual understanding or a misunderstanding.

Toward Relationships as Units of Analysis

One of the most basic questions for communication theory and research is whether to study the information-exchange *relationship* between two or more persons as the unit of analysis, or to study the participants as *individuals*. The S–M–C–R model of communication, for example, explicitly separated the source and the receiver. It treated messages as objects (as opposed to information) which one individual sends to the other. Research based on this linear model broke up the communication process into a set of isolated variables, each associated with one of the four component elements (S, M, C, and R) in the model (plus feedback). The model proved useful for designing and organizing experiments on the individual effects of messages on receivers. Such components research exemplifies the atomistic–mechanistic approach of classical physics which was at first borrowed inadequately by communication scholars.

The feedback loop, which improved the S–M–C–R model, is insufficient because it only carried (by definition) knowledge of the effects back to the source for his/her evaluation. This linear model excluded the effects of the source's messages on the source, an effect which may often be greater than the effect on the "receiver." Also excluded were the social effects of communication on other individuals who at the time are not considered the primary receivers of the source's message, even though these social effects sometimes are greater than the immediate effects on the primary receiver. Realization of such indirect effects gave rise to the two-step flow and multistep flow hypotheses in mass communication research; they deal with the relay of the source's original message to second, third, fourth, and other levels of "receivers." Communication research focused on the source's message to the initial receiver, although the recognition of multistepped flows suggested the greater complexity of the human communication process.

In comparison to the focus of past communication research on a components approach to communication effects on individuals as the units of analysis, we advocate a different approach in this book. The convergence model of communication calls for an opposite kind of communication research than did the linear models of the past. First, the unit of analysis is usually the information-exchange relationship between two individuals, or some aggregation of this dyadic link to the level of the personal communication network, clique, or system. For instance, the data-set that we utilize throughout our future chapters to illustrate communication network analysis, consists of 21,072 information-exchange links among 1,003 women living in 24 Korean villages. Our unit of analysis is these 21,072 links in certain analyses; elsewhere it consists of the hundred or so cliques composed of these 21,072 links, or else the

24 systems. Rarely do we utilize the 1,003 respondents as units of analysis, and even then we use network variables to explain their behavior (as in chapter 5). The individuals provided the data, so they are the units of response. But the typical respondent reported about 21 communication links with her fellow villagers. These 21,072 links are our basic units of analysis. Links, not individuals, should be the fundamental unit in any type of research based on the convergence model of communication.

Network data have an unusual quality. The basic data, of course, are a type of information about individual respondents: the identification of other individuals in the system with whom each respondent communicates. The solution to any network analysis problem requires that we discover certain properties of the communication structure [20] of the system, composed of the aggregate of the individual respondents. So network analysis is "quite different than other statistical problems. It cannot be solved by the incremental accretion of information, observation by observation, as [many] other statistical problems are. Rather it requires an overview of an entire structure. It is truly a problem in which the whole is greater than the sum of its parts" (Alba, 1972b). This principle of holistic interaction is the reason why systems theory is consistent with our conception of communication network analysis and with the convergence model of communication.

The basic difference in the unit of analysis is the point of departure between communication research based on linear models and that based on a convergence model. Several other important differences follow from this shift in the unit of analysis.

From Atomistic–Mechanistic to Holistic Approaches

Communication effects research has been much too atomistic–mechanistic, as argued previously. Inquiry based on the convergence model tends to be holistic. Instead of focusing mainly upon audience effects among individuals, a broader look at the communication process also considers the effects (1) on the "source" and on others not initially defined as participants, (2) on how others interpret the information that is exchanged, and (3) on the changes in behavior of the initial participants in the communication process. On many occasions individuals purposely say or do not say something to someone (silence as well as nonsilence) because they are aware of the effects of doing so on others who are not present and who do not participate initially in the communication situation.

How can the convergence model of communication, which is essen-

---

[20] *Communication structure* is the arrangement of the differentiated elements that can be recognized in the patterned communication flows in a system (chapter 3).

tially "sourceless" and "receiverless," be applied to mass communication campaigns? For example, when an automobile company aims television ads at prospective car-buyers, this situation might seem to be a source transmitting a persuasive message through a mass medium to an audience of receivers. Not necessarily. It depends on whether one defines communication as linear or convergent. Research based on a narrow, linear model of communication would ignore the effect of the advertisement on the managers of the auto company, on their competing companies, on what members of the "audience" say about the product to one another, and on the thousands of auto agency salespersons throughout the country who eventually talk with potential customers. What these other participants in the communication process do with the advertisement is as important as its effects on the more narrowly defined "target audience." Can those who sponsor or conduct applied communication research afford to leave these participants out of their investigations? We maintain that communication research would be amiss to do so. A more encompassing model of the communication process would not ignore these important components, their interrelationships, and the information which they create.

The convergence model of communication considers the full matrix of relationships in which the communication participants exist, and which functions as the context in which human communication occurs. The aggregation of the individual effects of communication messages is not the same as network effects, as we have defined them. The concept of pluralistic ignorance [21] helps make this distinction clear. In intact, natural social systems (as opposed to experimental laboratory groups), it makes a great difference whether or not individuals correctly know what others know, and vice versa.[22] If an individual thinks that "everybody's doing it," he is more likely to follow this same behavior (as we show in chapter 5).

One of the early problems with national family planning programs was to convince individuals who had already practiced family planning to share information about their experience with others. In many nations, the topic of family planning was taboo because of its relationship to sexual behavior. Adoption of family planning in Korean villages, for

---

[21] *Pluralistic ignorance* is the degree to which individuals hold incorrect conceptions of the behavior of other individuals in collectivities to which they belong.

[22] It is possible, of course, to re-create the phenomena of pluralistic ignorance in a laboratory and to determine its effects, as shown by the experiments of Professor Solomon Asch. He arranged small groups in a laboratory setting that were composed of one naive subject and several shills. After the shills reported counterfactual information (that one line was longer than another, although the opposite was actually the case), the naive subject would often agree, despite his own knowledge to the contrary. The Asch experiments also show the potential influence of the network on an individual's behavior (chapter 5).

example, was often done in secrecy. Without public knowledge of the fact that their peers had adopted, the rate of adoption of contraception was slower (chapter 6).

Shared understanding and agreement by means of communication is a prerequisite for the "takeoff" point in the rate of adoption of an innovation in a system. What others think and do through mutual understanding and collective action has important consequences on what each individual member of a system thinks and does (chapter 5).

We emphasized throughout this chapter that human communication is a holistic process. It almost always involves many other individuals than just a "source" and a "receiver," even at its most elemental level of the communication event. Past communication research has been grossly oversimplified by focusing mainly on the receiver effects of a source's message. But past scholars who acknowledged an uneasy feeling about this atomistic–mechanistic research approach, driven by linear models, often lacked the methodological–conceptual tools to capture the holistic aspects of human communication. We argue that network analysis provides one means to study communication structure, and thus to cope more realistically with the holistic reality of human communication.

One research area where it would seem particularly difficult to ignore this holistic reality is the study of *mass* communication; obviously, a mass of individuals must be participants. Strangely, past inquiry about mass media communication has been strikingly individualistic.

Mass Media Communication

Communication research has been, at best, remarkably narrow in its central focus, and consequently, in the selection of conceptual variables, data-gathering techniques, and analytical procedures (Guimarães, 1970, p. 3). Almost all past communication investigations in the United States, perhaps 90 percent or so, focus on communication effects, and television has been the concern of about 75 percent of these mass communication researches (Comstock and others, 1978).

Until about 1960, most such research found that the mass media had very limited effects, at least those that were direct and measurable (Klapper, 1960). In the twenty years since then, using more sophisticated multivariate research methodologies and looking for answers to somewhat broader research questions, communication scholars have generally found that the media, especially television, can have effects in certain contexts and with certain individuals. Many of these effects are indirect (that is, the effects are not immediate impacts on knowledge, persuasion, and overt behavior change), such as different uses of leisure time and sleep by the audience, agenda-setting (in which the media tell receivers what to think *about,* but not what to think), and changes in the functions of other media (for example, television seems to have altered the way in which Americans use radio and film). Direct (and indirect) effects have been found for certain subaudiences within the public, such as television effects on children, and the consequences of political communication on certain voters. In the 1970s, mass communication researchers began to look beyond effects, at audience motivations for receiving certain messages (this research approach is called "uses and gratifications"). Also, several investigations have centered on how mass media institutions obtain, process, and output news and other information to their audiences.

Generally, this body of U.S. mass communication research conducted in the 1960s and 1970s represented few major breakthroughs or important reconceptualizations. Rather, the general picture that emerges is one of a cautious, careful cumulation of rather small advances, theoretically and empirically. Exciting new directions have not emerged. The "revolutionary paradigm" launched by Shannon and Weaver in 1949 led to formation of an invisible college of communication researchers that is impressive in its present size and command of research resources. But its original intellectual excitement has evolved into an established research tradition that is gradually accumulating additional knowledge, mainly about the effects of linear communication.

The convergence model when applied to mass media communication implies that one should investigate more than just the direct effects of mass media messages on individual audience members. Also important are such research questions as how these direct effects spread among the networks of audience members, and how the media messages are given meaning by the "receivers" through their interaction with other individuals. Past media researchers have usually recognized that network relationships among an audience determine the effects of mass communication, but they lacked the methodological tools to understand these network variables that intervene on direct media effects.

A further implication of the convergence model in mass communication research is to focus on the mass media institutions that produce the messages. Here, we move back up the linear communication process to investigate the "source," to understand how mass media institutions obtain, give meaning to, and transmit information. Our previous illustration of the Sahel drought showed how the communication relationships among the six national governments, international agencies like FAO and U.S. AID, and the two prestige newspapers, determined the way in which the world news agenda for the Sahel disaster was set. So a convergence process was happening within and between the two mass media institutions, and their context, resulting eventually in a definition of the West African drought as major news. Past communication research on audience effects would have ignored this agenda-setting process (although it might have investigated how *The New York Times* and *Le Monde* each set the agenda for their audience, by convincing them that the Sahel disaster was important news). The narrowness of past research, based on linear models, simply has not been useful in helping us understand how meda institutions function in news-gathering and in information-processing.

Our definition of communication as convergence implies that the sharing of information creates and defines a relationship between two or more individuals. Thus, communication behavior itself should be studied as the dependent variable in communication research. Here a main research question (explored later in chapter 7) is "Who is linked to whom?" In comparison, most past communication research utilized communication dimensions as the independent variables to predict dependent variables that indicated such communication effects as voting, consumer behavior, violence, and so on. These dependent variables were largely borrowed by communication scholars from other behavoral disciplines (for example, political science, marketing, psychology, etc.). And the results of communication research were often useful to these other disciplines. But until communication research began to focus on *communication* behavior, rather than the various effects of communication on other types of behavior, a coherent discipline of communication could not begin to emerge.

Communication Network Analysis

Communicaton network analysis is a method of research for identifying the communication structure in a system, in which relational data about communication flows are analyzed by using some type of interpersonal relationships as the units of analysis.

The essence of much human behavior is the interaction through which one individual exchanges information with one or more other individuals. Any given individual in a system is likely to contact certain other individuals, and to ignore many others (particularly when the system is large in size). As these interpersonal communication flows become patterned over time, a "communication structure" (or network) emerges that is relatively stable and predictive of behavior.

Communication structure is the arrangement of the differentiated elements that can be recognized in the patterned communication flows in a system. One objective of communication research using network analysis is to identify this communication structure, and thus to understand the "big picture" of human interaction in a system. This research objective is holistic, in marked contrast to the study of communication effects on individuals.

Communication network analysis describes the component linkages (and their interrelationships in the interpersonal communication structure. A *communication network* consists of interconnected individuals who are linked by patterned flows of information.

Network analysis allows tracing specific message flows in a system, and then comparing this communication structure with the social structure of the system in order to determine how such structure is interrelated with the communication network. The information-flow data bring life to the otherwise static nature of the social structural variables; network analysis permits understanding the social structure as it channels the process of communication.

Most past communication research on the effects of communication forced a conceptual distinction between communication sources and receivers (which is somewhat easier to do in the case of mass media communication, but more difficult and less meaningful for interpersonal exchanges). In network analysis, no sharp distinction is made between source and receiver. Information flows occur among participants in the network, each of whom are both, in turn, transmitters and receivers. In the research conception underlying network analysis, communication is more truly a process of mutual information-exchange. That is why the convergence model and network analysis fit so well together. Theory and method complement one another more adequately than in the case of effects research based on a linear model.

Communication network analysis is one of the several research approaches utilized to study human behavior in light of the convergence model. The unit of analysis thus shifts from the individual audience member to the communication relationship between two or more individuals (dyads, personal communication networks, cliques, and total systems). Use of such units of analysis better allows a study of convergence. The main question being asked by communication researchers changed from "What is the effect of communication?" to "What do humans *do* with communication?" In essence, communication behavior becomes the dependent variable in such investigations, rather than an independent variable (or variables) to predict the effects of communication.

Further, communication network analysis has a particular advantage in allowing investigators to determine a "second dimension" of communication effects: the distribution of the consequences of human communication among the members of a clique or system, including the consensus or agreement that emerges among individuals in a network. In chapter 6, for example, we investigate how communication flows in Korean villages lead to a convergence in the villagers' knowledge, attitudes, and overt behavior regarding family planning. We show that mutual information-sharing about family planning in a village seems to lead to convergence (measured as a decreased variance in knowledge, attitudes, and practice). In this research the village, rather than the individual, is the unit of analysis. Unfortunately, there are as yet very few other applications of network analysis at the level of the clique or system, where the objective is to study how convergence occurs.

Network analysis has not completely effectuated all aspects of the convergence model in the operations of communication research. Most past network analyses utilized data from one-shot sociometric surveys, and hence do not incorporate the over-time·processual nature of communication as convergence. Needed are comparisons of the communication structure in a system as it changes over time; such research must be based on data-sets gathered at more than one point in time. Here the central question to be answered is "How stable are network links over time?" We synthesize the available research evidence bearing on this question in chapter 7.

Past investigations of communication networks have been amiss in largely ignoring the communication contents that flow through network links. Accumulated evidence to date (summarized in chapter 7) shows that somewhat different network structures occur for one topic (such as family planning diffusion in Korean villages) than for another topic (for instance, abortion, a relatively more taboo topic). We need to combine the research method of content analysis of communication messages with the techniques of network analysis to better understand how individuals give meaning to information that is exchanged through the communication process.

Comuunication network analysis has a long way to go in investigating two aspects that are implied by the convergence model: (1) the over-time, dynamic nature of human communication, and (2) the content of information-exchanges. But we feel that network analysis is one promising means of implementing the implications of the convergence model in the operations of communication research. Clearly, we do not just need "more of the same," further narrow studies of communication effects based on linear models. Such is the main message of this chapter, and of the present book.

However, we do not feel that linear models of communication have zero utility in the future. Undoubtedly, communication scholars will choose to conduct effects-oriented research in certain situations where communication is indeed linear, direct, and simple.

By no means, to date, have the majority of communication scientists or practitioners swung from linear models to convergence models, but "the beginning of the beginning" has begun, we believe. We feel that the philosophy and techniques of network analysis will assist in implementing these convergence models in communication research.

SUMMARY

In this chapter, we are frankly critical of the limitations and biases of linear models of human communication, especially the consequences of the psychological bias and the limits of mechanistic causation in communication research. These biases could be resolved by returning to the often-neglected principles of cybernetics, particularly the process of convergence, those cycles of under-and-over corrections converging on a goal. This principle leads to redefining *communication* as a process in which participants create and share information with one another in order to reach a mutual understanding. *Information* is a difference in matter–energy which affects uncertainty in a situation where a choice exists among a set of alternatives. Information is different from the meanings that individuals give to the information that is exchanged. Our conception of communication can be represented by a series of converging circles of information-exchange between two participants who approach, but never arrive at exactly, the same point of understanding. *Convergence* is the tendency for two or more individuals to move toward one point, or for one individual to move toward another, and to unite in a common interest or focus.

In what ways does the convergence model of communication represent a shift toward a new paradigm for communication research? A change of paradigm for scientific research calls for a change in the nature of the research questions, new research designs, new instruments for observation and measurement, and new methods of data-analysis and statistical inference.

The convergence model initiates just this kind of shift. Some of the new research designs and methods which go with the convergence model will be described in our discussion of communication network analysis in chapters 3 and 4. Examples of how this shift in perspective affects research will be presented in chapters 5, 6, and 7.

There are many social problems and areas of communication research to which the network/convergence paradigm can make a fruitful contribution. Unfortunately, the methods for network analysis and the study of convergence are not well known by very many social scientists, nor are these tools readily available. The community of social scientists who share elements of the new paradigm have only recently begun to organize. The next two chapters on the methods of network analysis are intended to help overcome this main obstacle to the growth and development of the network/convergence paradigm.

3 COMMUNICATION NETWORK ANALYSIS

Of all the potential contributions of [Claude Shannon's] information theory to mass communication, perhaps the most promising is in the study of communication networks.

William Schramm (1955b)

Networks will probably become as important to sociology as Euclidian space and its generalizations are to physics.

Francoise Lorrain and
Harrison White (1971)

The main purpose of this chapter is to present the general philosophy of network analysis as an approach to research on human communication and behavior change.

Most publications about communication networks are not very useful to social scientists because (as we pointed out in the Preface) most of this work is (1) abstractly methodological without much demonstration of the potential utility of network analysis techniques, and (2) very difficult to understand by most social scientists because it is so over-mathematized. We hope that the present chapter is a step forward in overcoming both of these problems of the past literature on network analysis.

A NETWORK APPROACH TO COMMUNICATION

The Data-Cube: Units of Analysis, Variables, and Time

Three main types of data should be included in any social science analysis of human behavior: (1) the *units of analysis* (individuals or their relationships), (2) *variables*, and (3) *time* (Figure 3–1). When the first dimension on the data-cube consists of individuals, examples of the second dimension of individual variables are education, attitude toward some issue, or the individuals' overt behavior (for instance, whether they have adopted family planning). Illustrative of relationship variables are who talks to whom in a system, joint membership of two or more individuals in a group or organization, and whether a respondent has a higher or lower status than some other individual (all of these examples

79

Figure 3–1. Data-Cube, Showing How a Social Science Analysis of Human Behavior Should Include: (1) Units of Analysis (Individuals or Relationships), (2) Variables, and (3) Time.

UNITS OF ANALYSIS
(Individuals or relationships)   VARIABLES

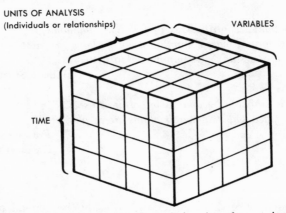

TIME

Note: Contemporary social research typically includes data from a large sample of individuals on a large number of variables (characteristics or attributes of the individual), and ignores time. In network analysis, the units of analysis are relationships describing information-exchanges (dyads, cliques, or systems, for example) and the variables describe attributes of these relationships. Thus, network analysis is particularly consistent with the convergence model of communication (described in chapter 2).

Source: Based on Cattell (1952), whose data-cube consisted of individuals, variables, and occasions. He showed that R-type factor analysis (as well as the usual uses of analysis of variance and multiple correlation) begins on the variables axis and sums over individuals; Q-type factor analysis begins on the individuals axis and sums over variables.

of relational data show that at least two or more individuals are involved). Time must be included in behavioral analysis in order to bring in process; otherwise the behavior being investigated can only be treated cross-sectionally, as if it were "stop-action" activity.

In the typical social science study, such as a survey, a great number of individuals are selected as respondents, and numerous variables characterizing each individual are measured. One (or more) of these dimensions are identified as dependent variables (meaning that they are the behavior of primary interest for the researcher to explain), and the other (independent) variables are correlated with them in a cross-sectional data-analysis, usually utilizing a computer to handle the relatively large number of variables and units of analysis. Little or no attention is usually given (1) to obtaining data about the respondents' relationships with other individuals, or (2) to the over-time processual nature of the behavior being investigated.[1] The individual is usually the unit of analysis.

Or our typical social science study may follow a laboratory experimental design, in which one or more independent variables are manipulated by the researcher in order to ascertain the associated changes in the dependent variable. In this case, the total number of variables may be somewhat smaller than in a survey, but they are usually characteristics or attributes of the individual respondents. Relational data and time are usually ignored or deemphasized. While change in the dependent variable is usually measured at t_1 and t_2, the t_1-t_2 period is usually very short, and time itself is not measured as a variable. The individual is almost always the unit of analysis.

Such typical studies as surveys or experiments are the main "stuff" of social science. They certainly are representative of the great majority of communication researches. In fact, they typify most of the past investigations completed by the two authors of this book. Recently, we (and other researchers) have begun to question this dominant approach because there is much that such investigations cannot tell us about human behavior.

For example, little can be learned in the common research approaches just described about the causes of the behavior being studied. The time-order of the variables cannot be determined because time is not included directly in the data-gathering.[2] Likewise, the individual's relationships with others in his/her environment are not measured. So it must be assumed that the social structure of the system in which the individual is a member is largely unimportant, or treated as irrelevant, in understanding his/her behavior. So too are the other individuals with whom the individual communicates about the topic of study. This dominant approach to social research stresses computer analysis of many variables (each usually measuring a characteristic of the individual) so that much of the investigator's time and resources are devoted to data-analysis, with correspondingly less attention to data-gathering. The net result is often a lack of direct understanding of the respondents' behavior that is being studied. The research that results is often a kind of "antiseptic," once-removed-from-reality kind of abstraction. What passes for most communication research today has become disappointing to the present authors. Its overemphasis upon studying communication effects with a linear

[1] Occasionally in such research, the time dimension is measured somewhat indirectly by asking each respondent to indicate the approximate date at which some event occurred in the past, for instance, the year in which an innovation like family planning was adopted.

[2] Although the individuals' sex, race, or age may be considered as occurring prior to the attitudes or overt behavior that are treated as the dependent variables in such analyses.

model of communication is only a small part of the real scope of communication research.[3]

We here describe various alternatives to the dominant social research approach of the past. Most of our alternatives deal with how to capture relational data and put them into behavioral research on communication. Unfortunately, in this volume we are not yet able also to put equal stress on how to utilize over-time data,[4] although we shall repeatedly call for this to be done.

Communication Network Analysis

Communication network analysis is a method of research for identifying the communication structure in a system, in which relational data about communication flows are analyzed by using some type of interpersonal relationships as the units of analysis. This analytical approach is particularly valuable to social researchers because it allows them to trace specific message flows in a system, and then to compare this communication structure with the social structure of the system in order to determine how this social structure is interrelated with the communication network. The communication flow data bring life to the otherwise static nature of the social structural variables.

The essence of much human behavior is the interaction through which one individual exchanges information with one or more other individuals. Any given individual in a system is likely to contact certain other individuals, and to ignore many others (particularly when the system is large in size). As these interpersonal communication flows become patterned over time, a "communication structure" (or network) emerges, and is relatively stable and predictive of behavior. Communication network analysis describes the linkages created by the sharing of information, and their interrelationships, in the interpersonal communication structure. A *communication network* consists of interconnected individuals who are linked by patterned communication flows.

[3] The nature of most recent communication research is illustrated by the present authors' analysis of the 102 journal articles appearing in a random sample of three issues from 1974–1977 of *Public Opinion Quarterly*, the *Journal of Communication*, *Communication Research*, and *Human Communication Research* (four leading journals in the field of communication). Of the 75 articles that featured independent and dependent variables as an approach to their data-analysis, 86 percent measured both independent and dependent variables at the individual level, 7 percent utilized at least one independent variable that was relational, and 8 percent featured a dependent variable that was relational. So much communication research is individualistic and nonrelational.

[4] However, we do feature studies of change and stability in network behavior in chapter 7. Relatively few such investigations have been completed to date, and more such research is certainly needed. We should recognize the dynamic, temporal nature of a communication link in a network; unfortunately, much past network analysis has treated communication links as if they were static.

In network analysis, no sharp distinction is made between source and receiver. Communication flows occur among "transceivers" in the network, each of whom are both, in turn, transmitters and receivers (Pool, 1973, p. 9). In the research conception underlying network analysis, communication is a mutual exchange. That is why the convergence model and network analysis fit so well together. Theory and method are made for each other.

In the past, communication research was usually concerned with "trees," rather than "forests." Owing in part to intellectual influences from the physical sciences, social scientists have generally studied specific parts of a system in order to understand the whole system (or so they thought). Now we realize that this piece-by-piece approach was too reductionistic, mechanistic, and atomistic. It simply does not fit the realities of most human communication.

An alternative approach was provided by "general systems theory," defined as the science of wholeness. The credo of systems theory is the statement that the whole is more than the sum of its parts. Our description of the convergence model of communication (in chapter 2) draws on systems theory and cybernetics, a more holistic approach to human communication than the linear model.

Communication network analysis usually consists of one or more of the following research procedures.

1. Identifying *cliques* [5] within the total system and determining how these structural subgroupings affect communication behavior in the system.
2. Identifying *certain specialized communication roles* such as liaisons,[6] bridges,[7] and isolates.
3. Measuring various *communication structural indexes* (like communication connectedness, for example) for individuals, dyads, personal networks, cliques, or entire systems. We will describe these procedures in detail in chapter 4.

Do Networks Matter? Effects on Human Behavior

A basic proposition of social psychology, sociology, and social anthropology is that individual behavior is influenced through relationships of the individual with others. The communication networks in which an individual is embedded thus offer a basic explanation for the

[5] Defined as a subsystem whose elements interact with each other relatively more frequently than with other members of the communication system.
[6] Defined as an individual who links two or more cliques in a system, but who is not a member of any clique.
[7] Defined as an individual who links two or more cliques in a system from his or her position as a member of one of the cliques.

individual's behavioral change. Evidence that networks matter comes from a wide variety of behavioral researches and other sources, several of which are illustrated here (further evidence is presented in chapter 5).

Some of this evidence is inferential, rather than being very explicit, because while networks can be measured by researchers, they are otherwise not visually obvious in many cases. Nevertheless, they are quite real in their effects on human behavior.

One of the authors of the present book was once a faculty member in a university department that was sharply divided into two conflicting cliques. When he first joined this department, the author was unaware of this internal division. But he immediately began to notice many puzzling events. Discussions at faculty meetings were unusually bitter, and voting was almost predictably along "party" lines, whatever the issue. When all of the author's colleagues were invited to a reception or a faculty dinner, only half of them came. Finally, after several months of these inexplicable activities, the author realized that much of such otherwise puzzling behavior could be explained by the clique divisions within the faculty. Eventually, in fact, the author was forced into membership in one of the two cliques, even though he tried to avoid such categorization. The internal division of this department led to many problems, and lessened its effectiveness, until the department was finally terminated by the university's administrators.

There is much empirical evidence of the importance of networks on human behavior. Durkheim's (1925) "egoistic" suicides were presumed to occur among individuals without interpersonal network relations that would have prevented suicide. Isolation from their social context encouraged these individuals to take the unsocial act of suicide. A comparison of isolates with nonisolates provides a very gross indication of the influence of networks on individual behavior. Roberts and O'Reilly (1978), for example, found that the isolated workers in a large organization had lower job satisfaction, organizational commitment, and job performance than their more integrated peers.

In certain special situations, being an isolate in a system may amount to a life-or-death matter. For instance, a common research finding on the post–heart attack careers of cardiac cases is that those individuals who live isolated from a primary network of spouse and children are less likely to take their daily medicine (which often has very unpleasant side effects). As a result, the isolates are less likely to survive over a period of years than are postcardiac men whose wives and children provide daily reinforcement to take the unpleasant medicine. For example, Finlayson (1976) found that cardiac husbands recovered more quickly and were able to return to work sooner when their wives had more sources of network support, and when this support came from a wider range of sources. Similarly, Smith (1977) found that chronically disabled workers recovered more rapidly if they were integrated into networks of family and peers.

Not only are network isolates less likely to recover from illnesses like heart attacks which require continued medication or treatment but isolates are less likely in the first place to seek treatment for certain health problems like mental illness. For example, Hammer (1963) and Kadushin (1969) found that individuals with kin and friendship network connections were more likely to be referred for psychiatric help. Horwitz (1977) found that individuals connected to others who had psychiatric experience were more likely to be referred to psychiatrists.

Further, some psychiatrists use network strengthening as a tool for curing mental illness. The typical approach here is to work with the patient's immediate network of family and friends, rather than just with the patient as an individual, especially in the case of schizophrenics (Speck and Attneave, 1973; Speck and Rueveni, 1969). Again, networks make a difference; "network therapy" results in more rapid recovery and less rehospitalizaton of the mentally ill.

There is a parallel in the basic approach of such therapeutic communities as Alcoholics Anonymous, Weight Watchers, and Smokenders. Their main strategy is to integrate an individual with a problem (such as alcoholism) into a tight network with other individuals who have overcome it. The personal communication network that is thus provided helps change behavior, give reinforcement, and continue the changed behavior over time (especially by involving the individual in helping change the behavior of others).

A network approach is also used in constructing mass media messages for preventive purposes. There is increasing awareness that a target audience should not always be treated just as an aggregate of separate individuals. For example, mass communication campaigns in the United States aimed at drunken drivers have not been very successful in changing behavior. In recent years such mass media campaigns have aimed their messages at friends, family, and party hosts in preventing drunken driving (Swinehart, 1968), rather than at the drunken driver alone.

A similar illustration is provided by a 30-second television spot advertisement, "Do It for Them," featuring a hypertensive man, his wife, and children in a scene of family togetherness. The audio message is as follows:

ANNOUNCER: If you have high-blood pressure, here are good reasons to stay on your medication.
SINGERS: Do it for her. Do it for him. Do it for your loving wife if you won't do it for yourself. Do it for all the loved ones in your life.

The final visual is a prescription medicine bottle with the directions, "Take daily as directed for them," superimposed over a happy family scene.

Another use of personal networks for behavior change occurs in the People's Republic of China, where almost every adult is a member of a "study group" composed of 12 to 20 individuals. The study groups include work associates, neighbors, and friends, individuals who are linked in strong multiplex ties. Each group is led by a cadre, a politically dedicated leader who has undergone special training. Each cadre is responsible for reading the *People's Daily,* the Communist Party newspaper in China, and for interpreting this news to his study group members, who discuss it and seek to apply the message to their daily lives. Group members are asked to criticize their own behavior and that of others, so as to motivate behavior change. It is mainly through the internal dynamics of the study groups that individuals are persuaded to behave in ways that are helpful to society (for example, to wait to get married until they are at least 25 years of age, to limit their family size to only two children, to accept a work assignment in a city distant from their husband or wife, etc.). Often these changes are not of the individual's choice, but are accomplished through persuasion and coercion in close-knit personal networks.

The importance of networks was recognized by Georg Simmel (1964, p. 140), writing about sixty years ago, who stated: "The groups [networks] with which the individual is affiliated constitute a system of coordinates, as it were, such that each new group with which he becomes affiliated curcumscribes him more exactly and more unambiguously." So the idea of network effects on behavior has been around for a long time. Network analysis formalizes this research approach and provides more standardized ways of conducting this research.

For Simmel (1964), the essential question for understanding behavior change is "to whom is the individual linked by communication ties?" Although using different terminology than that of today, Simmel, writing in 1922, was clearly one of the first network analysts, as is shown by the title of his most noted work, *The Web of Group-Affiliations.* Simmel's intellectual concern was with how an individual's "group-affiliations" (that is, links) in "social circles" (that is, networks) affect the individual's behavior. "Simmel is thus the Freud of the study of society" (Hughes, 1964, p. 9).

Network links represent potential influences on our behavior, and, in reverse, how we may affect the larger system: "Society affects us largely through tugs on strands of our networks—shaping our attitudes, providing opportunities, making demands on us, and so forth. And it is by tugging at those same strands that we make our individual impacts on society—influencing other people's opinions, obtaining favors from 'insiders,' forming action groups" (Fischer and others, 1977, p. viii).

One form of evidence for the importance of networks in explaining behavior comes from the study of *system effects*, the influences of others in a system on the behavior of an individual member of the system. For example, Alexander (1964) investigated the role of friendship cliques on student drinking behavior in an English high school. Most of each clique's members were either all drinkers or all teetotalers. In the rare case of a nondrinking member of a drinking clique (or of a drinker in an otherwise nondrinking clique), the deviant from the clique norm was less connected (sociometrically) than were the nondeviant individuals.

Yet another illustration of the importance of networks comes from a study by Laumann and Pappi (1973) of 51 community elites in a small German city. Based on sociometric data obtained in personal interviews with these influentials, a network influence score was computed for each individual. When these influence scores were averaged for the proponents versus the opponents for each of five community issues, the researchers were able to predict correctly the winning side for all five issues. Again, it seems, network variables do make a difference.

Similar evidence of the importance of networks has been found in explaining (1) academic success among school children (Hurt and Preiss, 1978), (2) tolerance of ethnic differences (Alba, 1978), and (3) upward social mobility (Anderson, 1974).

During the 1970s, several disciplines recognized the potential of network analysis in explaining the yet-unexplained variance in their dependent variable(s) of central interest. For example, marketing has moved to a new theoretical perspective, focusing upon dyadic exchange rather than treating buyers and sellers as isolated actors (Bagozzi, 1978). Anthropologists began to investigate (1) relationships rather than things, (2) process rather than form, and (3) elementary phenomena rather than institutions. These theoretical trends "lead inevitably toward a network model" (Wolfe, 1978). "Network analysis provides the investigator with pathways into the heart of social systems (Whitten and Wolfe, 1974, p. 719).

Political scientists and sociologists like Lazarsfeld and others (1948) pioneered in discovering the role of interpersonal communication in determining how citizens vote in an election; unfortunately, more recent voting research in the intellectual tradition of the University of Michigan's Survey Research Center has largely ignored the communication flows in election campaigns, assuming that voting is an individualistic act (Eulau, 1978). Sheingold (1973) criticized these individualistic studies of voting behavior, and called for the use of network analysis. Burstein (1976) has shown the unique advantage of network variables in explaining voting choices.

Sociologists have long felt that modern society has brought a weakening of intimate and supportive social bonds, a decline of community; network analysis offers a means of measuring the individual's ties to society and thus whether community solidarity is declining (Fischer and others, 1977, p. viii).

An example of how a network approach can provide new insights to an established research field comes from the study of self-disclosure, the act of revealing one's self to others. This concept has mainly been investigated in the past as if it were an individual attribute. Not very much variance in measures of self-disclosure have been explained by these individual variables. Balswick and Balkwell (1977) reconceptualized self-disclosure as a relational variable; obviously, an individual may disclose certain information about himself to one person but not to another. The research results led the researchers to conclude: "Self-disclosure exhibits definite patterns that are clearly relational in character."

Another field belatedly adopting a network approach is the study of community power and decision making. Conventional research on community elites focused almost entirely upon the characteristics of individual elites, which lost sight of the central research questions regarding the structure of the relationships among the elites. Illustrative of recent network analyses of the structure of community elites is Laumann and others' (1974) study of a small German city (mentioned previously in this section).

Each of these disciplines and research fields has, belatedly, recognized the potential of network analysis in explaining behavior change. Communication network analysis is a research paradigm whose time has come.

"Schools of Urban Life for Migrants to a Mexican Slum"

One illustration that networks matter is provided by the numerous studies of migration to cities. A common finding is that most individuals move to a community where they already have network ties (such as former neighbors, friends, or relatives). Thus, patterns of migration are distinctly nonrandom. One can predict which city a villager will move to by knowing where the villagers' acquaintances live. For instance, one survey of Mexican immigrants in a northern California community showed that almost all came from the *same* village in central Mexico, located over two thousand miles away! And once a rural family has moved to a city slum, friendship networks are the "schools of urban life" that teach the migrants what they need to know in adjusting to their new surroundings: where to find housing, work, food. An urban slum is thus a "network of networks."

One illustration of the importance of networks to rural–urban migrants is Lomnitz' (1977) investigation of a shantytown in Mexico City, composed of about 200 families that share an "equality of poverty." All of these households are extremely poor, and their sources of income are very unstable. How do they survive? Through a system of close-knit network relations in which money is borrowed and lent, information about possible jobs is shared, and emotional support and diversion are provided.

Most of the families in the shantytown originally migrated from the same village in rural Mexico. First one family came; it was followed by some relatives and friends, who were assisted by the earlier migrants in finding housing and work. Then the acquaintances of *these* migrants followed. So the migration stream itself is largely explained by network links, and through these ties, once he/she arrives in the city, each migrant is assisted in his/her adjustment to urban slum life.

Many of the later migrants simply add another room to the existing house of a relative in the shantytown. As a result, many families reside in a joint kinship arrangement in which up to four or five nuclear families live under a common roof, often around a courtyard; these individuals are tied in a pattern of reciprocal exchanges that add protection and stability to their precarious life. Thus, the social system of the shantytown consists of a set of closely knit kinship networks. Understanding these networks is essential to comprehending the nature of life in the shantytown.

Networks can act as liabilities, as well as assets, for migrants. "Since ethnic members who sponsor migrants have limited network contacts, they tend to channel the newcomers into particular types of jobs, which then become ethnic specializations" (Anderson and Christie, 1978). For instance, Portuguese immigrants to Toronto are channeled by ethnic networks into construction and janitorial jobs, although they were initially recruited as farmers and railway workers (Anderson, 1974). So ethnic networks often lead the new migrant into dead-end occupations and into ethnic ghettos, which provide immediate assistance, but which are usually a long-term liability.

Lomnitz (1977), using the research methods of most social anthropologists, was only able to study her Mexican respondents' "little networks" (extended family households, in the present case). The method of participant observation allowed the investigator to diagram the individuals and nuclear families in each extended household, and to describe the linkages among them in great detail. But without utilizing mathematical methods of network analysis, the "macronetwork" of all 200 families in the shantytown could not be identified.

However, such a macronetwork analysis has been conducted by Morett-Lopez (1979) for women in two shantytowns in Monterrey, Mexico. Sociometric data were obtained via personal interviews with a census of about four hundred female respondents; then Richards' (1976) NEGOPY computer program was used to identify the cliques within each of the shantytowns. The results of this network analysis, shown in chapter 7 of the present book, demonstrate the understandings that can be gained by mathematical analysis of large-sized networks.

Network communication is especially important whenever individuals are involved in exchanging information in order to reduce their uncertainty: when they are in a new job or organization, when they are learning about a new idea, when a major news event has just happened. Social science researches show that in all of these situations where individuals want information, and where the information is especially likely to change their behavior, they depend heavily on interpersonal communication messages that are transmitted through networks.

Korzenny and Farace (1978) synthesized 21 studes of communication networks and behavior change in developing countries (usually these investigations focused on the village as the system of study). The basic proposition that "the degree of interpersonal communication is positively related to the degree of behavior change" was generally supported by 111 tests of this proposition in the 21 studies, but the evidence was not very overwhelming. Nevertheless, we see that interpersonal communication through networks is a factor in human behavior change.

All of these varied researches and experiences, just reviewed, lead us to conclude that *the behavior of an individual is partly a function of the communication networks in which the individual is a member.* For a communication researcher, knowledge of individuals' network links allows interpretation of their social behavior.

The above generalization about network effects on behavior is of limited value in understanding human behavior, because it is so general. But it does represent a point of departure for communication research, directing network analysts to develop specific hypotheses and empirical tests about exactly *how* communication networks influence individuals' behavior. "Network analysis has made what were latent ideas manifest and specific and has provided a conceptual structure and method of study where there were once only loose applications" (Fischer, 1977, p. 20). Certainly the methodological advances in network analysis have helped move this field from talking about networks as a loose metaphor, to using network concepts as analytical tools.[8]

In chapters 5 and 6 we shall provide further evidence for the above proposition from our Korean data-analysis. In such a research design, network dimensions are utilized to predict or explain some communication effect. Network dimensions can also be considered as the human behavior that is to be explained or understood (as we demonstrate in chapter 7).

Now we turn to the historical origins of network analysis.

Historical Background of Network Analysis

Network analysis is certainly not a recent development, although the main emphasis it has received from social scientists has occurred primarily in the past few years.

[8] Several authors credit Barnes' (1954) article as the turning point in shifting the network concept from metaphor to analysis.

What really constitutes the network approach? "As so often happens with something seemingly new, closer examination reveals that network analysis consists of, at least in part, some rather old ideas that have been refurbished and made more attractive by being combined with sophisticated and quantitative tools (that is, sophisticated for sociology and anthropology)" (Laumann and Pappi, 1976, pp. 17–18).

The Rise and Fall of Sociometry

If the German sociologist Georg Simmel were one of the first to recognize the theoretical significance of networks in understanding behavior change,[9] it was Jacob L. Moreno, often called "the father of sociometry," who provided the basic methodological tools to measure network variables (Moreno, 1934). *Sociometry* is a means of obtaining quantitative data about communication patterns among the individuals in a system. Moreno's sociometric measurement techniques and the sociograms that resulted from his data-analysis afforded the first graphic realization of Simmel's call for a "geometry of social relations." Moreno acknowledged Simmel's influence on his conceptualizations of communication networks (Levine and others, 1976).

Moreno's research dating from the early 1930s certainly hepled provide the foundation for much of present-day network analysis. Moreno's approach typically asked the individual in some system (for example, a school or a classroom to select certain other members of the system that were his/her best friends, that were most attractive as potential work partners, or most knowledgeable about some topic. Such sociometric data were then typically cast in the form of a *sociogram,* a graphic means for displaying the patterns of communication or social choice in a system.[10]

---

[9] Even prior to Simmel's time, early sociologists had regarded communication between two individuals as the elemental unit in sociological analysis. They called this communication relationship "the social act," the smallest unit of directly visible action which has a shared meaning for both members of the dyad. Several sociological pioneers set up a polar typology of these dyadic relationships, such as Cooley's (1902) "primary" and "secondary" relationships; examples of the former are husband–wife and friend–friend relationships, and of the latter are clerk–customer and officer–subordinate relationships. Unfortunately, this conceptual apparatus has not proven to be very useful in the empirical investigations by sociologists in the past seventy-five years since Cooley's taxonomy. One reason is that dyadic relationships have very seldom been the units of analysis in such research, so the primary/secondary quality of communication links could not be a useful dimension in research until the beginnings of network analysis in recent years. Lacking were methodological and conceptual tools for linking the microlevel study of the communication relationship with the macrolevel concerns of much social science (especially sociology): "Sociometry, the precursor of network analysis, has always been curiously peripheral—invisible, really—in sociological theory. . . . We have had neither the theory nor the measurement and sampling techniques to move sociometry from the usual small group level to that of larger structures" (Granovetter, 1972).

[10] In addition to constructing sociograms, Moreno and his students also pioneered in computing network indices of the system's communication structure in order to

Although Moreno was not the first to use sociometry,[11] he certainly provided the main impetus for introducing sociometric measurement into the scientific literature. In fact, Jacob Moreno promoted sociometry with a missionary enthusiasm, describing his major book, *Who Shall Survive?*, as "a bible for social conduct, for human societies. It has more ideas packed in one book than a whole generation of books" (Moreno, 1934, p. lxvi). He saw his book as a religious tract, as well as a methodological text, and felt that sociometry was a scientific tool that should be utilized to ameliorate societal problems [12] (Boguslaw, 1975). Indeed, there have been many practical uses of Moreno's sociometry, from assigning students to small work groups to selecting groups of men (rather than individuals) as replacements in U.S. Army units in World War II.

But while Jacob Moreno provided communication scientists with a measurement tool (sociometry) of great usefulness even today, his main data-analysis technique of drawing sociograms was limited to a network with a maximum size of 80 to 100 individuals. Even then, the drawing of a sociogram is a highly arbitrary and time-consuming task.

The convention in constructing sociograms is to arrange individuals so that the distances between them indicate their degree or amount of communication (that is, their proximity). For example, the points of two individuals choosing each other (this is a reciprocal choice) should be closer than if the choice is only one way, which, in turn, should be closer than if the two individuals did not choose each other.

A sociogram helps one identify cliques, isolates, and liaisons in the communication structure of a network. The visual portrayal of this structure provides valuable insight into the nature of a communication network. Levine (1972) stated, "The value (or deceptiveness) of a [sociogram] lies in what it suggests, in its ability to stimulate thought." Moreno (1934) noted the immediate impact of a sociogram on the members of the network it represents; the two-dimensional Euclidian space speaks very strongly to individuals' feelings about their communication patterns (Roistacher, 1974).

The only problem is that the sociogram may be wrong. An infinite number of sociograms can be constructed from one set of network data, each of which may convey a *different* picture of the communication structure. There is no objective, standard procedure for drawing sociograms.

---

measure such concepts as cohesion, prejudice, status, and leadership. Index analysis, based on converting dimensions of communication structure to variables, is an important part of contemporary network analysis.

[11] For instance, the psychometrician Louis M. Terman asked sociometric questions of school children in a research study in 1904.

[12] Moreno (1934) stated: "The historians of the year 2000 will probably credit sociometry as the true beginning of a meaningful and useful sociology."

For example, one of the authors collected sociometric data in the early 1950s on the diffusion of an agricultural innovation in Collins, a small Iowa rural community. No computer-based methods of network analysis were then available, and so the author, after a careful reading of Moreno's (1934) book, *Who Shall Survive?*, sought to construct a sociogram from his sociometric data. After several weeks of frustrating effort, the author gave up. The 150 individuals could be arranged and rearranged in an endless variety of patterns, none of which clearly showed the communication structure of diffusion in the system.

Today, the clique structure of this rural community could be printed out by a computer in a few seconds of running time and at the cost of a dollar or two. But until the methodological breakthrough of network computer programs (like NEGOPY, which we shall discuss shortly), insights into network data were to remain locked in the complexity of such data.

After several decades of scholarly interest in Moreno's sociometric approach in the 1930s and 1940s, including the launching in 1937–1938 of the scientific journal *Sociometry*,[13] Moreno's approach became passé among social scientists.

The Influence of Computers

One reason was the rapid rise of computers as data-analysis tools, and the consequent influence of such machines on the nature of social research. The use of computers facilitated large-scale surveys of individual respondents; usually the data were punched on IBM cards with each individual as the unit of analysis. This psychological unit forced investigators to measure individual-level variables, and to look within the individual for explanations of communication behavior.[14] As we argued in chapter 2, the possibility of using communication *relationships* as units of analysis was generally overlooked. Linear models of the communication act, large-scale survey research, computer data-analysis, and the use of individuals as units of analysis, were all forces that worked directly against sociograms as data-analysis tools, and, less directly, that discouraged any type of network analysis (until, in the 1970s, computer-based network analysis techniques became available).

---

[13] A journal which continued through 1977, when it was renamed *Social Psychology*, as the journal now includes relatively few articles dealing with sociometric network analysis. The death of *Sociometry* was certainly not due to any lessening of scientific interest in network analysis; in fact, two new journals, *Social Networks* and *Connections*, began publication in 1978.

[14] Throughout all this (survey research) one fact remained. . . . The *individual* remained the unit of analysis. . . . As a result, the kinds of substantive problems on which such research focused tended to be problems of 'aggregate psychology,' that is, within-individual problems, and never problems concerned with relations between people" (Coleman, 1958).

A typical graduate student in most of the social sciences today (and certainly in the fields of communication and social psychology) is unlikely to encounter many network publications, or to be taught the methods of network analysis in his/her courses in statistics and research methods. He/she typically learns to use a standard computer package like SPSS (Nie and others, 1975) that does not contain any statistical routines designed explicitly for analyzing network data (although a factor analysis routine is included, which, as we show in chapter 4, can be used for network analysis purposes).[15] Then is it any wonder that most newly minted social scientists do not include network analysis in their repertoire of methodological skills?[16]

Not until recent years, beginning in the 1970s, has there been a resurgence of scientific interest in network analysis,[17] accompanied by the wider availability of computer methods for such data-reduction, and by a greater stress on theoretical formulations of communication as a process of convergence. So computers, through their influence on the nature of social research, first helped the decline of Moreno-type sociometry in the 1950s and 1960s. Then they led to the rise of computer-centered network analysis in the 1970s.

In the years since Simmel and Moreno, and especially in very recent years, communication network analysis has come a long way. The distance it has come, at least in amount of research effort expended, is illustrated by a recent bibliography (Freeman, 1976) on social networks[18] that includes over 1,600 publications, and a bibliography by Klovdahl (1978) of 750 network publications.

Alba and Kadushin (1976) attribute the current renewal of scientific

[15] Most of these statistical methods (like zero-order and multiple correlation, analysis of variance, and chi square), as well as the dominant theoretical models, encourage social scientists to think in such non-network terms as dependent and independent variables, with individuals as the units of analysis. If one accepts a systems viewpoint in communication research, which implies that all of the elements in a total system are interdependent, the search for mechanistic cause–effect relationships (as is indirectly implied in conceiving of human communication as independent and dependent variables) is futile; instead, one should be concerned with the study of "wholes" (Rogers and Agarwala-Rogers, 1976a).

[16] Our colleague Bill Richards (1976, p. 255) has suggested the need for NPSS, a Network Package for the Social Sciences. Unfortunately, this package does not yet exist.

[17] Two types of sociometric experiments were exceptions to this 1950s–1970s malaise in network research: (1) the laboratory experiments on small networks, as reported by Bavelas (1950) and Shaw (1964), and (2) the quasi-field experiments on the "small world problem" (Milgram, 1969) which are reviewed later in this chapter. However, neither of these research approaches appear to be very alive today, nor have they contributed a useful body of generalizations about human communication.

[18] We do not make much of a distinction in this book between "communication networks" and "social networks," although one might imagine a social network relationship, such as between a military general and a private, or between individuals in a kinship network, in which interpersonal communication rarely or never occurs. However, most network relationships among individuals are, directly or indirectly, of a communication nature.

attention in network analysis (1) to computers, and (2) to theoretical interest in communication structure: "[Network] study was abandoned for a time because the technology necessary for its pursuit was lacking. Its revival is attributable not only to technological innovations, ultimately reachable to high-speed computers, but also to an increasing recognition of the importance of networks in bridging the conceptual gap between micro and macro structure."

Bott's Study of Small Networks

One of the oft-cited studies that contributed to the resurgence of communication network analysis was Bott's (1955 and 1957) investigation of 20 families in London. This scholar originally set out to explain the husband–wife allocation of household tasks in terms of social class and neighborhood of residence. Unexpected inconsistencies in her data forced Bott to look for alternative explanations, such as in the interpersonal communication of her respondents with friends, neighbors, and kin. Following the lead of Barnes (1954),[19] Bott concluded that the network connectedness of her respondents intervened between the independent variables of social class and neighborhood, and the dependent variable of household task allocation. Thus, again, we see that networks made a difference.

This viewpoint of individual behavior as influenced by network relations, espoused by Bott (1957), was later followed by English anthropologists at the University of Edinburgh and the University of Manchester (Mitchell, 1969), and by Dutch anthropologists at the University of Leiden and the University of Amsterdam (Boissevain and Mitchell, 1973; Boissevain, 1974). These scholars concentrated on investigations of a few very small networks, often located in African nations. Such microanalyses were consistent with these anthropologists' concern with a holistic approach to their respondents' behavior. Network analysis allowed them to understand such behavior in its totality, and as part of an interrelated system of behavior. Unlike sociologists and social psychologists, the anthropologists were not so wedded to utilizing individuals as the units of analysis, or to using compters to handle quantitative data.

These early network researchers are often called "the Manchester School" of British social anthropologists because many of its leading members were at one time or another connected with the University of Manchester. The Manchester School took useful steps toward creating a set of concepts for network analysis, and are usually credited with moving "network" from metaphor to analysis.

A recent review of anthropological network research by a sympathetic critic (Foster, 1979) concluded: "Although the anthropological

[19] Professor John Barnes, in his investigation in a small Norwegian community, defined a social network as "a set of points joined by lines . . . which indicate which people interact with each other" (1954, p. 43).

network people laid out an important theoretically-motivated problem area and had a general vision of how it might be investigated, they encountered serious methodological problems. They could treat neither the network structure nor the individual action aspects of the problem satisfactorily."

Communication Networks in Organizations

Meanwhile, starting in the early 1950s, organizational scholars at the University of Michigan launched a tradition of research on network analysis of organizational communication (Jacobson and Seashore, 1951; Weiss and Jacobson, 1955; Weiss, 1956). In these investigations, a major thrust was to computer-analyze the interpersonal communication flows among the members of an organization, in order to identify cliques, the liaisons and bridges linking these cliques, and other aspects of the communication structure.[20] Then this informal communication structure was overlaid on the formal organizational structure, in order to determine inconsistencies between the two, "one of the true delights" of many organization scholars (Perrow, 1972, p. 62).

After seventeen years of dormancy, network analysis of organizational communication was again picked up by communication scholars (Schwartz, 1968), and during the 1970s has become a very popular tool in studies of organizational communication (MacDonald, 1971; Shoemaker, 1971; Allen, 1970; Betty, 1974; Amend, 1971; Chavers, 1976; Rogers and Agarwala-Rogers, 1976; Farace and others, 1977; Schwartz and Jacobson, 1977). A recent review of organizational communication calls the Jacobson/Seashore/Weiss research "an important turning point in the study of communication in organizations" (Rogers and Agarwala-Rogers, 1976, p. 124).

Today, communication network analysis is utilized in a wide variety of research contexts: Indian and Brazilian villages (Yadav, 1967; Guimarães, 1972), high schools (Lin, 1968), Mexican slums (Kincaid, 1972; Morett-Lopez, 1979), family planning diffusion in Korea (Lee, 1977; Dozier, 1977), an old folks' home in Michigan (Danowski, 1975).

MEASURING COMMUNICATION NETWORK LINKS

A *link* is a communication relationship between two units (usually individuals, although the nodes may be groups, organizations, nations,

[20] This research represented several important methodological advances in network analysis: (1) a modification of matrix analysis procedures previously described by Forsyth and Katz (1946), (2) displaying relational data about communication patterns in a who-to-whom matrix (sometimes called a "communimatrix"), and (3) use of a computer for data-analysis, which allowed the researchers to find the communication structure in a relatively large organization with several hundred members.

etc.) in a system. The link is the basic datum in any type of network analysis. Without knowing the existing links among the units/members in a system, no type of network analysis is possible.

Three main methods of measuring these communications links have been utilized in past research: (1) survey sociometry, (2) observation, and (3) unobtrusive methods.

Survey Sociometry and Sampling Network Links

By far the most frequently used means of obtaining network data is survey sociometry. Previously, we defined *sociometry* as a means of obtaining and analyzing quantitative data about communication patterns among the individuals in a system by asking each respondent to whom he/she is linked. Obviously, network analysis can be no better than the data it analyzes. How are such data obtained?

Measurement by Asking Sociometric Questions

A direct communication link is usually operationalized in survey sociometry by asking a question of respondents such as: "With whom in this system have you talked most frequently about [topic X]?" The form of this sociometric question is specific to a topic or issue (like family planning, or work-related matters, for example); an alternative is to ask respondents with whom they talk most frequently without specifying a particular topic. Moreno (1934) felt that concrete, rather than abstract, questions yield more meaningful sociometric data. Some researchers have found that asking a sociometric question with a very narrow content width can result in many respondents not providing any data about their communication links. For example, if a respondent does not discuss family planning (or some other very specific topic) with anyone else in her system, she will not report any links in answer to this question.[21] If there are many such respondents, a network analyst will learn that the sociometric topic is not widely discussed (which may indeed be an important finding in itself), but the researcher will not be able to conduct a network analysis of the communication structure of the system because the data-matrix will have too many "holes" (nondata) in it.

For example, Braun (1975 and 1976) encountered this problem in his sociometric survey of five Colombian villages; many of his respondents

---

[21] Most sociometric questions inquire about a respondent's verbal behavior (for example, "With whom have you discussed family planning?"), but in some cases sociometric questions ask who the respondent perceives as the model for his/her behavior, whether or not verbal communication with this model individual has occurred (for example, "Who in this village do you regard as an example of good farming practices?").

simply did not discuss either of the two specific topics dealt with in his questions. The resulting network data were so sparse that the communication structure in each village mainly consisted of numerous unconnected small cliques. Morett-Lopez (1979) encountered the same difficulty with one of his sociometric questions about family planning in two Mexican slums; many female respondents just did not talk about this topic. In two Korean villages, the topic of abortion was relatively taboo, and so few village women discussed it that a sociometric question yielded few reported links (Rogers, 1979). Similarly, asking a housewife an irrelevant question like "Whom do you talk with about job-related matters?" may not be relevant if she does not consider her household work to be a "job."

How can an investigator avoid these measurement difficulties, so as to obtain meaningful data from respondents with appropriate sociometric questions? At the heart of this problem is the practical difficulty of knowing how specific versus general a sociometric question should be on the basis of the topic's frequency of discussion among one's respondents. If one does not already know the degree of such discussion, extensive pretesting of the sociometric instrument is obviously necessary in order to understand the audience's discussability of the topics studied. The pretest instrument should include a variety of sociometric questions, covering the range of content width on the topic of study. The interviews might begin with a very general ("funnel") question about the broad topic, and then successively narrow down to more specific questions about the topic. For instance, in our Korean village study we asked sociometric questions about whom the respondent talked with most, discussed female health problems with, discussed family planning with, and discussed abortion with. Thus, the range of pretest questions bracketed the respondents' range of content width. Also important in coping with this problem of data-gathering are such standard survey techniques as employing skilled, same-sex interviewers, and training and supervising them thoroughly. In the past, network analysts have not always given enough attention to the important task of obtaining high-quality data. Without such data, sophisticated network analysis techniques are futile.

The maximum number of sociometric contacts that may be named can be specified for the respondent ("Who are the *three* other women in this village with whom you have discussed family planning?"), or else left unlimited. Moreno (1934) argued that respondents should be allowed an unlimited number of sociometric choices, presumably because not all individuals interact with exactly three, or four, or five others about some topic.

One type of unlimited sociometric choice is the "roster study," in which each respondent is presented with a list of all other members of the system, and asked whether he/she talks with each of them.[22] The roster technique has the advantage of ensuring that each respondent is presented with the opportunity of indicating his communication with each other individual in his system.[23]

After identifying with whom he/she talks, a respondent may be asked about the frequency of such communication: "Do you talk with [Mrs. X] daily, about once a week, once a month, once a year, or less often?" Thus, two types of information may be obtained about each possible link: (1) whether or not it occurs, and (2) the frequency with which the linked individuals communicate. The former is just a cruder expression of the latter.

The advantage of a roster-type sociometric approach in capturing weak ties (low proximity links) was demonstrated by Killworth and Bernard (1974b), who performed a cumulative series of network analyses with their CATIJ computer program (explained in chapter 4). First, they included only the stronger ties (in which communication between the pair of dyadic partners was more frequent) in their network analysis. It was not until the weak ties were also included in the network analysis that a communication structure emerged for the relatively small network they investigated (a women's prison) that "made sense" to professors Killworth and Bernard on the basis of their ethnographic observations. This result is exactly what one would expect on the basis of Granovetter's (1973) theory of the strength of weak ties: The weak ties (low-proximity links) tend to bridge between the cliques in a network.[24] Until they are included in a network analysis, the communication structure may be badly distorted.

An alternative to the relatively time-consuming (in a personal interview or questionnaire) roster technique of measuring network links, is to ask respondents a sociometric question in which about seven links are

[22] A special version of the roster study is the diary method of sociometry. An illustration of the diary method of gathering network data is provided by Tushman (1977). Each of the 345 R and D professionals in a large corporation reported their communication links for one sample day per week for 15 weeks. The name of each interaction partner was recorded in the respondent's diary after such interaction occurred. About 93 percent of the personnel provided these data, and 68 percent of the links reported were corroborated by the other dyadic partner (thus suggesting the validity of this diary method of data-gathering).

[23] Actually, this is usually not such a problem as one might expect because most respondents say they interact with only 19 or 20 others at most, even in a large system.

[24] This advantage of finer measurement of the less frequently occurring communication links helps to overcome one of the deficiencies of past network analysis, the lack of studying "weak ties": "Most network models deal, implicitly, with strong ties, thus confining their applicability to small, well-defined groups. Emphasis on weak ties lends itself to discussion of relations *between* groups and to analysis of segments of social structure not easily defined in terms of primary groups" (Granovetter, 1973).

reported. Killworth and Bernard found, at least for the network they studied, that with about seven choices per respondent, the weak links were measured as well as the stronger links.

The general point suggested by Killworth and Bernard's (1974b) work is that greater care and attention should be given by network scholars to measuring low-proximity links; these links are often ignored, which is unfortunate because they make a unique contribution to the nature of the communication structure that is obtained in network analysis.

However the sociometric question may be put, it seeks to elicit a rather sensitive type of information from the respondent. It is the authors' experience that sociometric questions often receive a somewhat higher rate of refusal and "no answer" responses than most other questions in a personal interview. Certainly skilled and well trained interviewers, who are able to gain rapport and trust with respondents, are necessary to obtain high-quality sociometric data.

One reason respondents perceive such information to be sensitive is that these data are somewhat private in nature; a respondent might feel that such data would be embarrassing if known by others in the system. Thus most researchers assure their respondents of confidentiality, and take special precautions to protect the privacy of their sociometric data (often sociometric partners are only identified by a code number, as one means of such protection).

Sociometric questions may imply reciprocal links (that is, respondent A chooses respondent B, and vice versa), or they may imply nonreciprocal links (where the two individuals are linked only by a one-way choice, which is not reciprocated). Most sociometric queries about information-exchange imply reciprocity (for example, "Who are the three individuals in this system that you talk with about topic X?"), although it is not always so reported by respondents.[25] For example, respondent A may choose respondent B as one of his three dyadic partners, but respondent B may not choose respondent A because B talks about topic X more frequently with individuals C, D, and E than with A.[26]

[25] "Data collected concerning a naturally symmetric [reciprocal] relationship are sometimes asymmetric. . . . Frequently in such situations, the analyst is justified in assuming that an asymmetric relationship in the data is, in reality, symmetric" (Alba and Kadushin, 1976). In fact, in later chapters we make just such an assumption in the data-analysis of our Korean network data, thus forcing reciprocity on all communication dyadic links, whether or not they are so reported. The alternative procedure, of discarding nonreciprocated links in the data-analysis, is less desirable as it loses valuable information. When a network analyst only includes reciprocal links in a network analysis, "weak ties" (that is, low-proximity links) tend to be eliminated, thus distorting the nature of the network structure that emerges because the weak ties are often bridging links between cliques (Killworth and Bernard, 1974b).

[26] Whether or not a link is reciprocated may also depend in part on the proximity of the two individuals. Shulman (1976) found that more proximate pairs of indi-

Reciprocity in a link depends on whether one or both individuals initiate communication. A very microanalytic approach to network analysis has been proposed by Harary (1971), Harary and Havelock (1972), and Rosengren (1975), focusing on the "demiarc," or half-link, as a unit of analysis. A communication link (AB) can be conceptualized as composed of two parts: a "male" demiarc going *from* an individual A toward another (B), and a "female" demiarc going *to* an individual (B).

In terms of initiative, individual A is more active than B in this example. If the AB link were reciprocated, A and B would both be active in initiating communication, and each would be involved in a male and a female demiarc. Theoretical work on demiarcs has just begun, and empirical study faces important problems which have yet to be solved.

An example of a sociometric question that implies nonreciprocity is "Who are the three individuals in this system that you regard as most expert about topic X?" Here, we would not usually expect both partners in a dyadic link to name each other. And the question inquires about an expert model, rather than directly about communication flows.

Validity is the degree to which an instrument measures what it is supposed to measure. Questions can certainly be raised about the validity of certain sociometric data, and often we lack a clear-cut criterion for assessing validity. One advantage of gathering data from both individuals in a dyadic link is that a kind of validity check on the network data is thus provided by reciprocity.

The reliability (that is, the degree to which an instrument measures the same variable consistently over time) of sociometric data is sometimes questioned. Critics argue that asking a single sociometric question is equivalent to measuring an attitude with a single-item scale (a measure with unknown reliability). It is possible, of course, to ask several sociometric questions of each respondent, and combine the responses, so as to increase the measure's reliability.[27] Actually, few sociometric surveys have been repeated at two or more points in time, so measures of

---

viduals were more likely to share a common view of the relationship, and to reciprocate sociometric choices.

[27] In a pilot study of 78 respondents in northern California, Fischer (1977) first asked a general sociometric question (typical of those asked in previous sociometric surveys): "Who are the people you think of as your closest friends?" Next, 12 specific sociometric questions were asked, such as which individuals helped the respondent find housing, provided advice on personal problems, etc. The single, general question elicited an average of 4 dyadic links per respondent, while the 12 specific questions (when combined) yielded 17 different links per respondent; only 14 percent of the single-question dyads were kin, compared to 41 percent of the 12-question dyads (Jones and Fischer, 1978).

over-time reliability are rarely available (chapter 7). And as network structures are often fluid, a certain amount of instability in sociometric measurement should be expected.

Another way to categorize measures of network links is whether they are (1) nominal (for instance, "Whom do you talk with?"), (2) ordinal ("Rank the members of your system in order of the frequency with which you talk with them. Give a '1' to the individual you talk with most frequently, a '2' to the individual you talk with next most frequently, etc."), or (3) ratio ("Please indicate how much time, in hours, that you spent with each member of your system this month"). Another type of ratio measure would ask each respondent to indicate his/her frequency of talking with each other member in the system on the basis of about once a month (scored "1"), about once a week (scored "4"), or about once a day (scored "30"). Ratio measures require more time for the respondent to provide the data, but they allow the use of certain statistical methods of data-analysis that are not justified with either nominal or ordinal measures.

So one of the core problems in survey sociometry is measurement (Holland and Leinhardt, 1973). The other is sampling.

Sampling Network Links and Limited Generalizability

Random means that every unit in a population has an equal probability of being drawn in a sample. Then characteristics and relationships of the sample can be generalized to the larger population by means of statistical inference. Most statistical methods of data-analysis (like correlation, analysis of variance, and chi square) can only be correctly utilized when this underlying assumption (of the data being based on a random sample) is met. Classical sampling theory is best suited to sampling individuals, rather than network relationships.

Random sampling is usually very difficult with network data, as it is often impossible to obtain a sampling frame of communication *links* in a system at the time of selecting the sample: such links are invisible, and only the two individuals who are linked usually can provide data about themselves and the link.[28] Links cannot talk. So they cannot usually be sampled directly, or be units of response.

Without a basis in random sampling, network analysis cannot (1) adequately justify the use of statistical methods based on statistical inference,[29] or (2) provide a sound basis for generalizing the research results to some larger population.

The sample designs for network analysis, as compared to monadic analysis,[30] provide (1) less basis for using statistical inference to gen-

---

[28] For discussions of the problems of sampling network links, see Denzin (1976), Granovetter (1976 and 1977), Beninger (1976), and Morgan and Rytina (1977).
[29] As Alba and Kadushin (1976) and Laumann and others (1974) pointed out.
[30] In monadic analysis, the individual is the unit of analysis.

eralize the research results to a larger population, but (2) *a greater capacity to understand the nature of communication structure.* In order to study a communication structure, network analysis must sample either intact structures, or at least the parts of them relevant to the research objectives.

A Sample of One

In reality, the statistical basis for generalizability is severely limited in almost all social science research by what Campbell and Dunnette (1968) call the "N = 1 problem." For instance, let's say that a scholar has selected a random sample of 321 respondents who are residents of a small city of 20,000 people. The research results may be generalized, according to the rules of statistical inference, from the sample of 321 to the population of 20,000. But this city is really only a sample of one, in that there is no *statistical* basis for generalizing the research findings to all cities of this size, or to any other sample. Most "samples" in social science research are of this N = 1 variety, and thus allow a legitimate use of statistical methods of data-analysis (that are based upon the assumption of a random sample of units from a larger population). But the population to which the results are generalized is usually not *socially* significant, and wider generalization (to a socially significant population) has no basis in statistical theory. It can only be done intuitively and at great scientific risk. Obviously, the researcher cannot claim generalization of his findings past his limited population "of one." Obviously also, the reader of the research report, who may be responsible for putting the results into practice, must *intuitively* generalize more broadly. Such generalization rests on "plausible inference," not on formal statistical inference: here the decision criterion is the utility of the data, not the quality of the data (Cronbach, 1977). The reader of the research is forced by practical circumstances to make inferences and generalizations beyond the one small population that was randomly sampled (1) to other, perhaps similar, populations, and (2) to future years when the sampled system may be quite different.[31]

In comparison with this "N = 1 problem," a network analysis of one intact system is only a little worse in the sense of generalizability, and at least it provides an in-depth network analysis of communication exchanges. So at least much can be learned about a little, rather than the usual social science approach of learning a little about a lot (and where the "lot" may still not be very socially significant).

It is usually impossible to obtain a random sample of network links. The practical objective of network sampling is thus to maximize the capacity to generalize, by minimizing known sampling biases. Four main "least–worst" alternatives are available for sampling network links: (1)

---

[31] Here the data represent only a sample of one in a time sense.

sampling intact systems, (2) quasi-sociometry, (3) snowball sampling, and (4) nonsampling.

Sampling Intact Systems

Most survey sociometry is based upon a sample of one or more "intact systems": villages, old folks' homes, schools, organizations, and so on. Usually, all of the members of each system are respondents, or at least all the members that meet certain qualifications: for instance, we feature a sociometric data-set in this book that was gathered from all of the 1,003 married women of reproductive age in a representative sample of 24 Korean villages with mothers' clubs purposively selected from a random sample of 24 rural counties.[32] Sampling intact systems is particularly advantageous for sociometric measurement: data about the characteristics of *both* the respondent and the respondent's dyadic contacts are thus available because everyone is interviewed. The accompanying disadvantage of saturation sampling of intact systems is that generalization of the research results is thus limited. For example, a much greater basis for generalizability of the results of our Korean survey could have been obtained if the 1,003 women had been sampled from 1,003 villages, rather than from just 24 villages. But if our theoretical/analytical interest were in the intact system of a village, any sampling design that did not respect the entire set of information-exchange relationships in a village would necessarily distort or missrepresent this research interest. When an investigator is mainly interested in a system (like a village or an organization), it would be inappropriate to sample individuals or links. A systems approach to research implies that the context would be seriously altered if the researcher only studied part of the entire system; this partial analysis of a component element or elements would thus create an unnatural situation precluding analysis of information-exchange relationships among the elements.

In many research situations, an important question underlying the operationalization of a network, is: "Where does a system stop?" (Burt, 1978b). If a network scholar is studying a system with a relatively fixed boundary (like a Korean village or a formal organization), this question might seem to have an easy answer. But even then there is often ambiguity. What about the links that cross the boundary of the village or the organization? There are always such links, unless the system is completely closed. Should data also be gathered from these individuals in

---

[32] Strictly speaking, this sample design does not provide a basis for statistical inference to generalize the results from the sample to the population of all Korean villages. Tests of statistical significance, however, will be reported for the reader's convenience. Our main purpose in using this sample of 24 villages is to demonstrate the advantages of network analysis for better understanding human behavior, rather than to generalize the results to all Korean villages.

the system's environment, and included in the network analysis? The answer will always be arbitrary; ultimately, it depends upon the objectives of the research. It is usually possible to learn how many and with whom these links are made outside the system of interest without directly interviewing them.

Quasi-Sociometry

Sociometric measurements can be utilized even with random samples of individuals through an approach that might be called "quasi-sociometry" in which the respndent is asked a sociometric question, but the individuals that he sociometrically names are not also respondents. Thus, data are obtained only from one individual in each dyadic partnership. The unit of analysis here could be an individual or dyad, but it is usually the respondent's personal communication network.

An illustration of such a one-sided sociometric technique was utilized by Kincaid (1972) with a random sample of 197 slum dwellers in Mexico City. Each respondent was asked to name his five best friends ("Who are the five persons that you talk with most frequently?"). Then the respondent was asked the occupation and physical location of these five friends, and his frequency of interaction with each of them. Finally, each respondent was asked whether each of the five friends was a friend of the other four friends, thus allowing Kincaid to measure the degree of integration [33] of the respondent's personal communication network.[34] This researcher was also able to measure each respondent's diversity as the standard deviation of the occupational prestige scores of the five friends. Kincaid concluded that these network variables intervened between the individual respondents' characteristics (such as their socio-economic status) and their personal efficacy (defined as the degree to which they felt able to control their lives). His research results generally suggested the importance of personal networks in helping new immigrants adjust to life in an urban slum (a point mentioned earlier in the present chapter).

By selecting the random sample of 197 slum dwellers, Kincaid was able to generalize his research results to all of the individuals in the Mexican slum that he studied. But this shantytown still only represented a sample of one slum from among the hundreds of such slums (each of them quite different) in Mexico City, and the hundreds of thousands of such slums in the world. So quasi-sociometry is not a complete solution to all sampling problems when studying communication networks. But it

---

[33] *Individual integration* is the degree to which the members of an individual's personal communication network are linked to each other.
[34] Defined as those interconnected individuals who are linked by patterned communication flows to a focal individual. Thus a personal communication network is anchored onto an individual—in the present case, the respondent.

is a useful means of providing a mathematical basis for generalizing the research results from network analysis to a larger population that has been sampled (at least when the objective is to study personal networks).

The assumption necessary in the quasi-sociometry surveys of personal communication networks is that the respondent accurately knows his best friends' education and status, and who their friends are.[35] Laumann's (1973) study in Detroit provides evidence that this was a safe assumption. In a similar approach to Kincaid's (1972) Mexican study, Laumann determined each of 1,013 respondents' three best friends, and then their characteristics and their friendships. The researcher then checked the validity of these data by telephone interviewing each of a subsample of 188 of the respondent's friends, and asking them their education, best friends, and so on. The two data-sets displayed a rather high degree of agreement, indicating that the quasi-sociometric data were valid. A similar methodology was followed by Shulman (1976) in Toronto, who found greater validity of the quasi-sociometric data for more proximate dyads.

Bernard and Killworth (1978a) found a modest degree of accuracy in their respondents' (the crew and scientists on a small oceanographic ship) ability to estimate the links of the other individuals in their personal communication networks. The estimates by each respondent about their links' links (that is, their dyadic partners' links) were compared to the links' links as reported by the links. Agreement occurred for one-half to two-thirds of the links' links. Further, the closer the proximity between the respondent and one of his/her links, the greater the accuracy with which the respondent knew the links' links. Bernard and Killworth concluded: "One must know a direct link *well* to know his links with any accuracy." Perhaps this tendency not only to "know whom he knows" but also to "know whom those he knows know" is limited to a fairly small system (there were only about 40 individuals on the oceanographic ship) in which a great deal of interaction takes place.

"The Small World Problem"

In 1979, one of the authors of this book was a visiting professor at the Universidad Iberoamericana in Mexico City, when he was approached by a communication major, Pedro Felix Hernandez, for advice about graduate study

[35] And, of course, it is assumed that the respondent accurately reports who his links are with; this assumption is also necessary with any other kind of sociometric measurement, but in the case of quasi-sociometry there is no easy check on the accuracy of these sociometric data because the respondent's dyadic partners are not also respondents. Laumann (1973, p. 85) argued that even if the respondent is not entirely accurate in reporting about his friends' characteristics, subjective perceptions may be more important than objective data. Perhaps measures of subjective homophily/heterophily are more valuable than their objective counterparts.

at Stanford University. While we chatted over a cup of coffee, the author commented on the excellence of Pedro's English language ability. He replied that it was due to his having lived with an Iowa family as an exchange student.

Rogers: "Oh, where in Iowa did you live?"

Pedro: "With a farm family in Collins."

Rogers: "Collins? That's the community I studied for my Ph.D. dissertation at Iowa State University! What is the family's name?"

Pedro: "Robert Badstubner."

Rogers (*in amazement*): "Why, that farmer was one of the opinion leaders in my investigation of the diffusion of 2,4-D weed spray!"

Rogers and Pedro (in unison): "What a small world!"

The statistical chance of one of 70 million Mexicans knowing an acquaintance of one of 220 million Americans is minuscule, yet the "small world" situation happens quite often. Actually, of course, the Mexican student is not just one out of 70 million random Mexicans, but one of the 6,000 students at an elite Mexican university, and one of perhaps a hundred or so such students with excellent English who wished to study in the United States. And the American was perhaps one of only a handful of visiting professors in Mexican universities in 1979.

Further, as we state elsewhere in this book, the average individual has about 1,000 acquaintances (someone whom you would recognize and could address by name if you met him/her). Usually, we grossly underestimate the number of our acquaintances: "People make fantastically poor estimates of the number of their own acquaintances" (Pool and Kochen, 1978). With a personal communication network of 1,000, an individual's friends of friends would number about 1 million if there were no overlap (there is, of course, due to interlocking personal networks). Thus, the small world event is not so surprising, once we begin to understand the nature of communication network probabilities (Pool, 1973, p. 17; Pool and Kochen, 1978).

Professor Stanley Milgram has ingeniously pioneered a research technique called the small world method (Milgram, 1967 and 1969; Korte and Milgram, 1970; Travers and Milgram, 1969; Erikson with Kringas, 1975; Feinberg and Lee, 1975; Guiot, 1976; Lin and others, 1977 and 1978; Stoneham, 1977; White, 1970; Lundberg, 1975; Bochner and others, 1976a and 1976b).* Milgram and his followers ask a respondent to advance a message from a randomly selected starter to an assigned target person by sending it via any acquaintance that the respondent thinks is more likely than himself/herself to know the target person. Rather surprisingly, Milgram (1969, p. 112) finds that an average of only 5.5 intermediaries are needed to transmit the message from, for example, a widowed clerk in Omaha to a stockbroker in Sharon, Massachusetts.

---

* An excellent review and criticism of the small world research literature is provided by Bernard and Killworth (1978c).

The links typically are homophilous—for example, from females to females, blacks to blacks, and so on.

Milgram (1967) stated the small world problem thus: "Starting with any two people in the world, what is the probability that they will know each other?" Most small world researches consider the effect of social structure on communication networks. For example, structure would be involved if Milgram's research question were asked as: "What is the probability that any two investment brokers will know each other?" (Bernard and Killworth, 1978c). Or, for instance, "Are any two black Americans more likely to know each other, than any black/white pair?"

Small world researches are usually amazingly cheap to conduct. For instance, Milgram's (1967) original investigation was budgeted at only $680!

The small world method has been utilized to trace communication networks between students, faculty, and administrators at Michigan State University (Shotland, 1976; Hunter and Shotland, 1974). The average distance within this megauniversity of 50,000 students was about five intermediaries, with students and administrators being most distant. Another ingenious application of the small world method by Bernard and Killworth (1978b) is what they call a "reverse small-world experiment": a sample of "starters" were given a list of 1,267 "targets," and asked to indicate their choice of a first link in a chain leading to each "target." Data on sex, occupation, and ethnicity were given to each respondent for all 1,267 targets. The hypothetical data about first links to each target from each respondent were then analyzed for the degree of homophily/heterophily. "Instead of many starters and one target, we presented each starter with a long list of targets. For each target, we provided a variety of information, and we asked the starter to tell us to whom he would send the (mythical) folder if he were initiating a small-world experiment" (Killworth and Bernard, 1978b). These researchers were able to persuade 58 respondents to complete the instrument, a task which required an average of eight hours per respondent.

Other investigators provide an incentive to encourage intermediaries to pass on the message to others; for instance, Arndt (1968) awarded a free one-pound can of coffee at a local store to housewives who told their peers about the free price. Then he traced the diffusion chains that resulted.

One methodological problem with the small world method is that the dropout rate is often very high. For instance, in Milgram's (1967) first study only 44 out of 160 chains (from starters in Nebraska to a target person in Massachusetts) were completed. The average *completed* chain length of 4.21 intermediaries would have been 6.21 if dropouts had not occurred (White, 1970). The "dead" chains tend to bias the average chain length to a shorter distance (because longer chains require that a greater number of individuals cooperate in passing along the message). This bias should be kept in mind when interpreting the results of small world studies. Often the rate of noncooperation and dropout is very high. For example, Bochner and others (1976b) found that 29 residents in a high-rise building in Sydney, Australia, refused to serve as starters, and of the 17 respondents who agreed to pass along a message within the building, only six of the messages went beyond the starter. After reviewing all small world researches, Bernard and Killworth (1978c) concluded that the Lin and others' (1977) data are probably the richest available in the small world literature because of their "high" chain completion rate of 30 percent.

There is a direct parallel between snowball sampling and the small world method: the former studies are a post hoc tracing of how a message has diffused (and presumably would in the future through the patterns of communication links), while the small world studies consist of planting and directing a hypothetical message. Both types of investigations measure the proximity of average links (chapter 4) in a system, and thus the connectedness of the system. The more cliquishness that exists in a system, the longer the chains of intermediaries will be to connect any two given individuals. Insight is thus provided into the nature of the communication structure of the system by the small world method.

The chance meetings of two individuals that lead to the "small world" exclamation are a clue to the inherent connectedness of society, and to an understanding of society as a network of personal networks.

Snowball Sampling

The Laumann (1973) study in Detroit illustrated another research approach called "snowball sampling," in which an original sample of respondents are asked to name their sociometric peers, who then become respondents in a second phase of data-gathering, their sociometric contacts thus nominated become respondents in a third phase, etc. (Goodman, 1961). After a randomly selected beginning, further sets of respondents are determined by following out the interpersonal chains at one remove, two removes, and so on. Thus, the sample grows like a snowball rolling downhill. Snowball sampling follows a multistage design in which respondents at each phase sociometrically determine who the respondents are at the following stage.

Snowball sampling has been used in several studies of the diffusion of innovations. For instance, Palmore (1967) traced the spread of family planning methods among low-income women in Chicago. Similarly, Agarwala-Rogers and others (1977) studied how four teaching innovations diffused from a set of several thousand college professors who were initially informed about them, to a sample of "secondary receivers," from them to a sample of their "tertiary receivers," and so on.

As the small world, and other, illustrations show, snowball sampling utilizes the sociometric data about network relationships to determine who in a system should be the respondents in a research study, rather than gathering data from all of the respondents in an intact system, or from a randomly selected sample (as in most sample surveys).

There are certain disadvantages of snowball sampling designs. Obviously, isolates are not included (except in the random, first-stage sample). Individuals with many links tend to be overrepresented in the later stages of snowball sampling. Small cliques not well connected into the total network are underrepresented. In short, a multistage snowball sample only randomly represents all *individuals* in the system at the initial phase, and other individuals nonrandomly *linked to* these random "starters" at the subsequent phases.[36] For certain purposes, however, such as investigating the sequential spread of a message in the system, a snowball sample is most appropriate.

Comparison and Summary

In this section we have reviewed "least–worst" alternatives in sampling network links:

1. To sample intact networks, thus obtaining a sample of relatively large chunks of network data. Here the units of sampling are intact systems, but the units of analysis may be individuals, personal communication networks, dyadic links, cliques, or entire networks (an example is the Korea data-set from 24 villages).

2. To follow a quasi-sociometry sampling design in which the units of sampling are individuals, and the associated personal communication networks attached to each such individual that is sampled. Here the unit of analysis is usually the individual respondent's personal communication network, with certain network variables measured by data obtained about the personal communication network from the individual respondent.

3. To utilize a snowball sampling design in which dyadic links (or chains of interpersonal communication links in multistage snowball sampling) fan out from a random sample of "starters." Here, the unit of analysis can be the individual or the chain, but it usually is the dyad.

4. Yet another alternative in survey sociometry is not to sample at all. Most laboratory experiments in the social sciences follow this alternative of simply not worrying about sampling and generalizability. So do some network studies. Every member of a single intact system (an organization, a village, etc.) is a respondent. Then the unit of analysis can be the individual, the personal communication network, or the clique, but not the network (as $N = 1$).

These four alternatives are summarized in Table 3–1.

36 It is possible to select randomly the second-stage individuals from the total pool of such individuals identified by the "starters," but it is often inconvenient to do so, and in practice it is seldom done.

TABLE 3–1.   Alternative Designs in Sampling Network Links.

Sampling Design	Unit of Sampling	Unit of Analysis
1. A random or representative sample of *intact systems*	Each system and every member of each intact system that is sampled	1. Individual 2. Dyad 3. Personal network 4. Clique 5. Network
2. *Quasi-sociometry* (a random sample of individuals is asked for data about their sociometric partners)	The personal communication network attached to each of a random sample of individuals	Personal network
3. *Snowball sampling*	Each of a random sample of "starters," and then a multistage sample of individuals that they identify with sociometry	Dyad (can also be the individual or the personal network)
4. *Nonsample* of a single intact system (also called a "census" or a "saturation sample")	A single network	1. Individual 2. Dyad 3. Personal network 4. Clique

There are particularly serious consequences of the usual methodological shortcomings of survey research when sociometric measurement is involved. For example, most survey research organizations today regard a 90 percent response rate as very satisfactory. But in survey sociometry, such a response rate is disastrous because it leaves huge holes in the who-to-whom data matrix, and hence in the communication structure. When 10 percent of the sampled respondents are missing from a frequency table, a bias may be injected in the results of tabulating some individual-level variable (especially if the nonrespondents are distinctive from the respondents). When 10 percent of the network links in a system are missing, the entire communication structure is distorted (in fact, when even one individual is removed from a network, our experience indicates that the communication structure usually is altered, unless, of course, the individual is an isolate).

Observation

One alternative to survey sociometry is to gather network data by means of *observation,* in which the researcher identifies and records the communication behavior in a system. A main advantage of observation

over direct questioning of respondents about their communication relationships is that the observed data are usually assumed to have greater
validity.[37] Individuals may, or may not, tell the exact truth about whom
they communicate with about a particular topic (although they are more
likely to be expected to do so when the data are gathered in privacy,
when the respondent can be assured that his/her data will be confiden-
tial, when a high degree of rapport is present between the respondent
and the researcher, and when the topic is not particularly taboo).

If communication links between respondents are appropriately observed, there can be little doubt about whether they occur or not. The
possible disadvantages of observation are mainly practical and logistical.
For instance, it may be necessary for the observer to be very patient if
the communication behavior that he/she wants to observe occurs only
with rare frequency.

Observation is most practical as a measurement technique when the
system is small.[38] Bernard and Killworth (1973) observed the communication exchanges on an oceanographic ship at sea; data were recorded
at regular intervals over several weeks for the ship's crew of 53 individuals. These investigators were able to check the accuracy of their
ethnographic observations against survey sociometry data that they obtained from their shipmates by means of questionnaires. Similar multimeasurement of communication links in a small, closed system was
reported by these same authors for another oceanographic ship at sea
(Bernard and Killworth, 1978a), for a women's prison in West Virginia
(Killworth and Bernard, 1974a), and for two offices (Bernard and Killworth, 1977). In one of the latter studies, an observer walked through
the office every fifteen minutes for several days, noting all occurrences of
individuals talking to each other.

In addition to the limitation that observation can only be utilized in
small systems, random sampling is almost impossible. Thus, observation
is a method that suffers even more than survey sociometry in its limited
basis for generalizability to a larger, socially significant population.

Observation was also utilized by Marshall (1971 and 1972) to
measure the interpersonal communication patterns among the 100 households in one Indian village. It was especially useful to this anthropologist to observe the small male cliques who regularly smoked a waterpipe
(hooka) together in the evenings. Such network data provided Marshall

[37] Although, as we discuss later, the presence of a measuring instrument (the observer, in this instance) often greatly affects what is being measured. Thus observation of human communication almost always becomes, at least partly, *participant*
observation. We define *participant observation* as a commitment by the researcher
to adopt the perspective of the respondents by sharing in their day-to-day experiences (Denzin, 1976).
[38] Bales (1950) provided a set of 12 categories for observing and classifying the
roles (but not the content) displayed in small group interaction.

(1971) with a basis for explaining why a contraceptive method (the IUD) diffused so much more slowly in his village of study than did a new "miracle" wheat variety. But in order to gather such observational data, it was necessary for Marshall to live in his village for more than one year.

In addition to its time-consuming nature, observation has another important disadvantage: its obtrusiveness. This difficulty may be especially important in a small system like a peasant village or a ship's crew, and over an extended period of time (both small systems and a lengthy period of study are conditions under which observation is most likely to be used). In fact, Bernard and Killworth (1978a) actually considered themselves participants as well as observers; they are included as two of the 45 crew members in sociograms of the oceanographic ship's crew. Naturally, such obtrusiveness of the network measurement technique may be a cause for scientific concern that the participant observation changes the behavior that is being investigated. On the other hand, observation can provide a rich kind of direct understanding of network behavior that has often been sorely lacking in most past network analysis, where the high degree of quantification has essentially dehumanized the data.

In comparison to observation, survey sociometry has been utilized much more widely in past research on communication networks. Even more rare are unobtrusive methods of measurement.

Unobtrusive Methods

An *unobtrusive method* is a measure that directly removes the observer from the events being studied (Denzin, 1976). A variety of such unobtrusive methods (Webb and others, 1966) are available for measuring communication links in a system. These unobtrusive techniques have only been utilized infrequently. A great deal of ingenuity (and some degree of good fortune) are often needed in order to capitalize on the potential of unobtrusive methods.

One example is provided by Bernard and Killworth (1977), who obtained network data about the frequent telephone conversations among the 21 blind individuals belonging to a special teletype "conference" hookup in the Washington, D.C., area. The date and time of each such link were automatically recorded, and the researchers were able to analyze these data in comparison with survey sociometry data obtained by personal interviews (with the permission of the participants).

A similar study involved the recorded interactions among 15 futurologists located throughout the United States who were linked for a six-month period by a computer linkup (Vallee and others, 1975). Such over-time data allow determination of the temporal stability and change of network relations (an issue that has been little researched in the past). Another computer teleconference called the "Network Network" began operation in 1978, with financial support from the National Science Foundation, linking the 40 leading scholars of network analysis in the United States (Freeman, 1977a). This teleconferencing network is like a giant chalkboard that each participant can reach with a long piece of chalk. Because all of the messages are exchanged via telephonic connections of computer terminals, a complete printout was available for analysis; the results show that the teleconferencing led to more connectedness among the network scholars (Freeman and Freeman, 1979).

Other unobtrusive "scratches" might be utilized as a source of network data: appointment calendars of officials in an organization, the lists of individuals to whom memos and other written messages are circulated, the names listed on interorganizational mail envelopes, and so on. A somewhat less unobtrusive technique is to ask individuals to keep logs of their communication activities (sometimes at a random sample of time periods during each day); previously, we pointed out that this diary method is essentially similar to a roster sample.

Bernard and Killworth (1977) gathered unobtrusive data from 54 amateur radio operators (called "hams") in the West Virginia area (1) by tape-recording all the radio conversations for 27 days (individuals were identified by their "call" letters and numbers, which they are required to use by law and by convention), and (2) by gaining access to the logs that most ham radio operators keep of all their conversations. Further, the researchers obtained survey sociometry data from the 54 individuals by mailed questionnaire. Thus, the unobtrusive data provided a check on the accuracy of the survey sociometry data on communication links.

Burt (1975) argued that in addition to their nonreactive nature, unobtrusive measures from archival records have the advantage of providing network data about individuals or organizations that are not available in surveys or to observation: individuals who refuse to be interviewed, persons who are dead, corporations which are dissolved, and so on. Burt (1975) demonstrated this point by performing a network analysis of individual/corporation relationships from 1877 to 1972; the network data were content-analyzed from *The New York Times*. A special advantage of network data from archival records is that such information is often recorded at distinct intervals of time (for example, in a daily newspaper), thus facilitating study of network stability over time (Burt and Lin, 1977).

Another example of unobtrusive measurement of communication networks is legislative roll-call analysis, in which the analyst clusters legislators into cliques on the basis of the similarity of their voting records (assuming that such similarity usually indicates that communication about the issue has taken place). An illustration is Stokman's (1977) study of the formation of a Third World voting block in the United Nations' General Assembly from 1950 to 1968; a network analysis was performed on the data about voting on colonial and socio-economic development issues to show the emergence of a clique of Latin American–African–Asian nations in the UN.

"Interlocking Directorates"

One unobtrusive measure of communication links is utilized in the "interlocking directorate" type of network analysis. A researcher will typically obtain publicly available data about the identity of the members of boards of directors of the largest industrial corporations (often the "*Fortune* 500," those firms with highest annual sales volume) (Sonquist and Koenig, 1975). Each director who is common to two corporations is considered as a communication link between them at the policy-making level. The greater the number of common directors between any two corporations, the more proximate they are considered to be. The typical corporation board of directors has from 10 to 15 members, a seminar-sized group that can meet comfortably in a board room. Most directors of U.S. corporations are "outsiders" to the firms, usually officers and directors of other corporations. For example, John A. Mayer, president of Mellon National Bank and Trust Company, was on the board of H.J. Heinz Company in the mid-1960s. Henry J. Heinz, II, chairman of the Heinz Company, was on the board of Mellon (Bearden and others, 1975). The Mellon Bank owned about 30 percent of the stock of Heinz Company (although many board interlocks are not accompanied by ownership ties). Boards of directors are important; they set the policies for the corporation and make all major decisions. In essence, the board members are the trustees for the owners of the corporation.

Board intermarriage suggests a cozy kind of coordination and control that exists among the major corporations in America, where three-fourths of total corporate manufacturing assets are in the hands of the 500 largest firms. The Federal Trade Commission (FTC) has a duty to police the Clayton Act of 1914, which prohibits directorate interlocks between direct competitors, and the Federal Trade Commission Act, which outlaws interlocking directorates that may lead to unfair competition.

Despite such restrictive legislation and the activities of watchdog agencies like the FTC, a great deal of directorate interlocking has been found by most network analysts. For example, Vance (1968, p. 73) found that one out of every eight corporate interlocks is with a potential competitor; if indirect interlocks (where a director from corporation A and a director from corporation B meet on the board of corporation C) are counted, about 80 percent of all big corporations are connected with at least one competitor and with innumerable potential suppliers and customers. The network analysis of Sonquist and Koenig (1975) showed that major U.S. corporations were "one big clique." When they utilized two or more common board members as a minimum measure of proximity, a tightly connected core of 401 U.S. corporations was found. Within this core, Sonquist and Koenig identified 32 cliques; more than 80 percent of these cliques had a bank as the central corporation. Banks also play a crucial role in connecting one clique with another (Sonquist and Koenig, 1975; Bearden and others, 1975). More than half of all interclique liaisons are banks.

At the center of the 32 cliques, Sonquist and Koenig found one large clique that included the First National City Bank, the Chemical Bank of New York, A T and T, Con Edison, U.S. Steel, Woolworth, New York Life, Colgate Palmolive, and seven other central members. All but one were headquartered in New York City, with liaison connections to major corporations in other cities. All of the 32 cliques had a distinct regional base.

So the general picture that emerges from the interlocking directorate studies is that the giant U.S. corporations are linked in a web of close connections evidenced through directorate interlocks and by indirect links through a third-party firm. The data base for these network analyses is huge; for example, Sonquist and Koenig based their investigation upon data from 797 corporations, 8,623 individuals, and 11,290 directorships. Computer programs obviously must be utilized to cope with such information overload, to derive a general pattern of the communication structure out of the maze of direct and indirect links.

The usual measure of proximity in these interlocking directorate studies is the common director between two corporations. In his network analysis of 70 industrial corporations and 14 banks, Levine (1972) found, for example, that the Mellon National Bank and Trust Company was closer to Gulf Oil (four directors in common) than to ALCOA (three directors) or Standard Oil of New Jersey (zero links). Note that in the interlocking directorate studies, the corporation is the "node" * in the network, and the individual director represents a link. Obtaining such network data is completely unobtrusive as the lists of directors for each corporation are a matter of public record in the United States.

The interlocking directorate method of network analysis can be carried out in a smaller system than that consisting of all U.S. corporations. For instance, McLaughlin (1975) investigated the interlocking directorates in one city, Phoenix. A tightly connected inner circle of 32 enterprises included "all the banks, all the law firms, and the two savings and loan associations . . . , along with the city government and the [governor] of the state government."

Obviously, these unobtrusive data about interlocking directorates are not enough to give a complete picture of the complexities of intercorporate connections (Levine and Roy, 1975). Observation and personal interviews with the interlockers could enrich our understanding and interpretation of how one corporation affects another. Much of the story that is only suggested by the interlocking directorates could be told by supplementary data: membership in elite clubs like the Bohemian Club (in San Francisco) and in intellectual groups like the Council on Foreign Relations, acquaintances made at elite resorts and through philanthropic enterprises, and old school ties formed at select private schools.

* A *node* is a unit in a network that is connected to certain other nodes by links.

The basic methodology of the interlocking directorate approach can be extended to the leaders or the members of any particular type of organization. For instance, a researcher might determine the network relations among formal organizations in a community on the basis of the number of common members for each possible pair of organizations. To the knowledge of the present authors, this type of network analysis has not yet been done. Here, the organizations would be treated as nodes and the individual memberships as links.

Or, to reverse the roles played by organizations and individuals, the individuals could be considered nodes and a common organizational membership could be considered as a communication link (assuming that interpersonal communication presumably occurs at the organization's meetings). For example, a possible measure of network proximity in our Korean villages of study could be whether or not two respondents both belong to the village mothers' club; they are more closely linked than another pair of individuals where one belongs to the club and the other does not, or where neither belongs.

Such an interlocking membership approach could be fairly unobtrusive if the data were obtained from organizational membership lists. Even if the individual respondents must be directly questioned about the organizations to which they belong, such data are likely to be less sensitive, and perhaps more accurate, than direct sociometric questions.

An unusual use of network analysis was reported by Cox and others (1975) who analyzed the "interlocking directorates" among 19 scientific journals in business and economics. The strength of each possible link in the 19-by-19 matrix was measured by the relative number of cross-citations from 1966 to 1970. For instance, an article appearing in journal A cites articles that have appeared previously in journals B, C, and D. The norms of scholarly publication require that authors acknowledge through their citations all connections between their research on a particular topic, and papers previously published on the same subject. So a citation indicates that communication has occurred between two journals, through the author of an article. This cross-citation index is thus an unobtrusive measure of network links.

Cox and others (1975) found the network of 19 journals was divided into two cliques, one for economics and one for business. At the heart of the former clique was a tight cluster of four journals centering on the *American Economic Review;* these four are the oldest and highest prestige journals in the field. For instance, *Administrative Science Quarterly* and the *Academy of Management Journal* were "close" to each other (meaning that articles in one journal most frequently cite articles in the other journal),[39] but both were far from the *American Economic Review.*

The analysis of data about journal citations could be carried out for authors, instead of journals. A main advantage of such types of network analyses is that they are completely unobtrusive.

Toward Multimeasurement of Communication Links

We have described in this section three main methods of measuring network data: (1) survey sociometry, (2) observation, and (3) unobtrusive methods. Each of these approaches has certain advantages and particular disadvantages (Table 3–2). *No one approach to measuring*

[39] The location of the 19 journals in two-dimensional space was determined by multidimensional scaling procedures, which are described in chapter 4.

TABLE 3–2   Advantages and Disadvantages of Three Main Methods of
Measuring Communication Network Links.

MEASUREMENT METHOD	ADVANTAGES	DISADVANTAGES
1. Survey sociometry (including samples of intact systems, quasi-sociometry of personal communication networks, snowball sampling, and a census in one intact system).	Large samples are possible. Some basis for generalizability of the results (depending on which sampling design is used).	The sociometric data may be of unproven validity and reliability.
2. Observation	Usually unquestioned validity of the data. Direct understandings are provided to the researcher.	Limited to relatively small systems. The behavior about which data are desired may occur only infrequently. The data-gathering may be obtrusive.
3. Unobtrusive methods (including interlocking directorate studies)	Usually unquestioned validity of the data. The data-gathering is not obtrusive.	The network data are limited to those recorded for other purposes.

*network links is best for all research situations, and in fact a combination
of two or more measurements in a multimethod design is usually superior
to the use of any single method* (Sieber, 1973). As Webb and others
(1966, p. 1) stated, "Interviews and questionnaires intrude as a foreign
element into the social setting they would describe, they create as well
as measure attitudes, they elicit typical roles and responses, they are
limited to those who are accessible and will cooperate, . . . But the
principle objection is that they are used alone."

One illustration of a multimethod approach to measuring communication networks is Parsons' (1973) investigation of 123 respondents in
one Filipino village These women were asked 18 different sociometric
questions about their communication patterns in five different interviews
over a fourteen-month period in 1971–1972. The validity of the 2,969
communication dyads thus identified was checked against the observation of interpersonal links by three different researchers. Generally, a
rather high degree of correspondence was found between the results of
survey sociometry and observation. Such triangulation in measuring
communication links is very seldom found in network studies, which are
almost universally of a unimeasure nature.

Obviously, every network analyst knows that there is a certain degree of "noise" or error in the sociometric data that he is analyzing. Some respondents may report a network link that does not actually exist because they think it is socially acceptable to do so. For instance, an isolate may report one or more links because he/she feels that it would enhance his position. Or a respondent may report being linked to a leader in his system because he/she feels that such a link will reflect well on his/her position in the network structure.

Many network analysts in the past have expressed some skepticism regarding the validity and reliability of their measures of network links. But until very recently, a systematic research attempt to determine the quality of network measurement has not occurred. Noteworthy among this contemporary methodological work is a series of ingenious investigations by professors Russell Bernard and Peter Killworth. Bernard is a Professor of Anthropology at West Virginia University and Killworth is a quantitative theoretician in the Department of Applied Mathematics and Theoretical Physics at the University of Cambridge in England. Their long-distance collaboration has resulted in an important series of four papers on the measurement accuracy of network links. Unfortunately, their results are generally bad news about the validity of measuring links with sociometric questions. Their disquieting findings suggest the need for network scholars to return to "start" in creating improved measurements.

Using a multimeasurement approach, Bernard and Killworth (1977) investigated four small networks: (1) 60 blind persons in the Washington, D.C., area who were linked by teletype, (2) 52 ham radio operators in the West Virginia area, (3) a small research office with 45 employees, and (4) 34 individuals in a graduate program at West Virginia University. A variety of (1) unobtrusive measures (for example, the teletype logs for the blind respondents, and tape recordings of the ham radio operators' conversations), (2) observation (such as a researcher who walked through the research office every fifteen minutes), and (3) survey sociometry questionnaires were utilized.

The conclusions reached by Bernard and Killworth (1977) are very sobering for network analysts: "People do not know, with any accuracy, those with whom they communicate." Further, none of the three methods of obtaining the data were particularly more accurate than the others.

Killworth and Bernard (1979) analyzed their data from a teletype network of deaf persons in the Washington, D.C., area to assess the accuracy of links obtained by a sociometric question, when compared with the unobtrusive data on links obtained from a three-week log of the teletype messages. This multimeasurement approach showed only a modest degree of agreement between the two types of data, leading Killworth/Bernard to suspect the accuracy of their sociometric measurement.

In a further study, Bernard and others (1979) compared sociometric data for their different networks (the ham radio operators, a college fraternity, office workers in a small research firm, and a university department) with the data obtained by observation (as recorded by an observer, for example, who walked through the fraternity at fifteen-minute intervals). The data were not only in disagreement at the dyadic level, but also when aggregated to the clique level. These results are discouraging for sociometric measurement (Bernard and others assumed that their observational data were accurate): "Any conclusions drawn from data gathered by the 'Who do you . . .?' are of no use in understanding behavioral social structure." This conclusion may be stated much too strongly, given the facts that (1) the systems of study were all rather small-sized (a necessity when using visual observation to measure network links), and (2) the observer only sampled the interactions that he could observe at the fifteen-minute intervals over a period of several weeks. Nevertheless, the investigations by Professors Bernard and Killworth cast some serious doubts on the usual sociometric measurement of network links, and suggest the need for much greater emphasis upon their improvement.

If the magnitude of noise that Professors Bernard and Killworth find in their methodological studies is characteristic of most sociometric measurement in other networks, serious questions are raised not only about such measurement techniques, but also about the utility of computer-based network analyses that are based on the assumed accuracy and precision of network data. "Attempts to filter out noise in a sociometric network matrix by using sophisticated software are likely to be unproductive. This is because such manipulations assume a much lower level of noise than actually occurs" (Killworth and Bernard, 1976).

The bad news from Professors Bernard and Killworth must be taken with at least a few grains of salt. They assume (1) that their unobtrusive measures and observations are of unquestioned validity, and (2) that the sociometric data ought to be perfectly related to these nonsociometric data, if the former were completely valid. Both assumptions can be seriously questioned. First, it must be pointed out that Bernard/Killworth's observation data are but a sample in time, once each fifteen minutes. What about the other fourteen minutes in each quarter hour? Data from a sociometric question thus might be considered as more valid, and when it is not closely correlated with the observations, one might question the validity of the observation data (Richards, 1979).

The unobtrusive and observation data are "objective," in that they do not depend on the respondents' perceptions; sociometric data are subjective. If the two types of data are not in complete agreement (as Professors Bernard/Killworth report for their four systems of study), the "validity" of each (in these investigators' view) may not be as relevant as which of the two are better predictors of human behavior. Certainly we would bet on the subjective, rather than the objective, data about network links. How individuals perceive a situation, whether objectively accurate or not, determines their behavior.

Nevertheless, the measurement studies of Professors Bernard and Killworth suggest that much greater efforts are needed to improve the measurement of communication links. Generally speaking, past researches on communication networks have overemphasized data-analysis, while short-changing the research attention given to measurement.

In order to correct this imbalance in the future, network scholars should obtain multiple measurements of communication links. At the least, these measurements could provide "convergent validity" checks on each other. Further, the multiple measures could also be subjected to tests for "discriminant validity." Unfortunately, the multitrait–multimethod approach [40] has not been utilized to date in measuring communication links.

In past network research, survey sociometry has been most widely used to measure network links. In part, this is because much past network data-gathering was simply a sociometric component of a larger data-gathering operation; one or several sociometric questions were included in a questionnaire or personal interview that was mainly designed for other purposes.[41] We foresee that much greater use of unobtrusive measurement should be made, at least to provide a multimethod validity check on survey sociometry data.[42]

---

[40] The "multitrait–multimethod matrix," proposed by Campbell and Fiske (1959), is a technique for determining the convergent and discriminant validity of operational measures of two or more concepts. The procedure consists of administering to the same sample of respondents two or more measures of two or more concepts. Then the four or more measures are intercorrelated. Convergent validity is the degree to which the two or more measures of the same concept correlate highly with each other. Discriminant validity is the degree to which each of the two or more measures of a single concept do not correlate with the parallel measure of a different concept. In other words, different measures of the same concept should be highly intercorrelated, while similar types of measurement (for instance, direct questions, observational ratings, etc.) of different concepts should not be intercorrelated (Agarwala, 1978).

[41] In such a situation, sociometry often seems so simple, but only until the researcher tries to analyze the data.

[42] A unique approach to validating the data obtained from survey sociometry was reported by Hurt and Preiss (1978), who analyzed sociometric data from 118 students in four classrooms. After these scholars had constructed a sociogram for each class, they showed it to the students and the teacher involved, and asked these respondents to help interpret its meaning and to explain why the communication structure of cliques and isolates occurred. These ethnographic data helped Hurt and Preiss understand their quantitative network analyses.

LEVELS OF ANALYSIS

As pointed out previously, the typical social science study uses the individual as the unit of response and as the unit of analysis.[43] One (or more) IBM cards are simply punched for each individual respondent. Thus, there is a unity parallel between the unit of response and the unit of analysis.

But in communication network analysis, five main types of units of analysis can be utilized: (1) individuals, (2) personal communication networks, (3) dyads, (4) cliques, or (5) systems (networks). A basic unit of measurement for network analysis in all of these cases is the dyadic communication link (as discussed in the previous section of this chapter), but data about such links can be easily transformed to such levels of units of analysis as individuals, personal networks, or systems.

Here we illustrate each of these five units of analysis, with the examples taken from well known network analyses.

Individuals as Units of Analysis

In chapter 2 we criticized most past communication research for its unquestioning use of individuals as the units of analysis. But it is not always inappropriate to use individuals as the units in network analysis. For example, for certain purposes it may be advantageous to measure some network variable at the individual level; thus, one might measure opinion leadership (a network-type variable) for individuals in a system.

Opinion Leadership as a Dependent Variable

Opinion leadership is the degree to which an individual is able to informally influence other individuals' attitudes or overt behavior in a desired way with relative frequency. A usual measure is the number of sociometric choices received by each individual in answer to a question (asked of all respondents) like: "From whom in this system did you receive information about [topic X]?"

The concept of opinion leadership was originated by Lazarsfeld and others (1948) in their study of the 1940 presidential election in Erie County, Ohio. Since then, numerous researches have sought to advance understandings of this concept by determining the communication behavior and social characteristics of opinion leaders, as distinctive from

---

[43] Although in some cases the data provided by individual respondents is aggregated to the group or system level, and these collectivities are utilized as the unit of analysis.

that of their followers.[44] This approach was only a slight extension of the usual monadic analysis in the direction of a more relational type of analysis, in that the individual was still the unit of analysis. We learned from these studies about how opinion leaders differed from nonleaders, but not about the *process* through which ideas flowed from opinion leaders to their followers.

An early illustration of using the sociometric links of an individual to explain his/her behavior is Newcomb's (1943) classic "Bennington Study." Bennington College is a small, elite girls' school in Vermont. The students came from rich families, and had conservative political attitudes when they entered as freshmen. Soon, many of the students became extremely liberal. Professor Newcomb sought to explain this attitude change. One explanation involved leadership (measured as the number of sociometric links received by each student), which was related to political liberalism and to upper-classman status. In other words, the leaders typified the liberal norms of Bennington College, and served as role models for the incoming freshmen students, who soon followed their lead.

A similar relationship of sociometric leadership, system norms, and individual behavior change has since been found in many other studies of opinion leadership (Rogers with Shoemaker, 1971).

Opinion leadership as the number of sociometric choices received directly by an individual in a system is one indication of influence. Another measure of opinion leadership is the number of direct choices received by an individual *plus* the number of indirect sociometric choices (in which one other individual links the opinion leader to a follower). Using such a measure, Laumann and Pappi (1973) found that the most influential individual in the small German city they studied could reach, in two or fewer steps, 91 percent of the other 50 elites for community affairs isues. Such a two-step measure of opinion leadership is obviously more comprehensive and precise than the count of direct, one-step choices typically used (depending, of course, on the amount of distortion that occurs in the second step).

From Opinion Leadership to Communication Structure

When scholars began to plot sociograms of communication among the members of a system, they could use communication relationships (such as sociometric dyads) as the units of analysis. This advance allowed the data-analysis of a "who-to-whom" communication matrix, and facilitated inquiry into the identification (1) of cliques within the total system and how such structural subgroupings affected behavior, and (2) of

---

[44] A synthesis of several hundred of these opinion leadership studies can be found in Rogers with Shoemaker (1971).

specialized communication roles such as liaisons, bridges, and isolates, thus allowing communication research to proceed beyond the relatively simpler issue of just studying the correlates of opinion leadership. Now it was possible to identify and investigate the interpersonal communication structure of a system, a task far more complex than just measuring the degree of opinion leadership of individuals in the system. Now the set of individuals following each opinion leader could be identified, and the degree to which different follower sets overlapped could be assessed. Thus the study of opinion leadership moved from focus on this concept as an individual *trait*, to a more realistic analysis of how opinion leaders fit into the larger communication structure of the entire network.

Once communication scholars began to look at the "forest" of communication structure in a system, instead of just the "trees" of individual-level opinion leadership, they could recognize and identify such other individual communication roles in the structure as (1) *liaisons* (who link two or more cliques, without being a member of a clique), (2) *bridges* (who are a member of one clique, and link it with another clique), (3) *isolates*, and (4) *cosmopolites* (who relate the system to its environment by providing openness).[45] Each of these specialized communication roles perform an important function for the system.

Research has often concentrated on determining the characteristics of individuals performing such communication roles as liaisons, much as has been done for opinion leaders. The general picture that has emerged from such studies is that liaisons are not particularly distinctive in their lifestyle or in other personal characteristics, but they may have special qualities stemming from their unique substructure-bridging function (Rogers and Agarwala-Rogers, 1976, p. 138). For example, Yadav (1967) found that liaison farmers in two Indian villages were intermediate in agricultural innovativeness[46] between the norms of the two cliques that they linked. A liaison linking an innovative and noninnovative clique was typically somewhat less innovative than the progressive clique and somewhat more innovative than the backward clique. This behavior of liaisons is what one might expect for individuals marginal to two or more cliques; their in-between behavior is ideal for the easy flow of information from one differing clique to another.

Predicting Individual Behavior with Network Variables

Obviously, opinion leadership is not the only network-type variable that has been analyzed with individuals as the units of analysis. For example, most investigations of personal communication networks find it

[45] *Openness* is the degree to which a system exchanges information with its environment.
[46] *Innovativeness* is the degree to which an individual is relatively earlier in adopting new ideas than other members of a system.

convenient to utilize personal network dimensions (such as the individual respondent's connectedness with his network, and the diversity or heterogeneity of the members of the network) as independent variables to predict the individual's behavior. As explained previously, Kincaid (1972) followed this quasi-sociometric approach in his investigation of Mexican slum-dwellers, to explain their adoption of family planning methods.

Another illustration of explaining individual behavior with network-type variables (and non-network variables) is Lee's (1977) study of family planning adoption by Korean villagers, which is described in detail in chapter 5. Lee found that such personal network variables as interconnectedness and integration explained aspects of contraceptive adoption that could not be explained with other, non-network variables.

In researches such as those just reviewed, the central research question is how the clique or the network influences behavior change on the part of individual members. "Why is it that one person is easily influenced by the group to which he belongs, while another person can for a long time successfully resist such influences?" (Festinger and others, 1950, p. 8). This question is a particular version of a research issue discussed previously: "Do networks matter?" The answer depends in large part on the nature of the individual's communication relationships with the cliques and networks in which he is a member. Not surprisingly, the measurement of various dimensions of these network connections of the individual with a larger unit is one of the central concerns of communication network analysis.

In these studies, network links are measured (via survey sociometry methods) and converted into network-type variables for each individual respondent. The dependent variable is still an effect of communication (knowledge, attitude, or overt behavior), as in the usual past research following a linear model of communication. Thus, such research is a special half-form of the new approach to communication inquiry that we recommend in this book. It uses networks for measurement purposes, but not as the units of analysis. It does not follow a convergence model of communication. It is still pretty much "business-as-usual."

To escape this "mental cage" inherited from past research, communication scholars must move more directly into relational analysis, by using the dyad, personal network, clique, or system as the unit of analysis.

Dyads as Units of Analysis

A *dyad* is composed of two individuals connected by a communication link. Information about the two individuals, and about the nature of the link, can be obtained (1) from either individual (as in quasi-socio-metry), or both individuals (as in study of the members of an intact system), or (2) by observation or unobtrusive measures. Survey socio-metry has been most frequently used.

The shift from the predominant use of individuals as units of analysis, toward network analysis, usually begins with dyads as units of analysis. But realization of this potential has been relatively rare: "Most social research, particularly quantitative research, treats social relation-ships, if at all, as attributes of individuals or groups. . . . An alternative approach . . . is to treat not the individual but the interpersonal rela-tionship as the unit of analysis" (Blau, 1962).

The Homophily Principle

A basic research question in past investigations of dyadic communi-cation has been to determine how the degree of similarity of the two individuals affects their interaction. *Homophily* is the degree to which pairs of individuals who interact are similar in certain attributes, such as beliefs, values, education, social status, and the like (Rogers with Shoe-maker, 1971, p. 210).[47] The opposite of homophily is *heterophily*, the de-gree to which pairs of individuals who interact are different in certain attributes.[48]

The most fundamental principle of human communication is that *the exchange of ideas most frequently occurs between transceivers who are homophilous*. Why does homophily happen so frequently? Because *more effective communication occurs when the transceivers are homo-philous*. When two individuals share a set of similar characteristics, common meanings, and a mutual value position, communication between them is likely to be effective, which is rewarding, thus encouraging homo-philous communication.

The Strength of Weak Ties

While such homophilous communication is facile, it may be dys-functional for the diffusion of new ideas. Innovations usually enter a hierarchical system at the top, through individuals who are of relatively higher socio-economic status. If all communication dyads were com-pletely homophilous on socio-economic status, the new ideas would only spread horizontally within the system and there would be no "trickle-down" (Rogers with Shoemaker, 1971, p. 212). As a result, one might

[47] This concept was named by Lazarsfeld and Merton (1964, p. 23), although the basic notion was noted much earlier by Tarde (1903, p. 64): "Social relations, I repeat, are much closer between individuals who resemble each other in occupation and education."
[48] Measures of the degree of homophily–heterophily at the dyadic level are provided by Coleman (1958) and Signorile and O'Shea (1965).

think of a kind of "optimal heterophily" in which information-seeking dyads connect individuals of somewhat dissimilar status (but yet similar enough to facilitate effective communication). Numerous researches suggest the generalization that *for new ideas to diffuse, dyadic communication must connect individuals who are somewhat heterophilous.*

Thus, human communication typically entails a balance between similarity and dissimilarity, between familiarity and novelty. Research on this issue is called "the strength of weak ties" (Liu and Duff, 1972; Duff and Liu, 1975; Granovetter, 1973; Rogers, 1973). The "strength" is informational, and the "weak" ties are heterophilous. The basic proposition here is that *the information-exchange potential of dyadic communication is related to the degree of heterophily between the transceivers.* In other words, a new idea is communicated to a larger number of individuals, and traverses a greater social distance, when passed through somewhat heterophilous links (as in radial personal networks) [49] rather than through homophilous links (as in interlocking personal networks).[50] There is less informational strength, then, in interlocking personal networks. "Weak ties" enable innovations to flow from clique to clique via liaisons and bridges.

Network analysis of the diffusion of a family planning method (the IUD) in the Philippines demonstrated the information strength of weak sociometric ties. The innovation spread more easily in dyads linking housewives of very similar social status (Liu and Duff, 1972). But heterophilous dyads were necessary to link the cliques composed of homophilous dyads; usually these "weak ties" connected two women who were not very close friends, and who differed in social status. So an occasional heterophilous dyad in the network was a structural prerequisite for rapid diffusion of the innovation.

Granovetter (1973), in an important network study described previously in chapter 2, traced the dyadic links through which a sample of individuals had obtained information leading to their obtaining a new job.[51] Generally, he found that dyads linking close friends who were highly homophilous, were much less important in transmitting job information than dyads between heterophilous individuals who were not close friends. Usually, the individual already knew the same job information as his close friends; he had to break outside of this interlocking

[49] A *radial personal network* is one in which an individual interacts with a set of dyadic partners who do not interact with each other.

[50] An *interlocking personal network* is one in which an individual interacts with a set of dyadic partners who interact with each other.

[51] Granovetter's (1973) methodology is an interesting variant on quasi-sociometry. First, he selected a sample of individuals who he knew had obtained a new job within the past year. Then he personally interviewed each such individual to retrospectively trace the communication dyads through which such job information had been obtained.

personal network to obtain new information. Instead of being a close friend, the job informant was usually "only marginally included in the current network of contacts, such as an old college friend or a former workmate or employer, with whom sporadic contact had been maintained" (Granovetter, 1973). Sometimes chance meetings or mutual friends reactivated such weak ties, so as to transmit the job information.

Most individuals located their jobs through a very casual acquaintance, not someone they saw regularly as a social friend. Only 17 percent of the respondents said they found their job through close friends or kin (Granovetter, 1974, p. 54). Interestingly, many of the respondents were unaware of the general pattern of weak ties in employment information; they felt that the way in which they found their job was somewhat out of the ordinary, an unusual occurrence (Granovetter, 1974, p. 147).

Naturally, the exact importance of weak ties in searching for some type of information probably varies on the basis of the tabooness or confidentiality of the topic (Boorman, 1975).[52]

Granovetter's (1973) notion of weak ties contains a methodological lesson for measuring network links: the importance of including weak ties (low-proximity links), along with strong ties, in network analysis. Evidence of this point is provided by Killworth and Bernard (1974b). As Granovetter's (1973) theory would lead us to expect,[53] the weak ties are uniquely crucial in bridging between cliques in a network. If the weak ties are not measured in a network investigation, the network analysis results seriously distort the communication structure. Killworth and Bernard recommend that weak ties be measured (1) by using a roster technique in which each member of a network is asked how frequently he/she interacts with each other individual, or (2) by asking a nonroster sociometric question in which each respondent provides data about seven links or so with others. In either case, Killworth and Bernard recommend that nonreciprocated as well as reciprocated links be included in the network analysis, because the nonreciprocated links tend to be weak ties.

The strength of weak ties theory suggests the importance of heterophilous dyas in information-exchange.

"Weak Ties" as a Measure of Proximity

Later in this book (chapter 4) in our discussion of *communication proximity* (the degree to which two individuals in a network have personal communication networks that overlap), we shall argue that "weak

[52] Boorman (1975) and Delany (1978) describe a mathematical model for simulating the search for a job via weak versus strong ties.
[53] As pointed out previously in our section on measuring network links, Granovetter (1973) argues that in survey sociometry when the respondent is allowed only a limited number of choices (for example, "Who are the three members of this system . . .?"), weak ties are unlikely to be reported.

ties" are really equivalent to a low degree of proximity.[54] Figure 3–2, which is adapted from Granovetter's (1973) illustration, shows how the link between individuals A and B is a weak link (of low proximity in that A's and B's personal networks have no overlap, except for each other). Strong ties link the members of both clique I and clique II; communication among the members of each clique is easy and frequent. But there is not much new information for them to exchange; they all know what their other clique-mates know.

The A–B link is the only connection between the two cliques, and thus functions to provide a bridge [55] across them. Obviously, it is a crucial

Figure 3–2. Low-Proximity Links Are Important Channels for the Flow of Information Between Cliques in a Network.

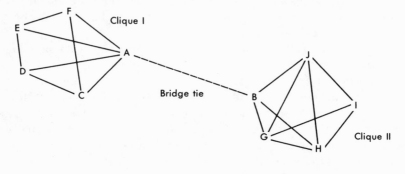

––––– "Weak tie" (low proximity)
–––––– "Strong tie" (high proximity)

Note: The bridge tie from individual A to individual B has low communication proximity because there is no overlap between the personal communication networks of individuals A and B. This communication link would play a crucial function in the flow of any information in this network; if it were removed, the network would collapse into two unconnected cliques.

[54] Granovetter (1973) suggests the following operational measures of a "strong tie": (1) the amount of time invested in the communication link, (2) the emotional intensity of the link, (3) the intimacy or mutual confiding between the dyadic partners, or (4) the reciprocity of the dyadic choices. He regards the degree of overlap of two individuals' personal networks, which we here consider to best measure proximity, as a separate variable that is related to the strength of ties (but that is not the same thing). In addition to the greater parsimony of our terminology, we prefer to use the more abstract concept of "communication proximity" rather than "strength of ties," as proximity can be measured in a precise mathematical formula (discussed later).
[55] In the words of Harary and others (1965, p. 198), a bridge is a link which provides the *only* path between two individuals in a network. Granovetter (1973) prefers the term "local bridge" for a link which is the only path between two individuals in a localized section of a network. We define a *bridge* as an individual who is a member of one clique and links it with another clique. Hence to us a bridge is an individual, rather than a link. By our definition, a bridge individual has an inter-

pathway for the flow of new information. If it were removed, the network would collapse into two unconnected cliques.

Our reformulation of weak ties as proximity suggests the following propositions, based on the research and writings on the strength of weak ties:

1. *The degree of proximity in communication dyads is negatively related to their information-exchange potential.*
2. *The degree of heterophily in communication dyads is positively related to their information-exchange potential.*

An extrapolation of these two propositions suggests a third proposition: That *the degree of proximity in communication dyads is positively related to their degree of homophily.* This notion was stated by Alba and Kadushin (1976): "A natural theme of proximity studies is . . . that the closeness [proximity] between the members of a pair is both a cause and a consequence of their similarity [homophily] in certain respects," and implied by Homans (1950): "Persons who interact with one another frequently are more like one another in their activities than they are like other persons with whom they interact less frequently."

Balance and Strain in Communication Dyads

While dyads with relatively high proximity may have a lower potential for information-exchange, an individual in such a proximity dyad has a greater potential for changing his partner's behavior. Such a "stronger" tie has more potential for influencing behavior change because a "psychological strain" is caused if the dyadic partners differ in their attitude toward some object (Newcomb, 1961). An unbalanced dyad of this type can be pictured as:

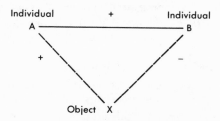

Assume that individual A and individual B are a proximate communication dyad, but that A is favorable to object X while B is unfavorable. Perhaps X is family planning, and A is an adopter and B is not. Our

---

clique link with very low proximity (individuals A and B illustrate this characteristic in Figure 3–2). A *liaison* (an individual who links two or more cliques without belonging to any clique) has at least two links of very low proximity.

expectation is that the dyad will seek to ease this psychological strain either (1) by individual B adopting family planning, (2) by individual A discontinuing family planning, or (3) by the dyad becoming less proximate.

Rogers and others (1976a) followed this model in investigating the effect of unbalanced dyads over time in leading to the adoption of family planning by Korean village women. Their prediction was generally successful (further details on this analysis are presented in chapter 5).

It is possible, of course, that "object X" may be a third individual; thus, the unit of analysis becomes a triad (Granovetter, 1973). The tendency toward balance in such relationships has been documented by Davis (1970) and Newcomb (1961, p. 160).

The basic idea of balance is utilized in everyday conversation, and is often expressed in such aphorisms as (1) "a friend of a friend will be a friend, not an enemy," and (2) "an enemy of a friend will be an enemy, not a friend." [56]

Balance theory has its basis in an article by the psychologist Fritz Heider (1946) in which he argued that an individual perceiver tends toward balancing his positive and negative attitudes toward another individual and a third object. Cartwright and Harary (1956) carried Heider's theory one step further by expressing a summary mathematical role for balanced interpersonal relationships, arguing that such "structural balance" would occur in systems with a single homogeneous clique, or two opposing cliques (each composed of individuals who like each other) (Leinhardt, 1977, pp. xvi–xvii). Numerous articles by professors James A. Davis, Paul W. Holland, and Samuel Leinhardt (reprinted in Leinhardt, 1977) have followed up on these leads in recent years, seeking to specify the nature of structural balance in triads.

The proposition summarizing the general viewpoint expressed in this section is that: *The degree of proximity in communication dyads is positively related to their potential for behavior change on the part of the dyadic partners.*

Spatial Distance and Dyadic Communication

One of the main research questions that has been asked in past research utilizing dyads as the units of analysis is: "What variables determine whether any given pair of individuals in a system are linked or not linked?"

---

[56] Former President Richard M. Nixon indicated his awareness of balance in communication networks in his national television address, announcing his acceptance of an invitation to visit the People's Republic of China on July 15, 1971: "Our action in seeking a new relationship with the People's Republic of China will not be at the expense of our old friends. It is not directed against any nation. We seek friendly relations with all nations. Any nation can be our friend without being any other nation's enemy." Obviously, Nixon was thinking about Russia (China's enemy).

Frequently, the answer is that the pair of linked individuals are (1) relatively homophilous on certain dimensions, such as their personal characteristics, and (2) spatially contiguous. Numerous researches have established (1) the importance of spatial distance in determining whether or not any given pair of individuals in a system are linked or not, and (2) the greater stability of spatially proximate links (Morett-Lopez, 1979). We return to explore this issue in greater depth in chapter 7.

Comparative Analysis of Dyadic Communication

Another research question frequently probed is: "How does dyadic communication for one topic differ from that for another topic?"

An illustration of such comparative analysis is Bhowmik's (1972) study of two types of communication dyads in eight Indian villages: (1) those linking friends, versus (2) those through which agricultural innovations diffused. As our previous discussion would lead us to expect, the friendship dyads were more homophilous (on social status, education, and other variables), while the innovation–diffusion dyads were more heterophilous.

Parsons' (1973) sociometric survey in a Philippine village, discussed previously, indicated that communication networks were different for the diffusion of contraceptive methods than for the communication of other innovations. In the case of family planning diffusion, personal experiences with the innovation were not conveyed, and an opinion leadership structure did not emerge. Marshall's (1971) study in an Indian village, mentioned previously, also showed that the network for a family planning method was markedly different than that for a new wheat variety. Dyads for family planning communication were very highly homophilous in terms of age, sex, and social status, and so the contraceptive diffused very slowly. Evidently, family planning ideas are often perceived as relatively taboo,[57] and this perception restricts the communication networks through which these ideas can spread.

The comparative analysis of dyadic links implies that some links provide a channel for the flow of more than one kind of content; these are "multiplex" links.

Multiplex Links

There is a direct equivalence between the *multiplexity* [58] of communication links (that is, the degree to which multiple message contents flow through a dyadic link between two individuals [59]) and the *poly-*

---

[57] *Taboo* communication is a type of message transfer in which the messages are perceived as extremely private and personal in nature because they deal with proscribed behavior (Rogers, 1973).

[58] Some authors refer to multiplex links as "multistranded." The opposite concept is called "unistranded" or "uniplex."

[59] And hence the degree to which the two individuals have multiple role relationships (for example, father–son and boss–employee).

morphism of opinion leaders (the degree to which an individual acts as an opinion leader for multiple topics). The only difference is that multiplexity is a characteristic of links, and polymorphism of individuals. Obviously, polymorphic individuals have multiplex links.

An important issue in past research on opinion leadership is whether there is one set of all-purpose opinion leaders in a system, or whether there are different sets of opinion leaders for each topic. Katz and Lazarsfeld (1955, p. 334) found that one-third of the opinion leaders among housewives in Decatur, Illinois, exerted their influence on more than one of the four topics of fashions, movies, public affairs, and consumer products. These investigators, however, interpreted their results to stress the monomorphism of opinion leadership: "The hypothesis of a generalized [polymorphic] leader receives little support in this study. There is no overlap in any of the pairs of activities" (Katz and Lazarsfeld, 1955, p. 334). Marcus and Bauer (1964) reanalyzed the Decatur data to show that the frequency of polymorphic opinion leadership was greater than could be due to chance.

By the time this reanalysis was published, however, several generations of students in communication had been taught that opinion leadership was monomorphic, and this general belief continues to the present day. There is a substantial "primacy effect" in beliefs about scientific truths in that a great deal of evidence is necessary to refute an original erroneous impression (Maccoby and Jacklin, 1974, p. 12).

Probably the degree of polymorphism in opinion leadership (and the multiplexity of links) is, in reality, highly situational, depending upon such matters as the diversity of the topics on which opinion leadership is measured, the nature of the network being investigated, and so on. Needed, as part of future research on multiplexity and polymorphism, is a standardized measure of polymorphism and of multiplexity.

Individuals connected by a multiplex dyadic link are presumably less able to withdraw from one another, and so the potential degree of influence or control of each individual over the other is greater (Laumann, 1973; Mitchell, 1969; Fischer and others, 1977, pp. 50–51). In many parts of the world, dyadic partners seek to convert a uniplex link to a multiplex link, so that they can count on its stability. For instance, in India, where the advantages of nepotism are widely understood, the president of a company usually appoints his closest relative (such as a son or younger brother) to be his treasurer; the possibility of financial misbehavior is thus minimized.

Personal Communication Networks as Units of Analysis

A *personal communication network* consists of those interconnected individuals who are linked by patterned communication flows to a focal individual. Thus a personal network (also called an "egocentric network" by some scholars) is anchored on an individual. It is each person's private communication environment.

In a previous section, we reviewed such studies as Kincaid's (1972) in which certain dimensions of an individual's personal network were utilized to predict the individual's behavior. But the individual was still the unit of analysis.

A logical next move would be to use the personal communication network as the unit of analysis. Unfortunately, our search of the literature discloses few such studies.

One of the most important dimensions of a personal communication network is the *integration* of the focal individual, the degree to which the members of an individual's personal communication network are linked to each other. The usual measure of individual integration is the number of links among the members of the personal communication network, divided by the total number of possible links (chapter 4).

Instead of using this conceptual variable of personal network integration, some scholars prefer to utilize the polar typology of radial versus interlocking networks (Figure 3–3). A *radial personal network* is one in which an individual interacts with a set of dyadic partners who do not

Figure 3–3. Radial Personal Networks Are Less Integrated and More Open Than Interlocking Personal Networks, and Thus Are More Effective in the Exchange of New Information.

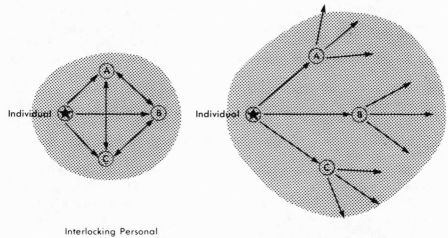

Interlocking Personal
Network

Radial Personal Network

Note: *Individual integration,* defined as the degree to which the members of an individual's personal network are linked to each other, is measured as the number of such links, divided by the total number of possible links. For example, for the interlocking personal network shown above, the integration score is 3 (the number of actual links among A, B, and C)/3 (possible links among these three individuals), or 1.0. The integration score for the radial personal network shown above is 0/3, or 0.

interact with each other. An *interlocking personal network* is one in which an individual interacts with a set of dyadic partners who interact with each other (Laumann, 1973, p. 113; Rogers, 1973). So interlocking personal networks are more integrated than radial personal networks.

Usually one's friends are friends with each other, thus constituting an interlocking personal network. Such interlocking personal networks are more numerous than radial networks. The reasons for this tendency toward integration in personal networks may be the same as those facilitating the homophily principle (discussed previously): similarity in meanings and life experiences which make homophilous communication facile and self-rewarding. *Interlocking personal communication networks are usually composed of homophilous links.*

Unfortunately, the ingrown communication patterns in interlocking personal networks discourage the exchange of new information with the environment beyond the personal network. Interlocking personal networks lack *openness,* the degree to which a unit exchanges information with its environment. So interlocking networks may simply facilitate the pooling of ignorance among the individual members. As in our previous discussion of "the strength of weak ties" for dyadic links, *the degree of individual integration in personal communication networks is negatively related to their potential for information-exchange.*

"Measuring Integration in Personal Networks"

Integration of a personal communication network is the degree to which communication links exist among the members of an individual's personal communication network. Such integration is usually measured as the number of links among the members of the personal network, divided by the total number of possible links.

Measurement of such personal network integration is no problem when sociometric data are obtained from all of the members of intact systems; then, for example, each of the four individuals in the personal communication networks shown in Figure 3–3 are respondents and report with whom they are linked.

But if a quasi-sociometry sampling design is utilized, only the starred individual in the personal networks shown in Figure 3–3 is a respondent; he can report his link with individuals A, B, and C, of course. But in order to measure integration, we also need to know whether A–B, B–C, and A–C are linked or not. Kincaid (1972), McCallister and Fischer (1978), and Jones and Fischer (1978) asked the respondent in each personal network whether his friends (A, B, and C) are friends of each other. To help the respondent provide these data, the researchers asked their respondents about each of these possible links, one at a time.

For example, Jones and Fischer (1978) and McCallister and Fischer (1978) first asked each respondent 12 specific sociometric questions, and obtained 17 different links per respondent. Five of these 17 individuals were selected randomly for each respondent, who was then asked about the existence of the 10 possible links among the five individuals. The interview questionnaire included the following format to assist the interviewer in obtaining these data (from which the measure of personal network integration could then be computed).

List the 5 selected names down the column: List the first 4 of them across the top, in the same order, in the spaces provided. Ask about all relationships in column 1; then about all relationships in column 2, etc.

	Do 1. __MARK__ and (2, 3, 4, 5) know each other well?	Do 2. __CLAUDE__ and (3, 4, 5) know each other well?	Do 3. __ED__ and (4, 5) know each other well?	Do 4. __LINTON__ and (5) know each other well?
1. __MARK__				
2. __CLAUDE__	Yes .... (1) No 2			
3. __ED__	Yes .... (1) No 2	Yes .... (1) No 2		
4. __LINTON__	Yes .... (1) No 2	Yes .... 1 No .... (2)	Yes .... (1) No 2	
5. __GEORGE__	Yes .... 1 No .... (2)	Yes .... 1 No .... (2)	Yes .... 1 No .... (2)	Yes .... (1) No 2

The integration score for the respondent's personal network shown above is 6/10 or 6.

The proposition on page 136 is illustrated in Lee's (1969) study of the search for an abortionist by American women (this at a time when abortion was illegal). Most respondents went first to their most intimate friends, who unfortunately were members of interlocking personal networks with the respondent, so they seldom could provide information about abortionists that the respondent did not already have. For example, one woman sought the name of an abortionist from several close friends, her mother, and a family doctor. All provided the name of the same abortionist.

Just as comparative analysis can be conducted of communication *links* for different topics, a similar analysis can be made of personal communication networks for varied topics. An illustration is Laumann's (1973, p. 125) study of urban men in Detroit. Such issues as voting and what kind of car to buy were discussed in less integrated personal networks (that is, more radial networks). But these same men talked about more sensitive topics, like a serious medical problem, only in interlocking personal networks, which were composed of more intimate relationships, and which were more closed. Perhaps these men feared that such private information would spread outside of their personal network if it were discussed in more radial networks.

Cliques as Units of Analysis

One of the fundamental purposes of most network analysis is to identify the cliques within a total system or network.[60] A *clique* is a subsystem whose elements interact with each other relatively more frequently than with other members of the communication system.[61] Clique identification is crucial to network analysis because cliques represent such an important aspect of the communication structure of a system. The identification of such individual roles as liaisons, bridges, and isolated dyads rests on the prior identification of cliques. Even the measurement of various communication network indices like connectedness can better be understood if the cliques in a system are first mapped.

Some network scholars use "group" and "clique" as synonymous terms. We do not follow this convention in the present book because "group" has a particular, different meaning to sociologists and social psychologists: a *group* is a relatively small number of individuals who share a sense of common identification and who are in direct, face-to-face interaction. A clique *may* have these same qualities, but often it does not. For example, some cliques contain more than 15 to 20 members, the number usually considered maximum for a group. The boundaries of a clique may seem indistinct or fuzzy to its members, because each individual can "see" only his/her direct contacts and may not recognize the clique members who are linked only indirectly through intermediaries. For instance, Kadushin (1976) found that American elite intellectuals were members of cliques, but most of their descriptions of their cliques were wrong. Groups often give themselves a name, whereas the clique structure in a network is often invisible to the system's members, although a network analyst is able to identify it. In part, this situation is a case of the forest and the trees; the network analyst's wider vision derives

---

[60] "One of the central problems in sociometry is that of partitioning groups [systems] into subgroups [cliques]" (Nosanchuk, 1963).

[61] A more precise set of three criteria for identifying cliques will be presented in chapter 4.

from his use of network analysis techniques which help illuminate the communication structure of the sytem.

During the 1940s, several different sets of social scientists "rediscovered the primary group," in the words of Katz and Lazarsfeld (1955, pp. 34–42). Industrial psychologists and organization scholars found that industrial work performance was greatly influenced by the work group, in the famous Hawthorne studies. Research on American soldiers in World War II found that the primary group was a key factor in motivating combat behavior. Communication scholars found that the mass media changed audience behavior when the media messages were passed along via interpersonal channels (chapter 5).

In all of these intellectual paradigm shifts, a halt was called, midway in an investigation, when a previously held, mechanistic model of human behavior was found to explain inadequately the reality that was being observed. In network terms, these "rediscoveries" amounted to a belated realization that individual behavior depends, in part, on the cliques to which the individual belongs.

However, none of these classical social science studies could go much further than to register dismay with their previous model, and to posit a clique explanation of behavior change. They lacked adequate research techniques for precisely measuring the effect of these cliques on individual behavior change.

In many cases the clique is a more precise predictor of individual behavior than the larger network of which the clique is a part. The individual is directly tied to the clique (by definition) through communication links, and may only be indirectly connected to the network.

One illustration of using cliques as units of analysis is reported by Berlo and others (1972, p. 14). Twenty-seven cliques were identified in a federal agency in the Pentagon. An index of *average clique connectedness*, defined as the degree to which the average member of a clique is linked to other individuals in a clique,[62] was computed for each clique. The index of clique connectedness ranged from 85 percent (this clique was centered in the agency director's office) down to 11 percent (for a clique in the planning office, where the need for individuals to work in close collaboration was much less). This latter clique was relatively large, with 17 members; it is obviously more difficult for everyone in a large clique to communicate with everyone else. The highest degree of connectedness was for work groups of from seven to 10 members. So the Berlo and others (1972) study suggests the proposition that *clique connectedness is inversely related to clique size*.

---

[62] An average clique connectedness index was computed as the average number of links for each individual member of the clique to other clique members, divided by the number of such possible links. Thus, in a five-member clique with six links, the index is $6/5 \div 10$. The number of possible cliques is $N(N-1)/2$, where N is the number of individuals in a clique.

Systems or Networks as Units of Analysis

A total network consists of all the individuals and other units in a system, such as an organization or a village. We use the terms "network" and "system" interchangeably.

Obviously, an entire system can be utilized as a unit of analysis (1) in a case study, or (2) in an investigation where a sample of such intact groups (that is, at least two) have been studied (such instances are relatively rare in past research).

One illustration comes from Guimaraes' (1972) investigation of 20 Brazilian villages. For each village, typically comprised of about 80 farmers, the degree of average system connectedness was computed as the degree to which the average member of a system is linked to other individuals in the system. The diffusion of agricultural innovations was more rapid in villages with a higher degree of system connectedness.

A somewhat similar approach was followed by Betty (1974) in an investigation of family planning clinics in the Philippines. Here, the clinic was the unit of analysis, and an index of system connectedness was computed for the communication links among the clinic staff. This measure was expected to be related to clinic productivity (measured as the number of family planning adopters secured by the clinic each month), and Betty's findings provided some support for this proposition relating connectedness and productivity.

Professors Marta Dosa and Bissy Genova of the School of Information Studies at Syracuse University are utilizing network analysis in a rather unusual way. Their study is a field experiment to evaluate the impact of a computer-based information system that was introduced to serve the 45 health agencies in the Syracuse, New York, area. Network data about the information-exchanges among each pair of agencies were gathered before the new information system was installed, and then one year later. Professors Dosa and Genova expected that the system of health agencies would become more interconnected as a result of the information system, that cliques would break down, and that isolates would disappear. Their $t_1 - t_2$ comparison of the system utilized network analyses in order to indicate the communication situation pre- and post-intervention. Note that network variables are the dependent measures, rather than the independent variables (as in most past studies of communication networks).

SUMMARY

This chapter presented a general philosophy of network analysis as an approach to research on human communication and behavior change. *Communication network analysis* is a method of research for identifying the communication structure in a system, in which relational data about communication flows are analyzed using some type of interpersonal relationships as the units of analysis. A *communication network* consists of interconnected individuals who are linked by patterned communication flows. The usual procedures of communication network analysis consist (1) of identifying cliques within the system, (2) of identifying specialized communication roles (liaisons, bridges, and isolates) in the communication structure, and (3) of measuring various indexes of communication structure (for example, connectedness) for individuals, personal networks, cliques, or systems.

Research evidence is synthesized to show that *the behavior of an individual is partly a function of the communication networks in which the individual is a member.*

Historically, the German sociologist Georg Simmel provided the original theoretical stimulus to network analysis, but Jacob Moreno's sociometry was the main methodological contribution. *Sociometry* is a means of obtaining and analyzing quantitative data about communication patterns among the individuals in a system by asking each respondent to whom he/she is linked. It provided a network analytical tool in the 1940s and 1950s, but the rise of computers in social research led to abandoning Moreno's approach. But later, computer techniques for large-scale network analysis were developed, which led to a resurgence of interest in networks. This new intellectual paradigm for communication research began to command the attention of a growing "invisible college" in the 1970s.

A *link* is a communication relationship between two units (usually individuals) in a system; it is the basic datum in any type of network analysis. Such links are usually measured by sociometric questions that ask a respondent to indicate the others with whom communication links exist. Other alternatives are (1) *observation,* in which the researcher identifies and records the communication behavior in a system, and (2) *unobtrusive methods,* in which the method of measurement removes the observer from the events being studied. *No one approach to measuring network links is best for all research situations, and in fact a combination of two or more measurements in a multimethod design is usually superior to the use of any single method.*

The sample designs for network analysis, as compared to monadic analysis, provide (1) less basis for using statistical inference to generalize the research results to a larger population, but (2) a greater capacity to understand the nature of communication structure. Most random sampling techniques better fit the selection of individuals than of links. In fact, it is usually difficult to obtain a random sample of network links. Four ways of dealing with this problem are: (1) sampling intact groups, (2) quasi-sociometry, (3) snowball sampling, and (4) nonsampling.

Five main types of units of analysis can be utilized in network analysis: (1) individuals, (2) dyads, (3) personal networks, (4) cliques, and (5) systems (networks). Individuals can be the units of analysis when network variables (like opinion leadership) are measured at the individual level. A *dyad* is composed of two individuals connected by a communication link. *For new ideas to diffuse, dyadic communication must connect individuals who are somewhat heterophilous. Heterophily* is the degree to which pairs of individuals who interact are different in certain attributes. The *information-exchange potential of dyadic communication is related to the degree of heterophily between the transceivers. Proximity* is the degree to which two individuals' personal communication networks overlap. We suggest that *both (1) the degree of proximity and (2) the degree of heterophily in communication dyads is positively related to their information-exchange potential.* So *the degree of proximity in communication dyads is positively related to their degree of homophily. Homophily* is the degree to which pairs of individuals who interact are similar in certain attributes. *The degree of proximity in communication dyads is positively related to their potential for behavior change on the part of the dyadic partners. Multiplexity* of communication links is the degree to which multiple message contents flow through a dyadic link between two individuals.

Another unit of analysis is the *personal network*, consisting of those individuals who are linked by patterned communication flows to a focal individual. In a *radial personal network*, an individual interacts with a set of dyadic partners who do not interact with each otther. In an *interlocking personal network*, an individual interacts with a set of dyadic partners who interact with one another. Individual *integration* is the degree to which the members of an individual's personal communication network are linked to each other. So interlocking personal networks are more integrated than radial personal networks. *Interlocking personal networks are usually composed of homophilous links. The degree of individual integration of personal networks is negatively related to their potential for information-exchange.*

A *clique* is a subsystem whose elements interact with each other relatively more frequently than with other members of the communication system. *Average clique connectedness* is the degree to which the average member of a clique is linked to other individuals in the clique. *Clique connectedness is inversely related to clique size.*

A network consists of all the individual and other units in a system. It is also utilized as a unit of analysis.

4 METHODS OF NETWORK ANALYSIS

Compared to complicated and unruly sociograms, matrices are very well-behaved.

William D. Richards, Jr. (1976, p. 36)

The structure of sociometric data matrices uniquely distinguishes them from other types of social science data.

Richard C. Roistacher (1974)

As stated previously, the objective of network analysis is to determine the communication structure in a system. There are several main methods of network analysis, which we describe and compare in this chapter. One of these, William D. Richards' NEGOPY, is the network analysis procedure that seems to fit best with the theoretical/methodological concerns of communication research. Here we shall show NEGOPY's strengths and weaknesses in comparison with four other methods of network analysis: direct factor analysis, smallest-space analysis, SOCK/COMPLT, and blockmodeling. In order to understand these five methods, we must first understand the proximity measures on which they are based.

All methods of network analysis are, first and foremost, means of coping with the major problem in understanding communication network data: information overload.[1] When a system has a very small number of members (or a small number of links among them), one of Jacob Moreno's sociograms can be a helpful means of untangling the "unmanageable thicket of information" (Levine, 1972). If the system is larger, there is no alternative but to use a computer-based network analysis program.

WHY ARE COMPUTERS NECESSARY IN NETWORK ANALYSIS?

In chapter 3 we traced the history of research on communication networks (1) from the sociometric era of Jacob Moreno and his followers, in the 1940s and 1950s, (2) through the decline of this approach in the 1960s, as computer-based analysis of behavioral data obtained in large-scale surveys focused mainly on the individual as the unit of analysis, (3)

---

[1] *Information overload* is the state of an individual or a system in which excessive communication inputs cannot be processed and utilized, leading to breakdown.

to relational analysis of communication networks in order to better understand the communication structure of a system. Computers first led to
the fall of Moreno-style sociometry in the second era, and then to the
resurgence of network analysis when computer programs for analyzing
communication networks were developed.

Why are computers necessary?

One of the practical problems facing communication network analysis is the immensity of the task. In a system of 100 members, each of the
100 individuals can talk to the 99 others, so that 9,900 communication relationships are possible.[2] In a 200-member system, 39,8000 communication dyads are possible, and in a system with 5,000 members, nearly 25
million, which would exceed the processing capacity of most modern
computers.[3] Most such dyadic links do not occur, of course, but enough
of them do to make computers an essential tool in network analysis.

Up to recent times, efforts aimed at studying communication networks have been hampered by the inability to manually handle and analyze the great amounts of data necessary to identify the communication
structure of relatively large-sized systems. Recent methodological advances in computerized network analysis (such as those detailed in the
present chapter) now allow us to understand many added dimensions of
communication networks that were previously hidden.

For instance, Figure 4–10 (which appears later in this chapter)
shows the communication structure for the diffusion of family planning
innovations among the 39 women in a Korean village. This network
analysis was first completed by hand methods, and then checked by the
computer procedure (NEGOPY) that we will describe later in this chapter. Even when the sample size is relatively small, as in the present case,
network analysis required the work of three researchers for two months.
When we checked our results with those obtained by using NEGOPY, a
computer program for communication network analysis, only about half
a second of execution time [4] was required (at a cost of only two dollars).

Even without having used these procedures of network analysis, it
would have been apparent that individual #13 in Figure 4–10, plays a
key role in the communication structure. Judging from the 11 other

---

[2] Half of which would be duplicated, so the general formula for the number of
links in a system actually is $N(N-1)/2$.

[3] This amazing proliferation of possible network links can be expressed in another
way, in terms of the size of the personal communication network of the typical individual. Pool (1973, p. 17) reports that the average adult has from 500 to 2,000
close acquaintances, with an average of about 1,000. One's friends of friends would
number about 1 million, if there were not much overlapping due to interlocking
personal networks. One's friends of friends of friends would number 1 billion. Thus,
it is understandable how a randomly assigned starter person in Nebraska can reach
a randomly selected target individual in Massachusetts in only 5.5 steps, in the "small
world" studies of Milgram (1967) and others (as was described in chapter 3).

[4] The computer in this case was a Control Data Corporation computer of the 6000
series.

women who said they talked with her about family planning (in answer to a sociometric question), one might have assumed that she has a great deal of influence with her peers, and is an opinion leader. Without computer analysis to display the communication structure of the village, however, it would have been extremely difficult to determine that individual #13 (1) is an opinion leader *only* for her own clique, and (2) is a bridge in linking her clique to another clique in the village. Thus, network analysis helps illuminate communication structure.

The computerized methods of network analysis that we describe here employ strict mathematical criteria for explicitly identifying cliques and individual communication roles. This formalization and utilization of precise criteria eliminates the major problem in using manual or visual methods of analyzing sociograms: different communication roles and cliques are often identified by different investigators when examining the *same* set of data. With the mathematization of computational rules executed by a standard computer program, such judgmental errors can be eliminated, and inter- and cross-network comparisons are facilitated. We illustrate these particular advantages of our methodological procedure for network analysis here and in later chapters.

Richards' NEGOPY procedure for network analysis is an "algorithm." An *algorithm* is a set of rules or directions for obtaining a specific output from a specific input. The distinguishing feature of an algorithm is that all vagueness must be eliminated; the rules must describe operations that are so well defined that they can be executed by a machine like a computer. Thus all subjectivity is removed from a set of analytical procedures; the results will be the same if a number of different analysts utilize the same computer program on the same data-set. Subjectivity goes. Only objectivity remains.

In summary, we see that computers are necessary in network analysis because:

1. They enable the researcher to cope with the information overload caused by the great number of communication links that are possible, even in a small-sized system.
2. They make it possible to understand otherwise hidden aspects of communication networks.
3. They follow strict mathematical procedures, and thus standardize the otherwise subjective nature of determining communication structure in a network.

NETWORK ANALYSIS AND COMMUNICATION STRUCTURE

Network analysis is a means of identifying the communication structure in a system. What is communication structure? It is one type of *structure,* defined as the arrangement of the components and subsystems within a system. Structure exists in a system to the extent that the units (such as individuals, cliques, etc.) in the system are differentiated from each other. If there were no structure in a system, all of its parts would be randomly distributed. Structure is a property of the system, rather than of the individual members of the system. One function of structure is to provide stability, regularity, and predictability to the system (Rogers and Agarwala-Rogers, 1976, p. 80). Structure is reflected in the patterns of behavior in a system that are relatively stable and that change only slowly.

One particular type of structure is *communication structure,* defined as the differentiated elements that can be recognized in the patterned communication flows in a system. One can imagine a network in which all the individual members are connected with each other via direct communication links. This system would have complete connectedness. It would have no communication structure, in that no differentiated elements could be recognized in the patterned flows. The network would consist of one gigantic clique. There would be no liaisons, bridges, or isolates. Only one communication role, clique member, would exist. All the individuals would be homogeneous in terms of their roles in the communication structure.

In a system of any size, such lack of structure due to complete connectedness does not occur; neither does the opposite kind of structureless situation, in which no one is linked to anyone else in the system. Most real-life systems fall somewhere between these two hypothetical extremes, in that they have some degree of communication structure.

Network analysis techniques are designed to identify and describe this communication structure. A fundamental step in such network analysis is to identify the cliques and the various individual communication roles in the structure, and to measure various dimensions of communcation structure through indices of connectedness, integration, diversity, and openness (as we detail in a later section of this chapter). The five main network analysis techniques utilized in this chapter are all means of clique identification. Cliques are the most important single aspect of communication structure in a system. They represent the subsystem components, as do the individual communication roles (1) of isolate and liaison (who do not belong to a clique), and (2) of bridges and liaisons (who link cliques). The basis of clique identification is *proximity,* the relative nearness of a pair of individuals to each other in a communication sense. The underlying logic of each network analysis technique rests fundamentally on the way in which it measures the proximity of dyads.

In the present book we see communication structure as multi-dimensional, and thus measure such structure in terms of such conceptual variables as connectedness, integration, diversity, and openness. Some network scholars view communication structure as being unidimensional, and measure the degree to which a network's communication structure departs from complete randomness (where there would be no communication structure). Richards (1976, pp. 118–145) argues for calculating the degree of communication structure as the proportion of triangles (that is, linked triads) occurring in a system, to the number of such triangles that are possible.[5]

In addition to communication structure, there are other types of structure in a system: social structure, economic structure, and so on. Each of these other aspects of structure can be brought into network analysis by determining how they are related to the communication structure. For instance, a favorite research approach in organizational communication studies is to determine the overlap (and nonoverlap) of the informal communication structure with the formal organizational structure as indicated by an organizational chart (which specifies who is supposed to talk with whom in an organization). For instance, an employee is usually prohibited from communicating directly with his/her boss' boss. But of course such forbidden bypassing frequently occurs in most organizations. Pointing out the discrepancies between the communication structure and the formal organizational structure is "one of the true delights of the organizational experts" (Perrow, 1972, p. 62).

In chapter 7 we explore the research question of who is linked to whom in a network. Explanation is sought mainly in the nature (1) of social structural variables and (2) of physical structure (that is, in physical distance between individuals). In chapter 7 we shall overlay the communication structure of networks on the social structure and physical structure in order to draw inferences and conclusions about how social and physical variables determine who interacts through network links.

MEASURES OF PROXIMITY

Proximity is the relative nearness of a pair of individuals to each other in a communication sense. All methods of network analysis rest directly and fundamentally on the measure of proximity that they utilize to index the relative nearness (or its opposite, distance) of a pair of individuals in the system being analyzed. The communication structure that is identified by a network analysis technique depends, obviously, on how the technique indexes proximity.

Network analysts have displayed considerable ingenuity in constructing various measures of proximity. The five main network analysis techniques explained and utilized later in this chapter incorporate three

[5] This measure would not perform reasonably at the upper extreme of a completely connected system.

main types of proximity indices, each of which has two (or more) variants (Table 4–1).[6] Each of these proximity measures has certain advantages and disadvantages, but we shall argue that the communication proximity measure utilized in the NEGOPY network analysis program is most appropriate for determining the communication structure of communication networks. However, on the basis of the limited evidence presently available (reviewed later in this section), we shall conclude that these various proximity measures are highly intercorrelated and hence seem to be indicators of the same basic dimension, proximity.

Three basic questions underlie our evaluation of the proximity measures described in Table 4–1.

1. Should a proximity measure include only the direct link between dyadic partners, or should it also include indirect links between the two dyadic partners?
2. If indirect links are included, how many "removes" (that is, steps) from the two individuals should be measured in the proximity index?
3. Should a proximity measure include the similarity of the two individuals on their nonlinks, as well as on their links?

Direct Links Versus Direct-Plus-Indirect Links in Proximity Indices

In communication network analysis, where human interaction is the crucial process being studied, the ideal measure of proximity should index (1) whether two individuals communicate directly, and (2) how closely tied they are through other individuals (that is, the overlap of their personal communication networks). By thus measuring communication proximity, we are also operationalizing the fundamental unit of communication structure in a system; as Killworth and Bernard (1978) stated: "Whatever 'structure' is, it is composed of overlap between people's [personal] networks."

The argument for including indirect as well as direct links in a proximity measure is a shortcoming of the linkage distance indices of proximity described in Table 4–1. *Linkage distance* is the number of links or steps in the shortest path joining two individuals. The simplest, crudest kind of linkage distance measure is whether or not a direct link exists be-

---

[6] In addition to these proximity indices, one might imagine alternatives: (1) common membership of two individuals in the same group (for example, a mothers' club) or in the same social category (for instance, religion or occupation), (2) one of the various measures of nonweak ties suggested by Granovetter (1973), such as (a) the amount of time invested in a communication link, (b) the emotional intensity of the links, (c) the intimacy or mutual confiding between the dyadic partners, and (d) reciprocity of the dyadic choices.

TABLE 4–1. Comparison of Indices of Proximity Utilized by Various Network Analysis Techniques.

Proximity Index	Definition	Network Analysis Techniques Using Some Version of the Proximity Index	Means of Operationalizing the Proximity Index
1. *Communication proximity*	The degree to which two individuals in a network have personal communication networks that overlap.	(1) Richards' (1976) NEGOPY	Overlap in personal communication networks for two individuals with a direct network link.
		(2) Alba and Kadushin's (1976) SOCK	Overlap in personal communication networks for all pairs of individuals in a system, whether or not they have a direct network link (this index is called "SIMMEL").
2. *Linkage distance*	The number of links or steps in the shortest path joining two individuals.	(1) Direct factor analysis	Binary linkage distance: whether or not a direct network link exists between two individuals (scored as 1 or 0).
		(2) Lin's (1968, 1975, and 1976) and Guimarães' (1970) Network Routine, and various other computer programs	The minimum number of links separating all pairs of individuals in a system.
3. *Correlational similarity*	The degree to which two individuals have like patterns of links and non-links.	(1) Lingoes' (1972) Smallest-Space Analysis (SSA)	Zero-order Pearsonian correlation between the columns (or rows) in a who-to-whom matrix indicating the two individuals' pattern of links and nonlinks with others in the system.
		(2) Breiger and others' (1975) blockmodeling with CONCOR	Same as for SSA (above), but with the correlation computed across multiple networks for the two individuals.

tween two individuals; this index is used in direct factor analysis of networks (Table 4–1). It ignores all indirect links, and thus, while simple to compute and understand, suffers from the lack of precision depicted in Figure 4–1, which shows two communication dyads, AB with relatively low proximity and CD with relatively high proximity (computed as the degree of overlap of personal communication networks). If proximity were computed simply as linkage distance, the AB and CD dyads would be equal; both have a direct link, and hence a linkage distance of 1.

But clearly in our example the "communication distance" between A and B is greater than between C and D, who are connected by a direct link plus four indirect links. In this illustration, linkage distance is too crude a measure of proximity, due to its incompleteness (it only counts indirect links if there is no direct link between two individuals). By incorporating indirect links as well as the direct link, our measure of com-

Figure 4–1. Communication Proximity Is the Degree to Which Two Individuals Have Overlapping Personal Communication Networks.

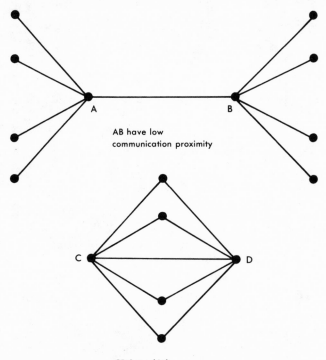

Source: Adapted from Alba and Kadushin (1976).

munication proximity is more precise and better reflects the realities of human communication flows.

An illustration of the 0/1 measure of linkage distance is shown in Figure 4–3 (see page 164) for eight selected respondents in a Korean village.

The alternative type of linkage distance (Table 4–1) is computed as the minimum number of links or steps separating all pairs of individuals in a system. The assumption underlying this measure of proximity is that communication flows only follow the shortest path, and that all other paths are irrelevant. Further, most linkage distance measures disregard multiple pathways of the same number of links; for example, a linkage distance of "3" means that three steps separate two individuals, but we do not know if there is one pathway of three steps, or ten pathways of three steps.

Figure 4–2a shows this type of linkage distance measure for the same eight selected respondents in a Korean village (that we show in Figure 4–3 for the 0/1 measure of linkage distance).

The linkage distance index of proximity, such as that provided by

Figure 4–2a. Linkage Distance Matrix for Eight Selected Respondents in Village A.

		#10	#18	#36	#13	#44	#48	#49	#47	Total Linkage Distance	Average Linkage Distance
					"Whom"						
	#10	—	1	2	1	2	2	3	3	14	2.00
	#18	1	—	1	1	2	2	3	3	13	1.86
	#36	2	2	—	1	1	2	3	3	14	2.00
"Who"	#13	1	1	1	—	1	1	2	2	9	1.28
	#44	2	2	1	1	—	2	3	3	14	2.00
	#48	2	2	2	1	2	—	1	1	11	1.57
	#49	3	3	3	2	3	1	—	1	16	2.29
	#47	3	3	3	2	3	1	1	—	16	2.29

Note: These data, taken from Figure 4–5, have been arranged in order by NEGOPY to facilitate comparison and to make cliques I and II (the two triangles) stand out. The linkage distance matrix is symmetrical, as the links are reciprocal, so average linkage distance for rows and columns are the same. The right-hand column shows that individuals #13 and #48, who are bridges between the two cliques (Figure 4–6), have the lowest average linkage distance scores; they are most proximate (least distant) from all other members of the network.

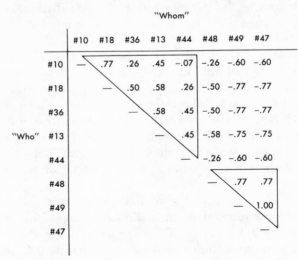

Figure 4–2b. Matrix of Correlational Similarity
for Eight Selected Respondents in Village A.

"Whom"

	#10	#18	#36	#13	#44	#48	#49	#47
#10	—	.77	.26	.45	–.07	–.26	–.60	–.60
#18		—	.50	.58	.26	–.50	–.77	–.77
#36			—	.58	.45	–.50	–.77	–.77
"Who" #13				—	.45	–.58	–.75	–.75
#44					—	–.26	–.60	–.60
#48						—	.77	.77
#49							—	1.00
#47								—

Note: These data, taken from Figure 4–5, have been arranged in order by NEGOPY to facilitate comparison and to help make cliques I and II stand out. This correlational similarity matrix is symmetrical, so the bottom half is not shown. Notice the generally positive correlation within cliques, and the negative correlations elsewhere. The way in which these correlations is computed is shown in Figure 4–12.

Lin's (1975, 1976, and 1978) Network Routine (as well as most other linkage distance programs), is computed by matrix multiplication methods (which are explained in a following section). Because of the shortest-path assumption, mentioned previously, the closest distance (that is, the greatest proximity) that can be measured is a direct link, scored as a "1." Wider distances between a pair of individuals include indirect links. But if the pair is a dyad (that is, if they have a direct link), maximum proximity is scored as "1" and all indirect links between the linked pair are ignored (Figure 4–2a). So this linkage distance considers indirect links only for pairs of individuals who are not directly linked.

Richards' (1975) NEGOPY program computes communication proximity in an opposite way. If the AB and CD pairs of individuals were not directly linked (as they are in Figure 4–1), Richards' (1975) NEGOPY program would not compute a measure of communication proximity; this index is only tabulated for dyads with a direct link. The advantage of this procedure is that NEGOPY can handle a very large-sized system (of $4,096 \times 4,096$ individuals); most large who-to-whom matrices are filled with many zeros, as the typical individual (even in a very large system) only interacts directly with a fairly small number of others. The disadvantage of the NEGOPY type of communication index is that many dyads who are not linked directly may have some indirect connections through other individuals, and this kind of indirect proximity is ignored.

In comparison, Alba and Kadushin's (1976) SIMMEL measure of communication proximity includes these two-step, indirect linkages for all individuals in a system, whether they interact directly or not. Despite the extra computer capacity thus needed, the SOCK computer program can handle very large-sized systems (up to 9,999 × 9,999 individuals).

Nevertheless, we prefer the NEGOPY communication proximity index that uses common links, rather than also including nonlinks (that is, "1's" rather than "0's" in a who-to-whom matrix), over Alba and Kadushin's (1971) SIMMEL measure, expressed as the proportion of the number of overlapping individuals to the total number of members in the two personal networks. Alba and Kadushin (1976) argue that proximity should be measured not only by the size of the intersection of two individuals' personal networks, but also by the size of their nonoverlapping parts. In other words, the Alba–Kadushin proximity index includes in its formula, as one component, the number of nonoverlapping links between dyadic partners; an example would be the eight links of A and B (other than the AB link) in Figure 4–1.

These nonoverlapping links cannot affect communication between the dyadic partners for the obvious reason that no messages flow through these links between the individuals, either directly or indirectly. So the Alba–Kadushin proximity index is less useful for the study of communication. However, this limitation is no criticism of their index for the purpose for which it was proposed: to measure affiliation, not communication.

We conclude the present discussion with an answer to our question #1: *A proximity measure should include both the direct link between two individuals as well as any indirect links they may have.* For this reason we prefer (1) communication proximity measures to linkage distance indices of proximity, and (2) Richards' (1975) communication proximity index to Alba and Kadushin's (1976) SIMMEL, which also computes proximity for pairs of individuals who are not directly linked.

Higher-Order Personal Networks in the Communication Proximity Measure

How many "removes" (from the individual respondent) should be included in the N-step personal communication networks for which communication proximity is measured? The answer is rather arbitrary, and rests on the number of steps through which communication messages that affect human behavior are actually transmitted (Alba and Kadushin,

1976). Undoubtedly, this number varies on the basis of the message content and its complexity, the nature of the system, the quality of trust in the dyadic relationships, and so on. Granovetter (1973) concluded that two-step personal networks are wide enough to describe the main flows of job-related information among individuals in a Boston suburb. Probably only rarely does much important information flow more widely than through second-order links, due (1) to the distortion that may occur in such sequential interpersonal flows, and (2) to the low probability that such messages will be passed along in more than two steps.

One type of evidence bearing on the question of what order of personal networks should be included in communication proximity indices, is provided by Lee (1977). He computed the individual-level connectedness scores for the 39 respondents involved in family planning diffusion in one Korean village (depicted later in Figure 4–10) at three levels:

1. First-order personal communication networks.
2. Second-order personal communication networks.
3. Third-order personal communication networks.

Figure 4–2c shows the first-order, second-order, and third-order communication links for a typical respondent (the second-order and third-order links shown are only the unique links, that is, links to individuals

Figure 4–2c. First-Order, Second-Order, and Third-Order Personal Communication Networks for Individual A.

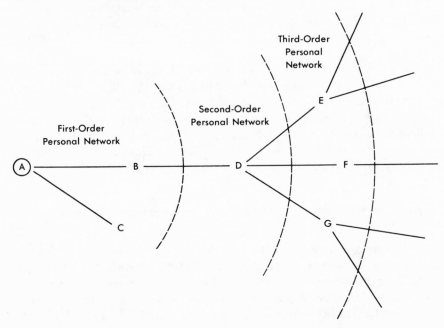

not already included at a previous order). Lee (1977) found that first-order connectedness shared a co-variance of 90 percent with second-order connectedness, but this latter variable shared a covariance of only 34 percent with third-order connectedness. In other words, the individual connectedness fell off sharply after the second-order personal network (that is, the friends of friends). Generally similar results were obtained when the first-, second-, and third-order connectedness scores were correlated with the individual-level dependent variable of family planning adoption (Lee, 1977).[7]

This analysis suggests an answer to our question #2 about indices of proximity, that *measures of communication proximity can adequately be based upon no more than second-order personal communication networks*. More data should be brought to bear on this important issue in future research.

Measuring Similarity of Two Individuals in Their Nonlinks, as Well as Links

The coefficient of correlation between the two dyadic individuals' rows and/or columns in a who-to-whom matrix is a correlation similarity measure. The correlation expresses the covariance or similarity of the patterns of communication (and noncommunication) of the two individuals (see Figure 4–12, later in this chapter, or Figure 4–2b, for illustrations of how correlational similarity is computed). The serious shortcomings of such correlations as an indicant of proximity is that they include noncommunication (zeros in the who-to-whom matrix) as well as communication links. Thus, two individuals in a dyad may have a high correlation because they do *not* communicate with the same set of individuals (their rows and columns have zeros in the same places), as well as because they *do* communicate with the same set of individuals. "Counting the absence as well as the presence of connections is not desirable when matrices are very sparse, as they typically are with network data. In such cases, counting absences means overestimating the closeness [proximity] of some pairs" (Alba and Kadushin, 1976). Correlation does not behave correctly as a measure of communication proximity; correlation can be negative even when two personal networks overlap.

---

[7] Support for this statement is also provided by our data-analysis of the 21,072 pairs among the 1,003 women in our 24 Korean villages. Proximity for each pair, measured as linkage distance (the number of links or steps in the shortest path joining two individuals), was correlated with measures of homophily–heterophily on age, mothers' club membership, and other variables (these are reported in chapter 7). The expected correlations did not change very much after the second-order links or steps were included in the linkage distance measure. That is, adding third-order links or steps did not seem to add much extra precision to our proximity measure.

Further, it can be higher for a pair of personal networks that do not overlap than the correlation for two personal networks that do overlap (Alba and Kadushin, 1976). In short, correlation is a measure of *similarity* of communication behavior, but not of communication *proximity*. As we saw in the previous discussion, similarity and proximity are not exactly the same.

So we conclude, in answer to question #3, that *a proximity index should measure only the degree of direct and indirect links between dyadic partners, but not their similarity of nonlinks with other individuals in their system*. This logic represents a disadvantage of correlational similarity measures (Table 4–1), which are used (1) by Lingoes' (1973) Smallest-Space Analysis, and (2) by Breiger and others' (1975) blockmodeling with CONCOR.

Interrelationships Among Proximity Measures

Our arguments for preferring Richards' (1975) communication proximity index over the five alternative indices described in Table 4–1, are mainly on logical grounds, rather than on the basis of empirical evidence.

The variety of proximity measures that we have just described might seem to be quite different in their nature. They certainly are in a conceptual sense. But empirically, they seem to measure the same basic dimension (of proximity). Several investigators have correlated two or more proximity measures for the same data-set. They generally find very high relationships.

1. Alba (1975) computed five proximity measures (linkage distance; RELATE, an index of the number and length of paths connecting each pair of individuals; and three SIMMEL measures of proximity, each indexing the overlap of personal communication networks for those individuals directly linked and not linked) for two sociometric matrices (friendship and interaction about community affairs) for the leaders in a small German city. These data were originally gathered by Laumann and Pappi (1976). All five proximity measures were correlated .70 or above; the SIMMEL proximity index correlated .90 or above with the linkage distance measure.

2. Later in this chapter, we show that five different network analysis techniques, each using a different measure of proximity (communication proximity, linkage distance, and correlational similarity), identify about the same communication structure for two Korean villages. Clearly, this result could only obtain if the proximity measures each index the same basic dimension.

3. A comparison of three measures of proximity was computed for the eight selected respondents in village A that are shown in Figure 4–3:

X_1 = Binary linkage distance ("0" or "1" between each of the pairs of eight individuals, shown in Figure 4-5).

X_2 = Stepped linkage distance, measured as the minimum number of links separating each of the pairs of eight individuals (shown in Figure 4-2a).

X_3 = Correlational proximity, measured as the correlation between the two dyadic individuals' columns (or rows) in a binary linkage distance matrix (Figure 4-5); the matrix of correlations is shown in Figure 4-2b.

These three types of proximity measures are highly interrelated; correlations (computed for each of the 28 pairs among the eight respondents) are:

$$r_{12} = .81$$
$$r_{13} = -.88$$
$$r_{23} = -.83$$

These three intercorrelations represent covariances (r^2) among the three proximity measures from 66 percent to 77 percent; the two correlations are negative only because of a mathematical artifact: the two distance indices (X_1 and X_2) measure negative proximity. While these three indices do not yield identical results, they are quite similar.

METHODS OF ANALYZING A COMMUNICATION MATRIX

All computer methods for network analysis (and a number of non-computer methods as well) are based on the use of a matrix to order the data about "who-to-whom" communication links. In such a matrix, each individual appears on the vertical ("who") dimension and also on the horizontal ("to whom") dimension; thus there is a row and a column for each individual in the system (an example appears later in Figure 4-3). In this binary matrix, if individual A has a communication link with individual B, a "1" is entered in row A/column B. If there is no communication link between individual A and individual B, the entry for row A/ column B is "0."

Reduction of data about communication links to a who-to-whom matrix has several advantages. First, a great deal of data can be packed into a small space, and in a format that is easier to comprehend visually than when the data are not so organized. Second, such matrices can be handled and analyzed using the techniques of matrix algebra, a special type of mathematics. Third, computers can be easily programmed to analyze data in matrix form for purposes of further analysis.

The main alternative to the matrix handling of sociometric data is the sociogram (discussed in chapter 3), which is only practical with small systems of up to one hundred members. Perhaps Roistacher (1974) said it all: "The natural structure of sociometric data is a matrix."

Matrix Multiplication Methods

There are basically two ways to analyze network data in matrix form: (1) matrix multiplication, and (2) matrix manipulation. Matrix multiplication methods consist of squaring a who-to-whom matrix by multiplying it by itself (a cumbersome procedure by hand unless the matrix is very small, but an easy task by computer), by cubing the matrix, or by raising it to higher powers. The results of such matrix multiplication are very convenient in a communication sense. For when a who-to-whom matrix is squared, the entries in the resultant matrix indicate the presence or absence of two-step links between each pair of individuals (that is, how individual A and individual C are linked through their ties to individual B), and direct links appear on the main diagonal. Similarly, cubing a who-to-whom matrix indicates the three-step links between pairs of individuals.[8] Such matrix multiplication methods of network analysis are thus very useful for measuring *linkage distance*, the number of links in the shortest path joining two individuals. And once such linkage distances have been computed for each possible link in a who-to-whom matrix, a variety of different computer[9] and noncomputer[10] techniques are available to rearrange the individuals on the row and column dimensions so that the communication structure becomes more easily apparent: cliques, liaisons, bridges, and isolates.[11] But it is important to remember that the criterion for rearranging the individuals (so as to better understand the communication structure) is linkage distance. This criterion might seem to be a sensible measure of communication proximity. But for reasons discussed previously (and diagrammed in Figure 4–1), we generally prefer a different measure, one indicating communication proximity, that is derived from a matrix manipulation procedure.[12]

[8] A special problem with cubing a matrix (or with raising it to higher powers) to measure linkage distance is "looping back." For example, a path from individual A to individual B, back to A, and then back to B again, is a linkage distance of 3; however, the correct linkage distance (the number of links in the shortest path joining the two individuals) is 1. To prevent looping back, most matrix multiplication computer programs measure linkage distance as the first power on which an element in the who-to-whom matrix becomes nonzero.

[9] Examples are Hubbel (1965), Guimarães (1968 and 1972), and Lin (1968).

[10] Examples are Luce and Perry (1949), Festinger (1949), Festinger and others (1950), and Harary and Ross (1957).

[11] The rearranged who-to-whom matrix is sometimes called a "distance matrix."

[12] While NEGOPY uses a matrix manipulation measure of proximity, it uses a matrix multiplication component (based on a distance matrix that is raised to successively

Matrix Manipulation Methods

Matrix manipulation methods of network analysis consist of rearranging the individuals in the rows and columns of a who-to-whom matrix so that communication dyads (the nonzero entries in the matrix) with greater proximity are as physically adjacent in the matrix as possible. A communication proximity index for each dyad is computed in which a higher proximity score is awarded for a dyad on the basis of the degree to which their two individuals' respective personal communication networks overlap (that is, the degree to which the two individuals' rows and columns in the who-to-whom matrix are similar), rather than simply whether the two individuals interact more, or less, directly (that is, in terms of linkage distance).

In the matrix manipulation procedure, cliques may be visually identified by a pattern recognition technique, according to several criteria detailed in a following section, or the criteria can be applied by the computer. Such cliques lie along the main diagonal of the rearranged who-to-whom communication matrix (shown later in Figure 4-9). The role of the computer in matrix manipulation is mainly to compute the proximity scores for each dyadic relationship, and thus to provide the basis for rearranging the individuals in the who-to-whom matrix, although the NEGOPY computer program also can (1) identify cliques and individual communication roles in the network, and (2) compute various network indices (such as for connectedness, integration, etc.) at the individual, clique, and network levels.

Historical Background of Matrix Manipulation Methods

A small flurry of matrix analysis procedures for network data were proposed by scholars about 1950; [13] most were published in the journal *Sociometry* and a number were remarkably far-sighted. Typically, these authors argued for matrix manipulation approaches in order to detect cliques (perhaps because computers were not yet widely available, or thought to be very appropriate, for matrix multiplication). The criterion for clique membership was typically the presence of direct mutual choices among the individual members. For instance, Festinger and

---

higher powers) once individuals have been tentatively assigned to cliques, to test whether each such clique meets the stated criteria for being a clique (Richards, 1975, pp. 39–46).

[13] In addition to the publications about matrix multiplication procedures cited previously, this early literature included the following work using a matrix manipulation approach: Forsyth and Katz (1946), Katz (1947), Beum and Criswell (1947), Bock and Husain (1950), Jacobson and Seashore (1951), Weiss and Jacobson (1955), and Weiss (1956). All of these publications deal with noncomputer methods of analyzing communication matrices.

others (1950) defined a clique as a subsystem of three or more individuals in mutual communication with each other. This proximity criterion of direct mutual choice is a kind of linkage distance measure, of course; one that we feel is inferior to the overlap of personal networks as a proximity measure (for reasons that were explained in our previous discussion of proximity).

After the early 1950s, a hiatus occurred in the number of network analysis procedures being proposed, until the 1970s. The more recent analytical approaches are all computer-based. And their proximity measure has shifted away from direct mutual choice (Roistacher, 1974).

Beum and Brundage's Approach

The pioneering piece in recognizing the advantages of using overlapping personal networks as a measure of dyadic communication proximity is by Beum and Brundage (1950). While this forward-looking article did not utilize our present terminology of "communication proximity" and "overlapping personal networks," the mathematical procedures outlined, and illustrated with a hypothetical network of six individuals, are almost identical to those underlying the NEGOPY approach recommended in this book, which were first set forth by Richards (1971), twenty-one years after the original work by Beum and Brundage.[14]

For many years, the Beum and Brundage approach did not seem to attract a following of network analysts. Then, after a lapse of a decade, Coleman and MacRae (1960) presented an analogous methodology that effectuated the Beum/Brundage network technique for networks of up to 1,000 individuals. A few years later, Borgatta and Stolz (1963) published an article that described a computer program for the Beum/Brundage approach.

Richards' NEGOPY Method

The network analysis methodology that we advocate at several places in the present volume, however, was independently reinvented by William D. Richards, Jr., in the 1970s. A direct intellectual influence on Richards was the noncomputer matrix manipulation of communication

---

[14] The basic similarities in computational procedures are (1) the individuals' identification numbers are arbitrarily used as weights, (2) the individuals (rows and columns) are rearranged in an iterative process, until the arrangement does not change further, (3) the measure of dyadic proximity is the degree of overlap of the two individuals' personal networks, and (4) proximity is computed only for pairs of individuals who are directly linked, unlike the network analysis procedures proposed by Alba and Kadushin (1976), which are otherwise similar to the Beum–Brundage and Richards approaches. Unlike Richards' NEGOPY approach, Beum and Brundage (1950) did not specify criteria for clique detection.

dyads by Eugene Jacobson.[15] Richards, then an undergraduate student in the Department of Communication at Michigan State University, was enrolled in Professor Jacobson's doctoral seminar in organizational behavior in the Fall of 1970. Richards' term paper in this course spelled out the basic elements of his NEGOPY approach, which was then presented the following year at the meetings of the International Communication Association in Phoenix (Richards, 1971).

In the early 1970s, a number of organizational communication scholars were involved in analyzing communication network data, but their efforts were generally hamstrung by the lack of a computer method for handling the large volumes of data that were involved. For instance, MacDonald (1971 and 1976) used a hand-run matrix manipulation procedure to investigate the 976 links among the 185 officials in a federal agency. His who-to-whom matrix required one entire wall of a university office, and untold hours of painstaking rearrangement of the rows and columns of the huge matrix.

So it was fortunate that Richards' NEGOPY model could be computerized, first at Michigan State University and then at Palo Alto, California (where he moved in 1971 to earn his Ph.D. in communication at Stanford University). Soon, Richards' NEGOPY had been utilized by thirty to forty network scholars at Stanford University, Michigan State University, the East–West Communication Institute, the University of Michigan, the State University of New York at Buffalo, University of Cologne, University of Zurich, University of Minnesota, and Florida State University. Its use would undoubtedly have been even more widespread but for the fact that (1) NEGOPY only runs on Control Data Corporation 6000- and 7000-series computers, rather large-sized machines, that are less widely available than IBM machines, and (2) no journal articles or books were published by Professor Richards about his network analysis technique; although he presented numerous papers at scientific meetings, his doctoral dissertation concerned network analysis philosophy (Richards, 1976), and two manuals for use of NEGOPY were published by the Institute for Communication Research at Stanford University (Richards, 1975; Rice, 1978a). But until the late 1970s, Richards' NEGOPY model had not yet entered the academic mainstream of work on network analysis.[16]

Richards' approach to network analysis has several distinctive aspects that lead us to advocate its use in the present book.

---

[15] This approach to analyzing communication networks is reported in Jacobson and Seashore (1951), Weiss and Jacobson (1955), and Weiss (1956), and discussed in Rogers and Agarwala–Rogers (1976) and Farace and others (1977).

[16] At least to the extent that alternative methods of network analysis (described later in this chapter) have been utilized by researchers and published in journal articles.

1. NEGOPY is the first network analysis computer program designed explicitly by a communication scholar for use in analyzing communication networks.

2. The network analysis model is based centrally on the measure of dyadic proximity that we feel is superior: the degree of overlap in the two individuals' personal communication networks.

3. The large capacity of the NEGOPY program. The existing versions of Richards' technique, which run on CDC computers, can handle a communication matrix with up to 4,095 individuals and 32,767 links (this capacity marks NEGOPY as the Guinness' record-holder for size in computer network analysis).[17]

4. Richards provides explicit criteria (1) for clique identification in a communication structure, thus standardizing the operational meaning of the concept of "clique," and (2) for various network indices, like connectedness, integration, and so on.[18]

Unlike certain other network analysis programs, the NEGOPY computer program does not printout a sociogram (or locate the individuals in two- or three-dimensional space, like the smallest-space analysis) and making it by hand can be very time-consuming, especially for a large system. One solution to this problem is to utilize NEGOPY to identify the communication structure in a system, and then to use smallest-space analysis as a basis for drawing a sociogram. An alternative is to utilize the NETPLOT computer program developed by Lesniak and others (1977 and 1978) at the State University of New York at Buffalo, Department of Communication. NETPLOT inputs the NEGOPY output and produces two kinds of visual output: (1) NETCHART, in which the sociogram of the interpersonal communication structure is imposed over a formal organization chart (limiting NETCHART's use mainly to organizational communication studies), and (2) NETLINK, in which the sociogram consists of a circle with cliques on the circumference (within-

---

[17] This incredible capacity is possible because proximity measures are only computed by NEGOPY for actual communication dyads (that is, the nonzero entries in the matrix), which typically number less than 100,000 in a 4,095 by 4,095 matrix, although almost 18,000,000 dyads are theoretically possible, and would occur in a completely connected network. NEGOPY takes advantage of the many "holes" that appear in a large network; its capacity is 32,767 links.

[18] This important advantage of NEGOPY in providing standardized criteria for the identification of the communication structure in a network, claimed by Richards (1975 and 1976), can be abrogated by a researcher who chooses to adjust the NEGOPY parameter that each clique member must have at least 50 percent of his/her links within the clique. When this parameter (or a number of other NEGOPY parameters) is varied, a variety of communication structures are produced for a given network, as Rice (1978a, 1978b, and 1979) shows. The 50.1 percent parameter is the usual convention among most network analysts, and is reflected in Richards' (1975 and 1976) conceptual definition of a clique; this parameter setting should generally be used unless the researcher knowingly wishes to determine the effects of changing the standard definition of a clique.

clique links are not shown). NETPLOT is limited to one computer installation at Buffalo, to about 500 individuals per plot, and it is fairly expensive to run.

NETWORK ANALYSIS PROCEDURES FOR NEGOPY

In this section, we first provide a "mini-illustration" of how Richards' NEGOPY procedures work with an exercise including eight of the individuals in village A, the Korean village in our 1973 survey of 24 villages with the highest rate of adoption of family planning methods. Then we move from this simplified network analysis with only eight individuals, to a parallel analysis of all 39 women in village A and in village B (which has the lowest rate of adoption of family planning methods of our 24 villages of study).

Our purpose in these examples is to demonstrate the details of how the NEGOPY computer "works." We have computed the network analysis presented here by cumbersome hand methods, and then checked them by computer analysis.

A Microillustration of How NEGOPY Works: Eight Individuals in Village A

In order to assist understanding of the NEGOPY network analysis procedures, we here provide a small-scale illustration with eight individuals selected from village A, one of the two Korean villages that we analyze in detail later in this chapter. As can be seen (later) in Figure 4–10, these eight women are members of two cliques (clique I or clique II), so the procedural steps we follow here will eventually end in assigning individuals #10, #13, #18, #36, and #44 to clique I and individuals #47, #48, and #49 to clique II. Now let us go back to the beginning and see how NEGOPY rearranges individuals in a communication matrix so as to make this communication structure become apparent.

The eight respondents provided data about 22 sociometric choices (11 reciprocal links)[19] among them in the diffusion of family planning ideas (the other links from the eight women to others in their village are not shown here for the sake of simplicity).

These data are arranged in a who-to-whom communication matrix

---

[19] If any of the 11 dyadic ties were not reported by the respondents as being reciprocated (that is, both-way), we converted them to be so, on the basis that information was really exchanged in both directions in each dyadic link, even if it was not reported as such by both respondents in their personal interviews.

IDENTIFICATION NUMBER OF RESPONDENTS	HAS COMMUNICATION LINKS WITH
#10	#13, #18
#13	#10, #18, #36, #44, #48
#18	#10, #13, #36
#36	#13, #18, #44
#44	#13, #36
#47	#48, #49
#48	#13, #47, #49
#49	#47, #48

in Figure 4–3. One can detect a tendency toward two cliques, clustering along the main diagonal; this tendency is simply an artifact of our assigning the respondents' identification numbers on the basis of their household locations on a map of the village, and the fact that many of the dyadic links are between spatially close-by individuals. As was explained in chapter 3, spatial proximity is often closely associated with communication proximity.

Our next analytical task is to reorder the eight individuals on the basis of their communication proximity with one another, so that more proximate individuals will gradually be pulled together into cliques (that is, rearranged in the who-to-whom matrix so as to lie closer together along the main diagonal). In a previous section of this chapter, we ex-

Figure 4–3. Who-to-Whom Communication Matrix for the Diffusion of Family Planning Ideas among Eight Selected Respondents in Village A.

"Whom"

		#10	#13	#18	#36	#44	#47	#48	#49
	#10	—	1	1	0	0	0	0	0
	#13	1	—	1	1	1	0	1	0
	#18	1	1	—	1	0	0	0	0
"Who"	#36	0	1	1	—	1	0	0	0
	#44	0	1	0	1	—	0	0	0
	#47	0	0	0	0	0	—	1	1
	#48	0	1	0	0	0	1	—	1
	#49	0	0	0	0	0	1	1	—

Note: These data are a subset of the 39 respondents in Village A, who are shown in Figure 4–10.

plained our measure of communication proximity as the degree to which the dyadic partners' personal networks overlap.

The analytical mechanism for sequentially reordering the individuals in the who-to-whom matrix is accomplished simply by computing the mean of the identification numbers of the individuals with whom each respondent interacts. Why the average of the contactees' identification numbers? At first thought, such a mathematical technique seems almost ridiculous. An identification number is completely arbitrary as a quantitative "name" for a respondent. It is at a nominal level of measurement, and to add such numbers and then divide them, so as to obtain their average, would seem to be completely meaningless.

But in the present case it is not. Consider the members of a known clique. Let us flash ahead for a moment to clique II (which will eventually emerge from our present procedures). This clique will be composed of individuals #47, #48, and #49 (Figure 4–6). For these individuals to form a clique, by definition they must tend to interact mostly with each other. So each of the three members will talk with much the same set of individuals, and thus the mean identification numbers for the three individuals should be quite similar. For clique II, all three members will have a mean identification score of about 48 (the average of 47, 48, and 49). Any individual with a mean identification number of approximately 48 probably belongs to clique II.[20] Since other individuals talk to other sets of contactees (that is, they have other individuals in their personal communication networks), their means will be different than those for the individuals in clique II. The mean identification numbers provide a convenient "rough cut" at partitioning a network of individuals into cliques.

So the sequential steps in NEGOPY network analysis are:

1. Calculate the mean identification number of the contactees of each individual in the system.
2. Rank-order the individuals on the basis of these mean identification numbers.
3. Rearrange the individuals (that is, the rows and columns) in the who-to-whom matrix on the basis of the rank-order of their mean identification numbers.
4. Repeat steps 1, 2, and 3 above so as to continue rearranging the matrix, until a stable solution is obtained.
5. Examine the resulting communication structure to identify cliques, bridges, liaisons, and so on.

We can speed up this sequential reordering process by adding a weighting factor so that within-clique links count more heavily than extraclique links (in computing mean identification scores). The prac-

[20] Although a respondent could also have a mean identification number of 48 by interacting with individuals #33, #56, #57, and #58, none of whom are in clique II.

tical problem in using these weights is that we do not yet know what cliques will emerge, so we cannot know which links are within-clique and which are not. But a good approximation is provided by the number of shared contactees that dyadic partners have in common (the degree to which their personal networks overlap). Here we see how our measure of communication proximity comes into the NEGOPY procedures; the weighting factor is the number of direct (one-step) links between the dyadic partners (this weight is one for every dyadic link, by definition) plus the number of the two-step links that also connect the two individuals (Figure 4–1).[21]

As an illustration, let us compute the mean identification number for individual #10 in Figure 4–3.

$$\text{Mean identification number for individual }\#10 = \frac{(1)\ \#10 + (2)\ \#13 + (2)\ \#18}{1 + 2 + 2}$$

$$= \frac{72}{5} = \#14.40$$

Here we explain each term in this equation:

1. Individual #10 is included in the formula for the mean identification number for herself, and has a weighting factor of 1 because indivdiual #10 cannot have two-step links with herself. So "1 (#10)" goes in the numerator.

2. Individual #10 has a direct link with individual #13, and the weighting factor is 2 because in addition to this direct link, individuals #10 and #13 have one two-step link through individual #18 (Figure 4–3). So the second term in the numerator is "(2) #13."

3. Individual #10 also has a direct link with individual #18, and the weighting factor is 2 because, in addition to this direct link, individuals #10 and #18 have one two-step link through individual #13 (Figure 4–3). So the third term in the numerator is "(2) #18."

4. The denominator is the sum of the weighting factors, or $1 + 2 + 2 = 5$.

So the reordered mean identification number for individual #10 is #14.40. If we had not utilized the weighting factors (which are based on our measure of communication proximity), the reordered mean identification score for individual #10 would have been 13.7 (#10 + #13 + #18, divided by 3). Use of the weighting factors makes the reordering process work faster, by bringing in more information to the calculations (communication proximity scores for each link, rather than just the direct links).

---

[21] It would also be possible to weight each dyadic link by other indicators of communication proximity, such as the frequency of interaction that is reported (for example, once per day, once per week, etc.). In fact, Richards' (1975) NEGOPY program has a provision for including the interaction frequency of each link.

In other words, we include in our calculations of the mean identification scores all of the two-step links for individuals who have one-step (direct) links.

By a similar procedure to that just demonstrated for individual #10, the mean identification score for individual #13 is:

$$\frac{(1)\ \#13 + (2)\ \#10 + (3)\ \#18 + (3)\ \#36 + (2)\ \#44 + (1)\ \#48}{1 + 2 + 3 + 3 + 2 + 1}$$

$$= \frac{331}{12} = \#27.58$$

The mean identification numbers for the other six individuals in our present illustration can be computed by similar procedures, and are shown in Figure 4–4 for the reordered communication matrix. The main change in rank-order of the eight individuals (on the basis of the first reordering of their mean identification scores) is individual #13, who moves from second place in Figure 4–3 to fourth place, and individual #47, who moves from sixth place to eighth (in Figure 4–4). The major

Figure 4–4. Who-to-Whom Communication Matrix for the Diffusion of Family Planning Ideas in Part of a Korean Village, after the First Reordering.

		"Whom"							
		#10	#18	#36	#13	#44	#48	#49	#47
	#10	—	1	0	1	0	0	0	0
	#18	1	—	1	1	0	0	0	0
	#36	0	1	—	1	1	0	0	0
"Who"	#13	1	1	1	—	1	1	0	0
	#44	0	0	1	1	—	0	0	0
	#48	0	0	0	1	0	—	1	1
	#49	0	0	0	0	0	1	—	1
	#47	0	0	0	0	0	1	1	—
Mean Identification Score (weighted)		#14.40	#18.62	#24.87	#27.58	#28.40	#42.17	#47.80	#48.20
Rank-Order		1st	2nd	3rd	4th	5th	6th	7th	8th

Note: These eight individuals are the same as those in Figure 4–3, but they have been rearranged in the matrix on the basis of the mean identification numbers of their personal networks.

"break" in the progression of reordered mean identification scores is between individual #28.40 (originally #44) and individual #42.17 originally (#48); this gap suggests that the future division between cliques will probably occur here (in fact, it does, as we see in Figure 4–6 and Table 4–2a).

Now we are ready for a second reordering of the eight individuals on the basis of further computation of their second reordered mean identification scores, based on the first reordered mean identification scores. For individual #10, the equation is now:

$$\text{Second reordered mean identification number for individual } \#10 = \frac{(1)\ \#14.40 + (2)\ \#27.58 + (2)\ \#18.62}{1 + 2 + 2}$$

$$= \frac{106.80}{5} = \#21.36$$

The only difference from our computations for the previous mean identification score is that we have substituted the newer and more precise (first reordered) identification scores for the earlier (original) ones; for instance, #10 has become #14.40 in the equation above (instead of #10).

The results of our second reordering of the eight individuals is shown in matrix form in Figure 4–5, and as a sociogram in Figure 4–6. Five individuals are included in clique I and three in clique II. Individual #13 is a bridge between her clique (I) and the other clique. Now the communication structure of this mininetwork of eight Korean women has become apparent, thanks to the NEGOPY procedures.

The criteria for placing the eight respondents into *cliques* (defined

TABLE 4–2a. Sequential Reordering of the Eight Individuals in a Part of Village A, by Means of the NEGOPY Network Analysis Procedures.

RANK-ORDER OF THE RESPONDENTS	ORIGINAL ORDER	SEQUENTIAL REORDERING OF INDIVIDUALS			CLIQUE MEMBERSHIP
		First	*Second*	*Third*	
1st	#10	#10 → #10 → #10			
2nd	#13	#18 → #18 ↘ #13			
3rd	#18	#36 ↘ #13 ↗ #18			CLIQUE I
4th	#36	#13 ↗ #44 ↘ #36			
5th	#44	#44 ↗ #36 ↗ #44			
6th	#47	#48 → #48 → #48			
7th	#48	#49 ↘ #47 ↘ #49			CLIQUE II
8th	#49	#47 ↗ #49 ↗ #47			

Figure 4–5. Who-to-Whom Communication Matrix for the Diffusion of Family Planning Ideas in Part of a Korean Village, after the Second Reordering.

	Original Identification Number	"Whom"							
		#10	#18	#13	#44	#36	#48	#47	#49
	#10	—	1	1	0	0	0	0	0
	#18	1	—	1	0	1	0	0	0
	#13	1	1	—	1	1	1	0	0
"Who"	#44	0	0	1	—	1	0	0	0
	#36	0	1	1	1	—	0	0	0
	#48	0	0	1	0	0	—	1	1
	#47	0	0	0	0	0	1	—	1
	#49	0	0	0	0	0	1	1	—
Second Re-ordered Mean Identification Score		#21.36	#22.44	#23.82	#26.66	#28.81	#31.62	#45.63	#45.71
Second Rank-Order		1st	2nd	3rd	4th	5th	6th	7th	8th
Third Reordered Mean Identification Score		#22.78	#24.28	#22.80	#26.38	#24.81	#39.28	#40.06	#40.04
Third Rank-Order		1st	3rd	2nd	5th	4th	6th	8th	7th

Note: These eight individuals are the same as those in Figures 4–3 and 4–4, but they have been rearranged in the matrix on the basis of their second reordered mean identification numbers. The third reordered mean identification numbers are also shown at the bottom of the figure.

as subsystems whose elements interact with each other relatively more frequently than with other members of the communication system) are:

1. Each clique must be composed of at least three members.
2. Each clique member must have at least 50 percent of her links within the clique.
3. All members of a clique must be directly or indirectly connected by a path (that is, by a continuous chain of dyadic links lying entirely within the clique).

A fourth criterion, recommended by Richards (1975), but difficult to apply in some situations, is that if any one member were removed from the clique, it would remain intact (and not fall apart).

In the present example we halted our reordering procedure after only two iterations. When we computed a third reordering (shown at the bottom of the communication matrix in Figure 4–5), the arrange-

Figure 4–6.   Sociogram of the Diffusion of Family Planning Ideas in Part of a Korean Village, after the Second Reordering.

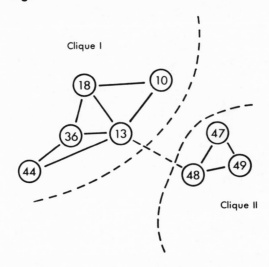

ment of the eight individuals is not changed very much, except for some switching back to previous positions (Table 4–2a). Usually several more reorderings are necessary, but in the present illustration the number of individuals is small, the cliques in the communication structure are rather starkly defined, and the original communication matrix was already partially ordered due to the fortuitous reflection of spatial proximity in the assignment of the original identification numbers. We find that, on the average, about five, six, or seven iterations (reorderings) are usually needed to reach a stable communication structure with the NEGOPY procedure when hand methods are used, or four iterations when the computer is utilized.[22]

We thus see how the Richards' network analysis approach consists of a series of gradual approximations. One might think of each of the individuals in a network as a billiard ball, connected in dyadic links by rubber bands and otherwise pushed apart by springs (Richards, 1976). The NEGOPY procedure gradually allows the rubber bands to pull the billiard balls tighter together, in cliques, and the springs to thrust the unconnected pairs of individuals farther apart. In analysis of variance terms, the NEGOPY approach encourages the minimization of within-group variance (on communication proximity) and a maximization of between-group variance.

[22] Four iterations are sufficient with the NEGOPY computer program because its routines are more complicated and utilize more information about the links than do the simpler hand methods used here to demonstrate the reordering process.

This process of gradual, iterative convergence, illustrated here in simplified and quantitative terms, occurs almost instantly inside the computer that is programmed for Richards' (1975) NEGOPY program. Then we can deal with up to 4,095 individuals in a network, rather than the eight individuals in our present illustration.

Now let us move from our oversimplified exercise with eight individuals to all 39 women in village A in Korea.

NEGOPY Network Analysis for Villages A and B

Sociometric data on family planning diffusion in two Korean villages (the highest and lowest in terms of the adoption of family planning methods among our sample of 24 Korean villages) were subjected to Richards' network analysis [23] in which the main procedures are as follows:

1. The sociometric data for the 39 respondents in each village are arranged in a who-to-whom matrix with each row representing the choosers and each column representing the individuals chosen (the matrix for village A is shown in Figure 4–7). Each entry (indicated by a solid square) in this communication matrix is a communication dyad.[24]

2. The individuals in the matrix are reordered into cliques by a gradual approximation process, described and illustrated previously for the eight individuals in village A. Figure 4–8 shows that this procedure (after two reorderings, which are not shown) tends to concentrate the respondents' communication relationships in village A toward the diagonal of the who-to-whom matrix, and thus is beginning to arrange the respondents in cliques. Further iterations of this basic procedure, in which the respondents are given new identification numbers after each reordering, makes the clique structure bcome increasingly apparent (Figure 4–9).

We terminated the reordering process when less than 10 percent of the respondents changed their position on one dimension of the who-to-whom matrix from one iteration to the next. We terminated the reordering process after six iterations (Figure 4–9).[25]

This concluded the process of gradual approximation through which the 39 women in village A were reordered in the sequential who-to-whom matrices on the basis of communication proximity, thus preparing the

[23] The Richards approach to network analysis is compared with four other selected methods of network analysis later in this chapter; each of these alternative approaches was also used to analyze the same two-village data.

[24] As explained earlier, we consider each communication relationship to be reciprocal, whether it is reported as such by the respondent or not, as each such dyadic interaction usually involves a certain degree of two-way information-exchange.

[25] We performed these clique identification procedures by hand methods, but the NEGOPY computer program was utilized later on our data, with similar results. NEGOPY was also utilized with our data by Danowski (1976) to identify essentially similar cliques, but with some relatively minor differences in the exact criteria utilized to assign individuals to cliques.

Figure 4–7. Who-to-Whom Matrix for Interpersonal Communication About Family Planning in Village A.

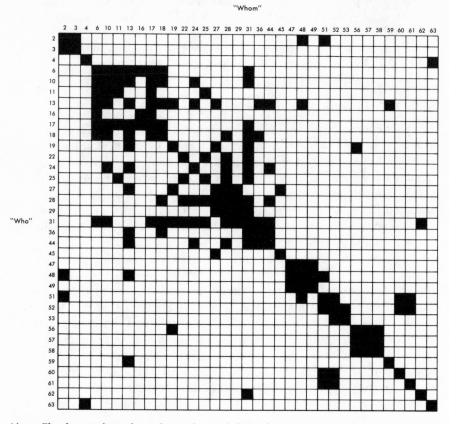

Note: The four isolates have been dropped from this matrix, in order to show more clearly the communication structure.

way for the assignment of these women to cliques. We placed the respondents into cliques following the three criteria specified by Richards (1975), and illustrated in our previous example of eight women.

One of our villages of study (village A, with the relatively more successful family planning program) has one large clique of 20 individuals (clique I), plus two smaller cliques and four isolates (Figure 4–10). The other village has two larger cliques of 15 individuals each, plus a small clique and four isolates (Figure 4–11).

3. Sociograms were constructed to visualize the sociometric data about interpersonal diffusion. Each sociogram presents (in an easily recognizable form) the main features of the interpersonal communication structure: (1) cliques, (2) liaisons, (3) bridges, and (4) isolates, indi-

Figure 4–8. Who-to-Whom Communication Matrix for Interpersonal Communication About Family Planning in Village A after Two Reorderings.

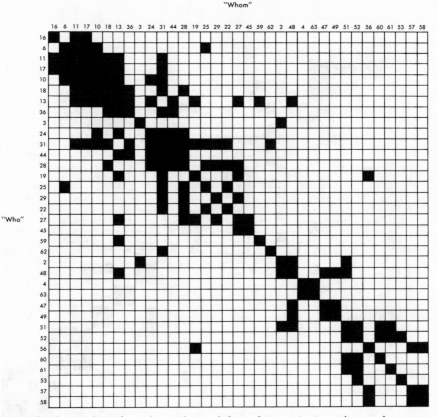

Note: The four isolates have been dropped from this matrix, in order to show more clearly the clique structure.

viduals who do not communicate with anyone (Figures 4–10 and 4–11).[26] We also identify the members of the family planning mothers' club and the club leader in each of the two village sociograms, so as to enable contrasting the formal relationships (membership and leadership) of the

[26] An alternative approach to identifying communication roles in a network, which may be appropriate for certain research problems, is to duplicate individuals who are members of overlapping cliques, so that individuals appear in simple chains with everyone to whom they are linked (Spilerman, 1966). Thus each clique is completely distinct, as liaisons and bridges are "eliminated" by the duplication procedure. Spilerman argues that his approach allows the investigator to make posteriori partitions of cliques, rather than imposing a priori rules for clique identification on the network data. The disadvantage with Spilerman's strategy is a loss of standardization, of objectivity.

Figure 4–9. Who-to-Whom Communication Matrix for Interpersonal Communication About Family Planning in Village A after Six Reorderings.

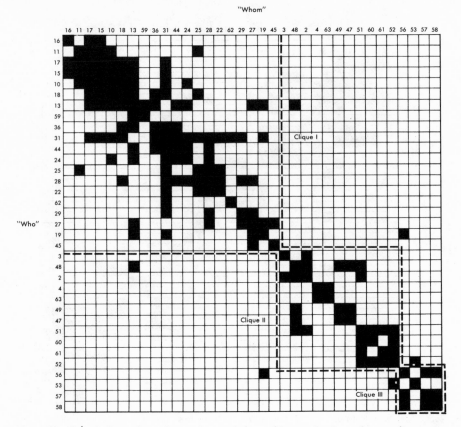

Note: The four isolates have been dropped from this matrix, in order to show more clearly the clique structure.

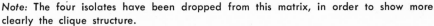

mothers' club with the informal communication structure of family planning diffusion.[27]

4. Various indices of communication structure can be constructed. In addition to clique identification, network analysis can provide measures of interpersonal communication structure at the individual, clique, or system level: connectedness, integration, and openness. For example, we can compute an index of *average system connectedness,* defined as

---

[27] We also identify the informal opinion leaders on the sociograms (Figures 4–10 and 4–11). These opinion leaders are those individuals sociometrically nominated by at least 10 percent of the other respondents in their village.

Figure 4–10. Sociogram of the Interpersonal Communication Relationships About Family Planning in Village A.

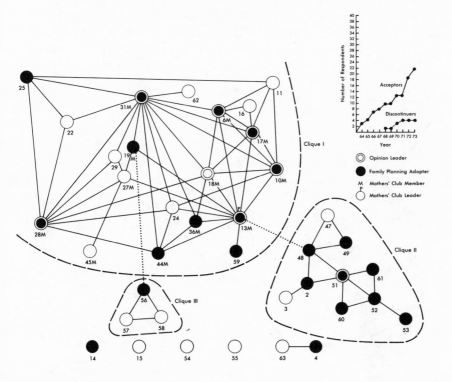

Source: Rogers and others (1976c). Adapted with permission of The East–West Communication Institute, copyright © 1976.

the degree to which the average member of a system is linked to other individuals in the system. The formula is:

$$\text{Average System Connectedness} = \frac{\text{Number of actual communication links in a system}}{\text{Number of possible communication links in a system}}$$

The denominator is $\dfrac{N(N-1)}{2}$ or 741 in each of our two villages of 39 individuals. The connectedness index for village A is 86/741 or .116 and for village B it is 102/741 or .137. Thus village B is somewhat more connected than village A.

Figure 4–11.   Sociogram of the Interpersonal Communication Relationships About Family Planning in Village B.

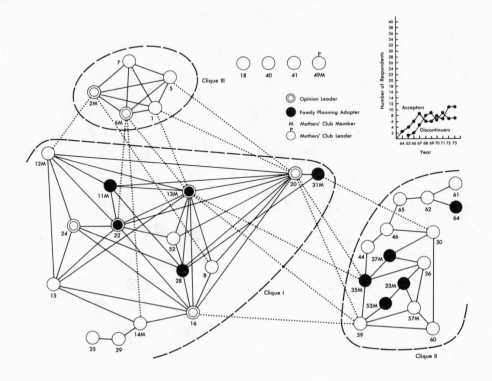

Source: Rogers and others (1976c). Adapted with permission of The East–West Communication Institute, copyright © 1976.

Average connectedness can also be indexed at the clique level; for example, the average clique connectedness index for clique III in village B (Figure 4–11) is 1.00, which is greater than the index of .37 for clique I in village B.

A system may not always partition into two or more cliques; in fact, the authors of this book have encountered numerous such cases. This outcome might not necessarily be considered a problem. Undoubtedly, there are many highly connected systems where no distinct subsystems exist. Actually, the detection of cliques (and the exact number of cliques) depends in part on the somewhat arbitrary criteria of clique separation set by the investigator. For example, Richards' NEGOPY computer program has several parameters which may be set by the researcher, such as the cutoff criteria of the 50.1 percent minimum for within-clique links; this parameter can be raised to 60 percent, 65 percent, or more, in order to break out cliques in a system. The resulting communication structure is strongly affected by changing this parameter setting (Rice 1978a, 1978b, and 1979). By changing it, the researcher is actually altering the theoretical definition of a *clique* (a subsystem whose elements interact with each other relatively more frequently than with other members of the communication system), and is destroying the standardization that is provided by the NEGOPY program. But setting the clique cutoff parameter at arbitrarily higher levels may be appropriate if a researcher wants to determine if there is even a minor degree of structure in a highly connected network. In any event, any report of communcation network analysis research should include an explicit listing of the parameter settings and cutoffs chosen (Rice, 1978b).

Indices of Communication Structure

We define *communication structure* as the differentiated elements that can be recognized in the patterned communication flows in a system. We have demonstrated, in the previous section, one approach to identifying the communcation structure in a network through the use of NEGOPY. Here we show how certain dimensions of communication structure can be measured by indices, and then used in data-analyses. The indices help us convert the nature of communication structure into quantitative variables.

Past writings about communication networks have proposed a hopeless thicket of concepts and indices of communication structure. "The terminological jungle, in which any newcomer may plant a tree, is evidence for the basic simplicity of the idea of a network" (Barnes, 1972, p. 3). And confusion. Certainly the field of network analysis does not need additional conceptual labels for its main network variables. As we explained in the Preface to this book, the same variable may be called by several conceptual names, and the same concept may be measured as several different dimensions. We should strive to standardize concepts and their measures, as "an effective defoliant for this untoward undergrowth" (Mitchell, 1974). In the present section, we seek to present a succinct set of concepts for analyzing communication structure in networks. Indices of this structure can be calculated at three levels: (1) individual, (2) clique, and (3) system. We focus our measures of communication structure on four concepts: connectedness, integration, diversity, and openness.[28]

---

[28] One research approach to the validation of communication structure indices is by simulating artificial data-sets that are originally constituted to represent different types of communication structures (Edwards and Monge, 1977).

Individual-Level Indices

At the individual level (including personal communication networks), an important structural characteristic is the degree to which a person is connected to the rest of the network in which he/she is a member. This degree of linkage is an important variable in explaining how much influence the system has on the behavior of the individual, as we show in chapter 5. For example, isolates in a network (who have, by definition, zero connectedness) usually have been found to display different behavior than nonisolates; isolates would not be expected to be much influenced by a system to which they are not connected. *Individual connectedness* is the degree to which a focal individual is linked to other individuals in the system. This concept is indexed as the actual number of links between the focal individual and the other members of the network, divided by the number of possible links (which is the number of individuals in the system minus one).[29]

Mrs. Chung, the mother's club leader in the village of Oryu Li (Figure 1–2) is high in connectedness, having links with 27 of the other 68 women in the village (so her individual connectedness score is 27/68 or .40). In other words, Mrs. Chung is directly linked to 40 percent of the other women in her village. A more precise measure of individual connectedness might include the number of two-step links, as well as the number of direct (one-step) links. The empirical evidence for adding two-step links, but not three-step links, to a measure of individual connectedness was presented previously for one Korean village (Figure 4–2).

Notice that our formula for indexing individual connectedness is a ratio measure, with the number of possible links in the denominator so as to remove the effect of network size.[30] Ideally, a more precise index

[29] Although conceptually distinct, individual connectedness is indexed in a generally similar way to *opinion leadership*, the degree to which an individual is able to influence informally other individuals' attitudes or overt behavior in a desired way with relative frequency. The difference is that an opinion leadership index ought to count only the number of one-way links *to* the focal individual (in which the individual is named as a source of influence), while individual connectedness should count all links. Yet another concept very similar to connectedness is *centrality*, defined as the degree to which an individual has a short average distance to others in a network (Freeman, 1976 and 1979). Although measures of centrality usually consist of distance as measured by the average number of steps to every other individual in a network (one type of proximity, as discussed previously in this chapter), the concepts of centrality and connectedness are very similar, if not identical. So too are connectedness and *cohesion*, the degree to which an individual is bound to the system (Cartright and Zander, 1962), a favorite concept in small group research that is used to indicate a kind of attraction of the individual to the group.

[30] Generally, each of the indices of communication structure presented in this section seeks to remove the effect of size through the denominator. However, this approach does not completely or adequately compensate for the effect of size because the effect of size is not strictly linear: (1) in cases where the denominator is the number of possible links, there may be a practical limit on the number of links by an individual, independent of the size of the unit (for example, there is evidence that the

of individual connectedness should measure not just the dichotomous presence or absence of a link, but the frequency, duration, and/or importance of interaction in a link (Kim, 1978). Such more precise data can indeed be included in the formula for individual connectedness (and for the other indices presented in the present section), but their inclusion at this point would unnecessarily complicate our explanations. A practical issue to be resolved in future inquiry is whether the inclusion of these data would increase the precision of the indices commensurate with the additional computational effort required.

Individual integration is defined as the degree to which the members of an individual's personal communication network are linked to each other. This concept is measured as the number of indirect (two-step) links between the focal individual and the members of his/her personal communication network, divided by the possible number of such links.[31] The greater the number of these indirect links, the greater the degree of integration of the focal individual with his/her contactees. What contributes to the existence of more indirect links? The more an individual's contactees communicate with each other, the greater will be the number of indirect links between the individual and his/her contactees (and hence the higher the degree of communication proximity, on the average, between the focal individual and each of his/her direct contactees). Individual integration indexes the degree to which an individual's personal communication network is interlocking, rather than radial. The individual integration score for an individual in a completely interlocking network is 1.0 (Figure 3–5), while the individual integration score for an individual in a completely radial network is 0.0.

We can analyze the relationship between the degree of individual integration and the likelihood of the person receiving a new idea, and whether or not he/she will adopt. Research on "the strength of weak ties" (chapter 3 and chapter 5) implies that individual integration is negatively related to learning about new information. Individual integration captures the degree of homogeneity in information-exchange in a personal communication network. Low integration indicates that the focal individual has a greater heterogeneity for such information-exchanges, and this quality is related to innovativeness in adopting innovations (Kincaid, 1972). When the individuals in a personal network are highly linked with each other, there is a higher frequency of information-

---

average individual in a very large system of 3,900 has about the same number of links as the average individual in a small system of 39), and (2) where the denominator is a function of the number of individuals in a unit, the number of links can increase at a much faster rate than the number of individuals in the unit.

[31] Other network scholars referred to a concept basically similar to our individual integration as "density" (Kincaid, 1972, p. 63; Boussevain, 1974, p. 37), "integrativeness" (Richards, 1975, p. 72), or "dispersion" (Bott, 1955).

exchange among them, they are more likely to possess the same information, and so any given message is more likely to be redundant (Danowski, 1976, p. 289).

Bridges in a network, because of their links to individuals in two or more cliques, have a lower degree of individual integration. Liaisons tend to have an even lower degree of individual integration than bridges, because (due to their unique location in the communication structure of the network) the members of their personal communication network have relatively few links to each other. This lower individual integration of liaisons may be the underlying explanation of why liaisons have generally been found by network scholars to have distinctive communication characteristics (MacDonald, 1976; Schwartz and Jacobson, 1977). For example, Yadav (1967) found that liaisons in an Indian village were farmers with agricultural innovativeness scores midway between the innovative and laggardly cliques that they linked; presumably, the liaisons were not highly tied into either of the two cliques that they linked, and so they could deviate somewhat from the norms of both cliques.

Individual diversity is the degree to which the members of an individual's personal communication network are heterogeneous in some variable. This concept is indexed as the standard deviation in some variable that is measured for each member of the focal individual's personal network. For example, Kincaid (1972, p. 64) measured the individual diversity of his respondents (who were household heads in a Mexican slum) as the standard deviation in occupational prestige scores for the five individuals linked to each respondent. Yum and Kincaid (1979) measured the ethnic diversity of their respondents (Korean immigrants in Honolulu) as the percentage of each individual's five best friends that were non-Koreans; these researchers found that this ethnic diversity measure was different than other measures of individual diversity, such as the standard deviation of occupation and prestige scores (as was described above). Such measures of individual diversity for a personal communication network are analogous to heterophily [32] in a dyadic link.

Clique-Level Indices

At the clique level of analysis, a variety of communication structural indices can be computed: (1) clique connectedness, (2) average clique connectedness, (3) clique integration, (4) clique diversity, and (5) clique openness. These concepts are defined in Table 4-2b, and are generally parallel to the communication structural indices at the individual level. One exception is clique connectedness, which should be distinguished from average clique connectedness.

---

[32] *Heterophily* is the degree to which pairs of individuals who interact are different in certain attributes.

TABLE 4–2b. **Concepts Measuring Communication Structure at the Individual, Clique, and System Level.**

CONCEPTS MEASURING COMMUNICATION STRUCTURE	Individual	Clique	System
		LEVEL OF ANALYSIS	
1. *Connectedness:* The degree to which a unit is linked to other units.	*Individual connectedness:* The degree to which a focal individual is linked to other individuals in a system. ———	*Clique connectedness:* The degree to which the cliques in a system are linked to each other. *Average clique connectedness:* The degree to which the average member of a clique is linked to other individuals in the clique.	*Average system connectedness:* The degree to which the average member of a system is linked to the other individuals in the system.
2. *Integration:* The degree to which the units linked to the focal unit are linked to each other.	*Individual integration:* The degree to which the members of an individual's personal communication network are linked to each other.	*Clique integration:* The degree to which the cliques linked to a focal clique are linked to each other.	———
3. *Diversity:* The degree to which the units linked to the focal unit are heterogeneous in some variable.	*Individual diversity:* The degree to which the members of an individual's personal communication network are heterogeneous.	*Clique diversity:* The degree to which the cliques in a system are heterogeneous in some variable.	
4. *Openness:* The degree to which a unit exchanges information with its environment.		*Clique openness:* The degree to which the members of a clique are linked to others external to the clique.	*System openness:* The degree to which the members of a system are linked to others external to the system.

181

Clique connectedness is defined as the degree to which the cliques in a system are linked to each other.[33] This concept is indexed as the number of links between the focal clique and all the other cliques in a system, divided by the number of possible links (Table 4–3). Clique connectedness measures the degree to which a clique approaches a state at which every individual is directly linked to every other member.

In contrast, *average clique connectedness* is the degree to which the average member of a clique is linked to other individuals in the clique. This concept is indexed as the average number of links for each individual member of the clique to other clique members, divided by the number of such possible links. For example, clique I in village B (Figure 4–10) has an average clique connectedness score of .37 (as pointed out previously).

So clique connectedness is the extent to which the cliques in a system are interlinked, while average clique connectedness is the connectedness of the average individual within the clique.

Clique openness is the degree to which the members of a clique are linked to others external to the clique. This concept is indexed as the number of links for members of a clique that cross the clique's boundary, divided by the number of such possible links. Most new information enters a clique from external sources, so a more open clique is expected to be more innovative.

System-Level Indices

The two main indices of communication structure at the system level are average system connectedness and system openness; both concepts have direct parallels to concepts and their operations at the clique level (Tables 4–2b and 4–3).

The 10 indices of communication structure that we have just reviewed are useful tools for shedding light on the basic research question of how interpersonal communication is related to behavior change.

SELECTED METHODS OF NETWORK ANALYSIS

NEGOPY is only one of the main methods of network analysis that can be used to analyze communication networks. To understand fully its unique advantages and disadvantages, we need to compare it to other

---

[33] A practical problem in computing clique connectedness is to determine just what constitutes a link between two cliques. For instance, does it matter whether two cliques are linked by one bridge or by ten? Does it matter whether the link between two cliques is through a bridge, or via a liaison? These same problems are involved in operationalizing concepts like system connectedness.

TABLE 4–3. Conceptual Definitions and Operational Measures of Communication Structure at the Individual, Clique, and System Level.

INDICES OF COMMUNICATION STRUCTURE	CONCEPTUAL DEFINITION	OPERATIONAL MEASURE
I. Individual-Level		
1. *Individual connectedness*	The degree to which a focal individual is linked to other individuals in the system.	The actual number of links between the focal individual and the other members of the network, divided by the number of possible links (which is $N - 1$, when N = the number of individuals in the network).
2. *Individual integration*	The degree to which the members of an individual's personal communication network are linked to each other.	The number of indirect (two step) links between the focal individual and the members of his/her personal communication network, divided by the possible number of such links.
3. *Individual diversity*	The degree to which the members of an individual's personal communication network are heterogeneous in some variable.	The standard deviation in a variable measured for each member of the focal individual's personal network.
II. Clique-level		
1. *Clique connectedness*	The degree to which the cliques in a system are linked to each other.	The number of links between the focal cliques and all the other cliques in a system, divided by the number of possible links.
2. *Average clique connectedness*	The degree to which the average member of a clique is linked to other individuals in the clique.	The average number of links for each individual member of the clique to other clique members, divided by the number of such possible links.

TABLE 4–3 (Cont.)

Indices of Communication Structure	Conceptual Definition	Operational Measure
3. *Clique integration*	The degree to which the cliques linked to a focal clique are linked to each other.	The number of indirect (two-step) links between the focal clique and the other cliques to which the focal clique is linked, divided by the possible number of such links.
4. *Clique diversity*	The degree to which the cliques in a system are heterogeneous in some variable.	The standard deviation in a variable measured for each clique in a system.
5. *Clique openness*	The degree to which the members of a clique are linked to others external to the clique.	The number of links for members of a clique that cross the clique's boundary, divided by the number of such possible links.
III. *System-Level*		
1. *Average system connectedness*	The degree to which the average member of a system is linked to other individuals in the system.	The average number of links for each individual member of the system to other system members, divided by the number of such possible links.
2. *System openness*	The degree to which the members of a system are linked to others external to the system.	The number of links for members of a system that cross the system's boundary, divided by the number of such possible links.

methods of network analysis. In this section, we describe such alternate methods of communication network analysis as:

1. Direct factor analysis.
2. Factor analysis of correlations, particularly smallest-space analysis.
3. SOCK and COMPLT programs.
4. Blockmodeling.

Direct Factor Analysis

Factor analysis is a statistical procedure for clustering similar observations together on the basis of their common variance. The result is a series of one or more "factors," each of which is a cluster of observations with a high degree of common variance. Thus, the conversion of a large amount of data into a small number of factors provides a useful means of coping with information overload. Such data-reduction is exactly what is needed for network analysis, so as to identify the communication structure in a network.

Social scientists originally utilized factor analysis methods on datasets in which the observations were a number of variables provided by a sample of respondents. A typical example is a factor analysis of responses to scale items, in order to determine the factors that are composed of similar scale items. This use is called "R-type" factor analysis in that the covariances between pairs of responses (variables) are analyzed across individual respondents (two of the dimensions of the datacube shown in Figure 3–1).

Respondents can also be factor-analyzed, so that they are grouped together on the basis of their similar values on a number of variables; this use is called "P-type" factor analysis. Here the covariances between pairs of individual respondents are analyzed into factors, across their responses (variables) (Figure 3–1).

Any kind of data on individuals' responses can be factor-analyzed. So it is possible to factor-analyze the network links reported by each respondent, in order to identify one or more factors of respondents, each of which is a clique. Each clique (factor) shares a high degree of common variance in proximity scores, with maximum differences in variance between cliques. An individual's membership in a clique is expressed as a factor-loading, a correlation which shows the strength of the individual's association with the clique (factor). These factor-loadings are a special type of proximity measure in that they measure the individual's closeness to the clique, rather than to another individual.

There are basically two types of factor analysis of network links: (1) direct factor analysis, and (2) factor analysis of correlations (including smallest-space analysis).

Direct factor analysis utilizes as input the raw data of a who-to-whom communication matrix, such as the 0's and 1's indicating whether or not a communication link occurs between any two individuals (as was shown in Figure 4–3 for eight Korean women, and is shown in step #1 in Figure 4–12). Hence the measure of proximity used in direct factor analysis is relatively crude: linkage distance expressed only in terms of whether or not a first order, direct link occurs between every possible pair in a network. This measure is inferior to the more precise measure of communication proximity advocated in this book. A further, and more serious, difficulty is that the cliques produced by factor analysis are composed of individuals with similar patterns of links and nonlinks to other individuals in the network, whether or not the individuals thus clustered together in a clique are linked to each other. This measure of proximity is not completely logical in a communication sense; for instance, it is not completely consistent with our present definition of clique (as a subsystem whose elements interact with each other relatively more frequently than with other members of the system). The computer printout from a factor analysis of network data describes abstract patterns of variance, but does not allow one to reconstruct which individuals in the system are linked to each other (Richards, 1977). However, a sociogram can be drawn by referring back to the original who-to-whom data on communication links, and in fact the direct factor analysis printout can assist in the usually difficult task of arranging the individuals in the sociogram because the printout shows which individuals should be classified together in cliques.

Just as R-type factor analysis has the problem of "naming the baby" (that is, deciding what each factor should be called in terms of its main components), so do all factor analysis methods of network analysis. The usual procedure for naming the factors in R-type factor analysis is to identify one or several variables that are "purely" loaded on a factor (that is, the variable has a high factor-loading on the factor of interest, and low loadings on all other factors). Similarly, in P-type factor analysis, the individuals with purest loadings on a factor (that is, a clique) represent that factor most distinctly, and suggest what may distinguish it from other factors. For instance, in his factor analysis of links in an "invisible college" of methodological and mathematical sociologists, Burt (1978c) identified Professors James Davis and David Heise as key figures in what he termed "the social psychology clique," Professors James Coleman and Seymour Spilerman in "the mathematical sociology" clique, and so on. Each clique (factor) was "named" on the basis of the intellectual specialty of the individuals with purest factor loadings on that factor.

Similarly, the four women in Korean village A (Table 4–4) with the purest loadings on clique I (individuals #6, #10, #17, and #28) are all

Figure 4–12.   Procedures for Computing a Matrix of Correlations for Input to Smallest-Space Analysis.

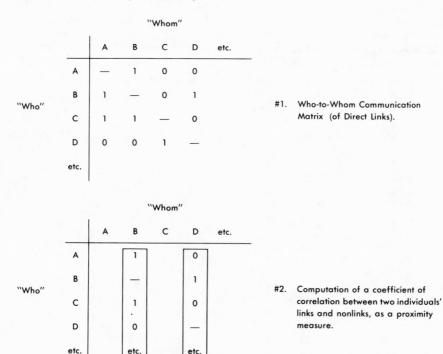

"Whom"

	A	B	C	D	etc.
A	—	1	0	0	
B	1	—	0	1	
C	1	1	—	0	
D	0	0	1	—	
etc.					

"Who"

#1.   Who-to-Whom Communication Matrix (of Direct Links).

"Whom"

	A	B	C	D	etc.
A		1		0	
B		—		1	
C		1		0	
D		0		—	
etc.		etc.		etc.	

"Who"

r = .23

#2.   Computation of a coefficient of correlation between two individuals' links and nonlinks, as a proximity measure.

	A	B	C	D	etc.
A	—	.56	.12	.47	
B	.56	—	.19	(.23)	
C	.12	.19	—	.31	
D	.47	(.23)	.31	—	
etc.					

#3.   Matrix of correlations (for input to smallest-space analysis).

Note: In direct factor analysis, the presence or absence of direct links in a who-to-whom matrix (#1 above) is utilized as a crude proximity measure in the factor analysis (to identify cliques in the network). In the factor analysis of correlations, however, a more precise proximity measure is used, the coefficients of correlation between two individuals' links and nonlinks (illustrated in #2 above). The resulting matrix of correlations (#3) is input to the factor analysis. The correlations are rather inappropriate measures of communication proximity as they index the similarity of all the links *and all the nonlinks* of each pair of individuals in a network.

TABLE 4–4. Direct Factor Analysis of the Communication Structure of Village A in Korea.

INDIVIDUAL IDENTIFICATION NUMBER OF RESPONDENTS	FACTOR-WEIGHTINGS WITH CLIQUES (FACTORS) * IDENTIFIED BY DIRECT FACTOR ANALYSIS			INDIVIDUAL COMMUNICATION ROLE IDENTIFIED BY DIRECT FACTOR ANALYSIS
	I	*II*	*III*	
# 2	0	1.00	0	Clique II member
# 3	0	.71	0	” II ”
# 4	0	0	0	Isolated dyad
# 6	1.00	0	0	Clique I member
#10	.72	0	0	” I ”
#11	.38	0	0	” I ”
#13	.49	.18	0	” I ”
#14	0	0	0	Isolate
#15	0	0	0	”
#16	.54	0	0	Clique I member
#17	.77	0	0	” I ”
#18	.56	0	0	” I ”
#19	.21	0	.34	” III ” †
#22	.54	0	0	” I ”
#24	.48	0	0	” I ”
#25	.42	0	0	” I ”
#27	.22	0	0	” I ”
#28	1.00	0	0	” I ”
#29	.65	0	0	” I ”
#31	.63	0	0	” I ”
#36	.27	0	0	” I ”
#44	.27	0	0	” I ”
#45	0	0	0	Isolate
#47	0	1.00	0	Clique II member
#48	0	.89	0	” II ”
#49	0	1.00	0	” II ”
#51	0	.83	0	” II ”
#52	0	1.00	0	” II ”
#53	0	.35	0	” II ”
#54	0	0	0	Isolate
#55	0	0	0	Isolate
#56	0	0	.82	Clique III member
#57	0	0	.82	” III ”
#58	0	0	1.00	” III ”
#59	0	0	0	Isolate †
#60	0	.50	0	Clique II member
#61	0	.50	0	” II ”
#62	0	0	0	Isolate †
#63	0	0	0	Isolated dyad

* Factor-weightings of less than .10 are shown as zeros, for the sake of clarity. The highest factor-weighting for each individual is in boldface.

† These individuals are classified in a different communication role by direct factor analysis than by the NEGOPY program (whose results were shown in Figure 4–10).

members of the mothers' club; none of the three women with purest loadings on clique II (individuals #47, 49,# and #52) or the three women
in clique III are mothers' club members. So we might label clique I the
"mothers' club" factor.

There is no standardized criterion in factor analysis for deciding
which individuals belong to one clique (factor) or to another. The usual
convention is to assign individuals to the factor on which they have the
highest and purest factor-loading. Occasionally, however, especially in a
highly connected network without clear-cut cliques, some individuals
(particularly bridges and liaisons) will have approximately equal loadings
on two or more cliques.[34] Then an arbitrary assignment must be made,
or else these individuals must be considered as liaisons. A further problem in assigning individuals to factors is that some individuals have only
a low factor-loading on one factor; there is no standard criterion for
cutoff between isolates and nonisolates, but one convention is to use a
level of factor-loading that is significantly different from zero at the 5
percent level. An example is individual #27 in village A (Table 4–4)
who has a factor-loading of only .22 on clique I.

A nonsymmetrical who-to-whom matrix will yield different factors if
the Q-type factor analysis is computed across the rows or across the
columns. This problem can be solved by forcing reciprocation in all links;
that is, by converting all nonreciprocated links into reciprocated links
(as is justified by the argument, presented earlier, that all communication
links are really two-way whether they are so reported by both individuals in a dyadic link or not).[35] Then the who-to-whom matrix will be
symmetrical.

There is one considerable advantage of direct factor analysis: computer programs for factor analysis are very widely available at university
computing centers.[36] This same advantage of course characterizes factor
analysis of correlations, a network analysis method which utilizes a somewhat more precise measure of proximity than direct factor analysis (as
is explained in the following section).

A disadvantage of factor analysis methods of network analysis is
that such computer programs have a rather limited capacity, usually
about 150 or so individuals (but sometimes up to 400 individuals). This
size limitation is far smaller than NEGOPY's 4,095 by 4,095 limit.

The network communication data for villages A and B were factor-

[34] An example is individual #19 in village A (Table 4–4) who has a factor-loading
of .34 on clique III and of .21 on clique I. This individual was classified as a bridge
by the NEGOPY program (Figure 4–10).
[35] Another solution to the nonsymmetry problem was demonstrated by Wright and
Evitts (1961) and Beaton (1966).
[36] And the costs of using direct factor are fairly cheap. Direct factor analysis of the
village A communication link data cost only $1.85 in computer time at the University
of Michigan, while the computer run for village B cost $1.94.

analyzed with SOC MET, a direct factor analysis computer program developed by Professor James Lingoes at the University of Michigan. The results for village A (Table 4–4) generally are similar to the NEGOPY network analysis shown previously in Figure 4–10; only three of the 39 women are categorized in a different communication role.[37] Individual #19 is classified in clique III by direct factor analysis and in clique I by NEGOPY (Figure 4–10 shows she is a bridge from clique I to clique III, Table 4–4 shows she has factor-loadings of .34 on clique III and .21 on clique I). Direct factor analysis shows individual #59 is an isolate, while NEGOPY puts her in clique I (where she has only one link); the case is similar for individual #62.

The two network analysis methods classify 38 of the 39 women in village B in the same communication roles (Table 4–5 and Figure 4–11);[38] direct factor analysis shows individual #8 has a factor-loading of .31 with clique III (although with a factor-loading of .14 with clique I), while NEGOPY puts this woman in clique I.

So the communication structure depicted by direct factor analysis and by NEGOPY are very similar.[39] However, this similarity may be in part due to the rather clear-cut cliques in these two villages, especially village A.

Table 4–6 shows that the results of direct factor analysis agree generally with those of NEGOPY and of blockmodeling. The latter method (discussed in a following section) classifies the 78 women in the two villages in the same communication roles as NEGOPY, with four exceptions.

One direct factor analysis computer technique called "CATIJ" (rhymes with "cabbage"), developed by Killworth and Bernard (1974a and 1974b), inputs roster-type sociometric data that measures proximity as the minimal number of links between each "i" (the chosen, or the "who" in a who-to-whom matrix) and "j" (the chosen, or the "whom"). Such minimal distance is more precise than the single "0" or "1" measure of proximity used in most direct factor analysis. To gain sensitivity in their proximity measure, Professors Killworth and Bernard follow a

---

[37] However, this similarity would be less if we allowed the factor analysis program to identify more factors; for instance, it is possible to break out two "subfactors" for clique I and three "subfactors" for clique II, making a total of six factors.

[38] Although this similarity would be much less if we allowed the factor analysis program to continue breaking out "subfactors," as explained previously for village A; in one computer run, we identified four "subfactors" for clique I, and four for clique II, making a total of nine factors.

[39] Katz and Powell (1953) provide a measure of the goodness-of-fit of one who-to-whom matrix with another (and thus of the similarity of two measurements of network *links*), and Hubert and Baker (1978) discuss an improvement, but our search of the literature did not yield a goodness-of-fit test for comparing two *communication structures* that result from two different network analyses of the same who-to-whom matrix.

TABLE 4–5. Direct Factor Analysis of the Communication Structure of Village B in Korea.

INDIVIDUAL IDENTIFICATION NUMBER OF RESPONDENTS	FACTOR-WEIGHTINGS WITH CLIQUES (FACTORS) * IDENTIFIED BY DIRECT FACTOR ANALYSIS			INDIVIDUAL COMMUNICATION ROLES IDENTIFIED BY DIRECT FACTOR ANALYSIS
	I	*II*	*III*	
# 1	0	0	.89	Clique III member
# 2	.15	0	.91	” III ”
# 5	.19	0	.78	” III ”
# 6	.37	0	.99	” III ”
# 7	0	0	.89	” III ” †
# 8	.14	0	.31	” III ”
#11	.56	0	0	Clique I member
#12	.68	0	0	” I ”
#13	.96	0	0	” I ”
#14	1.00	0	0	” I ”
#15	.71	0	0	” I ”
#16	.42	0	0	” I ”
#18	0	0	0	Isolate
#20	.74	0	.21	Clique I member
#22	.70	0	.15	” I ”
#24	.55	0	0	” I ”
#25	1.00	0	0	” I ”
#28	.96	0	0	” I ”
#29	.74	0	0	” I ”
#30	.30	.66	0	” II ”
#31	.71	0	0	” I ”
#33	0	.81	0	Clique II member
#35	.25	.54	0	” II ”
#36	0	1.00	0	” II ”
#37	.12	.60	0	” II ”
#40	0	0	0	Isolate
#41	0	0	0	”
#44	0	.75	0	Clique II member
#46	0	.98	0	” II ”
#49	0	0	0	Isolate
#52	.46	0	0	Clique I member
#53	0	.41	0	” II ”
#57	0	.58	0	” II ”
#59	.14	.59	0	” II ”
#60	0	.99	0	” II ”
#61	0	.52	0	” II ”
#62	0	.98	0	” II ”
#64	0	.52	0	” II ”
#65	0	.48	0	” II ”

* Factor-weightings of less than .10 are shown as zeros, for the sake of clarity. The highest factor-weighting for each individual is in boldface.

† This individual is classified in a different communication role by direct factor analysis than by the NEGOPY program (whose results were shown in Figure 4–10).

TABLE 4–6. Comparison of Communication Structures Obtained from Selected Methods of Network Analysis for Two Korean Villages.

Respondent Identification Number (Village A)	Individual Role in the Communication Structure (Village A)			Respondent Identification Number (Village B)	Individual Role in the Communication Structure (Village B)		
	1. NEGOPY	2. Direct Factor Analysis	3. Blockmodeling with CONCOR		1. NEGOPY	2. Direct Factor Analysis	3. Blockmodeling with CONCOR
# 2	Clique II member	—	—	# 1	Clique III member	—	(no blockmodeling of village B)
# 3	" II "	—	—	# 2	" III "	—	
# 4	Isolated dyad	—	—	# 5	" III "	—	
# 6	Clique I member	—	—	# 7	" III "	—	
# 10	" I "	—	—	# 8	Clique I member	Clique III member *	
# 11	" I "	—	—	# 11	" I "	—	
# 13	" I "	—	—	# 12	" I "	—	
# 14	Isolate	—	—	# 13	" I "	—	
# 15	"	—	Clique III member *	# 14	" I "	—	
# 16	Clique I member	—	—	# 15	" I "	—	
# 17	" I "	—	—	# 16	" I "	—	
# 18	" I "	—	—	# 18	Isolate	—	
# 19	" I "	Clique III member *	Clique I member	# 20	Clique I member	—	
# 22	" I "	—	—	# 22	" I "	—	
# 24	" I "	—	—	# 24	" I "	—	
# 25	" I "	—	—	# 25	" I "	—	
# 27	" I "	—	—	# 28	" I "	—	
# 28	" I "	—	—	# 29	" I "	—	
# 29	" I "	—	—	# 30	" II "	—	
# 31	" I "	—	—	# 31	" I "	—	

#36	" I "	—		
#44	" I "		—	#33	" II "
#45	Isolate	—		
#47	Clique II member	—		
#48	" II "	—		
#49	" II "	—		
#51	" II "	—		
#52	" II "	—		
#53	" II "	—	Clique III member *	
#54	Isolate	—	" III " *	
#55	"	—		
#56	Clique III member	—		
#57	" III "	—		
#58	" III "	Isolate *	—	
#59	Clique I "	—	Clique I "	
#60	" II "	—		
#61	" II "	—	Clique I "	
#62	" I "	Isolate *	—	Clique III " *	
#63	Isolated dyad	—		

(Right column listing)

#33	" II "
#35	" II "
#36	" II "
#37	" II "
#40	Isolate
#41	Isolate
#44	Clique II member
#45	" II "
#49	Isolate
#52	Clique I member
#53	" II "
#57	" II "
#59	" II "
#60	" II "
#61	" II "
#62	" II "
#64	" II "
#65	" II "

* This individual is classified in a different communication role by direct factor analysis or by blockmodeling, than by NEGOPY.

193

roster approach in which each respondent is asked to indicate how frequently he/she interacts with each of the other individuals in a closed network (like a prison, an oceanographic ship at sea, etc.). Such measurement
is rather time-consuming in interviews, of course, and is usually only
practical in relatively small-sized networks (CATIJ is limited to networks
of less than 150 individuals), but Killworth and Bernard (1974b) thus
measure "weak ties" (Granovetter, 1973) as well as "strong ties" (that is,
high-proximity links). The results of CATIJ analyses show that the communication structure of a network does not fully emerge until these weak
ties are included in the data-analyses, at least up to the point at which
each respondent is allowed to make about seven sociometric choices (at
this point the roster approach yields about the same communication
structure in a network as does a nonroster limited-choice sociometric
question like "Who are the seven other members of this system that you
talk with most often?" or an unlimited-choice question to which an
average of about seven links are reported by respondents). Killworth
and Bernard (1974b) also recommend against only including reciprocated
links in network analysis, which tends to eliminate "weak ties" and distort the communication structure that exists in the network because, as
Granovetter's (1973) theory would lead us to expect, the "weak ties" are
the bridge links between cliques, and are especially vital to understanding the communication structure (chapter 3). Professor Bernard is an
anthropologist and usually insists on checking the validity of the communication structure (that emerges from CATIJ) with his ethnographic
observation of the relatively small networks that he and Professor Killworth study.

The measure of proximity inputted to CATIJ is not based on reciprocal links, and so the who-to-whom matrix is not symmetrical. Killworth
and Bernard (1974a and 1974b) always factor-analyze by rows in the
matrix (the individuals chosen by a respondent) rather than by columns
(the individuals choosing the respondents).[40] They include all the individuals in a clique who have a factor-loading on that clique of at least
.60; this is an arbitrary level, of course, but at least it standardizes clique
identification across each of the systems that they analyze.

Despite the fact that CATIJ uses a different proximity measure than
we prefer in this book (which is the communication proximity index, as
explained previously in this chapter), we feel that CATIJ is the "least–
worst" direct factor analysis method based on a distance measure of proximity. Because the roster-type data about communication links obtained
by Professors Killworth and Bernard are relatively precise (especially
because they include the "weak ties"), CATIJ is able to identify the

[40] If Killworth and Bernard "forced" reciprocation of their data (by changing all
nonreciprocated links to reciprocated links in the who-to-whom matrix), it would
not matter whether CATIJ factored by rows or by columns.

communication structure in a network with considerable sensitivity. However, we feel that CATIJ suffers, for purposes of *communication* network analysis, from using a distance measure of proximity instead of inputting communication proximity, measured as the overlap of two individuals' personal communication networks.

Nosanchuk (1963) compared direct factor analysis to three other methods of network analysis, including Katz' (1947) matrix manipulation technique. While direct factor analysis was highest in computer costs (given, of course, the nature of available computers in the early 1960s), it provided the most objective results and the most meaningful partitioning of the network into cliques (measured as the ability to recover a preconstructed communication structure).

Lankford (1974) compared direct factor analysis with factor analysis of correlations and with smallest-space analysis (along with two other methods). This comparison showed that direct factor analysis produced similar results to factor analysis of correlations (for two different data-sets), although direct factor analysis was relatively more expensive.

Undoubtedly there is a potential for the direct factor analysis of network data that is not presently being fulfilled, especially at the many research locations where more sophisticated network analyses are not available.

Factor Analysis of Correlations and Smallest-Space Analysis

Instead of the relatively crude proximity measure used in direct factor analysis, it is possible to input a communication matrix in which the proximity measure is a coefficient of correlation. As explained previously in this chapter, such a proximity index has important disadvantages as a measure of communication proximity because it includes noncommunication (O's in the original matrix) as well as communication links (1's). Thus a correlation indexes the similarity (that is, the covariance) of all the links *and all the nonlinks* of every pair of individuals in a network. The procedure by which the correlations are computed was diagrammed in Figure 4–12.

But compared to the crudeness of the proximity measure in direct factor analysis, correlation as a proximity index is far superior because: (1) it measures the similarity of the dyadic partners' personal communication networks (unfortunately, it also measures the similarity of the two individuals' nonlinks), and (2) it is much more precise.

The first factor analysis of correlations as a method of network analysis was reported by Bock and Husain (1950), but network analysis of correlations did not have many users until a special type of such factor analysis came along called "smallest-space analysis." The input data in the form of a communication matrix of correlations is the same (actually this is usually the case, but one can also input data in other forms, like a linkage distance measure, to smallest-space analysis). But much of what follows is quite different from usual factor analysis methods.

Smallest-space analysis is sometimes referred to as a *nonmetric* factor analysis because the computer program converts the correlations to nonmetric "distances," in which the *rank-order* of distances between points is the inverse of the rank-order of the correlations.[41] The distances do not *equal* the inverse of the correlations; thus, some approximation of measurement (that is, of proximity in the communication matrix) results

Figure 4–13. Smallest-Space Analysis, a Type of Factor Analysis of Correlations, Expresses Proximity (Measured by the Correlations) as Two-Dimensional Distance.

	"Whom"			
	A	B	C	D
A	x	.8	.2	.1
B		x	.5	.3
C			x	.9
D				x

"Who" labels rows A, B, C, D.

Communication Matrix with Correlations Indicating Proximity

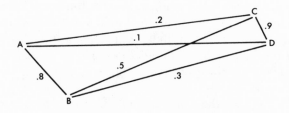

Smallest-Space Analysis with Distances Corresponding
in Inverse Rank-Order to the Correlations

Source: From *Survey Research Methods* (p. 330) by Earl R. Babbie. Copyright © 1973 by Wadsworth Publishing Company, Inc., Belmont, California 94002. Reprinted by permission of the publisher.

[41] The rank-order of distances is the inverse of the rank-order of the correlations because a high correlation indicates a close distance.

in a corresponding loss of information in the data. This approximation is necessary to fit the "distances" into two-dimensional space on a computer printout (like that in Figure 4–13).[42]

An example of the nonmetric nature of smallest-space analysis is shown in Figure 4–13. The six intercorrelations among the four individuals (at the top of Figure 4–13) are the input data to smallest-space analysis. The computer arranges the four individuals in such a fashion that the distances between them are the inverse of the rank-order of the correlation measures of dyadic proximity (as shown in the lower diagram in Figure 4–13). The longest distance, between individuals A and D, corresponds to the weakest correlation. The shortest distance, between individuals C and D, corresponds to the strongest of the six correlations.

As more and more correlations (and individuals) are included in a matrix, it soon becomes impossible to arrange the individuals so that the distances between them correspond exactly to the rank-order of the strength of the intercorrelations. Thus, smallest-space analysis is an approximation; the computer provides a measure of the degree of approximation (the coefficient of alienation) in locating the individuals in a network on a two-dimensional surface so that closer distances indeed correspond to higher correlations. The "coefficient of alienation" for the smallest-space analysis in Figure 4–13 is zero; the dyadic distances are in exact rank-order with the size of the correlations.

Certainly, one of the main advantages of smallest-space analysis for purposes of network analysis is that it provides a graphic representation of the communication structure. One of the main outputs from a smallest-space analysis computer program like Lingoes' smallest-space analysis (SSA)[43] is a two-dimensional mapping of the individuals in the communication matrix, plotted so that distance in the map corresponds to proximity. Dyadic links can then be drawn on this computer printout, so as to produce a sociogram in which the individuals are distanced on the basis of their measured proximity (as indexed by the strength of the correlations). Figures 4–14 and 4–15 show the results of smallest-space analysis for villages A and B. Individuals who are located near each

[42] Actually, smallest-space analysis is not limited to just two-dimensional space, but that is all that can easily be illustrated in this book. The objective of smallest-space analysis is to fit the distances into as few dimensions as possible (Lingoes, 1972, p. 52).

[43] SSA was originally developed by Professor Louis Guttman (1968) at Hebrew University in Israel, and then computerized by Professor James C. Lingoes at the University of Michigan, and is now widely available on university computers in the United States. The smallest-space analysis programs are described by Lingoes (1972 and 1973). Guttman–Lingoes' smallest-space analysis is a type of nonmetric multidimensional scaling, developed at Bell Telephone Laboratories by Shepard (1962a and 1962b) and Kruskal (1964a and 1964b). The purpose of nonmetric multidimensional scaling is to determine the spatial configuration of nodes which best summarizes the information contained in a set of data.

other on the two-dimensional space of the computer printout are more likely to belong to the same clique. Isolates tend to be near the center of the printout.

In everyday life we all use expressions that indicate we think of personal relationships in terms of a smallest-space type of proximity-distance. For example, "She is very close to the Preseident," or "We've grown more distant in the past year." The smallest-space analysis computer program utilizes this analogy to physical space in order to impose a kind of order on the communication structure of a network.

Once the links were drawn by hand between the individuals' locations on the computer printout in Figures 4–14 and 4–15, the clique structure became evident, and corresponds to that obtained by NEGOPY (Figures 4–10 and 4–11). Here we see the main advantage of smallest-space analysis: the graphical representation of the individuals in spatial

Figure 4–14. Computer Printout from Lingoes' Smallest-Space Analysis for Village A, with Links Drawn by Hand.

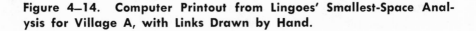

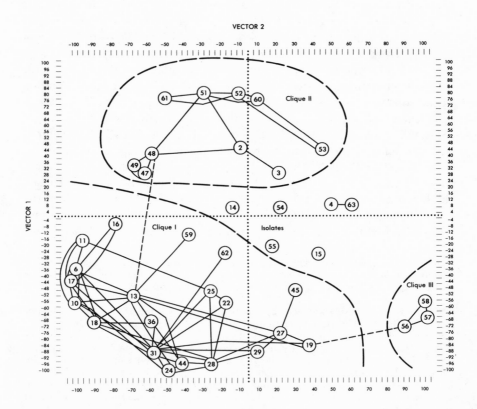

Figure 4–15.   Computer Printout from Lingoes' Smallest-Space Analysis for Village B, with Links Drawn by Hand.

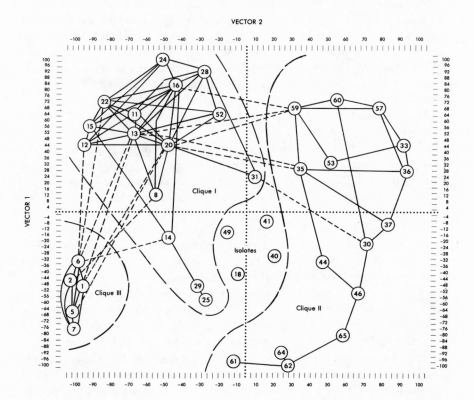

terms that corresponds to their location in the communication structure.

We find that the ability to visualize the communication structure is an important aid to understanding the nature of a communication network. Unfortunately, smallest-space analysis does not identify cliques, and so one must apply some type of clustering program to the SSA results. Johnson's (1967) heirarchical clustering technique is often utilized. Or NEGOPY could be used to identify cliques and provide indices of communication structure, in combination with using SSA to printout the location of individuals in that structure.

NEGOPY could be used in sequence with SSA for yet another reason: smallest-space analysis can only handle about 50 to 100 individuals, depending on the size of the computer (Bloombaum, 1970). So NEGOPY could be used first on a data-set, to break out the component cliques, each of which could then be analyzed with SSA. We show later (Table

4–8) that each of the methods of network analysis have certain advantages; using two or more methods on the same data, in sequence, has obvious advantages. But, to date, few multimethod approaches to network analysis have been conducted.

Kim (1977b) used Lingoes' SSA and NEGOPY on the network data from Oryu Li village (discussed in chapter 1). She found very similar results from both network analysis approaches. For instance, both techniques showed the great importance of residential contiguity in determining who was linked to whom. In fact, the SSA printout was almost a reproduction of the map of the village; that is, by knowing the network links one could almost reconstruct where the 69 women lived relative to each other (Figure 1–1).

A special type of smallest-space analysis computer program, SSA-II, should be used if the who-to-whom matrix is not symmetrical (due to unreciprocated links), and SSA-I should be utilized with symmetrical matrices (Lingoes, 1972). Hence, smallest-space analysis is not troubled by unreciprocated data, as is direct factor analysis. These two computer programs (SSA-I and SSA-II) are widely available in university computer centers, and operate at a relatively modest cost. For instance, SSA of village A cost $2.21, while village B cost $2.24.[44] Hence, SSA costs were somewhat higher than direct factor analysis.

The computer printout for each smallest-space analysis also provides a coefficient of alienation, which indexes how well the constructed dimensions actually fit the original data. The smaller the coefficient of alienation, the better the fit. SSA for village A showed a coefficient of alienation of only .04 and the comparable figure for village B is .06. These are very good fits; the convention is to regard a coefficient of alienation of .15 or less as a good fit. If a higher coefficient were obtained, it is possible to try a three-dimensionl smallest-space analysis, instead of two dimensions, but it is more difficult to understand the three-dimensional results and to present them clearly in a written report.[45]

During the 1970s a number of network scholars have utilized smallest-space analysis to visualize the communication structure of networks. For example, Laumann and Pappi (1973 and 1976, p. 168) used smallest-space analysis to study the community power structure and decision-making process in a small German city (we discussed certain of their findings in chapter 3).[46] SSA was used to printout the proximities of the top 46 leaders of the city. Then "fault lines" showing the consensus–cleavage structure were drawn onto the printout for each of five

---

[44] On the University of Michigan IBM computer.
[45] Although Laumann and Pappi (1976) have done so, using three-dimensional drawings.
[46] Lingoes' smallest-space analysis also was used in an interlocking directorate study of the power structure of Phoenix (McLaughlin, 1975).

community issues (on the basis of the community leaders' responses about where other leaders stood on these issues). The Laumann–Pappi analysis showed that these fault lines predicted almost perfectly how these five community issues were later resolved. The visualization of the network data made possible by smallest-space analysis greatly aided its understanding and interpretation. Visual inspection of the communication structure in a network is one means of coping with the information overload caused by the plethora of links.

SOCK and COMPLT

Professor Richard D. Alba, in collaboration with Charles Kadushin, at Columbia University developed a useful system of network analysis procedures that include two main computer programs called "SOCK" and "COMPLT." The input data for SOCK/COMPLT must be in binary form (that is coded as 0's and 1's) and the who-to-whom matrix must be symmetrical. The SOCK/COMPLT system has two main components. The first, SOCK, is a clique-identification procedure that allows the user options in choosing between (1) four proximity measures (called RELATE, SIMMEL 1, SIMMEL 2, and SIMMEL 3), and (2) two clustering techniques, a version of Johnson's (1967) hierarchical clustering routine or a kind of nonmetric multidimensional scaling (Kruskal, 1964a and 1964b). Essentially, SOCK inputs the who-to-whom data matrix and converts the 0/1 data into one of the three SIMMEL proximity measures, which index the degree to which each pair of individuals are linked to similar others, that is, the degree to which their personal communication networks overlap (Alba and Kadushin, 1976). Unlike the measure of communication proximity used in NEGOPY, however, the SIMMEL proximity measures are computed for each pair of individuals in a matrix, whether the pair is directly linked or not. We questioned SIMMEL-type proximity measures at the beginning of this chapter, at least for communication network analysis, where one usually only wants to measure proximity between the individuals in a network who are in direct communication.

SOCK has a very large capacity, being limited mainly by the size of the computer's memory and by the user's pocketbook; Alba and Guttman (1972) say that SOCK can handle networks of up to 9,999 (which would be much larger even than NEGOPY). If SOCK is utilized in combination with a Stromberg Datagraphics 4060 (as at Columbia University's computer center), machine-generated sociograms can be printed out.

The other part of the SOCK/COMPLT network analysis system is COMPLT, a graph-theoretical clustering program (Alba, 1972a). The proximity measure is based on graph theory (Harary, 1969). COMPLT follows the work of Luce and Perry (1949) in focusing on the structural properties of network data to identify cliques; the program first identifies all possible subgraphs, then discards certain of them that do not meet criteria, and then combines the subgraphs according to the user's directions (based on visual inspection of the overlaps among the subgraphs) to form cliques.

Because of its numerous options, the SOCK/COMPLT system is extremely flexible. In fact, it almost begins to approach being a "Network Package for the Social Sciences." The SOCK/COMPLT computer programs have been available since the early 1970s and are now running at several university computer centers.

Tichy and others (1978) reported using SOCK/COMPLT to reanalyze data previously gathered by Payne and Pheysey (1973) on organizational communication among the managers of three English factories. The reanalysis by Tichy and others (1978) and Tichy and Frombrun (1978) provided additional insight into the different communication structures of the three factories. Despite its size and flexibility in the several network analysis techniques that it provides, SOCK/COMPLT does not seem to have been widely used by network analysts, at least as reported in the literature.

Thanks to the kindness of Professor Alba, we were able to run our network data from villages A and B on the SOCK/COMPLT system. We chose to utilize SIMMEL 2 as the proximity measure, along with the hierarchical clustering routine and the nonmetric multidimensional scaling technique to cluster the respondents into cliques. Although limitations of space prevent our detailed presentation of these results here, the communication structure for villages A and B that emerged from using SOCK was almost identical to that resulting from NEGOPY (Table 4–6).

Blockmodeling with CONCOR

A somewhat distinctive approach to network analysis called "blockmodeling" has developed since the mid-1970s, centering around Professor Harrison White and his associates at Harvard University's Department of Sociology.[47] *Blockmodeling* is a network analysis technique for ob-

---

[47] The literature describing blockmodeling includes: Arabie and others (1978), Bonacich (1977), Boorman and White (1976), Breiger (1976a, 1976b, and 1979), Breiger and Pattison (1978), Breiger and others (1975), Heil and White (1976), Lorrain (1975), Lorrain and White (1971), Mullins and others (1977), Schwartz (1977), Snyder and Kirk (1979), White (1974 and 1977), White and Breiger (1975), and White and others (1976). Critical reviews of blockmodeling may be found in Chubin (1979) and Sailer (1978). Schwartz (1977) noted that Professors Louis L. McQuitty and James A. Clark (1968) at Michigan State University independently invented iterative, intercolumnar correlational analysis (the algorithm represented by CONCOR) at about the same time as Professors White and Breiger at Harvard University.

taining the structure for two or more networks composed of the same individuals. Each of the multiple networks typically represent a different sociometric question asked of the same set of individual respondents. Thus, blockmodeling is unusual among network analysis methods in enabling a researcher to analyze *multiplexity* (the degree to which multiple contents flow through a dyadic link between two individuals).

Blockmodeling categorizes individuals together (in "blocks") on the basis of their having similar communication links and nonlinks, and thus is based on a measure of "proximity" like the correlations utilized as inputs to factor analysis of correlations; the difference is that the correlation expresses similarity across *multiple* networks in the case of blockmodeling with the CONCOR computer program (Figure 4–16).

The blocks of individuals in blockmodeling are not the same as cliques, in the usual sense of a communication definition of clique as being composed of individuals who interact with each other relatively more than with nonclique members. A block need only contain individuals who have similar patterns of communication links *and nonlinks* (Breiger and others, 1975). Thus, two individuals in a block are linked to the same sets of other individuals, but they may not be linked to each other. This lack of direct contact between the members of a block is not consistent with a notion of *communication* networks, that each link in a network has at least some minimum degree of communication proximity. Professor White and his colleagues do not claim that blockmodeling is a technique for communication network analysis. Instead they argue that the basis for categorizing individuals in cliques is *structural equivalence,* defined as the degree to which two individuals are linked to the same set of other individuals but not necessarily to each other.[48] This measure of structural equivalence is generally similar to the communication proximity measure that we recommend in this book (the degree to which two individuals in a network have personal communication networks that overlap), except that the two individuals need not be linked to each other in the case of blockmodeling's structural equivalence (Figure 4–17).

However, the results of blockmodeling (with the CONCOR program) our communication network data for Korean village A, presented later in this section in Figure 4–18, are almost identical with the results of our NEGOPY network analysis (Table 4–5). This almost complete similarity in the communication structure that is obtained, suggests that the proximity measures for CONCOR and for NEGOPY must indeed be very similar, at least for village A (which has a rather clear-cut communication structure with few links between cliques).

[48] Two individuals in the same block are substitutable in regard to their links with other blocks (Sailer, 1978). Two individuals are structurally equivalent if they are related in the same ways to other individuals that are structurally equivalent.

Figure 4–16. Blockmodeling Is a Network Analysis Method for Obtaining the Communication Structure for Two or More Networks of the Same Individuals; the Measure of Proximity May Be a Correlation Computed for Two or More Topics.

	A	B	C	D	etc.
A	—	1	0	0	
B	1	—	0	1	
C	1	1	—	0	
D	0	0	1	—	
etc.		etc.		etc.	

Who-to-Whom Communication Matrix for Topic #1

	A	B	C	D	etc.
A	—	0	1	1	
B	0	—	0	1	
C	1	0	—	1	
D	0	1	0	—	
etc.		etc.		etc.	

Who-to-Whom Communication Matrix for Topic #2

	A	B	C	D	etc.
A	—	0	1	0	
B	1	—	0	0	
C	1	1	—		
D	0	0	1	—	
etc.		etc.		etc.	

Who-to-Whom Communication Matrix for Topic #3

$r = .41$

Note: The measure of "proximity" that the CONCOR blockmodeling computer program uses to assign individuals to blocks is *structural equivalence,* the degree to which two individuals are linked to the same set of other individuals but not necessarily to each other. The concept of structural equivalence is usually measured by CONCOR as a correlation between two individuals' columns (or rows) in a series of who-to-whom matrices (one for each sociometric topic that is being analyzed in the blockmodeling). This correlation is similar to that shown in Figure 4–12 for a single who-to-whom matrix, except that in the case of blockmodeling, it is for multiple matrices. The next step in blockmodeling with the CONCOR computer program is to create a new who-to-whom matrix with the r of .41 entered for BD and DB, and similarly computed correlations entered for all other intersections in the matrix. Then, a new correlation is computed for BD from this matrix of correlations. The process of computing correlations of the matrices of correlations continues until the process converges to a partitioning of the individuals into blocks at a specified cutoff level.

Figure 4–17.   The Difference Between Communication Proximity (Used in NEGOPY •to Identify Communication Structure) and Structural Equivalence (Used in CONCOR for Blockmodeling).

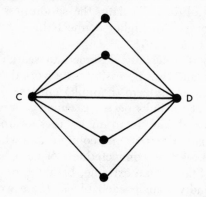

CD have high *communication proximity*, the degree to which two linked individuals in a network have personal communication networks that overlap, and also have high structural equivalence.

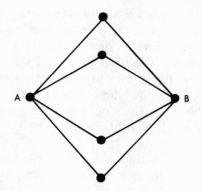

AB have high *structural equivalence*, the degree to which two individuals are linked to the same set of other individuals but not necessarily (directly) to each other. Thus, AB do not have communication proximity.

Note: The CD link above has high communication proximity (as shown previously in Figure 4–1), and high structural equivalence; the AB link has high structural equivalence but no communication proximity.

A possible problem with CONCOR occurs when each of the multiple network matrices inputted to compute the correlations between columns (or rows) (Figure 4–16) has different average system connectedness (that is, the average number of links per individual); the networks with higher connectedness will be weighted more heavily in the resulting correlations (Schwartz, 1976). To date, the seriousness of this unintended weighting of networks with higher connectedness has not been investigated (Arabie and others, 1978).

Blockmodeling is especially designed to search for the "holes" or "gaps" in a network, and thus necessitates network data that are relatively "sparse," that is, with many zero (nonlink) entries. A block composed of zeros, indicating that no links occur, is called a "zeroblock." The basic approach in blockmodeling is to make these zeroblocks as large as possible by rearranging the rows and columns in a who-to-whom matrix.[49] A zeroblock has an average connectedness of zero, as there are no links in it. One can imagine, at one extreme, breaking down network data so there is only one individual in each block; there would be many zeroblocks (but the results would be meaningless, of course). At the other extreme, one can imagine putting all the individuals in the network into one big block (this too would be meaningless). The task of blockmodeling is to choose a cutoff point somewhere between these two extremes that maximizes the size of the zeroblocks while allowing as few "errors" (that is, nonzero entries or links) as possible in the zeroblocks. CONCOR can be adjusted to any given cutoff point. In fact, a succession of different cutoff points can be specified, to provide different sets of blocks. There is no standard convention as to what this cutoff should be; instead blockmodelers usually prefer to experiment with a succession of various cutoff levels, so as to break down the who-to-whom matrix into a series of finer and finer blocks. This approximation process stops when the researcher has obtained a set of blocks that fit his purposes and his understanding of the network data.

CONCOR yields (1) a graphic image of the blocks, and (2) a hierarchical clustering [50] of the individual members of the network that represents the blocks in the network structure. Once the blocks in a network are determined, other data are usually brought into the blockmodeling analysis. For example, it is customary to compute the average

[49] In the early days of blockmodeling, this permuting of rows and columns was done by hand in a trial-and-error procedure. Then a computer program for such matrix multiplication called "BLOCKER" was developed by Heil and White (1974) to search for true zeroblocks. BLOCKER demanded that the network analyst provide a hypothesis about the blockmodel, and then it sought to derive the blocks that had been expected from the network data. In recent years, the CONCOR computer program is used by almost all blockmodelers, rather than BLOCKER.
[50] "Hierarchical clustering" refers to the successive levels of blockmodel refinement, not to any kind of vertical structure in the network.

connectedness scores [51] for each block. Other characteristics of the individual members of each block are then determined to see how each block differs from others. For instance, Mullins and others (1977) computed the average publication records of the four blocks of biological researchers that were found in one invisible college. Similarly, we shall shortly present the percent of mothers' club members and of family planning adopters for each of the blocks in village A (Table 4–7).

Blockmodeling is one means of coping with information overload, by aggregating the individuals in a network into categories (blocks) on the basis of their structural equivalence. Then the personal and social characteristics of these blocks can be investigated to better understand the nature of networks. We stress that blockmodeling handles network multiplexity by analyzing the network structure for a set of individuals who provide linkage data for more than one communication topic.

An alternative procedure in using blockmodeling is to blockmodel the who-to-whom matrices for the same topic across various points in time. For instance, White and others (1976) blockmodel the sociometric responses from the 17 students in Newcomb's (1961) fraternity house (described in chapter 7) that were obtained at weekly intervals, so as to determine when the network stabilized.

Professor Ronald L. Breiger (1976b) at Harvard University performed a blockmodel analysis with the CONCOR program for the 39 women in village A for 10 different communication topics. Despite the fact (1) that nine other topics [52] in addition to family planning diffusion were included in the blockmodeling analysis, and (2) that we did not force the network links to be reciprocal, the resulting blockmodel (Figure 4–18) is amazingly similar to the communication structure obtained from NEGOPY (shown in Figure 4–10). Both CONCOR and NEGOPY found three blocks/cliques, containing identical individuals except for several minor differences.[53] And because direct factor analysis, smallest-

---

[51] Usually called "density" by most blockmodelers.

[52] These nine networks ("i" is the respondent and "j" is her dyadic link) are: (1) i gives information or advice about children's education, (2) i receives information or advice about purchasing clothes or furniture, (3) i gives information or advice about purchasing clothes or furniture, (4) i gives information about induced abortion, (5) i gives information or advice when a family member is ill, (6) i receives information or advice when a family member is ill, (7) i's husband talks most with j's husband, (8) i would seek j for information and advice about a new contraceptive, and (9) i talks most with j. The who-to-whom matrices for all ten network topics are very similar (chapter 7), especially (1) the "talks most with" topic and (2) the family planning discussion topic (which we have been analyzing throughout the present chapter).

[53] Individual #55 was dropped from the CONCOR analysis because she was an isolate on all 10 sociometric questions, and individual #53 was assigned with others in block II by CONCOR (Figure 4–18) to clique II (block I) by NEGOPY (Figure 4–10). The bridge links identified by NEGOPY appear as two of the three links that mar the zeroblocks in Figure 4–18.

TABLE 4–7. Characteristics of Respondents in Three Blocks and Eight Sub-Blocks in Village A.

Block/Sub-Block *	Number of Women	Member of Mothers' Club		Adopted Family Planning		Own TV Set		Attended Middle School	
		Number	Percent	Number	Percent	Number	Percent	Number	Percent
Block I	9	0	0	7	78	3	33	4	40
Sub-block Ia	(5)	(0)	(0)	(5)	(100)	(2)	(40)	(2)	(40)
Sub-block Ib	(4)	(0)	(0)	(2)	(50)	(1)	(25)	(2)	(50)
Block II	8	0	0	3	38	0	0	3	38
Sub-block IIa	(4)	(0)	(0)	(2)	(50)	(0)	(0)	(0)	(0)
Sub-block IIb	(4)	(0)	(0)	(1)	(25)	(0)	(0)	(3)	(75)
Block III	21	13	62	12	57	5	24	8	38
Sub-block IIIa	(8)	(6)	(75)	(6)	(75)	(4)	(50)	(5)	(62)
Sub-block IIIb	(4)	(3)	(75)	(1)	(25)	(0)	(0)	(1)	(25)
Sub-block IIIc	(4)	(3)	(75)	(3)	(75)	(0)	(0)	(1)	(25)
Sub-block IIId	(5)	(1)	(20)	(2)	(40)	(1)	(20)	(1)	(20)
Total	38 †	13	34	22	58	8	21	15	39

* Sub-block Ia includes individuals #2, #51, #52, #60, and #61; Ib includes #3, #47, #48, and #49; IIa includes #4, #53, #54, and #63; IIb includes #15, #56, #57, #58; IIIa includes #6, #10, #11, #13, #16, #18, and #59; IIIb includes #14, #19, #27, #45; IIIc includes #24, #28, #31, and #36; and IIId includes #22, #25, #29, #44, and #62.
† Individual #53 is not included in the blockmodeling of village A.

208

Figure 4–18.   The Results of the CONCOR Blockmodeling of Matrices for Ten Network Topics in Village A Are Three Blocks That Correspond Closely to the Three Cliques Identified by NEGOPY on the Basis of Family Planning Discussion.

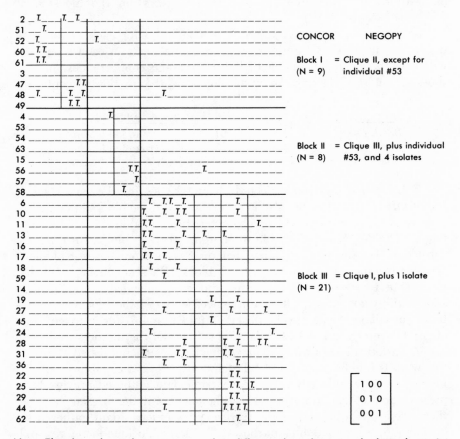

CONCOR	NEGOPY
Block I (N = 9)	= Clique II, except for individual #53
Block II (N = 8)	= Clique III, plus individual #53, and 4 isolates
Block III (N = 21)	= Clique I, plus 1 isolate

Note: The data shown here are somewhat different than the network data shown in Figures 4–9 and 4–10 for the 39 women in village A, because (1) these data are a composite for the 10 network topics, (2) individual #53 is an isolate in all 10 networks and is not shown here, and (3) these data were not forced to be reciprocal, so the matrix is nonsymmetrical. Nevertheless, the results from CONCOR and NEGOPY are very similar. Except for the two links in block I and one link in block II, there are perfect zeroblocks here.

Source: Breiger (1976b), adapted by permission.

space analysis, and SOCK also found a very similar communication structure to NEGOPY's, we conclude that all four methods yield about the same results, at least for village A (where the structure is admittedly rather clear-cut).[54] The CONCOR computer run cost about $5.00 (Breiger, 1976b), which is slightly higher than the computer costs for the other methods of network analysis.

CONCOR does not identify liaisons or bridges per se in the communication structure; they are shown as "errors" in the blockmodel diagrams (Figure 4–18).

Average connectedness scores were computed for each of the nine blocks in Figure 4–18 (as the number of actual links in each block, divided by the possible number of links). Average connectedness indices show that most of the links are within-block (with only three exceptions).

	BLOCK I	BLOCK II	BLOCK III
Block I	.22	.01	(rounded to zero)
Block II	0	.09	(rounded to zero)
Block III	0	0	.15

Table 4–7 shows four selected characteristics for the three blocks. CONCOR identified eight sub-blocks within the three blocks in village A, and we also show the sub-block characteristics in Table 4–7. One advantage of CONCOR is being able to compute the sub-blocks; in this case sub-block IIIa seems to be somewhat distinctive from the rest of block III (for instance, the members of sub-block IIIa seem to be somewhat more elite in socio-economic terms, and are somewhat more likely to adopt family planning). Other differences between the blocks and sub-blocks in village A can also be observed in Table 4–7; for instance, none of the 17 women in blocks I or II are members of the mothers' club.

A variety of uses of blockmodeling have been published. Most of this work is highly methodological, demonstrating the capabilities of this method of network analysis by reanalyzing data gathered previously in pre-blockmodeling days by earlier scholars. Until the present writing, there were no published works featuring sociometric data gathered especially for blockmodeling purposes. To date, blockmodeling research shows the utility of this tool in analyzing multinetwork data about scientific communication, a chism in a religious order, international relations (Snyder and Kick, 1979), change and stability in Newcomb's (1961) student residence, and work-related communication in the Hawthorne Plant of the Western Electric Company.

Burt (1978d) described a network analysis procedure somewhat comparable to blockmodeling in that "similar" individuals are classified into the same category in a who-to-whom matrix, and then the category's links with other categories are analyzed. The categorization utilized by Burt, however, is on the basis of proximity (measured by linkage distance

---

[54] Although for the network data on who i talks with more often, CONCOR found three blocks, while NEGOPY found five cliques.

as expressed in the minimum number of links between each pair of individuals in a system). Each category of one or more individuals is called a "role-set" by Professor Burt. The categorization is effectuated by a computer program called "STRUCTURE" (Project in Structural Analysis, 1977), which utilizes Johnson's (1967) hierarchical cluster analysis algorithm. Like blockmodeling, STRUCTURE categories individuals on the basis of one or more types of network links (for example, one or more different sociometric questions). The capacity of STRUCTURE is a 150×150 matrix, and up to nine different sociometric questions for these 150 individuals. Burt (1978d) illustrated his type of network analysis with data from 59 elite sociologists specializing in methodology and mathematical sociology. Not surprisingly (to any sociologist), Burt finds that the category of four social statisticians is of higher status than any of the other four clusters of elite sociologists.

OTHER NETWORK ANALYSIS TECHNIQUES

Many other network analysis techniques exist, in addition to the five approaches illustrated previously in this chapter. Here are six examples of other network analysis approaches that have been proposed.

1. Hubbel (1965) developed a clique-identification technique based on raising a who-to-whom matrix to successively higher powers (by squaring, cubing, etc. the matrix). The criterion for clique identification rests on a linkage distance measure of proximity; individuals are classified into a clique if they have a high degree of direct and/or one-step communication with other members of the clique.

2. Lin (1968, 1975, and 1976) and Guimarães (1970) developed a computer program ("Network Routine") that provides various indices of communication structure, although it is not intended to identify cliques. Data are input as 0's and 1's, and a linkage distance measure of proximity is constructed (by matrix multiplication).

3. Foster and Seidman (1978) developed a network analysis package that contains a variety of clique-identification procedures based on different proximity measures. The package can detect cliques on the basis of matrix multiplication (Luce and Perry, 1949), overlapping personal networks (Alba, 1973), and graph-theoretic techniques (Harary, 1969). So, as in the case of SOCK/COMPLT, a variety of network analysis tools are provided by Foster and Seidman's system.

4. CLIQUE is a clique-detection computer program, based on graph theory, that only inputs reciprocated links in binary form (that is, each link must be expressed as either a 0 or a 1). The CLIQUE program is running at the University of Essex, England (Alt and Schofield, 1975).

5. McQuitty (1957) developed a method of clustering by rearranging the rows and columns in a correlation matrix so that pairs of individuals with the highest correlations (these are the same input correlations as in smallest-space analysis) are adjacent.[55] The rearranging is done by hand, through visual inspection, to find the highest correlation in the matrix; the pair of individuals that this highest correlation indicates are most proximate are then moved together in the matrix. Then these two individuals' highest correlations are identified, and the individuals involved in these correlations (called "first cousins" by Professor McQuitty) are rearranged so that they are adjacent to the original pair of individuals. Then, second cousins, third cousins, and so on are identified and rearranged in the matrix. McQuitty's clustering approach does not allow either clique overlap or isolates; each individual is placed in a cluster (clique).

6. Peay (1974) developed a hierarchical clustering computer program that is similar to Johnson's (1967) approach, except that Peay allows clusters (cliques) to overlap.

Most of these network analyses are only running on the developer's computer; these approaches have not been widely utilized by network analysts. But their existence—and there are many more like them not described here—suggest the tremendous variety of ways to go about analyzing network data.

COMPARISON OF THE FIVE NETWORK ANALYSIS METHODS

To date, there have been relatively few comparisons of the advantages and disadvantages of two or more network analysis techniques, so that often a potential user does not know which method best fits his/her network problem. Nosanchuk (1963) compared four methods of clique identification, but only one of his four (direct factor analysis) is utilized very widely today. Lankford (1974) compared five network analysis methods for clique identification, including direct factor analysis, factor analysis of correlations, and a type of smallest-space analysis (not Lingoes'). On the basis of his use of these three methods with two data-sets (one was a 67-by-67 matrix of binary data, and the other was a 29-by-29 matrix with data on the strength of each link), Lankford concluded that both direct factor analysis and factor analysis of correlations were superior to smallest-space analysis (which required about twice as much computer time). Direct factor analysis and factor analysis of cor-

---

[55] Lankford (1975) concluded that McQuitty's clustering technique yielded similar cliques to that provided by direct factor analysis.

relations produced identical cliques, but the latter method displayed certain procedural advantages, leading Lankford to conclude: "Factor analysis of the correlation matrix remains the most efficient general method of clique identification."

Table 4–8 provides a comparision of the five network analysis methods utilized with the data from villages A and B in this chapter. While each of these methods has certain distinctive aspects in terms of proximity measures, outputs, and so on, they are all intended to determine the nature of the communication structure of a network.

We conclude from the present comparison of network analysis methods across our two data-sets (especially on the bases of Table 4–6) that *NEGOPY, direct factor analysis, smallest-space analysis, SOCK, and blockmodeling (with CONCOR) all produce very similar communication structures for the same network data.* This similarity of results from the five network analysis techniques suggests that they all perform about the same basic function, even though their measures of proximity, data-reduction procedures, and clique-identification mechanisms are quite different. In the case of CONCOR, the input data were especially different, consisting of matrices for nine other sociometric questions in addition to our basic sociometric question about family planning diffusion. Despite these differences, the communication structure of cliques (blocks) identified by CONCOR is remarkably similar to that from NEGOPY and the three other network analysis methods. Clearly, our results in this chapter lead to the conclusion that *the method of network analysis utilized is not very important in affecting the communication structure of cliques, bridge-links, connectedness, and so on that is obtained.* Interestingly, the similarity of results generally holds for village B, where the communication structure is not so clear-cut (there are many more bridge-ties between the cliques, and so clique boundaries are not so sharp), as well as for village A. The similarity of results from the five network analysis techniques for villages A and B is supported by two other comparative uses of these techniques.[56] As mentioned previously, Kim (1977b) found almost identical results from two types of network analysis, NEGOPY and smallest-space analysis, for the 69 women in Oryu Li village (chapter 1). In addition to the highly similar communication structure obtained by NEGOPY and by CONCOR for family planning

[56] Although not by the findings (1) of Wigand (1976) who used NEGOPY, a version of smallest-space analysis, and hierarchical clustering with data from 69 health agencies, or (2) of Bernard and others (1979), who utilized three methods of network analysis (direct factor analysis, blockmodeling with CONCOR, and Alba/Kadushin's COMPLT) with four network data-sets (ham radio operators, a college fraternity, office workers in a small research firm, and a university department). The three algorithms produced different numbers of cliques in each of the four networks; for example, COMPLT found two cliques, CONCOR four cliques, and direct factor analysis 10 cliques, among the office workers in the research firm.

TABLE 4–8. Comparison of Selected Methods of Network Analysis Using Communication Network Data from Two Korean Villages.

CHARACTERISTICS OF NETWORK ANALYSIS METHODS	METHODS OF COMPUTER NETWORK ANALYSIS				
	1. NEGOPY	2. Direct Factor Analysis with SOC MET	3. Smallest-Space Analysis (SSA)	4. SOCK and COMPLT	5. Blockmodeling with CONCOR
1. Outputs	1. Clique identification 2. Indices of communication structure (connectedness, integration, etc.)	1. Clique identification, with a measure (factor-loadings) of each individual's connection with each clique (factor)	1. Visual representation of the communication structure in which spatial distance indicates proximity	1. Clique identification on the basis of 3 proximity measures and 2 clustering techniques	1. Blocks (not identical with cliques because block members are not necessarily linked with each other) 2. Connectedness of each block
2. Maximum size of communication matrix	4,096 × 4,096 individuals and 32,767 links	200 × 200	100 × 100	9,999 × 9,999	Multiple matrices, each of about 100 × 100
3. Measure of proximity on which communication structure is analyzed	Communication proximity (the degree to which two linked individuals in a network have personal communication networks that overlap)	Linkage distance expressed as to whether or not a direct link exists for each possible dyad	Correlations indicating similarity of dyadic partners' personal network links and nonlinks	SIMMEL, the degree to which dyadic partners' personal network links and nonlinks overlap	Correlations of correlations, each indicating the similarity of dyadic partners' network links and nonlinks
4. Availability of the computer program	Very limited (about 9 U.S. universities)	Almost every university computer center in the U.S.	Many university computer centers in the U.S.	Very limited	Very limited, at Harvard University
5. Costs in computer time (for a 39-member village)	About $2.00	$1.90	$2.23	—	About $5.00

diffusion in village A (Table 4–6), rather similar results were also obtained by NEGOPY and CONCOR for a general sociometric question about whom each respondent talked with most often (Breiger, 1976b).

Despite this general similarity of communication structure that emerged from using the five methods of network analysis, perhaps we should enter a minor caveat about our present results: both villages A and B are relatively small-sized systems with only 39 members. Would the five network analysis methods also yield similar communication structures with larger systems? We don't know. But in Oryu Li, a village with almost twice as many respondents, NEGOPY and smallest-space analysis provided similar results (Kim, 1977b).

Even though the five network analysis methods yielded similar communication structures in villages A and B, other important differences between those methods affect which one might be best utilized with a particular data-set.

1. On the basis of *accessibility,* direct factor analysis is found at almost every university computer center in the United States, and at most academic computer centers around the world.

2. If the researcher wants to *inspect visually* the communication structure, smallest-space analysis is ideal in that the printout displays the individuals in two- (or three-) dimensional space, so as to facilitate drawing a sociogram. NEGOPY with NETPLOT (Lesniak and other, 1977) and SOCK/COMPLT with a Stromberg Datagraphics 4060 plotter can generate sociograms, but at a higher cost than SSA.

3. If the researcher has a *large-sized* network, NEGOPY and SOCK are far superior to the other network analysis methods in capacity.

4. If the researcher wishes to determine *multiplexity* across two or more network topics, blockmodeling with CONCOR should be utilized.

5. If the researcher wants to obtain *indices of communication structure* like connectedness, integration, and so on, NEGOPY seems to be advantageous, although other network analysis methods provide certain indices that NEGOPY does not; for example, direct factor analysis prints out a factor-loading of each individual on each clique, measuring the strength of the individual's relationship with each clique.

6. If the researcher wishes to identify the *communication role* of each individual in the network (liaison, bridge, isolate, etc.), NEGOPY is preferable.

Cost differences in running the five network analysis methods (Table 4–8) are fairly minor, although with larger-sized networks these cost differences might become more pronounced. All of the costs (at least for these two small networks) are relatively low, thus suggesting the feasibility of a multimethod strategy in which two or more network analysis techniques are used with the same data-set so as to uniquely combine their various special advantages. For example, one might utilize smallest-space analysis to obtain a two-dimensional printout of the individuals in a network on the basis of their proximities to each other, then compute NEGOPY to identify the clique boundaries in a nonarbitrary way, and superimpose the results on the two-dimensional printout from smallest-space analysis.

Or a researcher might successively utilize two or more of the network analysis methods with the same network data-set. For instance, one could utilize NEGOPY first with a large network of, say, 1,000 individuals. Each of the "bite-sized" cliques resulting from the NEGOPY run could then be analyzed with one of the other network analysis methods.

On the basis of our network analysis of villages A and B, we feel that *NEGOPY is generally the most appropriate network analysis method for studying communication networks because of its advantages (1) in handling larger-sized networks, (2) the indices of communication structure that it provides, (3) its capacity to identify individual communication roles, and (4) its unique basis on a measure of communication proximity.*

The major shortcomings of NEGOPY are (1) it does not printout a sociogram (unless the NETPLOT routine, or smallest-space analysis, is utilized with NEGOPY), and (2) it lacks widespread accessibility in university computer centers. The latter disadvantage would in large part be overcome if a version of NEGOPY could be developed to run on IBM computers, a task to which Professor Richards, and others, are currently addressing themselves.

The present discussion is perhaps a first step toward an eventual "user's guide" to network analysis, which would specify the common features and the unique advantages and disadvantages of each network analysis technique. Also needed is a Network Package for the Social Sciences, in which a variety of proximity measures and clique-identification procedures would be included. At present (1) Charles Alba and Richard Kadushin's SOCK/COMPLT network analysis system, and (2) Brian Foster and Stephen Seidman's (1978) system, are the closest approximations to such an NPSS. When, and if, such a computer package is available, it would encourage network scholars to utilize a multimethod approach to network analysis.

However, a methodological advance of even greater moment, in our opinion, would be progress toward improved measurement of communication network links.

SUMMARY

This chapter shows how network analysis identifies *communication structure*, defined as the differentiated elements that can be recognized in the patterned communication flows in a system. One particular method of network analysis, William D. Richards' NEGOPY, is described in some detail and compared with four other network analysis methods. All of the five network analysis techniques utilized in the present chapter are computer-based. Computers are necessary in network analysis because they (1) enable coping with the information overload caused by the great number of communication links that are present in most systems, (2) provide understanding of otherwise-hidden aspects of communication structure in a network, and (3) follow strict mathematical algorithms and thus help eliminate researcher subjectivity in identifying the communication structure in a network.

All network analysis techniques rest directly and fundamentally on their measure of *proximity,* the relative nearness of a pair of individuals to each other in a communication sense. Three main types of proximity measures have been utilized by network scholars: (1) *communication proximity,* the degree to which two individuals in a network have personal networks that overlap, (2) *linkage distance,* the number of links or steps in the shortest path joining two individuals, and (3) *correlational similarity,* the degree to which two individuals have like patterns of links and nonlinks. An individual's behavior is influenced both (1) by direct communication flows with another individual, and (2) by indirect flows with individuals with whom he does not share a direct communication relationship. We conclude (1) that a proximity measure should include both the direct link between two individuals as well as any indirect links they may have, (2) that measures of communication proximity can adequately be based upon first- and second-order personal communication networks, and (3) that a proximity index should measure only the degree of direct and indirect links between dyadic partners, but not their similarity of nonlinks with other individuals in their systems. When various measures of communication proximity, linkage distance, and correlational similarity have been correlated for the same data-set, similar but not identical results are obtained. So these indices all seem to measure the basic dimension of proximity.

Network data are almost always handled in the form of a who-to-whom matrix, rather than in sociograms. There are two ways to analyze network data in matrix form: (1) matrix multiplication (squaring the matrix, or raising it to higher powers), (2) matrix manipulation, rearranging the individuals in the rows and columns of a who-to-whom matrix so that communication dyads with greater proximity are as physically adjacent in the matrix as possible. Matrix multiplication is useful in measuring linkage distance, while matrix manipulation is preferable for computing communication proximity (as the degree to which two individuals in a network have personal networks that overlap).

The communication structure of a network is identified by the

NEGOPY computer program by sequentially reordering the individuals in a who-to-whom matrix. The analytical procedure for this reordering is accomplished simply by computing the mean of the identification numbers of the individuals with whom each respondent interacts. This mean score is a convenient approximation of which individuals probably belong together in cliques. The individuals in a system are gradually pulled together into cliques by a process of computing the mean identification numbers of others with whom each individual interacts, reordering the individuals in the who-to-whom matrix on the basis of their mean identification numbers computed from the new identification numbers of others with whom each individual interacts, and so on, until the ordering of individuals in the who-to-whom matrix no longer changes very much. The resulting communication structure can then be examined to identify cliques, bridges, liaisons, and so on.

Individuals are placed into *cliques* (defined as subsystems whose elements interact with each other relatively more frequently than with other members of the communication system) based on three criteria:

1. Each clique must have a minimum of three members.
2. Each clique member must have at least 50 percent of his/her links within the clique.
3. All clique members must be directly or indirectly connected by a continuous chain of dyadic links lying directly within the clique.

Once the communication structure of a network is identified, various indices of communication structure can also be computed at the individual, clique, and system level.

Identifying and understanding this communication structure is one of the main tasks of network analysis. Unfortunately, the concepts and indices utilized to analyze communication structure in past network analysis have been confusing and contradictory; we focus on four main concepts: connectedness, integration, diversity, and openness. At the individual level, we define (1) *individual connectedness* as the degree to which a focal individual is linked to other individuals in the system, (2) *individual integration,* the degree to which the members of an individual's personal communication network are linked to each other, and (3) *individual diversity,* the degree to which the members of an individual's personal communication network are heterogeneous in some variable. At the clique level, we utilize the concepts of (1) *clique connectedness,* the degree to which the cliques in a system are linked to each other, (2) *average clique connectedness,* the degree to which the average member of a clique is linked to other individuals in the clique, (3) *clique integration,* the degree to which the cliques linked to a focal clique are linked to each other, (4) *clique diversity,* the degree to which the cliques in a system are heterogeneous in some variable, and (5) *clique openness,* the degree to which the members of a clique are linked to others external to the clique. Two main concepts index communication structure at the system level: (1) *average system connectedness*, the degree to which the average member of a system is linked to other individuals in the system, and (2) *system openness*, the degree to which the members of a system are linked to others external to the system.

In this chapter, we compared the results of NEGOPY with four other methods of network analysis: (1) direct factor analysis of network links (*factor analysis* is a statistical procedure for clustering similar observations together on the basis of their common variance), (2) smallest-space analysis, developed by Professor James Lingoes at the University of Michigan, (3) SOCK/COMPLT, a system of network analysis procedures developed by Professor Richard D. Alba and Charles Kadushin at Columbia University, and (4) blockmodeling, a network analysis technique for obtaining the structure for two or more networks composed of the same individuals, computed by the CONCOR program, developed by Professors Harrison White and Ronald Breiger at Harvard University.

NEGOPY, direct factor analysis, smallest-space analysis, SOCK, and blockmodeling (with CONCOR) all produce very similar communication structures for the same network data from two Korean villages. So the method of network analysis utilized is not very important in affecting the communication structure of cliques, bridge-links, connectedness, and so on that is obtained. A network analyst can decide which network analysis technique to utilize on the basis of accessibility of the computer program, the size of the network that the program can handle, its ability to handle multiplexity, and whether the researcher needs to identify individual communication roles and obtain indices of communication structure. We conclude that NEGOPY is the most appropriate network analysis method for studying communication networks because of its advantages (1) in handling larger-sized networks, (2) the indices of communication structure that it provides, (3) its capacity to identify individual communication roles, and (4) its unique basis on a measure of communication proximity. The major shortcomings of NEGOPY are that (1) it does not printout a sociogram, and (2) it lacks widespread accessibility in university computer centers.

5 NETWORK VARIABLES IN EXPLAINING INDIVIDUAL BEHAVIOR

Network analysis is . . . an attempt to reintroduce the concept of man as an interacting social being capable of manipulating others as well as being manipulated by them. The network analogy indicates that people are dependent on others, not on an abstract society.

Jeremy Boissevain and J. Clyde Mitchell (1973, p. viii)

Every time that a social phenomenon is directly explained by a psychological phenomenon, we may be sure that the explanation is false.

Emile Durkheim (1950, p. 104)

The central theme guiding this chapter is how network analysis can improve our understanding of individual human behavioral change, over the understanding that could be achieved without considering network variables. In other words, we seek to answer the research question: How important are communication network variables in uniquely explaining individual-level behavioral change?

Evidence to help answer this question will be taken from a variety of investigations, using different research approaches and seeking to explain various types of individual behavior change. Our most clear-cut evidence about network effects comes from several studies of the adoption of family planning in Korean villages, which we shall feature later in this chapter.

We bring several kinds of evidence to bear on our basic research question about the importance of network variables in explaining individual behavior.

1. Comparisons of isolates versus nonisolates in a system.
2. Personal communication network effects on individual behavior.
3. The effects of cliques on the behavior of individual members.
4. System effects on individual behavior.
5. Studies of the strength of weak ties.
6. Threshold effects on individual behavior.

Back in chapter 3, in a section entitled "Do Networks Matter? Effects on Human Behavior," we concluded that *the behavior of an indi-*

vidual is partly a function of the communication networks in which the individual is a member. In the present chapter, we present a detailed review of the available evidence bearing on this statement.

Figure 5–1 depicts the main concern of this chapter, in comparison with chapters 6 and 7. Here we center on the right-hand side of this diagram: the effect of network variables (especially connectedness) on individual behavior change. We utilize independent variables at the individual (and personal communication network) level, clique level, and system level to predict the dependent variable of individual-level behavior change (Figure 5–2). In chapter 6, we move up from this dependent variable of individual-level behavior change to a dependent variable of behavior at the group or system level. And in chapter 7, we shift to the left-hand side of the diagram in Figure 5–1 to explain the dependent variable of who is linked to whom (that is, to study the antecedents of network variables).

Here in chapter 5 we follow a rough order of presentation, moving out from the individual to the personal network, the clique, and the system. "We are each at the center of a web of social bonds that radiate outward to the people whom we know intimately, those we know well, those whom we know casually, and to the wider society beyond" (Fischer and others, 1977, p. vii).

COMPARISON OF ISOLATES AND NONISOLATES

One type of evidence for the importance of network variables on individual behavior is to compare certain behavior of the individuals in a system that have no network links (the isolates) with those individuals who are linked to others. This comparison gives us a crude cut at the effect of an individual having network links; the continuous variable of individual connectedness is simply dichotomized into two categories of zero-connectedness versus some-connectedness.

As obvious and direct as this type of investigation would seem to be, a search of the network literature shows only one study that compared isolates and non-isolates: Roberts and O'Reilly (1978) found non-isolates were more satisfied with their jobs, more committed to their organization, and higher performers than were isolates. Their respondents were 579 officers and enlisted men in three U.S. Navy organizations. The researchers concluded: "Overall the picture is one of dysfunctional aspects for individuals who are not [connected] into organizational communication networks" (Roberts and O'Reilly, 1978).

In our 24 Korean villages of study, we identified 85 isolates (and

Figure 5–1. Paradigm of Network Variables and Behavior Change.

NON-NETWORK VARIABLES $\longrightarrow$ NETWORK VARIABLES $\longrightarrow$ BEHAVIOR CHANGE VARIABLES

1. Individual characteristics (for example, age, socio-economic status, etc.)

2. Characteristics of network links (for example, their homophily/heterophily and/or spatial distance).

3. System characteristics (for example, aggregated individual characteristics like average years of education, global characteristics such as the number of members in the system, and leader characteristics).

1. Who is linked to whom (at one point in time, and over time).

2. Connectedness.

3. Integration.

4. Diversity.

5. Openness.

1. Individual behavior change (for example, the adoption of a family planning innovation).

2. Group or system performance (for example, the development achievements of a village).

Note: In this chapter we utilize non-network and network variables to explain the dependent variable of individual-level behavior change; chapter 6 utilizes these same independent variables to explain group or system performance. Chapter 7 uses non-network variables to explain who is linked to whom, and the stability of these links over time.

Figure 5–2.   Independent Variables at the Network, Clique, and Personal Communication Network Levels Are Utilized to Predict Individual-Level Behavior Change.

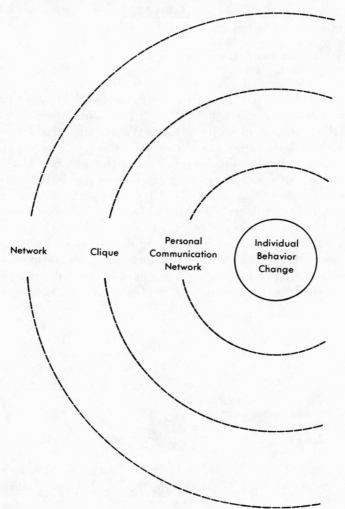

isolated dyads) among the 1,003 female respondents. These isolates are markedly different from the 918 nonisolates:

	ISOLATES AND ISOLATED DYADS	NONISOLATES
1. Percent who are adopters of family planning	10%	38%
2. Percent who are members of mothers' clubs	13%	48%

The isolates are only about one-fourth as likely to adopt (and currently use) family planning methods, and are only about one-third as likely to be members of mothers' clubs. These two variables are inter-related, as one of the objectives of mothers' clubs is to promote the adoption of family planning. We also investigated the personal/social characteristics of isolates and nonisolates, and generally found only minor differences. However, the homes of isolates were more likely to be located on the periphery of villages A and B and Oryu Li (the only three villages for which this spatial analysis of isolates was conducted).

As a further step in our analysis, we divided the 24 villages at the median level of adoption of family planning (35.6 perecnt) into "low-adoption" and "high-adoption" villages, in order to determine the effect of connectedness on the adoption of family planning by isolates and nonisolates:

	LOW-ADOPTION VILLAGES (N = 12)	HIGH-ADOPTION VILLAGES (N = 12)	ALL VILLAGES (N = 24)
1. Percent adoption of family planning by isolates and isolated dyads	3%	17%	10%
2. Percent adoption of family planning by nonisolates	29%	44%	38%

Only one of the 37 isolates in the low-adoption villages (3 percent) adopted, compared with 17 percent in the high-adoption villages; this difference suggests that the effects on individual adoption (1) of being isolated, and (2) of living in a low-adoption village, do not interact, but each has an independent effect on adoption.[1]

An individual's behavior depends in part on influences from his interpersonal environment. The individual's network links to others in

[1] Further evidence about the differences (in innovativeness) between isolates and nonisolates is described shortly from the Coleman and others (1966) study of the diffusion of an antibiotic drug in a local community of medical doctors.

his system represent the communication channels through which the norms of the system are conveyed to the individual, and thus these links have potential for affecting his/her behavior. If an individual is nominally a member of a system, as indicated by his/her membership in an organization or by residing in a community (like a Korean village), but if the individual is not linked to others in this system, the system has little direct effect on the individual's behavior. This situation represents a case in which the individual is "categorically-defined" in a network but evidently is not so "ego-defined" (Whitten and Wolf, 1974, p. 725), at least in terms of communication links. Isolates thus represent an interesting, albeit simple, test of the effect of network variables on individual behavior.

Our present conclusion, however, may be flawed by a serious tautology in our analysis (and that may exist in several of our other Korean data-analyses in this chapter) of the influences of network variables on individual adoption of family planning innovations: the network variables are measured with a sociometric question about family planning diffusion. Thus, one would expect that women who talked with others about family planning would more likely be adopters of this idea. However, the relationship of individual connectedness with adoption of the innovation was also supported when the connectedness measure was based on a sociometric question about who the respondent talked with most.[2]

PERSONAL NETWORK EFFECTS ON INDIVIDUAL BEHAVIOR

In this section, we mainly analyze the effect of the size of an individual's personal communication network on his/her behavior. This variable of size is one measure of our basic concept of *individual connectedness*, the degree to which a focal individual is linked to other individuals in the system. We expect that greater connectedness is positively related to behavior change. A similar relationship is expected with another network variable, *individual integration*, the degree to which the members of a focal individual's personal communication network are linked to each other. This concept is measured as the number of indirect (two-step) links between a focal individual and the members of his/her personal communication network, divided by the possible number of such links. The influence of an individual's personal communication net-

[2] In this analysis of villages A and B, we found that none of the isolates are adopters of family planning, as compared to 42 percent of the nonisolates. These results are comparable with those obtained when we measured isolates and nonisolates on the basis of the sociometric question about family planning diffusion.

work is expected to be stronger when this personal network is more highly integrated because these other individuals tend to form a consensus on norms and exert a consistent informal pressure on each other to conform to these norms (Bott, 1955 and 1957).

Perhaps the importance of personal communication networks as an influence on behavior was first recognized by the German sociologist Georg Simmel (1964), who published an influential article in 1922 entitled *"Die Kreuzung Sozialer Kreise,"* literally," "the intersection of social circles." Simmel felt that an individual's behavior could be understood if one knew his/her communication links to various others.

A personal communication network "forms a social environment from and through which pressure is exerted to influence [an individual's] behavior," said Boissevain (1974, p. 27). For example, Boissevain (p. 35) suggested the proposition that individuals with larger personal communication networks obtain more information from their networks, and hence are likely to respond to this informational input in their behavior. The information "strength" of individuals' personal communication networks varies on the basis of the nature of the networks (such as their diversity on certain relevant variables).

From this background of theoretical logic, we derive three propositions that are tested later in this section:

1. *Individual connectedness is positively related to individual behavioral change.*
2. *Individual integration is positively related to individual behavioral change.*
3. *Individual diversity is positively related to individual behavioral change.*

Past Research on Personal Network Effects on Behavior

Before we turn to our Korean data, let us review some illustrations from a variety of studies, all showing the effect of network variables on individual behavior. These researches are methodologically of three types:

1. Studies that compare the relative contribution of network variables with individual characteristics in explaining variance in some measure of individual-level behavioral change (such as innovativeness). From this type of research design, we shall conclude that network variables are approximately as important as individual characteristics in explaining the individual-level dependent variable, depending upon the specific nature of the variables that are measured. We can diagram this approach as follows:

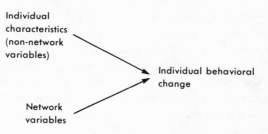

2. Researches in which network variables are investigated as they intervene or mediate between individual characteristics and the dependent variable of individual-level behavior change. Here we conclude that the network variables have important intervening effects.

3. Investigations in which the unique contribution of network variables is computed, usually with multiple correlation methods, in explaining the variance in individual-level dependent variables of behavioral change, while controlling on the contribution of individual characteristics variables. This research approach represents the "hardest" evidence of the importance of network variables.

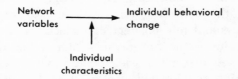

Network Variables Versus Individual Characteristics

Kincaid (1972) concluded from his investigation in a Mexico City slum that communication network variables (like individual connectedness, integration, and diversity) intervened between socio-demographic variables and the social psychological variable of efficacy (the perception by an individual that he/she has control over his/her future). Efficacy, in turn, was related to family planning knowledge and use. Kincaid (1972) stated that his findings demonstrated "the utility of constructing behavioral models which include communication network variables in conjunction with social and psychological variables."

Strong evidence for the importance of network variables in explaining the acquisition of instrumental information by Korean immigrants to

Honolulu was provided by Yum and Kincaid (1979). The dependent variable was the degree to which each respondent possessed information about the major social agencies in Honolulu providing assistance to immigrants. The investigators concluded "that the characteristics of the immigrants' communication networks [individual connectedness, integration, and diversity] are better predictors of information acquisition than the usual demographic variables [age, education, and occupation], except for English fluency."

One kind of evidence for the importance of network variables in explaining human behavior change comes from certain researches on the diffusion of innovations. The uncertainty that surrounds the evaluation of a new idea by an individual means that the individual's perception of the innovation is influenced not only by the concrete, material aspects of the innovation but also by the individual's peers, especially if they have already adopted the new idea (Burt, 1978a). Network influences on medical doctors' innovation decisions about a new antibiotic were especially strong, reported Coleman and others (1966, p. 32): "Apparently, testing at the expert level [by pharmaceutical companies and medical schools] cannot substitute for the doctor's own testing of the new drug; but testing through the everyday experiences of colleagues on the doctor's own level can substitute, at least in part."

Coleman and others found that medical doctors who had more friends and professional associates among other physicians (that is, the doctors with higher individual connectedness) were more innovative in prescribing the new antibiotic drug. Isolates were markedly less innovative in adopting the new drug than were nonisolates. However, the isolates were not completely unaffected by social networks; rather, the effect upon them just came considerably later in the diffusion process of the innovation. As a result of their being less connected to the local medical community, the isolated doctors were less responsive to the diffusion process in their system.

A variety of other diffusion investigations have found network variables, especially individual connectedness, related to innovativeness. For example, Guimarães (1972) found connectedness related to agricultural innovativeness in 20 Brazilian villages. Several investigations of educational innovativeness among schoolteachers in the United States found individal connectedness related to innovativeness (Lin, 1966; Allen, 1970). Sociometric isolates in less innovative high schools were especially low in innovativeness.

Individual connectedness, whether measured by a sociometric question about friendship or about seeking new information, was more highly related to adoption of an educational innovation among 272 faculty members at Ohio State University than a variety of individual measures of demographics, attitudinal variables, professional orientations, and scholarly productivity (Stern and others, 1976). Housewives in El Salvador with a high degree of individual connectedness with their village network were more innovative in adopting health and family planning innovations (Lin and Burt, 1975).

The generalization from past diffusion researches that individual connectedness is positively related to innovativeness may need to be qualified somewhat on the basis of the type of innovation. If the innovation is compatible with the norms of the system (a "normative innovation"), the generalization would be expected to hold because most of the information and influence about the innovation reaching the individual through his/her links would be positive. Most of the researches just cited focused on normative innovations (the family planning innovations that diffused in our Korean villages of study were also normative).

But if the innovation is disruptive to the norms of the system and if many of the interpersonal messages about the new idea are negative (such as about its undesirable side-effects from individuals that have discontinued its use), individual connectedness should be negatively related to innovativeness. Marginal individuals (like isolates) on the periphery of the network would then be most innovative (Burt, 1978a). An illustration of this point is provided by Becker's (1970) study of a normative innovation, measles immunization, and a non-normative innovation, diabetes screening, that diffused among the administrators of health departments. The latter innovation conflicted with medical and economic interests supportive of the health administrators. "Pioneer adopters of the [non-normative] innovation were identified as marginals, while earliest adopters of the [normative] innovation were found to be individuals with high [connectedness]" (Becker, 1970).

Intervening Effects of Network Variables

Network variables were found to be important in explaining voting in a national election in Israel by Burstein (1976). About one-third of the variance explained in voting behavior was added by inclusion of network variables (like the party preference of one's best friends) in the analysis, in addition to the variance explained by socio-demographic variables (like income). Further, the network variables also intervened between the background characteristics and voting behavior: "Much of the impact of background variables appears to operate through their impact on network ties to [political] parties" (Burstein, 1976). All in all, background and network variables seemed to be of approximately equal importance in predicting voting in Israel. Despite the general importance of networks in determining voting choice, most political research in the United States has ignored network variables (Sheingold, 1973; Eulau, 1978).

Network variables are related to academic success (final grades of middle-school students (Hurt and Preiss, 1978). Data were gathered from 118 U.S. students in four schools. Individual connectedness, measured sociometrically, was related to final grades in part through its intervening effect on communication apprehensiveness (the degree to which an individual was hesitant to participate in oral communication). The more apprehensive students remained quiet in the classroom or stuttered and stammered when the teacher asked them a question. The apprehensives had few network links with other students or with their teacher. As a result, only one apprehensive student received a final grade of "A" (her teacher liked her because she was quiet, even though they only communicated indirectly through other students).

Our review only disclosed these two past studies of the intervening effects of network variables. The results indicate that network variables seem to intervene between various independent variables and the dependent variables of behavior change. Thus, communication links act as a mediating influence in determining how particular antecedents affect behavior change.

The Unique Contribution of Network Variables

Chavers (1976) investigated individual characteristics versus network variables as predictors of educational innovativeness among 159 teachers at four boarding schools for American Indian high school students. Network variables and individual characteristics of the teachers together predicted about 47 percent of the variance in innovativeness, an increase of 11 percent over the individual variables alone. Thus the non-network variables were slightly more effective predictors than the network variables, but both sets of independent variables explained certain amounts of teacher innovativeness. The best single predictors among eight network variables were individual connectedness and clique integration, with the stability of individual links also of some importance.

Anomia and alienation are rather global concepts indicating an individual's perception of estrangement (that is, that those in power are unconcerned with the individual), unpredictability of the consequences of behavior, isolation in one's social relationships, powerlessness in achieving one's goals, and meaninglessness as a result of the deterioration of norms (Srole, 1956). One would expect that individuals lower in connectedness and integration would be more alienated and anomic; however, Parks (1977) found only weak relationships, perhaps because of the restrcted range in his data-set (his respondents were 58 undergraduates at Michigan State University). Nevertheless, Parks' (1977) research is pioneering in relating network variables to anomia and alienation; a large body of previous research on this topic mainly related only individual characteristics to anomia and alienation, generally with rather humdrum results.

A similarly pioneering attempt to introduce network variables into a major field of social psychological research is Alba's (1978) study of network diversity and prejudiced versus tolerant attitudes among a national sample of Americans. Instead of assuming (as in past research) that prejudiced attitudes are a function of social characteristics like social class and ethnicity, Alba (1978) investigated the relationship of the ethnic diversity of personal networks on tolerance. Although his measure of diversity (and of tolerance/prejudice) was limited (because Professor Alba was reanalyzing data gathered without a network approach in mind), Alba (1978) concluded that "subcultures cannot be understood apart from the networks which maintain them. To ignore the rootedness of each individual in a bed of concrete relationships to others is to fall willy-nilly into a view of the social world . . . of detached atoms moving randomly in relation to one another."

Alba's investigation, like the Parks (1977) study of anomia/alienation discussed previously, suggests the potential richness of introducing the network analysis paradigm into previous research fields that have reached an impasse in explaining a dependent variable by using mainly social characteristics of the individual. Although the full potential of this research strategy of incorporating network variables, and thus moving to another dimension on the data-cube (chapter 3), has not yet been demonstrated empirically, it offers an opportunity to rejuvenate now stale fields of behavioral research. Network variables may be able to explain uniquely additional variance in dependent variables, that has not been previously explained by variables measuring individual characteristics. But this potential has not yet been well established.

The results of past research on the unique contribution of network variables in explaining behavior change is a somewhat mixed bag; there are few such studies, and their findings do not clearly indicate whether network variables make an important, unique contribution. More clear-cut evidence is provided by our Korean data-set.

Effects of Personal Communication Networks in Korea

How do our Korean respondents' personal networks explain their decisions to adopt (and/or discontinue) the innovation of family planning, over time? Figure 5–3 illustrates how an increasing percentage of respondent #31's (in village A) personal network adopted family planning from 1969 to when she adopted in 1972. An individual is more likely to adopt family planning if a larger proportion of her personal network consists of individuals who have adopted previously. The percentage of the personal network made up of family planning adopters (a measure of diversity) was calculated for each of the 39 respondents in village A and in village B for each of the ten years (1964 to 1973) covered by our

Figure 5–3.   An Illustration of Respondent #31's (in Village A) Adoption of Family Planning as the Percentage of Adoption Increased in Her Personal Communication Network from 1969 to 1972.

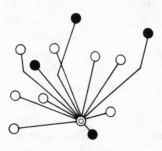

1969

Personal Network
Adoption 4/12 = 33%

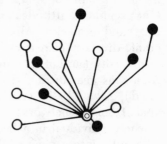

1970

Personal Network
Adoption 6/12 = 50%

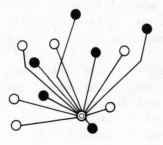

1971

Personal Network
Adoption 6/12 = 50%

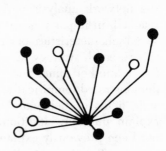

1972

Personal Network
Adoption 8/13 = 62%

Source: Rogers and others (1976c). Adapted with permission of The East–West Communication Institute, copyright © 1976.

survey data.[3] The personal networks for each year were adjusted to exclude women who were not yet married (and who were thus not usually resident in the village, nor likely to be regarded as adults). The cumulative data are categorized by the percentage of the respondents' personal networks who have adopted family planning. Figure 5–4 shows that of the women who have personal networks with 10 percent adopters or less, only 10 percent adopt family planning themselves. There is a steady increase in this percentage of women adopting as the proportion of their

[3] The measure of network diversity used here is a simple percentage. An improved measure might be a weighted proportion in which we would assign greater weight to links on the basis of their communication proximity.

Figure 5–4.   Percentage of Eligible Women Adopting Family Planning in Relationship to the Percentage of Their Personal Network Who Have Adopted Family Planning in Villages A and B in Korea.

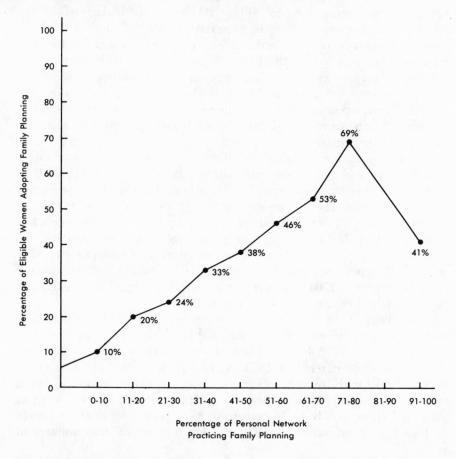

Percentage of Personal Network
Practicing Family Planning

Source: Rogers and others (1976c). Adapted with permission of The East–West Communication Institute, copyright © 1976.

personal networks who have adopted rises, reaching a maximum of 69 percent among women who have personal networks with 71 to 80 percent adopters; this trend is stronger and more consistent in village A than in village B, where family planning diffusion was less successful. We conclude that *an individual is more likely to adopt an innovation if more of the individuals in her personal network have adopted previously.* This is hardly a surprising conclusion, but it again suggests the potential of network variables in providing fuller understanding of the diffusion process.

The average percentage of personal networks adopting for all eligible women was calculated for each year from 1964 to 1973 in villages A and

B. The relationship of changes in the percentage of adopters in personal networks to the overall adoption percentage of the village was examined over time by plotting the two curves in comparison (Figure 5–5a for village A and Figure 5–5b for village B). For a particular year, if the mean percentage of adopters in personal networks is higher than the overall adoption percentage in the village, this suggests that the adopters are consulted more frequently than average and presumably have greater influence than the average village woman. On the other hand, if the mean percentage of adopters in personal networks is lower than the overall adoption percentage in the village, the adopters are consulted less frequently than average and presumably have less influence than the average village woman.

In village A, the average percentage of personal networks adopting was 20 percent in 1964, rising gradually to 48 percent in 1971 and then more steeply to 67 percent in 1973. The only declines were minor slumps in 1965 and 1969. These decreases do not represent an actual fall in the numbers practicing family planning (in fact, in 1965 there was one additional adopter), but are due rather to the arrival of new women in the village through marriage. The rate of family planning adoption roughly parallels the curve of changes in the personal networks, rising gradually from 14 percent in 1964 to 38 percent in 1968, leveling off until 1971, and rising rapidly thereafter to 56 percent in 1973.

In village B, by contrast, the average percentage of personal networks who have adopted family planning rises from 11 percent in 1964 to 37 percent in 1967, but then falls sharply to 18 percent in 1968, and rises again to 28 percent in 1973. As in village A, the adoption curve rises and falls with the percentage of personal networks adopting, rising from 9 percent in 1964 to 34 percent in 1967, dropping to 14 percent in 1969, and rising slowly to 27 percent in 1973. The drop in these curves in 1968 is due primarily to the increasing number of discontinuers in village B.

In both villages, adopters have a higher percentage of their personal network adopting than do nonadopters. The fact that the average percent of personal networks adopting family planning in village B is lower than the percentage of overall village women adopting in 1967–1969 indicates that adopters were consulted less frequently and presumably had less personal influence than the average women in these years. This is still true of village B for 1973, at the end of our ten-year diffusion period of study.

We would expect this to result in a slower rate of adoption within the village (as indeed occurred in village B). In village A, women high in personal influence tended to adopt first, and this appears to have hastened the adoption of family planning throughout the village. In general,

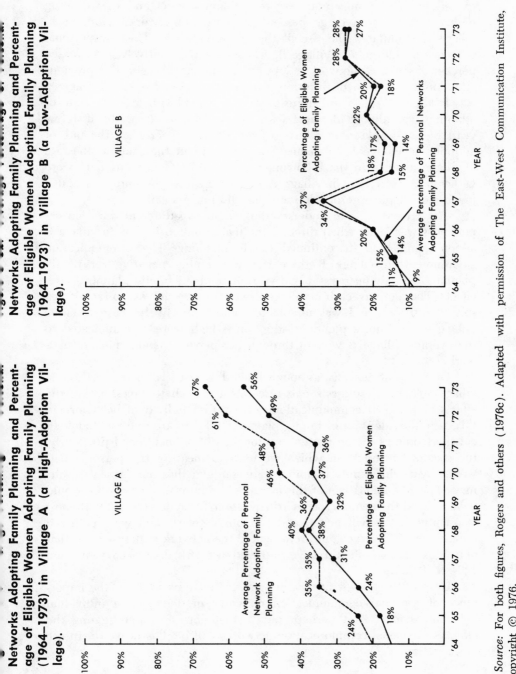

Networks Adopting Family Planning and Percentage of Eligible Women Adopting Family Planning (1964–1973) in Village A (a High-Adoption Village).

Networks Adopting Family Planning and Percentage of Eligible Women Adopting Family Planning (1964–1973) in Village B (a Low-Adoption Village).

VILLAGE A

VILLAGE B

Average Percentage of Personal Network Adopting Family Planning

Percentage of Eligible Women Adopting Family Planning

Percentage of Eligible Women Adopting Family Planning

Average Percentage of Personal Networks Adopting Family Planning

YEAR

YEAR

Source: For both figures, Rogers and others (1976c). Adapted with permission of The East-West Communication Institute, copyright © 1976.

235

the adoption of family planning by opinion leaders and the resulting higher figures for average percent of personal networks adopting in village A stimulated the rise of the adoption curve. The low personal influence of adopters in village B, reflected in the relatively low average percent of personal networks adopting, means that the effect of previous adoption on subsequent diffusion was much less (in any given year).

In the less successful diffusion village, called village B, the rate of adoption was almost identical with that in village A for the first few years of family planning diffusion from 1964 to 1967. Then the rate of adoption in village B "plateaued," and was about the same as the rate of discontinuance in the following years to 1973 (when our data were gathered).[4] However, in village A there were few discontinuers and a much more rapid rate of adoption that did not plateau.

The crucial year in understanding these two different diffusion experiences was 1968, when three of the main opinion leaders in village B adopted and then discontinued family planning. The communication environment in village B thereafter was highly negative for family planning, containing many negative rumors about family planning side-effects. The mothers' club in village B was not very active (in fact, it dissolved in 1975), and was unable to combat effectively these negative influences on family planning adoption, which were communicated to the average village B woman through her personal communication network.

Our present analysis, although limited to just two of our 24 Korean villages of study, suggests one research approach to investigating the effects of personal communication networks on individual behavior (in this case, the adoption of family planning). There are two methodological shortcomings of the present approach: (1) as mentioned previously, the sociometric question which we used to measure the personal networks dealt with family planning diffusion, and thus our present results may in part be an artifact of this measure (an improved procedure would have utilized the general socometric question "Who do you talk with most frequently in this village?"), and (2) our network data were gathered only in our 1973 survey, and represented the network structure as of that date (instead, we should have gathered network data each year from 1964 to 1973).

Despite these two caveats, our present analysis suggests the importance of personal communication networks in determining individual behavior change. And perhaps our methodology for investigating the effects of personal communication networks will be illustrative for future investigation.

---

[4] Figures 4–10 and 4–11 in our previous chapter show the rate of adoption and of discontinuance by year from 1964 to 1973 in village A and village B.

EFFECTS OF CLIQUES ON INDIVIDUAL BEHAVIOR

One means through which an individual's network links influence his/her behavior is through the cliques to which the individual belongs. If membership in the clique is important to the individual, the clique has potential for influence on the individual's decisions and actions. The general picture that emerges from past network studies, several of which were conducted with adolescents, shows that cliques influence individual behavior change. One analytical approach has been to study deviants from clique norms.

The role of cliques in reinforcing and supporting political deviants was investigated by Finifter (1974), in an unusual research design. Interviews were conducted with all of the members of 24 work groups (ranging from 10 to 45 members) in the large automobile factories in the Detroit area. These cliques were very heavily Democratic in their political orientation; for example, 82 percent of the auto workers voted for Kennedy over Nixon in the 1960 presidential election. The laborers belonged to the United Auto Workers, a union which actively supported the Democratic Party. Yet some members in each of the 24 work cliques were Republicans. How did these political deviants escape the overwhelmingly Democratic group influences? One method was to withdraw from political discussions with friends outside of the factory (the entire Detroit area is strongly Democratic). But within the factory, the Republicans were closely integrated into the work group, where they had more friends and chose attitudinally similar friends. Thus, the politically homophilous clique was a refuge for the Republican blue-collar workers.

Kandel (1973) found that peer influences through cliques were particularly important in influencing high school students to smoke marijuana. Peer influences were stronger than parental influences, but if both peers and parents were drug-users, a high school student was especially likely to smoke grass. Such network influences on individual behavior were even more important for marijuana use than for smoking cigarettes and drinking alcohol. Presumably the more deviant and taboo the behavior, the more important the network influences from cliques.[5]

Adolescents are relatively more peer oriented than children or adults, and so we would expect cliques to be especially influential in high school. Coleman (1961) found very strong clique effects in influencing teenagers' behavior in 10 Illinois high schools (we shall return to his study in a later section).

Previously, in chapter 3, we discussed Alexander's (1964) study of

---

[5] Andrews and Kandel (1979) found that attitudes toward marijuana were less effective predictors of using marijuana at a future time than were influences from an adolescent's peer network.

the effect of high school cliques on their members' drinking of alcohol. The cliques were very uniform on drinking behavior; most cliques consisted of all drinkers or of all teetotalers. In the nine cliques where one member deviated from the clique norm on drinking, the deviant had a low degree of connectedness with the clique, as one might expect. If this one-shot sociometric survey had been longitudinal in design, we would predict (1) that these deviants would drop out and join another clique with the opposite norm, or else (2) that the deviant would change his drinking behavior so as to conform to the norm of his clique.

The past researches reviewed here suggest that cliques seem to have an effect on the behavior of their individual members. Whether the uniformity of individual behavior among clique members results (1) from the initial selection of clique members, (2) from the group pressures on individual members' behavior, and/or (3) from dropping deviant members of a clique, is an issue that we shall explore in chapter 7.

"Rediscovering the Clique"

Today it is well established in behavioral science that much human behavior change results from interpersonal influence from an individual's close friends. Prior to the 1940s, however, the conventional wisdom of sociologists and other social scientists was that such tight-knit groups as the family and community were on the decline, and that the mass media were strong, direct influences on behavior change.

This model of behavior change was called the "hypodermic needle model" (or the "bullet theory"); it postulated that the mass media had direct, immediate, and powerful effects on a mass audience (Rogers with Shoemaker, 1971, p. 203). This version of stimulus-response behavior "pictured the mass media as a giant hypodermic needle, pecking and plunging at a passive audience" (Rogers with Shoemaker, 1971, p. 204). Mass society was conceived as a mass of disconnected, atomized individuals; personal contacts were thought to be of waning importance.

But this line of thought underwent a radical change because of a study of the 1940 presidential election by Professor Paul Lazarsfeld and others (1944) at Columbia University. This inquiry was designed with the hypodermic needle model in mind, and was sponsored by one of the largest mass media corporations in the United States. Data were gathered from panels of voters in Erie County, Ohio, each month for six months leading up to the election. In each interview the respondent was asked which candidate he intended to vote for; if a change in voting intentions from the previous month was reported, the respondent was asked what communication sources/channels led to the change. Voting was assumed to be an individual act.

To the surprise of the researchers, only one of their hundreds of respondents indicated a voting intention change due to the mass media. All of the other respondents said their change occurred due to interpersonal contacts from friends, neighbors, work associates, and kin. This finding came as something of a shock to the researchers. Lazarsfeld and others (1948) postulated an indirect role for the media in a "two-step flow of communication": the mass media directly contacted opinion leaders in society who then passed this information along via interpersonal channels to their followers.

The impact of the Erie County study was to put people back into the mass communication process, to recognize the effect of network links in changing individual behavior. Although Lazarsfeld and others (1948) did not gather sociometric data, their study was followed up by their Columbia University colleagues in a series of network investigations (Katz and Lazarsfeld, 1955; Coleman and others, 1966) that (1) further explored the role of opinion leaders in the two-step flow of communication, and (2) established the importance of cliques in individual behavior change.

Other rediscoveries of cliques were occurring at about the same time; for instance, Harvard University scholars were finding in the Hawthorne plant of the Western Electric Company (near Chicago) that cliques of work associates were a major influence on workers' production rates. Interpersonal relations were belatedly recognized as important in situations that were formerly conceptualized as strictly formal and atomistic.

The rediscovery of cliques by Lazarsfeld and others (1948) led to a paradigm shift in the behavioral sciences; researchers could no longer afford to ignore interpersonal links in their attempts to explain voting behavior, worker productivity in factories, and the diffusion of innovations. But specific research methods for analyzing such communication networks had to await the 1970s.

SYSTEMS EFFECTS ON INDIVIDUAL BEHAVIOR

Systems effects are the influences of a system's structure on the behavior of individual members of the system. As a simple illustration of systems effects consider two Korean women. Both are illiterate, married, have two children, and are aged 29. The husbands of both women are high school graduates, who operate farms of two acres. Neither are isolates in their village network. One might expect that both women would be about equally likely, or unlikely, to adopt family planning.

But the women are different in one crucial respect: they live in different villages, one in village A and one in village B. We have shown previously (chapter 4) that the rate of adoption is 57 percent in village A, and 26 percent in village B. Obviously, these two villages represent quite different communication environments for family planning behavior. Certainly, the social structure and the communication structure of these two villages will have a different effect on the family planning decisions of the two women, who are equivalent in their personal characteristics.

Investigating just how systems influence the behavior of their individual members is a rather complicated business. One of the complications is that the individual is also a member of the system, and hence represents one part of the whole whose influence on the part is being investigated. This part–whole problem is troublesome when computing characteristics of the system, which are then utilized to explain the behavior of individual members of the system. These kinds of system variables, constructed as the average or variance of the characteristics of individual members of the system, are called "aggregate" variables; an example is the average years of education of all the female respondents in a Korean village. Such an aggregate variable for the system might be expected to affect an individual's behavior because the individual talks with her fellow villagers, and so is influenced by their aggregated characteristics.[6] An illiterate in a village of high school graduates is different from an equally illiterate woman in a village of illiterates.

A second type of system variable is called a "global" variable in that it is a characteristic of the system, rather than an aggregation of its members' individual characteristics. An example is whether a village's mothers' club is active or not. Another illustration is whether a family planning clinic is located in the village, nearby, or at a distance.

Our literature search indicated few studies of systems effects, other than several researches on village effects on the adoption of innovations. One exception is Coleman's (1961) study of the systems effects of high schools on student academic achievement. This network study in nine Illinois high schools showed how the adolescent subculture was a strong deterrent to academic achievement (Coleman, 1961, p. 265). The boys in each school named as the best athletes and as most popular with girls were members of the "leading clique" (that is, the highest-prestige clique), as were the girls in each school who were named as best dressed and as most popular with boys. Boys and girls named as best students were not likely to belong to the leading clique in a school. Athletes were relatively more visible than scholars. The norms of the nine high schools on athletics over scholarship were conveyed to the average student by the clique structure of the school, in which the star athlete was on top. Coleman (1961) discusses the dysfunctional aspects of this antischolarly norm for U.S. education.

---

[6] The investigator must be cautious in interpreting research results about systems effects so as to avoid the "ecological fallacy" of mixing levels of analysis between the individual and the system (Robinson, 1950; Hauser, 1970). There is a vast social science literature dealing with the issue of moving up or down from one level of unit of analysis to another.

Several previous studies have analyzed the effects of village systems on the individual-level adoption (1) of agricultural innovations—Saxena (1968) in India and Davis (1968) in Nigeria—and (2) of family planning innovations—Anker (1977) in India, Freedman (1974) in several nations, and Hong (1976) in Korea. These investigations mostly utilized aggregate variables, and unfortunately did not include network variables. This lack is a major limitation in assessing the predictive power of village systems on individual behavior because the systems characteristics presumably have their influence on individual behavior through the communication links of the individual with his/her fellow villagers. We have already shown in a previous section that villages or cliques have less effect on their nominal members who are isolates. Individual connectedness is one means through which cliques and systems affect their members' behavior.

Kim and Palmore (1978) analyzed network data from 808 respondents in 11 Korean villages about the diffusion of family planning. Their 13 network variables included individual connectedness and individual integration, plus a special type of individual connectedness computed as the number of links to others who had adopted family planning. Fourteen individual variables explained about 34 percent of the variance in adoption, while the 13 network variables explained 8 percent.

Lee (1977) analyzed the data from the 1,003 women in 24 Korean villages in terms of three types of independent variables related to individual adoption of family planning.

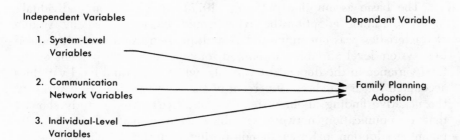

The data were first analyzed by examining zero-order correlations between each independent variable with the dependent varable. The results showed that individual-level variables were more strongly predictive of adoption than were system-level variables. Sixteen of the 25 individual-level variables, as against 12 of the 25 system-level variables, were correlated with the dependent variable (at a level significantly different from zero). Six individual-level variables had coefficients higher than any of the system-level variables: husband–wife communication about family planning, family planning field-worker contact, number of living sons, husband–wife communication about the number of children, membership in the mothers' club, and family planning knowledge.

Step-wise multiple regression analyses of both selected individual-level and system-level variables showed that three individual-level variables accounted for 18 percent of the total variance in family planning adoption: (1) husband–wife communication about family planning, (2) number of living sons, and (3) family planning field-worker contact. Only one system-level variable survived the step-wise regression analysis, adding only 1 percent to the explained variance in family planning adoption.

When communication network variables were added to the individual-level and system-level variables in a step-wise regression analysis, individual connectedness was the strongest single predictor of the dependent variable (accounting for 16 percent of the variance). Individual integration was the third best predictor, adding 3 percent to the explained variance (beyond the best individual-level predictor, husband–wife communication about family planning).

The multiple regression analysis demonstrated that individual-level independent variables accounted for 19 percent of the total variance, while system-level independent variables accounted for 2 percent of the total variance in family planning adoption. Communication network variables (individual connectedness and individual integration) explained 20 percent of the variance. The three sets of variables combined accounted for a total of 28 percent of the variance in family planning adoption.

The basic assumption of Lee's (1977) study, that an individual's family planning adoption behavior would be influenced by system characteristics, was not supported. A multiple regression analysis showed that system-level variables accounted for only about 2.5 percent of the total variance in the dependent variable, while individual-level variables accounted for as much as 19 percent of the total variance. In contrast to the negative finding about systems effects, Lee's (1977) study showed that communication network variables were associated with family planning adoption in Korea, demonstrating a substantial effect on adoption over and above the individual-level and system-level variables. One interpretation of these results is that system norms influence individual behavior through the individual's network links. This viewpoint was stated by Granovetter (1974, p. 4), who pointed out "the enormous, though often unnoticed, constraint placed on individuals by the social networks in which they find themselves." Further, Granovetter (1974, p. 98) noted: "Personal contacts are used simultaneously to gather information *and* screen out noise, and are, for many types of information, the most efficient device for so doing."

"To understand the individual in society, we need to understand the fine mesh of social relations between the person and society; that is, we must understand social networks" (Fischer and others, 1977, p. vii). Thus, "Network analysis . . . bridges the gap between individual and aggregate models of social life" (Fischer and others, 1977, p. 28).

THE STRENGTH OF WEAK TIES

Previously, in chapter 3, we reviewed the strength-of-weak-ties theory, based on the work of Granovetter (1973) and Liu and Duff (1972).[7] The general proposition summarizing this research is that: *The informational strength of communication links is inversely related to the degree (1) of proximity, and (2) of homophily in the dyad.* Or, in other words, information reaches a larger number of individuals, and transverses a greater social distance, when passed through weak ties rather than strong (Granovetter, 1973).

Each individual operates in his/her particular communication environment for any given topic, consisting of a number of friends and acquaintances with whom the topic is discussed most frequently. These friends are usually (1) highly homophilous (or similar) with the individual, and with each other, and (2) most of the individual's friends are friends of each other, thus constituting an interlocking network. This homophily and individual integration facilitates effective communication, but it acts as a barrier to prevent new ideas from reaching the individual. So there is not much informational strength in an interlocking network; needed are some heterophilous ties to the network from external sources, to give it openness. These weak ties enable information to flow from clique to clique via liaisons and bridges. The weak ties provide cohesive power to the total network.

Network analysis of the diffusion of the IUD in the Philippines demonstrated this strength of weak ties: the innovation spread most easily within interlocking cliques, among housewives of very similar socio-economic status (Liu and Duff, 1972). But heterophilous flows were necessary to link these cliques; usually these weak ties connected two women who were not close friends, and enabled the innovation to travel from a higher-status to a somewhat lower-status housewife. So a few heterophilous communication links in a network were a structural prerequisite for effective diffusion of the innovation.

[7] These two sets of authors independently discovered the strength of weak sociometric ties, and published articles with almost identical titles within a few months of each other in 1972–1973, although approaching the issue in somewhat different ways.

"The Search for an Abortionist"

The strength of weak ties is illustrated by Lee's (1969) study of women's search for an abortion, a real-life search process that is strikingly parallel to the hypothetical small world problem, described previously. Lee's investigation was conducted prior to the legalization of abortion by the U.S. Supreme Court in 1973, and abortion-seekers often tried several unproductive paths to an abortionist before one was found. The ultimately successful path to an abortion varied among Lee's respondents from one to seven links, with an average of five. The first attempt in searching for an abortionist was often with intimate friends in interlocking personal networks. Evidently, the female abortion-seekers were unaware of the proposition that strong ties with homophilous others are generally ineffective routes to new information.

The pressure to locate an abortionist within the limited time period of up to three or four months eventually led a woman to contact someone she did not know very well, but who she felt might possess the necessary information. Respondents with relatively larger and less integrated personal networks were more successful in finding an abortionist in fewer links.

Once a woman found an abortionist, she then became an important channel for other women. During the four years following her illegal abortion, the average respondent in Lee's study was contacted for help by 200 others. Thus, a vast underground network of interpersonal communication channels sprung up for abortion-seekers. Certain women that Lee called "abortion information specialists" were perceived by others as likely to be useful.

Abortion is a taboo topic, leading to initial search through strong ties. Most of Lee's (1969) respondents had to learn gradually through a trial-and-error process about the strength-of-weak-ties proposition.

Strong (proximate) links are not irrelevant for all purposes. They are unduly limited as a channel for new information, but they may be important as a means of influence and control over the individual's behavior. Epstein (1961) suggests that radial personal networks, which are usually larger in size, less integrated, and characterized by greater heterophily and diversity, are informationally rich (as the strength-of-weak-ties theory would imply). But interlocking personal networks, which are smaller, more integrated, and less diverse, play an important role in influencing individual behavior through communication with trusted peers and by the fear of gossip.

The role of weak and strong ties in how individuals sought psychiatric treatment was investigated by Horwitz (1977). The strong ties acted as "preventive medicine" in that individuals embedded in well integrated personal communication networks were less likely to need psychiatric treatment. Their network partners seemed to act as psychiatrist substitutes. Weak ties provided communication channels through which individuals were referred to formal psychiatric agencies; the function of weak ties was as an information-exchange, while the strong ties provided social control and support.

"The Strength of Strong Ties: *Palancas* in Mexico"

Most social science is "made in the United States," which unfortunately means that many theories of human behavior change may be culture-bound. This limitation may exist for the theory of "the strength of weak ties." In chapters 2 and 3 we concluded, on the basis of Granovetter's (1973) original formulation of this theory and of several researches, that the information-exchange potential in communication dyads in negatively related to their degree of proximity. Thus, the "strength" of "weak" ties is an information-exchange potential in low-proximity dyads.

Evidence for this theory was obtained by Granovetter (1973) from an investigation of how a sample of individuals in Newton, a Boston suburb, obtained information leading to their getting a new job (chapter 2). Close friends were relatively unimportant as sources of job information; they seldom knew of positions that were news to Granovetter's respondents. More important were scant acquaintances, individuals who were only weakly tied to the respondent.

The weak-ties theory may be an apt explanation of the flows of job information in the United States. But it doesn't work in Mexico. One of the authors of the present book collected a number of case studies on how individuals secured jobs in Mexico. In very few cases were weak ties involved. Usually, it was exactly the opposite. *Strong* ties were crucial in getting a job. The explanation for this contradiction with the weak ties theory lies in two important cultural differences between the United States and Mexico: (1) the nature of the employment process, and (2) the quality of interpersonal relationships.

In the United States it is assumed that an employer decides that he needs to hire someone in a specific position; usually a written job description is publicized, applications from qualified candidates are sought, they are interviewed, and their qualifications are evaluated by the personnel department in the employing company, with one applicant finally selected. Here, information-exchange is much more important than influence in the decision-making process. But in Mexico, the selection of the new employee rests much more on influence than on information. Perhaps, on the average, there are more qualified individuals available for any given job, as Mexico had an unemployment rate of almost 50 percent in the late 1970s (in contrast, the United States had an official unemployment rate of 5 or 6 percent). Thus, the Mexican job market is one of few "fisherman" and many, many "fish."

In any event, the typical employment process in Mexico goes something like the following. Start with an individual seeking employment, who perhaps has recently graduated from a Mexican university or returned from study abroad. This job-seeking individual goes to one or several companies in which he has *"palancas"* (literally, "levers" or individuals with whom he has very proximate relationships or who owe him a favor from a previous exchange). A *palanca* may be an uncle, or close friend of one's father, a good social friend, or someone who was helped previously when that individual was in need. The job-seeker activates the *palanca* to give him a job in his organization. If no such position exists (as is sometimes the case), one may even be created that is more or less appropriate for the job-seeker.

Following are some not untypical cases of how jobs are obtained in Mexico.

Case #4: Miguel G., after spending five years in a correctional institution for delinquents, was released on parole. His sponsor, a young Mexican woman who had supervised him in a therapy group in the correctional institution, approached her best friend's husband about hiring Miguel G. as an accountant in his import–export company. This potential employer contracted for part-time accounting services, and felt he could hire Miguel G. to do his company's accounting work at a lower cost. But he was concerned whether he could trust Miguel's honesty, on the basis of his delinquency record. Miguel's sponsor's father, who owned a steel factory and was an important customer of the import/export company, was convinced by his daughter that Miguel had been fully rehabilitated. So Miguel was hired on an initially provisional basis. The *palanca*-type favor was partly in exchange for a previous obligation to the steel magnate.

Case # 12: Cecilia H. graduated from a Mexican university with a degree in communication research, and then searched for employment for about a year while she completed her thesis research. Her former professor, meanwhile, was appointed as director of research in the government agency that overseas the radio, television, and film industries in Mexico. Cecilia asked the professor for a job; he invited her family to dinner (in his home) with his aunt, who was his boss as head of the government agency. Mexican presidents serve for six-year terms, and usually employ a new set of government officials when they take office. A new *sexanio* was just beginning, and so the government communication agency was searching for new employees. Cecilia's family had been friends with the aunt and her nephew (the professor) for many years, and had exchanged many *palanca* relationships in the past. She was offered a position to do audience research.

As a result of obtaining a new job via *palancas*, the new employee has put himself in a position of obligation to his helper; thus the new employee has become a potential *palanca* to those who helped him get a job, a possible fund of social capital for some future occasion. And who knows? Some day soon the potential *palanca* may be asked to create a new job for the nephew or cousin of his former *palanca*. There are different grades of *palancas*, ranging up to a *palancón* (a "big lever"). The job secured through *palancas*, especially if it is a government position, is often called a *hueso* (a "bone").

The Mexican government, of course, recognizes the inequalities involved in the *palanca* influence process, and the fact that unqualified individuals are often hired. In recent years the government has instituted various laws and regulations to rationalize the employment process and other decision-making processes. But Mexican observers say that these efforts have not greatly diminished the role of *palancas,* which of course are not limited to employment. Giving business contracts, getting admitted to a university, being sent to a conference. Wherever decisions are made, *palancas* are at work.

There are certain advantages of the *palanca* process; for example, new employees hired via this process have a high degree of communication proximity (and its accompanying homophily) with existing employees in their company. Their employers have multiple ties with them, and know that they can be trusted. The Mexican employer often feels it is more important to be able to trust the new employee than for the underling to have perfect technical qualifications for the job. Something like *palancas* may be found in other cultures, and even in the United States, a famous President appointed his brother as attorney general.

The impression one gains from the analysis of the typical employment process in Mexico is that it is activated by "the strength of *strong* ties." Influence through network ties is more important than informaion flows in getting a job. Rigorous network studies are needed in Mexico and in other cultural settings before the strength of the strong-ties proposition can be accepted as valid.* More generally, cross-cultural tests of "made in the U.S." behavior science theories are needed to determine the degree to which they are culture-bound.

In both the United States and Mexico, we conclude that networks are important influences on human behavior, but the function played by network links may be somewhat different in each country. Further, the fundamental basis of network links may be different in Mexico than in the United States. North Americans tend to respond to their network links with social friends and work associates in making many decisions. In Mexico, kinship ties are much more important in effecting many life decisions, and the quality of these links tends to be more stable and multiplex. Perhaps through future study of this fundamental quality of network links in various cultures, network analysts can better understand the role of cultural factors in human behavior.

* Langlois (1977) found support for the strength of weak ties only among those seeking upper-middle-class professional jobs (like Granovetter's Newton respondents) in his study of French-speaking people in Quebec.

Testing Propositions about the Strength of Weak Ties in Korea

We analyzed the network data from villages A and B to test the strength-of-weak-ties theory regarding family planning diffusion. Our analysis explored the strength of communication ties in five specific hypotheses, each derived from the original Granovetter (1973) statement, relating communication proximity to such variables as bridging ties, reciprocity,[8] homophily on mothers' club membership and on the adoption of family planning, and differences in family planning knowledge between dyadic partners. The unit of analysis is the network link. The strength of a tie between two dyadic partners is measured by communication proximity, the number of communication contacts which they share. Our analysis showed:

1. *Communication proximity (tie strength) and reciprocity.* Reciprocal ties are more proximate ("stronger") in both villages than are nonreciprocal ties. The 17 reciprocal ties in village A have an average proximity score of 3.8, compared to an average proximity of 2.6 for the 52 nonreciprocal ties.[9] The mean strength of the 18 reciprocal ties in village B is 3.8, while the 66 nonreciprocal ties average 2.9. So reciprocal ties are "stronger" (more proximate), as we expected.

2. *Communication proximity (tie strength) and bridging links.* The number of ties linking communication cliques is rather small, but in both villages they are weaker than are nonbridging ties. In village A, the two bridging ties have an average proximity score of 1.0, compared with 3.0 for the 67 nonbridging ties. Village B has 14 bridge-linking ties, averaging 2.4 in proximity, and 70 nonbridge ties with a mean proximity of 3.4. As hypothesized, the bridging links that connect cliques are "weaker" (less proximate) than are ties within cliques.[10]

3. *Communication proximity (tie strength) and communication between mothers' club members and nonmembers.* In village A, communication ties between a mothers' club member and a nonmember are weaker (less proximate) than ties between two members or between two nonmembers. In village B the reverse is true. Mean proximity in the heterophilous (on club membership) links of a member with a nonmember is 2.5 in village A, compared with a mean proximity of 3.1 for the homophilous relationships of member/member and nonmember/nonmember. In village B, the mean proximity of ties joining heterophilous members/nonmembers is 3.3, while the homophilous ties average 3.1.

We had expected stronger ties (greater proximity) in more homophilous links, but this hypothesis was not supported in village B.

4. *Communication proximity (tie strength) and communication between adopters and nonadopters of family planning.* In village A, the

[8] Reciprocal ties are communication relationships in which the partners choose one another.

[9] Our communication proximity scores were computed by a procedure illustrated in chapter 4.

[10] In both villages, we find that bridging links are less likely to be reciprocal. None of the bridging links in either village are reciprocal, while 25 percent of the nonbridging ties are reciprocal.

heterophilous ties between an adopter and a nonadopter are less proximate than the homophilous adopter/adopter and nonadopter/nonadopter links. Nonadopters are not well integrated into the family planning communication network of village A, whose norms are generally favorable to family planning. In village B, links between pairs of family planning adopters are strong (proximate), as are ties between adopters and nonadopters, but homophilous ties between nonadopters are relatively less proximate. Although our results are not completely consistent, again we see that homophilous ties are generally more proximate than heterophilout ties, as we expected.

5. *Communication proximity (tie strength) and heterophily on family planning knowledge.* The women in our two Korean villages were each asked a set of 10 "how-to" knowledge questions about family planning.[11] The difference in the number of correct responses by dyadic partners was calculated for each link. In village A, there is no consistent relationship between proximity and dyadic heterophily in family planning knowledge. In village B, mean proximity increased from 2.9 to 3.7 as dyadic knowledge differentials rose from 0 to 3 or more. So, contrary to our expectations, we found heterophily on family planning knowledge to be positively related to proximity in village B.

Our sample size of network links in the above analysis is only 296, and so these results should be considered as only illustrative of propositions about the strength of weak ties that can be tested. We conclude, tentatively, that stronger ties (more communication proximity) are related (1) to reciprocity, (2) to nonbridging links, and (3) to homophily on relevant variables.

THRESHOLD EFFECTS ON INDIVIDUAL BEHAVIOR

In our 24 villages of study in Korea, we found much indirect evidence of the effect of the village on individual adoption of family planning innovations. For instance, one of our 24 villages had 51 percent adoption of the IUD and only one vasectomy adopter; another village had 23 percent adoption of vasectomy; yet another is a "pill village." These village-to-village differences in the adoption of specific family planning methods are certainly not random, and probably reflect the impact of communication networks in each village in "standardizing" a common behavior among the members of each village (chapter 6). We noticed this tendency for there to be a pill village, an IUD village, and so on early in our Korean data-analysis. It led us to begin thinking about

[11] These questions included how often it was necessary to take contraceptive pills, if men could use the IUD, etc. (chapter 6).

threshold effects in the Korean villages, and how we might investigate them.

Through discussions with Professor Mark Granovetter, we became interested in studying "thresholds" as they influenced the diffusion of innovations in our 24 villages of study. What is a *threshold?* It is the number or proportion of other individuals in a system who must make a decision or take an act before a given individual will do so (Granovetter, 1978). The costs and benefits to the individual of making one choice or another depend in part on how many others in a system make the same choice. For example, the cost of joining a riot declines as riot size increases, since the probability of being apprehended is smaller as the number of rioters becomes larger.

Granovetter asks us to imagine 100 people milling around in a square in a potential riot situation. Thresholds for rioting are distributed as follows: one individual has a threshold of 0, one individual has a threshold of 1, one individual has a threshold of 2, and so on up to the last individual, who has a threshold of 99. Now the individual with a 0 threshold instigates the riot by breaking a window. This behavior activates the individual with a threshold of 1 to throw a rock through a window. The activity of these two rioters now triggers the individual with a threshold of 2, and so on, until all 100 individuals have joined the riot.

Imagine that we replaced the individual with a threshold of 1 with another person with a threshold of 2. Now if the instigator breaks a window, there is no one with threshold 1 to follow his lead. No riot will develop.

Granovetter (1978) argues that his threshold model of collective behavior ought to apply to such research problems as the spread of rumors and epidemics, strikes, voting, migration, and leaving a situation like a boring lecture. Certainly, thresholds must be at work in the diffusion of family planning innovations in our Korean villages of study. In order to investigate thresholds as they affect adoption behavior, one would need data on the number of adopters in each village by month and year. We possessed just such a data-set for the 1,003 women in the 24 Korean villages.

Dozier (1977) split the sample into 18 villages from which he computed multiple regression equations for thresholds of individual women. Then he used these equations with data from the other villages to predict threshold distributions, and then to predict the outcome of the adoption of family planning innovations. When this prediction was compared with actual rates of adoption, Dozier concluded that he was unable to explain much more of the variance in adoption than without using the threshold variables. But in any event, Dozier's methodology is suggestive of future approaches to investigating thresholds in the diffusion of an innovation in a system.[12]

The general notion of thresholds in determining behavior is important in the context of the present book because it is so consistent with our convergence/network paradigm. Obviously, thresholds allow us to predict collective action by the members of a system; presumably, threshold effects occur due to the network links among the individuals in a system.

"Using Threshold Effects in the People's Republic of China"

In the People's Republic of China, a threshold approach is utilized as one strategy for diffusing unpopular innovations. "Cadres" are the political, administrative, or technical leaders found at all levels of society; they are selected for their political devotion and most are members of the Communist Party. The cadres usually wear distinctive clothes of slightly better cloth than their followers' blue work clothes, and have a certain degree of special power and privilege. But their most distinctive quality is the respect with which they are held by their peer-followers. Part of this respect comes from being better informed, as each cadre is expected to read regularly the People's Daily (the official national newspaper of the Communist Party of China).

Cadres serve as institutionalized opinion leaders in diffusing innovations; they provide leadership by personal example. The cadres' early adoption of state-recommended innovations helps decrease the risk and uncertainty of these new ideas for their followers. For instance, in the early 1970s when sterilization was announced as an approved contraceptive method for couples with two children, the cadres "took the plunge" immediately. Then they told their followers that vasectomy and tubectomy had no serious side-effects (Rogers and Chen, 1979). Thus the cadres, motivated by a sense of altruistic responsibility and of internalized expectations, adopt an innovation first and help make it more acceptable for their followers by providing a group of early adopters who are respected by the masses. The cadres act to create a threshold for diffusion, and so act to speed up the S-shaped curve of adoption in the systems that they lead.

PLURALISTIC IGNORANCE

Pluralistic ignorance is the degree to which an individual incorrectly perceives the behavior of others. Such pluralistic ignorance (or its oppo-

---

[12] Other models and algorithms for thresholds have been described by Pitcher and others (1978) and Johnson and Feinberg (1977).

site, pluralistic knowledge) is one indicator of an individual's knowledgeability about the behavior of others in his/her system. Presumably, an individual will be less pluralistically ignorant if he/she is highly connected with others in the system. One consequence of network communication ought to be a lower degree of pluralistic ignorance.

There are two varieties of pluralistic ignorance: (1) the unfounded assumption that one's own attitudes and behavior are unshared, and (2) the unfounded assumption that they are uniformly shared (Merton, 1968, p. 431). The latter assumption of a "looking-glass perception" has been found to be most common (Fields and Schuman, 1976), the belief that others think the same as oneself.

The usual research approach to studying pluralistic ignorance in past investigations is illustrated by O'Gorman's (1975) and O'Gorman and Garry's (1975) study of racial prejudice. Respondents are asked two questions: (1) "How prejudiced are you?" and (2) "How prejudiced are other people who live around here?" The answers to the first question are aggregated (for example, averaged), and compared to responses to the second question. For instance, perhaps only 30 percent of the respondents say they are prejudiced, but these same respondents say that 60 percent of the other people in their area are prejudiced. Clearly, the average respondent seems to suffer from pluralistic ignorance.

Despite the obvious importance of interpersonal networks in creating or destroying pluralistic ignorance, network variables have not yet been included in this field of research.

Family planning behavior is a fertile field in which to study pluralistic ignorance because, like racial attitudes, it is not very visible to others; it also is a relatively taboo topic, and hence is less likely to be discussed. We found, not surprisingly, a good deal of pluralistic ignorance about family planning behavior in villages A and B. Each woman was asked whether each of her dyadic partners was an adopter or not, at the time of our 1973 survey. We checked the accuracy of these perceptions against the partner's reports (in their personal interviews) as to whether or not they were adopters. About 60 percent of the dyadic partners' adoption status was incorrectly perceived by respondents. Many of these village women were pluralistically ignorant as to whether "everybody's doing it," or not. For example, in village A, where 57 percent had adopted family planning, only 38 percent of dyadic partners were reported to be adopters. In village B, 26 percent had actually adopted, but only 18 percent of dyadic partners were reported to be such.

Some respondents were more pluralistically ignorant, while others were more pluralistically knowledgeable, about the family planning behavior of their dyadic partners. We found that the degree of pluralistic ignorance was negatively related to the communication proximity of network links, as might be expected. Future research on pluralistic ignorance could test other qualities of a network link (reciprocity and homophily–heterophily, for example) as they relate to the degree of pluralistic ignorance of the dyadic partners about each other's behavior.

The concept of mutual understanding, an important consequence of communication as convergence (chapter 2), is partly indexed by measures of pluralistic ignorance, suggesting the theoretical significance of research on pluralistic ignorance, driven by the convergence model of communication.

"Banjars in Bali: Breaking Down Pluralistic Ignorance"

The Province of Bali is one of the poorest and most densely populated areas in the world. The 2.4 million people on this tiny Indonesian island earn about $150 per capita, $30 less than the national average. Impossibly small farms are operated by about 1,100 people per square mile in rural areas.

In 1971, when the national family planning program began in Bali, the average number of births per woman was just under six. By 1976, five years later, this rate was reduced by more than one-third, to 3.8 births per woman. About 65 percent of eligible couples were using a contraceptive method in 1978, compared to the national average of 30 percent. Bali went from being one of the most fertile provinces in Indonesia to being the least fertile.

What caused this dramatic drop? *Banjars*. They are a traditional village assembly that meets monthly at the call of the village chief. For centuries, the *banjar* in each Balinese village has been meeting to discuss community issues every 35 days (the Balinese month). In mid-1975, the provincial government of Bali began encouraging the *banjars* to include discussion of family planning in their monthly meetings.

Nowadays, each household head answers the monthly roll call at the *banjar* with the contraceptive status of his wife. Further, a three-foot-by-four foot map of the village is posted in the *banjar* meeting hall. Each map shows the house of each village family, and whether or not they are adopters of family planning. The color code is blue for IUDs, red for the pill, and green for condoms. The visual impact of this *banjar* map helps overcome the illiteracy barrier for many villagers who cannot read.

The *banjar* map and roll call are, of course, communication strategies for breaking down pluralistic ignorance about family planning. In Bali, at least, everybody knows who's using family planning.

"Manipulating Network Links: The Mafia at Work in Sicily" *

Throughout much of this chapter the thrust of our analysis might seem to imply that the individual is a kind of passive recipient of network influences

* This illustration is adapted from Boissevain (1974, pp. 1–10).

from his/her communication environment. This relationship between the network and individual behavior actually works both ways. Individuals should be conceived of as actively exerting considerable influence on their networks (a viewpoint that we shall explore with data in chapter 7).

One of the ways in which a person influences the behavior of others is through manipulating networks in which he/she is a member. An illustration is provided by the case of *Professore* Volpe, whose eldest son was a high school student in a small Sicilian town. Volpe suspected that his colleague, a teacher in the school, was trying to fail his son so as to block his entrance to the university and thus bring shame on the professor's family. Eventually, this suspicion led to a confrontation with his enemy in front of his fellow teachers; before slamming out of the room, Volpe demanded an apology.

That evening, Volpe contacted one of his friends in the Mafia, and described how he had been insulted by his enemy. The *mafioso* said, "I'll see to it." Later, Volpe's enemy heard a knock on his door during the night, and a courteous but tough voice suggested that unless an apology to *Professore* Volpe occurred, there might be "unpleasantness." Two days later, *Professore* Volpe received a short note of apology in the mail.

When asked how much he had to pay the *mafioso*, Volpe said, "Nothing, of course," and told how the *mafioso* was the son of a man that Volpe's father, an important lawyer, had helped to keep out of jail forty years before. "He helped me for . . . friendship. Because of our father, we have friends all over Sicily."

So for every behavioral change that results from network links, we should suspect that another individual may be manipulating networks to bring about the change. Networks influence us, but we also control them.

CONCLUSIONS

The main question guiding this chapter was: How important are communication network variables in uniquely explaining individual-level behavioral change? Our general conclusion is that they are important, at the individual level (where we compared isolates with nonisolates), personal communication networks, clique level, and system level (where evidence on system effects, threshold effects, and pluralistic ignorance was reviewed).

We feel that *there is considerable intellectual potential in incorporating network variables as additional independent variables in explaining a dependent variable of individual-level behavior change.* This conclusion was most clearly demonstrated in this chapter for the dependent variable of innovativeness. Our Korean village data, and that reviewed from a wide variety of other diffusion investigations, clearly shows that *communication network variables make a unique contribution, in addition to individual characteristics, in explaining individual-level behavior change.*

More generally, we have seen in this chapter the potential fruitfulness of applying the network analysis/convergence paradigm to the investigation of a variety of types of individual behavior. For example, we have reviewed Park's (1977) study of anomia/alienation, Alba's (1978) research on prejudice/tolerance, and Burstein's (1976) election study in Israel. All of these works, and others cited elsewhere in the present book, suggest the richness of a research design in which the investigator incorporates network variables about information-exchange *relationships* as additional independent variables, along with previously studied *individual characteristics*, in explaining such dependent variables as voting, prejudice, anomia/alienation, and so on, thus moving to consider two of the three dimensions of the data-cube (chapter 3). Strong empirical proof of the advantage of adding these network variables, in terms of added variance explained in the dependent variable, is not yet available (except in the case of innovativeness). So the promise of incorporating network analysis in the previously atomistic research on individual-level change has not yet been adequately demonstrated. But we feel the potential is clear, certainly on theoretical grounds.

6 COMMUNICATION NETWORKS IN EXPLAINING GROUP AND SYSTEM PERFORMANCE

With individuals as units of analysis . . . it is not possible to study variations in social structure and their determinants. To do [so] requires that the collectivities whose social structure is under examination be made the units of analysis.

Peter B. Blau (1969, p. 51)

The purpose of this chapter is to demonstrate how group and system performance can be explained with communication network variables, compared with more conventional (non-network) explanatory variables. In chapter 5, we treated independent variables at the system and group level (as well as at the individual level) to explain individual behavior. Here we look at the behavior of whole systems or groups as our units of analysis (Figure 5–1). Specifically, we will use communication network variables to explain (1) the rate of adoption of family planning innovation, and (2) the rate of self-development in Korean villages.

RESEARCH ON GROUP/SYSTEM PERFORMANCE

A central theoretical issue for many social science disciplines (for example, political science, sociology, and economics) is why some systems have relatively higher effectiveness and performance than do others. Answers have often been sought in such independent variables as the social structure of the system. For example, it has been found that organizations with greater decentralization and less formalization (that is, less bureaucratization) are more innovative in adopting new ideas (Zaltman and others, 1973), and hence more effective. Recently, it has also been recognized that the communication structure of a system is one determinant of its performance (Rogers and Agarwala-Rogers, 1973). Here the main research questions would be: How is system connectedness related to system innovativeness and performance? How is system connectedness related to the degree of convergence among its members?

Research Approaches to Group/System Performance

In order to answer such questions, a researcher needs data from a sample of systems that vary in such network dimensions as connectedness, diversity, and so on, and in their performance. A case study of a single system (for example, a peasant village or an organization) cannot tell us much because there is no variation in the dimensions of study. A more appropriate research design would be the comparative analysis of two systems. A pioneering example of this design is Yadav's (1967) investigation of two Indian villages, one of which he knew to be much higher in agricultural innovativeness (it had won a national award for being a very progressive village) than his other village. The two villages were both in the Punjab, with similar soils and weather conditions, and both were populated by Sikh peasants. Yadav sought to explain the difference in innovativeness in the two villages on the basis of their contrasting communication structures. The more innovative village was more open to external ideas and its internal communication structure was more connected (thus facilitating the flow of innovations within the village).

A somewhat similar two-village comparative analysis of the diffusion of family planning ideas in Korea is presented in this chapter. A comparative system analysis can serve a useful research purpose in exploring the topic of study and in suggesting hypotheses/research questions for future study. But a two-system comparative analysis hardly provides strong answers to research questions, which must rest on data-analysis of a larger sample of systems.

Very few past studies have utilized systems like groups, villages, or organizations as their units of analysis. Even more rarely have such studies included independent variables that measure some aspect of the communication structure of the system (such as its connectednes or diversity). Exceptions are (1) Guimarães' (1972) study of agricultural innovativeness in 20 Brazilian villages, and (2) investigations of educational innovativeness in schools (Lin, 1966 and 1968; Allen, 1970; Shoemaker, 1971). The dependent variable in these investigations was innovativeness (the degree to which a unit is relatively earlier than others in adopting a new idea).

Why has there been so little research using groups/systems as the units of analysis?

1. A considerable amount of research resources are usually needed to gather data from all the individuals in a sample of groups/systems. Many scholars (for instance, a Ph.D. student) cannot afford to gather data from a thousand or so respondents in 25 systems.

2. The statistical analysis of such data, usually obtained from individual respondents but aggregated to the group/system level, is greatly complicated by the different levels of units of analyses that are possible.

3. When designing research on the group/system level, most social scientists have not thought of indexing the communication structure of the group/system as one type of variable. They fail to look past the individual as their unit of analysis.

Compared to the past researches (mentioned above), our two Korean data-analyses in this chapter feature (1) a somewhat larger sample of systems (that is, villages), (2) a wider variety of indices of communication structure, and (3) a multiple regression approach that allows us to detect the relative contribution of network and non-network variables in explaining group/system innovativeness and development.

Group Transformation as a Strategy of Change

Recently, development planners and social theorists have recognized that local groups at the village level are essential for effective rural development. This small group may be a farmers' credit cooperative, as in the Comilla Project in Bangladesh (Rahim, 1976); a credit group, as in the Puebla Project in Mexico (Diaz-Cisneros and Myren, 1974); a "study group" in China (Chu, 1977); a radiophonics school in Colombia (Beltran, 1976); a radio-listening group in Tanzania; a village assembly (*banjar*) in Bali, Indonesia; or a mothers' club in Korea (Park and others, 1974, 1976). Research in social psychology shows that such small groups are an effective means for changing individuals' attitudes and behavior, especially if there is a channel by which new ideas can come into the group from external sources. The processes of transformation which take place within a system, and which create a set of output resources from a given set of input resources, are fundamental in understanding system change (Coleman, 1971). In other words, the *way* that the individual members of a system obtain and process information to reach decisions and take action affects the performance of the system as a whole, and the rate and direction of change in the system (Kincaid, 1976). When a small group is formed within a village, for example, the village as a whole will not function in the same way that it did before. The change in the communication networks will affect both individual and collective decision making and action. This basic approach to change was clearly stated in the case of Mexico's highly successful Puebla Project: "Such a program can function efficiently only when the *campesinos* [farmers] are organized into groups, so that *campesino* leaders join the technical assistance agents in helping the *campesinos* improve their production practices" (Diaz-Cisneros and Myren, 1974, p. 127).

The strategy of social change through a group transformation in the communication structure can be contrasted with the analysis of the aggregate characteristics of social systems. The latter research approach was posed by Emile Durkheim at the turn of the century: "Given people who possess some particular characteristic, will they behave differently in groups which vary in the proportion having that characteristic?" (Durkheim, 1895). A half-century later, Kendall and Lazarsfeld (1950, pp. 195–196) reemphasized that "just as we can classify people by demographic variables or by their attitudes, we can also classify them by the kind of environment [such as the network] in which they live. The appropriate variables for such a classification are likely to be [system] data."

A pioneering study of the Great Books Discussion Groups in the United States by Davis (1961) directly influenced the design of our Korean study; it analyzed (1) the "compositional effects" (such as the heterogeneity in the group members' education), as well as (2) individual member effects on the activity, intellectual changes, increase in knowledge, and retention of group members. The Great Books Discussion Group program offered a research opportunity to study 1,909 members of 172 discussion groups (hence with an average membership of approximately 11 members). Davis (1961, pp. 216–217) concluded his evaluation: "We are not grinding sub-disciplinary axes when we conclude that throughout the analysis we have been struck by the importance of group discussion and group relationships as factors in program retention." The local discussion groups facilitated the national program of book-reading without having to provide an expensive staff of professional instructors. The group discussions and the network relationships in the Great Books program provided one of the major gratifications to individuals for their participation in the program. The main educational goal of the book-reading program was thus facilitated by the social effects of the small groups.

Similar forces operated in the activities of the mothers' club in the Korean village of Oryu Li (chapter 1). The members genuinely enjoyed each other's companionship and the bonds of friendship and goodwill that the club fostered within their village. The successful outcomes of most of their club projects and the club's increasing membership reinforced these network links and provided satisfaction to the club members. Our case study of one village, although useful for suggesting fruitful hypotheses, is inadequate for purposes of generalization to other villages. What about systems that are closer to, or farther away from, a city? Villages with larger or smaller populations? Or villages without such a charismatic leader as Mrs. Chung? The larger sample of 24 villages which represents rural Korea yields confidence that our conclusions can be more broadly generalized across villages with various levels of mothers' club inputs and activities, with different types of leaders, and with different characteristics, at the village level of analysis. In this chapter we shall also look at the communication structure of the New Village Movement development committees in another sample of 24 Korean villages to determine the role of network and non-network variables in explaining village self-development.

All analysis in this chapter is conducted with the group (for example, a mothers' club) or the system (a village) as our unit of analysis.[1] We

---

[1] The only variables measured at the individual level are those created to study the effects of the group's or village's leader on system-level performance. In this sense,

look specifically at the structure of village communication networks, the stable patterns of information-exchange which should predict system performance. Our main approach throughout the present analysis is to determine the relative importance of communication network variables in explaining system performance, compared to more conventional explanatory variables of a non-network nature. Thus, our work provides an assessment of that strategy of change represented by changing the communication structure of a system in order to facilitate the system's performance in innovativeness and development. Mothers' clubs in Korea are an example of the strategy of group transformation for change.

MOTHERS' CLUBS AND THE ADOPTION
OF FAMILY PLANNING INNOVATIONS IN KOREA

The Korean mothers' club program was initiated in 1968 by the Planned Parenthood Federation of Korea (PPFK). Their main purpose for organizing mothers' clubs in rural villages was to make use of the existing networks of interpersonal communication and local leadership to achieve the goals of the national family planning program. Also in 1968 the government family planning program introduced oral contraceptive pills, and the mothers' clubs were expected to distribute the pills in rural areas.[2] The family planning program employed township field workers, each responsible for approximately 2,200 eligible couples in over 50 to 60 villages. The mothers' club program would for the first time have someone responsible in each village for coordinating the supplies, activities, and information for the family planning program.

During 1968, 12,650 mothers' clubs were organized in about one-fourth of Korea's 48,000 villages. Originally, the membership of each club was limited to about 12 women under the assumption that a limited membership would increase the club's prestige within the village, and create a greater sense of solidarity and cohesiveness in the club. A member had (1) to be able to read and write, (2) to be affiliated with at least one other community activity, and (3) to be a mother between the ages of 20 and 45. In the beginning, mothers' club members tended to be older, and to have more education and social status, than other village women. The number of mothers' clubs had grown to over 23,000 (involving over 700,000 women) by 1973 when we collected our present data.

The specific objectives of mothers' clubs are (1) to encourage family

---

the characteristics of leaders are also the characteristics of the groups and villages themselves.

[2] From 1962, when the Korean family planning program began, until 1968, the IUD had been inserted in county health clinics; unlike the pills, this contraceptive method did not require monthly distribution to adopters.

planning practice and continuation by giving reinforcement and support to acceptors, (2) to aid the overburdened field workers in recruiting new adopters and in supplying contraceptives, (3) to aid in the introduction of oral contraceptive pills to the national family planning program, and (4) to encourage women's participation in community development activities (Park and others, 1976, p. 276). The basic idea of mothers' clubs was to facilitate interpersonal communication about family planning at the village level and to legitimize the practice of family planning among village women. In short, the promotion of mothers' clubs was an intervention in the communication structure of Korean villages.

Initially, each club was expected to hold at least four meetings a year. The expenses of each meeting could be covered by the sales of oral contraceptives. PPFK provides (1) special training programs for mothers' club leaders, and (2) public information, educational, and mass communification materials for the national family planning program. *Happy Home Magazine* is distributed monthly to mothers' club leaders; this house organ includes information for club leaders to introduce at their monthly meetings, so as to sustain the members' motivation for club participation, family planning, and home improvement.

The 1973 survey of club leaders and members (Park and others, 1974) showed that the mothers' clubs were generally very effective: "The high rates and regularity of attendance and record-keeping, the high percentage of clubs with low drop-out rates, and the large proportion of clubs who say family planning is the most important topic at meetings indicate that the goal of establishing a viable, voluntary movement of mothers on the local level has been achieved" (Park and others, 1976, pp. 279–280). Mothers' clubs seem to have contributed directly to the adoption of family planning and to the reduction of fertility in rural areas. How much the mothers' club program contributed to the adoption of family planning innovations was a somewhat controversial question (Park and others, 1976).[3] One of the main purposes for our present reanalysis of the data from the 1973 survey (Park and others, 1974) is to determine *how* the mothers' clubs affect family planning adoption, compared to other important variables, with special emphasis on the relationship of the mothers' club to the structure of the family planning communication networks within each village.

[3] Korea experienced a 33 percent decline in its crude birth rate from 1960 to 1970, and the annual growth rate was estimated at 1.9 to 2.0 percent in 1973 (Cho, 1973). Approximately 40 percent of this decline during the 1960s was due to changes in the age-sex structure of the population and to the rising age of marriage. In urban areas (where there are no mothers' clubs), 45 percent of the decline was due to reduced marital fertility, but in rural areas almost 60 percent of the decline was due to reduced marital fertility (Cho, 1973). Unlike almost all other nations in Asia, Africa, and Latin America, the Korean family planning program was relatively more successful in the rural sector.

The data used for the present network analysis come from a combination of random probability and purposive sampling procedures. In the 1973 study a probability sample of 450 mothers' club leaders was selected in three stages: (1) a random sample of 25 out of the 150 counties in Korea, (2) a random sample of two out of 10 townships within each of these 25 counties, and (3) a random sample of an average of nine mothers' club leaders from each county. To supplement the data from club leaders, a census of all married women up to age 49 was conducted in one representative village in each of the 25 counties selected for the leader survey. A total of 1,003 women were interviewed in 24 villages,[4] an average of approximately 40 women per village. So the analysis reported herein includes data from 24 representative Korean villages purposely selected from a random sample of 25 counties.[5]

A Brief Look at Two Villages in the Study

Before looking in depth at the statistical results from all 24 villages in our study, we briefly compare two of these villages: "village A" with a relatively high rate of family planning adoption (57 percent), and "village B," a very traditional village with a relatively low rate of family planning adoption (26 percent). Our comparative analysis of network and non-network variables in these two villages gives us a "first cut" at our data, and provides insight into why the outcome of a national diffusion program is irregular and varied at the local level. As in our case study of Oryu Li (chapter 1), a close look at villages A and B shows "what goes on" at the village level in response to a national family planning program including a planned intervention in village communication structure. Both villages A and B were exposed to the same national family planning program during the ten years before our study was conducted in 1973. Both villages are served by a township family planning field worker; both have mothers' clubs. Beyond these basic similarities, however, there are important differences (Table 6–1).[6]

Village A: Higher Family Planning Adoption

This village is located on the periphery of Masan City, a prosperous seaport in southern Korea, and in 1973 the village was legally annexed by the city. Several village men travel daily from the village to work in Masan City. The village is above average economically, as is evidenced

---

[4] One village had to be dropped from the present network analysis because data from the network questions were improperly coded; duplicate identification numbers were assigned to respondents.

[5] Findings in the present chapter can be generalized to other Korean villages with the limitations of the sampling procedures in mind.

[6] The communication networks of these two villages were presented in Figures 4–10 and 4–11.

TABLE 6–1.   Characteristics of Female Respondents in Village A and Village B.

CHARACTERISTICS OF THE RESPONDENTS	VILLAGE A (N = 39)	VILLAGE B (N = 39)
I. *Fertility and Contraception*		
1. Percentage of married women of reproductive age that have adopted family planning	57	26
2. Average number of living children	2.6	4.0
3. Ideal number of children	2.8	3.8
4. Percentage of women who have had an induced abortion	38	18
II. *Mass Media Ownership*		
1. Percentage owning a radio in their home	85	97
2. Percentage owning a television set in their home	23	3
III. *Mass Media Exposure to Family Planning (percentage)*		
1. Through radio	87	90
2. Through television	96	10
3. Through newspapers	31	18
4. Through magazines	36	23
5. Through posters	69	54
IV. *Mothers' Club*		
1. Date organized	1968	1971
2. Number of club members	13	14
3. Club meeting activity	Regular monthly meetings	Meets only during the slack work season
4. Funds in the club's credit union	$300	$175
5. Has club leader received training by PPFK?	Yes	No
6. Percentage of women reading *Happy Home Magazine*	26	15
7. Attendance of township family planning field worker at mothers' club meetings	Regular	Once or twice per year
8. Attendance of township chief at mothers' club meetings	Often	Seldom
9. Percentage of women contacted by the family planning field worker through home visits	38	69

to a visitor by the numerous television antennas sprouting over village rooftops.

Village A has existed for over 400 years, and has long prided itself on its cooperative spirit, which may stem in part from the occasional floods that devastate the village. The Choi clan dominates village A: 35 of the 70 village households presently belong to this family clan. An impressive shrine to their ancestors is maintained by the Choi clan, and the Choi clan leader is an important figure in the village.

A reverence for traditional values in village A contributed initially to resistance to family planning and to the mothers' club. This opposition by husbands, and especially by village elders, was gradually overcome by pride in the accomplishments of the mothers' club. The club annually provides a dinner and entertainment for the elders as one means of gaining their support. In fact, the powerful village chief is now a strong supporter of the mothers' club, and regularly visits the mothers' club leader.

Prior to the founding of the mothers' club in 1968, a traditional women's *kae* [7] existed under the leadership of Mrs. Choi, the mothers' club leader. She transferred leadership of this informal group to her aunt when she was appointed leader of the mothers' club, but Mrs. Choi regularly consults with her aunt about club affairs. Thus the aunt acts as a kind of unofficial sponsor to the mothers' club, and the club represents a formalization of the previously existing *kae*.

Mrs. Choi's husband is a liaison between the two main cliques of village men, and his crucial role in the village communication structure complements her position. Their home is located on the edge of the village, but Mrs. Choi (respondent #13 in Figure 4–10) is at the crossroads of the interpersonal communication flows in the village. Mrs. Choi receives more sociometric choices as a source of family planning information than almost any other woman in village A. This centrality stems in part from her perceived credibility about family planning and health matters. Mrs. Choi's brother is a medical doctor, and she delivers many of the babies in the village and stocks a supply of household medicines. She is 44 years of age (one of the oldest women in the mothers' club), and has two sons and two daughters. She has practiced family planning continuously since 1964, being one of the first adopters in the village. Her high school education marks her as one of the most highly educated women in village A.

Certainly the leadership of Mrs. Choi is one of the major reasons for the successful accomplishments of the mothers' club, along with the

---

[7] A *kae* is a voluntary, rotating credit association in which each member contributes a specific amount of money at monthly intervals, and in return receives all or part of the fund at one monthly meeting each year (Kurtz, 1973; Geertz, 1962).

socio-economic progress of the village and its cooperative spirit. Mrs. Choi has a harmonious leadership style, seldom forcing her decisions on the club, but actively encouraging the members in activities that they decide to take. She has participated in a leadership training course provided by PPFK in Seoul.

The mothers' club has conducted a number of community development activities in addition to its family planning accomplishments. The club's credit union is supported mainly by monthly dues of 100 *won* (about $0.25 U.S.) per member, and had assets of $300 in 1973. These funds in the past were mainly used for the benefit of the club members, rather than for the benefit of the entire village. For example, the club members chartered a bus to go on a sightseeing tour of Seoul.

The first family planning township field worker to serve village A was a young, single woman. Such work might imply that she was not a virgin (a value strongly held in Korea for unmarried women). In fact, this field worker did not inform her parents for several years that she was engaged in promoting family planning; she simply told them she worked on the staff of the county health clinic. However, this field worker was able to launch the mothers' club with the help of the village chief and Mrs. Choi (although the field worker did not attend the initial club meetings). The club has helped legitimize the discussion of family planning among married women in village A.

The young field worker was eventually able to exchange jobs with a tuberculosis field worker who also served village A. This woman was middle-aged, married, and a family planning adopter. She promoted family planning more aggressively than her predecessor in village A. In 1973, when village A was annexed to Masan City, another field worker, Miss Kim, was assigned to work there. Young and with only two years' experience as a field worker, Miss Kim had difficulty in promoting family planning in the village. The mothers' club leaders teased her that "we've educated you about family planning," a jest that is partly true.

Thus, the experience of village A shows how family planning field workers must depend on mothers' clubs as a means to multiply and legitimize their family planning communication activities.

Village B: Lower Family Planning Adoption

This village is located in the most conservative and traditional area of Korea, where Confucian ideals are very strong regarding filial piety, respect for elders, lineage loyalty, and "proper" behavior. Village B is the center for the Lee clan in this area, a clan noted for its noblemen (*yangban*) tradition of disdaining manual labor and individual initiative. Unfortunately, the wealth and landholdings of the Lee clan have dissolved in the past seventy years, and village B is in a general state of decline. But the Lee clan still dominates the village, as 50 of the 80 households are clan members.

There was very strong resistance to family planning and to mothers' clubs in the village. A family planning field worker was slapped and scolded by a village elder, although as a government official she was eventually allowed to work in the village. Family planning was taboo; one male village leader told us that "talk of family planning is equivalent to revealing to your neighbors the most intimate details of your wife's sex life . . . behavior extremely improper." Village men did not want to limit their number of children; the folksaying that "every child given by heaven brings his own food to the world" was often cited. Village elders pointed out that the population of village B, once consisting of over 300 households, had actually declined in past decades. In the face of these strong beliefs, the family planning field worker was extremely careful in approaching village women.

Because of resistance to family planning, the mothers' club was not initiated until 1971, three years later than in village A. The club has suffered from poor leadership. The club leader appointed by the village chief, when we approached her in the 1973 survey, quickly denied holding the office, and pointed to another woman as the club leader (actually this woman was the vice-leader of the club, and conducted most of the club meetings).[8] The leader (respondent #49 in Figure 4–11) is an isolate in the communication structure of the village, and has not adopted family planning herself. She is an inactive leader with little initiative to promote family planning innovations to her peers.

Despite this weak leadership and the conservative values of village B, the mothers' club had 14 members in 1973,[9] and its credit union had $175. Further, the club had completed several community development activities, and 10 of the 39 married women in the village were practicing family planning. However, eight women had discontinued family planning, and there were many negative rumors in the village about the side-effects of the IUD and pills. The mothers' club was unable to counteract these rumors effectively.

In 1975, the inactive club leader unilaterally decided to give a loan of $20 (U.S.) from the club's credit union to a village family. The borrowers migrated to the city and refused to repay the loan. The mothers' club members revolted against the inactive club leader by voting her out

[8] She also was an enthusiast for *kaes*, having organized seven of them prior to the beginning of the mothers' club. Unfortunately, this leader (jokingly called "Aunt *Kae*" in the village) perceived the mothers' club as just another *kae*, deemphasizing its family planning functions.
[9] Actually, there were 19 other club members who were 45 years of age or older, and hence were not interviewed in the 1973 survey. Officially, as we explained previously, such older women are not eligible to be mothers' club members.

of office, and replacing her with the former vice-leader (the *kae* enthusiast). One of the mothers' club's first acts under their new leader was to divide up the remaining funds in their credit union (about $15 per member), and then to dissolve the credit union . . . *and* the mothers' club. Our network analysis of women in village B in 1973 might have predicted the eventual demise of its mothers' club in 1975. Weak leadership and an inactive club were prerequisite to the financial crisis that terminated the mothers' club in village B.[10]

Various network variables help us understand why mothers' club performance was higher in village A than in village B: the overlap of the club with cliques, the position of the mothers' club leader in the village network, and so on (chapter 4). Now we explore these variables in all 24 Korean villages.

Explaining Family Planning Innovativeness in Korean Villages

The experience of the village of Oryu Li, and of villages A and B, offer useful ideas about how mothers' clubs contribute to the diffusion of family planning knowledge and the adoption of family planning in Korean villages. We now take a more quantitative approach to analyzing a large set of potentially useful variables for explaining family planning innovativeness in the 24 villages in our sample.

Table 6–2 presents the variables used in this analysis. The set has been divided first into 22 "conventional" explanatory variables of a non-network nature, and nine communication network variables, and then into three levels of analysis of the explanatory variables.

1. Independent variables characterizing the village as a system. The village population and distance from the nearest city, for example, apply to the village as a whole. Mass media exposure to family planning, on the other hand, is a composite variable based on the village average of the individual respondents' levels of exposure to family planning through radio, television, newspapers, posters, and so on. The communication network variables listed lower in the first column are four indices of the communication structure of the village as a whole.

2. The second column in Table 6–2 consists of variables measured at the mothers' club level of analysis. Field worker visits, for example, are the frequency with which the township family planning field worker visits the mothers' club (rather than the individual households in the village). *Happy Home* subscription is a measure of how frequently this magazine is received by the mothers' club (not the extent to which

---

[10] In a somewhat parallel analysis, Lincoln and Miller (1979) utilized the communication structure of a private research organization to understand its later conflict and division into two separate organizations.

TABLE 6–2. Non-Network and Network Variables for Explaining Family Planning Innovation in Korean Villages.

	VILLAGE VARIABLES	MOTHERS' CLUB VARIABLES	MOTHERS' CLUB LEADER VARIABLES	FAMILY PLANNING INNOVATION VARIABLES
I. *Non-Network Explanatory Variables*	1. Mass media family planning exposure 2. Distance from city 3. Number of households renting land 4. Economic level 5. Population 6. Educational diversity 7. Electrification rate	1. Field worker visits to club 2. Mothers' club membership rate (%) 3. Educational diversity 4. Financial subsidies 5. *Happy Home Magazine* subscription 6. Club activeness 7. Contraceptive supplies 8. Age heterophily	1. Leadership training 2. Length of village residence 3. Education 4. Age 5. Prestige 6. Influence 7. Family planning credibility	1. Family planning average knowledge and attitudes 2. Family planning adoption rate (%)
II. *Communication Network Variables*	8. Family planning communication network connectedness 9. General communication network connectedness 10. Overlap between family planning and general communication networks 11. Family planning advice index	9. Mothers' club members network homophily	8. Leader's family planning network connectedness 9. Leader's general communication network 10. Leader's family planning opinion leadership 11. Leader's family planning expertise	

individual mothers are exposed to hearing it read at club meetings). The members' network homophily, the only communication network variable at the club level of analysis, is the extent to which general communication network links connect club members with other club members, or non-members with other nonmembers.

3. The third column in Table 6–2 shows the variables defined at the mothers' club leader level of analysis. The connectedness of the leader within the family planning communication network, for example, is based on the same data as connectedness at the village level, but is limited only to the leader's average linkage distance from other club members.

The last column lists the two main dependent variables in our present analysis. The measure of family planning knowledge at the village level of analysis is the average knowledge of all the respondents in each village. Each respondent was asked if she knew about nine contraceptive methods: IUD, oral pills, condoms, vasectomy, diaphragm, tubal ligation, rhythm, basal body temperature, and withdrawal. If the respondent had heard of any of these methods, she was asked to describe how the method is used or how it prevents pregnancy. More points in the family planning knowledge scale were given if the respondent could describe how a method worked than if she had only heard of it. Family planning knowledge scores for all respondents in each village were then averaged to create the composite score for the village.

A family planning attitude scale was constructed on the basis of how "good" or "bad" each respondent thought these nine methods were; attitude scores for all respondents in each village were averaged to obtain the family planning attitude score for the village. The average scores for family planning knowledge and attitudes were highly corre- lated ($r = .87$) with the village as the unit of analysis, so they were combined into a single measure of knowledge/attitudes. This is our first dependent variable.

The family planning adoption rate for each village is measured by the percentage of respondents who said they were using at least one of the nine methods of contraception. These village adoption rates ranged from a low of 14 percent to 58 percent, with an average of 36 percent. The village level measure of knowledge/attitudes toward family plan- ning methods is moderately correlated ($r = .41$) with the adoption rate.

Knowledge/attitudes and adoption are the two main indicators of the performance of mothers' clubs in Korean villages.[11] A gap between (1) levels of knowledge and attitudes toward family planning, and (2) the adoption of family planning, has been found in most nations (Rogers,

---

[11] The ultimate measure of mothers' club performance, decreased fertility, is a longer-term impact of family planning, but we could hardly expect Korean mothers' clubs, which only began in 1968, to have much effect on fertility by the time of our 1973 survey.

1973). This gap implies that communication is mostly effective in raising levels of knowledge and attitudes, but that other variables are more important in determining the adoption of family planning. Our own measures of knowledge/attitudes, and adoption, are only moderately correlated (a 17 percent covariance).

In the following sections, we consider four sets of independent variables in order (communication network variables, village characteristics, mothers' club characteristics, and mothers' club leader characteristics) to determine their contribution in explaining variance in our two dependent variables. Our analytical procedure is cumulative in that certain of the communication network variables are also included in analyses of village characteristics, mothers' club characteristics, and mothers' club leader characteristics; thus we are able to determine the relative importance of communication network variables, in comparison with non-network variables, in explaining our two dependent variables.

Communication Network Variables

The communication networks of our 24 villages were operationalized by means of two different sociometric types of questions (Park and others, 1974).

1. Family planning: "Of the women living in this village, who do you talk with most about family planning? Please list the names of the five people you talk to most about this subject."

2. General: "Who are the people that you meet and talk with most in this village outside of your family?" These responses were also limited to the five most frequent links.

These sociometric data were then submitted to two network analysis computer programs: (1) the NEGOPY program described in chapters 3 and 4, and (2) a matrix multiplication program.[12]

Family planning network connectedness I is the average linkage distance separating each network member from all other members in the family planning communication network. NEGOPY provides a second measure of connectedness based on the number of reported communication links in each village divided by the possible number of such links $[N(N-1)/2]$: family planning system connectedness II (Table 6–3).

The average family planning network connectedness I scores for our 24 villages is .36, and ranges from .17 to .56. Average connectedness for the general communication network is .49, and ranges from .30 to .68. Thus, general communication structures show greater connectedness than the family planning communication structures. Average family planning

---

[12] The computer program that we used, Network Routine, was written by Guimarães (1970); another, similar program is Coleman's (1964).

network connectedness II is .11, indicating that for all 24 villages there is an average of 11 percent direct family planning communication links out of all possible links. Table 6–3 shows there is a moderate correlation (r = .59) between the two different measures of family planning network connectedness, and that both measures of family planning network connectedness are correlated at about the same level with general communication connectedness (r = .42 and .48).

Knowing the number of steps (linkage distance) between each individual and all other members of her network allows us to compare directly the similarity of two types of communication networks for the same set of individuals. For example, suppose that we know Mrs. Choi and Mrs. Lee are one step away from each other in the general communication network (that is, they directly communicate with one another). If these two women also communicate directly about family planning then,

TABLE 6–3. Correlation Among the Communication Network Variables (N = 24).

VARIABLES	ZERO-ORDER CORRELATION COEFFICIENTS								
	2	3	4	5	6	7	8	9	10
1. Family planning network connectedness I	.59	.42	−.03	.69	.29	.22	.29	.17	.68
2. Family planning network connectedness II		.48	.03	.37	.15	.31	.40	.38	.43
3. General network connectedness			−.47	.28	.26	.18	.23	.04	.28
4. Network overlap				.00	.03	−.19	−.24	−.05	.10
5. Leader's family planning network connectedness					.80	.54	.49	.34	.51
6. Leader's general network connectedness						.62	.53	.31	.35
7. Leader's family planning opinion leadership							.89	.58	.34
8. Leader's family planning expertise								.54	.40
9. Mothers' club network homophily									.20
10. Family planning advice index									—

for them at least, the general communication network and the family planning communication network are the same; they overlap perfectly. If we compare the linkage distances between all dyadic pairs in the family planning communication networks and the general communication networks, we obtain an overall measure of the degree of overlap in the communication structure of these two networks.

Correlation between the linkage distances of the 21,072 dyads in all 24 villages for the family planning communication network and the general communication network is .50. There are important differences in the degree of network overlap from village to village, however; correlations in the 24 villages range from .28 to .85, with a mean correlation of .64. These 24 correlations are squared to create our measure of network overlap (defined as the degree to which respondents in a village talk to the same women about family planning as they talk to most frequently about general matters). We expect such overlap to be lower in villages where family planning is still a relatively taboo topic.

The mothers' club leader's family planning opinion leadership (measured by the percentage of women in her village who report they consulted with her about family planning matters) is highly correlated ($r = .89$) with the club leader's family planning expertise (the percentage of women in the village who say that she is an expert in family planning). Both measures are highly correlated with the club leader's degree of connectedness in the family planning communication network and in the general communication network.

Network homophily measures the percentage of links in a village's family planning communication network in which the two linked individuals are similar with respect to mothers' club membership (that is, both are members or nonmembers). The network homophily variable ranges from 5 to 82 percent in the 24 villages.

The family planning advice index is a measure of the percentage of positive advice about family planning that is exchanged across all of the links in the general communication network. The advice index ranges from 13 to 68 percent for the 24 villages. The family planning advice index is rather highly correlated ($r = .68$) with family planning network connectedness I (as measured by the average linkage distance), and it is also highly correlated with the average connectedness of the mothers' club leader in the family planning communication network.

Table 6–4 presents the zero-order correlations of the communication network variables with our two dependent variables of family planning knowledge/attitudes and rate of adoption,[13] and the amount of variance

[13] Because of the high correlation between the two different measures of connectedness for the family planning network ($r = .56$) and the generally better performance of the linkage distance–based measures (in predicting other variables), only family planning network connectedness I is used in the analyses that follow.

TABLE 6–4.   Zero-Order Correlation and Increase in the Variance of Family Planning Knowledge/Attitudes and Adoption Explained by Communication Network Variables (N = 24).

COMMUNICATION NETWORK VARIABLES	FAMILY PLANNING KNOWLEDGE/ATTITUDES		FAMILY PLANNING ADOPTION RATE	
	Zero-Order Correlation (r)	Increase in Variance Explained (percent) (R^2)	Zero-Order Correlation (r)	Increase in Variance Explained (percent) (R^2)
1. Network overlap	.19	9 *	.51	26 *
2. Leader's family planning network connectedness	.23	5	.50	26 *
3. Club member network homophily	.35	2	.04	1
4. Leader's family planning opinion leadership	.27	2	.24	3
5. Family planning network connectedness I	.38	7	.40	1
6. Family planning advice index	.30	2	.25	4
7. General network connectedness	.14	—	—.18	2
8. Leader's family planning expertise	.39	15 *	.13	1
9. Leader's general network connectedness	.20	3	.41	1
Multiple regression of the best set of variables (asterisked above)	r = .49 R^2 = 24% Adjusted R^2 = 17%		r = .72 R^2 = 52% Adjusted R^2 = 47%	

explained by network variables in these two dependent variables.[14] The best predictors of family planning knowledge/attitudes are: (1) the family planning expertise of the mothers' club leader (15 percent of the variance explained), and (2) network overlap (a 9 perecnt increase), which together yield a multiple correlation coefficient of .49, accounting for 24 percent of the variance.[15]

[14] The statistical procedure that we utilized to determine the relative importance of each independent variable in explaining variance in a dependent variable is step-wise multiple regression. This computer procedure adds one independent variable at a time to a multiple regression, according to the amount of variance that it explains in the dependent variable. Independent variables are added in this way until the increase in variance explained is not statistically significant at the 5 percent level.
[15] A more conservative estimate of the total variance explained would be 17 percent, as computed by the formula for adjusted R^2: $R^2 - (k - 1/N{-}k)(1 - R^2)$, which takes into account the number of independent variables (k) in the regression equation

The best set of network variables for explaining the rate of adoption of family planning are (1) network overlap (26 percent) and (2) the leader's family planning network connectedness (26 percent increase). Together, these two variables account for 52 percent of the variance in the family planning adoption rates of our 24 villages.

Village Characteristics and Family Planning Innovation

Next we examine the relative importance of village characteristic variables (along with selected [16] communication network variables analyzed previously) in explaining our two dependent variables at the village level of analysis. Family planning communication connectedness I is negatively correlated with the distance of the village from the nearest city ($r = -.37$), with village population ($r = -.51$), and with the educational diversity of the network members and their husbands ($r = -.53$), as measured by the variance of their years of education. In other words, villages which have more highly connected family planning communication networks are closer to cities, have smaller populations, and have lower educational diversity. Educational diversity is higher in villages with larger population ($r = .41$), and in villages with higher rates of electrification ($r = .40$). Finally, villages with higher levels of exposure to family planning through the mass media are closer to the nearest city ($r = .37$), and have a higher economic level ($r = .38$).

The three best variables in explaining family planning knowledge/ attitudes (Table 6–5) are (1) mass media family planning exposure (44 percent of variance explained), (2) economic level of the village (a 16 percent increase), and (3) family planning network advice (a 10 percent increase). A moderate correlation exists between family planning network connectedness I and family planning knowledge/attitudes, but this independent variable does not increase the amount of variance explained when controlling for the first three independent variables. They account for 70 percent of the variance in family planning knowledge/attitudes within our 24 villages.

The best predictors of family planning adoption (Table 6–5) are (1) mass media family planning exposure (26 percent), (2) network overlap (a 16 percent increase), and (3) family planning network connectedness I (a 12 percent increase). Together, these three independent variables account for 55 percent of the variance of the rate of adoption of

---

relative to the small number of cases (N) represented by our 24 villages (Theil, 1971, p. 178). This adjusted R^2 is shown in all the following tables which report the results of multiple regression analysis.

[16] The four communication network variables included in Table 6–5 are measured at the village level; the other five communication network variables (in Table 6–4) are measured at the mothers' club or club leader level, and are brought into our following analyses when appropriate.

TABLE 6–5. Zero-Order Correlation and Increase in the Variance of Family Planning Knowledge/Attitudes and Adoption Explained by Village Characteristic Variables (N = 24).

Village Characteristic Variables and Communication Network Variables (in boldface italics)	Family Planning Knowledge/Attitudes		Family Planning Adoption Rate	
	Zero-Order Correlation (r)	Increase in Variance Explained (percent) (R²)	Zero-Order Correlation (r)	Increase in Variance Explained (percent) (R²)
1. *Mass media family planning exposure*	.66	44 *	.51	26 *
2. *Network overlap*	.19	2	.51	16 *
3. *Family planning network connectedness I*	.38	0.2	.40	12 *
4. *Distance from city*	−.20	0.6	−.10	5
5. *General network connectedness*	.14	0.2	−.18	2
6. *Number of farmers renting land*	.31	3	−.17	1
7. *Economic level*	.53	16 *	.09	0.6
8. *Population of village*	−.01	0.3	−.01	0.3
9. *Educational diversity*	.04	9	.15	0.3
10. *Electrification rate*	.12	4	.12	0.5
11. *Family planning advice index*	.30	10 *	.25	—
Multiple regression of the best set of variables (asterisked above)	r = .84 R² = 70% Adjusted R² = 66%		r = .74 R² = 55% Adjusted R² = 48%	

family planning. Communication network variables continue to be important predictors of both family planning knowledge/attitudes and adoption at the village level, even when village characteristics are also brought into the analysis. Mass media exposure to family planning has a very high zero-order correlation with knowledge/attitudes (r = .66) and adoption (r = .51) at the village level of analysis; it is more important in explaining knowledge/attitudes than adoption.

Mothers' Clubs Variables

The set of mothers' club variables contains only one communication network variable, the homophily of network links.[17] Network homophily

---

[17] As this is the only one of the nine communication network variables (Table 6–4) measured at the level of mothers' clubs.

measures the extent to which club members interact with other club members and nonmembers interact with nonmembers in the village. Network homophily is highly correlated with the percentage of women in the village who are members of the mothers' club ($r = .84$), as might be expected. Network homophily also has a rather strong correlation with the activeness of the mothers' club ($r = .52$). Interpersonal communication by members of more active clubs tends to be with other club members. Mothers' clubs with a greater percentage of members are more active ($r = .44$). The more active mothers' clubs also have a higher level of educational diversity ($r = .41$), that is, the members and their husbands vary more widely in their educational experiences (as measured by the sum of the variance of the members' education and the variance of their husbands' education).

The frequency of family planning field worker visits is negatively correlated with mothers' club membership ($r = -.53$) and the degree of network homophily ($r = -.37$), suggesting that field workers give more attention to mothers' clubs that have a smaller proportion of village women as members. Perhaps field workers visit less well organized villages because those better organized are more self-sufficient.

Table 6–6 shows that (1) the club membership rate, and (2) the activeness of the club, are both somewhat related to family planning knowledge/attitudes, but the most important predictor variable is the club members' network homophily (12 percent of the variance explained). The best predictors of family planning adoption are the frequency of field worker visits (23 percent) and the mothers' club membership rate (16 percent increase). Together, these two variables explain 39 percent of the variance of the family planning adoption rate of villages. In general, however, mothers' club variables are not as highly related to our two dependent variables as are communication network variables and village characteristics variables (discussed previously). Mothers' club variables may have indirect effects on family planning knowledge/attitudes and adoption through their direct effects on communication network variables, however.

Mothers' Club Leader Variables

The mothers' club leader's age is negatively correlated (at about the same level) with the leader's opinion leadership ($r = -.38$), her general communication network connectedness ($r = -.35$), and her family planning communication network connectedness $r = -.37$). Younger mothers' club leaders are more connected to other members in their village communication networks than are older leaders, and more village women go to younger club leaders for consultation about family planning matters. The average age of the mothers' club leaders in our 24 villages

TABLE 6–6.   Zero-Order Correlation and Increase in the Variance of Family Planning Knowledge/Attitudes and Adoption Explained by Mother's Club Variables N = 24).

MOTHER'S CLUB VARIABLES AND COMMUNICATION NETWORK VARIABLES (IN BOLDFACE ITALICS)	FAMILY PLANNING KNOWLEDGE/ATTITUDES		FAMILY PLANNING ADOPTION RATE	
	Zero-Order Correlation (r)	Increase in Variance Explained (percent) (R²)	Zero-Order Correlation (r)	Increase in Variance Explained (percent) (R²)
1. *Field worker visits*	−.09	0.2	.48	23 *
2. *Club membership rate*	.30	1	.09	16 *
3. *Educational diversity*	.08	4	.21	4
4. *Financial subsidy*	−.24	9	.02	4
5. *"Happy Home Magazine"*	.23	2	.12	5
6. *Club activeness*	.32	5	.22	5
7. **Club members' network homophily**	.35	12 *	.04	3
8. *Contraceptive supplies*	−.10	0.5	−.04	1
9. **Members' age heterophily**	.07	2	.02	0.1
Multiple regression of the best set of variables (asterisked above)	r = .35 R² = 12% Adjusted R² = 8%		r = .62 R² = 39% Adjusted R² = 33%	

is 42 years, considerably older than the average club member. In rural Korea, respect and influence come with age.

Family planning expertise, the percentage of women who say the club leader is an expert about family planning, is correlated with the leader's family planning credibility (r = .45), measured by her knowledge and attitudes toward contraceptive methods. Club leaders with more education have higher family planning credibility (r = .41), and somewhat more prestige in the village (r = .33). The leader's prestige (as indexed by the extent to which village-level and higher-level officials visit her) is related to the extent to which she travels to visit them, her family planning influence score (r = .45).

Table 6–7 shows that the leader's family planning credibility is highly correlated with the village level of family planning knowledge/attitudes (r = .59). In other words, the best explanation of village knowledge and attitudes toward family planning is the mothers' club leader's knowledge and attitudes.[18]

[18] The leader's score for knowledge/attitudes is included in the average scores for her village, but with an average of 40 respondents per village, the inclusion of the leader's score does not substantially affect the correlation coefficient.

TABLE 6–7.   Zero-Order Correlation and Increase in the Variance of Family Planning Knowledge/Attitudes and Adoption Explained by Mothers' Club Leader Variables (N = 24).

MOTHERS' CLUB LEADER VARIABLES AND COMMUNICATION NETWORK VARIABLES (IN BOLDFACE ITALICS)	FAMILY PLANNING KNOWLEDGE/ATTITUDES		FAMILY PLANNING ADOPTION RATE	
	Zero-Order Correlation (r)	Increase in Variance Explained (percent) (R²)	Zero-Order Correlation (r)	Increase in Variance Explained (percent) (R²)
1. *Leader's family planning network connectedness*	.23	0.4	.50	25 *
2. *Leadership training*	.11	4	.41	17 *
3. *Prestige*	.06	2	.44	15 *
4. *Leader's general network connectedness*	.20	1	.41	0.5
5. *Length of village residence*.	.17	2	.10	2
6. *Education*	.08	4	.22	1
7. *Influence*	.25	0.3	.22	1
8. *Age*	−.01	0.1	−.16	0.1
9. *Family planning expertise*	.39	2	.13	0.1
10. *Leader's family planning opinion leadership*	.27	2	.24	0.1
11. *Family planning credibility*	.59	35 *	.23	0.6
Multiple regression of the best set of variables (asterisked above)	R = .59 R² = 35% Adjusted R² = 32%		r = .76 R² = 57% Adjusted R² = 51%	

In order to affect the rest of her village, the club leader's knowledge and attitudes must be known to other village women. This seems to be the case. The leader's family planning credibility is substantially related to the percentage of village women who consider her an expert in family planning matters (r = .45). Her expertise is also highly correlated with village family planning knowledge/attitudes (r = .39).

The best set of club leader variables for explaining family planning adoption are the leader's family planning network connectedness (25 percent of the variance explained), leadership training (a 17 percent increase in variance explained), and the club leader's prestige (a 15 percent increase). These three independent variables explain 58 percent of the variance in family planning adoption at the village level. The best single predictor is a communication network variable (connectedness).

Best Explainers of Family Planning Knowledge/Attitudes and Adoption

As a final step in our analysis, we entered all of the network and non-network variables into a step-wise regression analysis in order to determine which independent variables are most important in explaining our two dependent variables. Table 6–8 shows only the best four predictor variables for both family planning knowledge/attitudes and adoption. The most important variable in explaining village family planning knowledge/attitudes is village-level exposure to family planning mass media (44 percent of the variance explained), followed by the economic level of the village (a 9 percent increase in variance explained), family planning communication network connectedness I (an 8 percent increase), and the club leader's credibility (an 8 percent increase). These four variables explain 69 percent of the variance in family planning knowledge/attitudes in our 24 Korean villages. Three different levels of measurement are included: two village-level variables, one club leader variable, and one communication network variable.

Communication network variables are even more important explainers of family adoption at the village level (Table 6–8). The best predictor of adoption is village-level exposure to family planning mass media (26 percent of the variance explained). The next two most important variables are communication network variables: (1) the mothers' club leader's connectedness in the family planning communication network (23 percent increase), and (2) the degree of overlap between the family planning network and the general communication network (a 17 percent increase). The fourth most important variable in explaining adoption rate is the frequency of field worker visits (a 9 percent increase).

The two communication network variables, village-level mass media exposure to family planning and field worker visits to the mothers' club, explain 75 percent of the variance of family planning adoption in our 24 villages. These two independent variables express the degree to which family planning information is input to a village. Mass media exposure and change-agent visits are highly related to the adoption of innovations at the individual level in previous researches (Rogers with Shoemaker, 1971). Our unusual finding is the two communication network variables that explain family planning adoption. These variables increase the variance explained in the family planning adoption rate by 40 percent, after controlling for the effect of exposure to mass media family planning. The two communication network variables of leader's family planning connectedness and network overlap explain a proportion of the

TABLE 6–8. Zero-Order Correlation and Increase in the Variance of Family Planning Knowledge/Attitudes and Adoption Explained by the Best Set of Independent Variables (N = 24).

Independent Variables (communication network variables are in boldface italics)	Type of Variable	Knowledge/Attitudes Family Planning		Family Planning Adoption Rate	
		Zero-Order Correlation (r)	Increase in Variance Explained (percent) (R²)	Zero-Order Correlation (r)	Increase in Variance Explained (percent) (R²)
1. Mass media family planning exposure	Village	.66	44 *	.51	26 *
2. *Leader's family planning network connectedness*	Network			.50	23 *
3. *Network overlap*	Network			.51	17 *
4. Field worker visits	Club			.48	9 *
5. Economic situation	Village	.53	9 *		
6. *Family planning network connectedness I*	Network	.23	8 *		
7. *Leader's family planning credibility*	Leader	.59	8 *		
Multiple regression of the best set of variables (asterisked above)		R = .83 R = 69% Adjusted R² = 63%		R² = .87 R² = 75% Adjusted R² = 70%	

variance in the rate of adoption of family planning innovations which has heretofore not been measured and taken into account. In short, *communication networks are important in explaining the rate of adoption of an innovation at the system level.*

What remains to be seen, however, is what factors account for the interpersonal communication structure of our villages. The connectedness of the village family planning communication network is highly correlated (1) with the mothers' club membership rate ($r = .50$), and (2) with the educational diversity of the club members and their husbands ($r = -.46$). In other words, villages in which the family planning communication network is more highly connected have (1) mothers' clubs with a higher percentage of membership, and (2) these clubs have members whose educational levels are more similar. These two variables together explain 60 percent of the variance in the connectedness of the family planning communication network ($R = .77$).

There is considerable evidence that the organization of village women in mothers' clubs has an important impact on the communication structure of the village network. The connectedness of the family planning network, network overlap, the amount of positive family planning advice, the homophily of network links, and the leader's opinion leadership are all affected by mothers' club variables. These five network variables, in turn, are substantially related to the rate of adoption of family planning innovations. The structure of the village communication network intervenes between the mothers' club variables and the rate of adoption of family planning innovations. The most important effects of the mothers' clubs on family planning adoption are indirect, operating through their direct effects on village communication networks. Communication network analysis has allowed us to ascertain the means by which the mothers' club program has achieved one of its primary objectives, the utilization of interpersonal communication networks in villages to promote family planning. Thus, *the formation of groups within systems is an effective intervention in changing the communication structure of the systems.*

Our main conclusions can be diagrammed as:

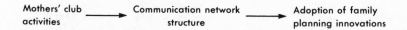

Mothers' club activities ⟶ Communication network structure ⟶ Adoption of family planning innovations

Communication Networks and Convergence

What do our Korean findings about communication networks and family planning diffusion have to do with convergence? The convergence model of communication, as described in chapter 2, treats communication as a process in which information is shared among members of a system in order to reach a more mutual understanding regarding some topic. Such mutual understanding may lead to mutual agreement and collective action. An important characteristic of the convergence model is the shift in perspective from the individual to the network of relationships among individuals in a system that is formed by sharing information. Communication network analysis is one of the important newer methods for studying the pattern or structure of communication that results from this process of information-sharing.

Previously in this chapter, we demonstrated an increased ability to explain system-level performance (innovation) by adding network variables describing communication structure to a set of conventional (non-network) variables. Our dependent variables were (1) the average levels of family planning knowledge and attitudes, and (2) the village-level rate of adoption of family planning. Now we complete this analysis by explaining the *convergence* in attitudes, knowledge, and contraceptive behavior in the 24 Korean villages, with communication network variables.[19]

Commonly, one measures the characteristics of the members of intact systems by using the rates or averages of variables that are aggregated from data measured initially at the individual level. Rates and averages are statistics, however, that do not indicate the degree of difference (or, conversely, similarity and agreement) existing among the members of a system. The appropriate indicator of the amount of homogeneity/heterogeneity (that is, similarity/dissimilarity of agreement) among the members of a system is the *variance* around the average for a given variable.[20] If several intact systems (such as villages) are studied, then the variance of individual responses within each system can be used as a variable to describe each system, just as averages and rates (percentages) were used previously in this chapter.

The variance around the average levels of family planning attitudes/knowledge for the 24 villages are relatively easy to compute by the same computer package from which we obtained the averages. Our variance-type statistic corresponding to the rate of adoption of family planning was suggested by our case studies of Oryu Li, and villages A

[19] Somewhat similarly, Moch (in press) has shown that clique members in an organization demonstrated a certain degree of convergence in work attitudes.

[20] Variance is based on the average deviation of individual responses from the mean:

$$s^2 = \frac{\sum\limits_{i=1}^{N} (X_i - \overline{X})^2}{N-1}$$

If, for example, one of our 24 villages had an average family planning knowledge score of 6.4, some individual respondents might have a score of 0 and others a perfect score of 10. Thus, in this village there would be a rather wide variance around the average.

and B. Family planning field workers refer to some villages as "pill" villages, to others as "IUD" villages, and so on because adopters in a certain village may prefer a particular type of contraceptive method over others. This tendency toward homogeneity in adopting family planning methods by our respondents in each village represents a convergence that results from the communication networks in the village.

An extreme example of this phenomenon in our data-set is that 89 percent of family planning adopters in one village chose the IUD (while only 8 percent adopted rhythm in this village). An opposite extreme is village B, where three women chose the rhythm method, three chose the oral pill, two chose condoms, and the remaining two adopters chose the IUD. There is no clear-cut preference in village B for any one method over others. The predominant choice of one family planning method is not a form of collective action resulting from a collective decision (like a referendum or a vote at a public meeting). Nevertheless, it is a form of collective action resulting from a process of within-village interpersonal communication over time in which individual actions gradually converge toward a mutually preferred choice of action. As a form of behavioral convergence, the predominance of one contraceptive method in a village is expected to be related to the communication structure for the discussion topic of family planning, especially the connectedness of this network.

To measure the degree of family planning method convergence in each village, we used the standard formula for entropy (1) from the field of thermodynamics, and (2) from information theory (Shannon and Weaver, 1949, pp. 50–51). *Entropy* is the degree of uncertainty in a system.[21] Negentropy is the opposite of entropy. Measures of entropy play a central role in research on information theory as measures of information, choice, and uncertainty.

The frequency distribution of contraceptive methods within each of our 24 villages corresponds directly to the probabilities of choice for one or more discrete outcomes of possible behavior. Equal probabilities across these outcomes (a similar percentage of adopters for each contraceptive method, as in village B) represent a system state of high entropy, or high system uncertainty. The predominance of one outcome over the others (as in our "pill village") represents a system state of low entropy, or conversely, of high negentropy, certainty, and system convergence.

The Korean village with the lowest degree of preference for any particular contraceptive method in our sample has an entropy score of

[21] Entropy (or H) $= - \Sigma \, p_i \log p_i / \log n$

where p is the proportion of adopters for each contraceptive method (i), and n is the number of different contraceptive methods adopted in a given village. Perfect entropy results in a score of 1.0, and perfect negentropy in a score of 0.

.99; it is village B, described previously. The village with the highest degree of convergence toward one method has an entropy score of .39. The average level of entropy across our 24 villages is .82 (and the standard deviation is .15). This measure of method convergence (negentropy) is not related to knowledge convergence or to attitude convergence.[22] Knowledge convergence and attitude convergence are highly correlated ($r = .64$), however.

What is the relationship between the communication network structure in our 24 villages and the degree of knowledge, attitude, and behavioral convergence? Zero-order correlation between the connectedness of the family planning communication network and knowledge convergence is .28. The correlation with attitude convergence is .06. Behavioral convergence, measured as the village negentropy score for family planning method preference, is positively correlated with the connectedness of the family planning communication network ($r = .39$). Villages in which the network of family planning communication is more highly connected have a greater preference for one method of contraception over others, as we might expect.

The relationship between network connectedness and the measures of knowledge and attitude convergence are partly confounded by the average levels of knowledge and attitudes in the same villages. We used partial correlation procedures to control for the effects of the average level of village knowledge and attitudes, on the relationship between network connectedness and convergence. After controlling for the effects of average village knowledge, the correlation between knowledge convergence and the connectedness of the family planning communication network is stronger ($r_{12.3} = .43$). When the average level of village attitudes toward family planning is controlled, the relationship between attitude convergence and network connectedness is also much stronger ($r_{12.3} = .56$). Controlling for the family planning adoption rate slightly reduces the measured relationship between method convergence and communication network connectedness ($r_{12.3} = .31$).

Overall, we conclude that a moderate but important relationship exists between the structure of the family planning communication networks in our 24 villages and the degree to which members of these networks converge in terms of their knowledge and attitudes of family planning, and their choice of family planning method. The generalization

[22] For ease of interpretation and presentation, these three measures are reversed so that a high score represents convergence. Thus, a low attitude variance score represents high attitude convergence, a low knowledge variance score represents high knowledge convergence, and a low entropy score represents a high level of method convergence. The signs (direction) of correlation coefficients have been adjusted accordingly.

here is that *system connectedness is positively related to system convergence*.

"Self-Development in Urban Slums"

An external threat to a system often results in changes in the communication structure within the system. This relationship can be observed in urban slums in developing nations, especially where the residents are squatters (and hence do not have a legal right to the land). The residents are often suspicious of government representatives or other officials, even when these individuals intend to help, because the squatters fear an attempt will be made to expel them from their homes. Because the squatters are clandestine residents on their land, they are usually considered as ineligible for any government services (such as police protection, roads, sewers, water, electricity, and schools).

Given these conditions, one might expect that the quality of life in urban slums in countries like Mexico and Colombia would be very poor. On the contrary, one of the surprises for most students of these squatter settlements is that, largely through the self-development efforts of the residents, a fairly "livable" community situation has been created, especially given the very poor economic resources of the families (for example, almost none of the household heads have regular employment). While many of the squatters' homes are constructed of packing box materials or plywood scraps, certain structures are rather well made of bricks or cement blocks. One of this book's authors remembers seeing certain homes in a Colombian squatters' community that almost approached the quality of middle-class housing. Investigation sometimes showed that the bricks had been "liberated" one at a time from a nearby industrial construction site. Neighbors often pitch in to help each other in building these slum houses. For example, when one of the authors was engaged in drawing a map (for sampling purposes) of a Colombian squatters' slum he found that his map, drawn the previous day, was already out of date. During the night, four new homes had been built by groups of neighbors.

In a similar fashion, local networks within a squatter settlement are activated to construct sewer lines and waterpipes, to lay out roads and soccer fields, to build schools and community halls, and to tap existing electrical power lines (often illegally). Community leaders are elected or emerge in other informal ways. Enterprises like grocery stores, privately operated taxis and buses, taverns, and repair shops often spring up.

Overall, the slum residents seek to cope with their lack of public services and the generally hostile environment by a variety of self-development activities. A "can-do" spirit is translated into altruistic action via the efforts of networks among the squatters. Belatedly, in the 1970s governments in developing nations began to recognize the potential of self-development as a means of raising the quality of life of their people.

THE NEW VILLAGE MOVEMENT
AND SELF-DEVELOPMENT IN KOREA [23]

Now we move from our analysis of the family planning performance of mothers' clubs to consider the role of communication networks
in self-develment. Our description of Oryu Li (chapter 1) showed
how villagers can improve the socio-economic development of their system through participation and leadership, with a certain degree of government support. Oryu Li's mothers' club program was an active component in the "miracle" of this village's development. The success story
of Oryu Li is a background for understanding the type of network analysis we present in this section.

Our purpose is to show how communication network analysis can
provide understandings of self-development. Unlike our previous network analysis of mothers' club performance, which was based upon data
from all of the eligible women in our 24 villages, here we utilize data
only from the leaders in each village in order to measure communication network variables among them that predict village self-development.
Having an average of only nine respondents per system, instead of the
average of 40 women respondents in our previous analysis, is a step
toward solving the logistical barrier (of inadequate research resources)
to sampling systems instead of individuals as units of analysis in network investigations. So the following analysis differs in purpose as well
as methodology from our previously presented analysis of mothers' club
performance.

Korea's New Village Movement

In 1971, the Republic of Korea launched a nation-wide campaign
known as *Saemaul Undong* or the New Village Movement.[24] Its primary
purpose was to reduce the gap in incomes and living standards between
rural and urban segments in the nation. This goal was to be achieved by
stimulating a new spirit of diligence, self-help, and cooperation in villages. When the late President Chung-Hee Park announced the New
Village Movement, he said that villagers could only improve their living
conditions if they did so themselves, and he promised to extend government support to those villages that were most active in self-development.

---

[23] The data reported in this section were collected and analyzed in collaboration with
Professor Il-Chul Kim, Department of Sociology, Seoul National University.
[24] When this program later spread into urban industrialized areas of Korea, it was
called the New Community Movement.

Korea's program was part of the trend toward emphasizing an integrated rural development approach in the 1970s in Asia, Africa, and Latin America. Korea's New Village Movement is one of the most successful of the integrated rural development programs in any developing country, perhaps because of the personal attention it received from the nation's former president. For example, in front of the main government office building in Seoul stand two flags. On one side is the national flag. On the other, flying at equal height, is a green three-leaf flag, symbol of the New Village Movement.

Two essential elements in integrated rural development programs are (1) the goal of rural–urban equality, and (2) local group action at the village level. Korea during the 1960s displayed one of the most rapid rates of economic growth of any nation in the world. But this progress mainly occurred through rapid industrialization and urbanization, while the wages of urban laborers and the incomes of villagers were kept at a low level. So much of the new wealth was concentrated in relatively few hands, causing a widening socio-economic gap in Korean society.[25] The basic definition of development changed about 1970, in Korea and throughout the world, to recognize that economic progress had to be accompanied by equality (Rogers, 1976b). The New Village Movement was thus designed to shift the government's development inputs from urban-industrial programs to rural areas.

Local Groups in Self-Development

Since 1970 it was increasingly recognized that for rural development programs to effectively close the rural–urban socio-economic gap, such inputs had to be channeled through local groups at the village level, so that government assistance created village self-develoment instead of dependence. For instance, instead of building a new school building, health clinic, or road for a village, Korea's New Village Movement was designed to provide bags of cement and other inputs so that the villagers themselves could then construct their own facilities. And the amount of these inputs was awarded to a village on the basis of its self-development accomplishments during the previous year (these annual achievements were "graded" by government officials so that each Korean village was categorized as "basic," "self-help," or "self-sufficient"). This reward system encouraged village self-development.

[25] During the 1970s, this rapid urban industrialization eventually created a labor shortage in the rural sector, which subsequently increased farm wages and the opportunity for women to be paid for their work on the farm. This economic advance for women in turn contributed to the power of women in mothers' clubs and in the process of village development.

Korea's integrated rural development program, like those in other developing nations, is designed to promote self-development, recognizing that real development consists of what villagers do *for themselves,* rather than what governments do for villagers. This 1970s-style conception of development is consistent with our convergence model of communication, recognizing that development communication consists of information-exchange (1) between a national government and its villagers, and (2) within a village, to reach mutual understanding and collective action.

Self-development has been going on in villages in Latin America, Africa, and Asia for a long time (where it has been called *"gotong royong"* in Indonesia and *"harambee"* in Kenya, for example). But village self-reliance in development was not given much attention by national governments until the integrated rural development programs of the 1970s. In Korea, as elsewhere, the success of the recent emphasis upon village self-development rested on activating village communication networks to pull together for common goals. Such connectedness rested, in part, on the activities of village leaders.

Volunteer village leaders are the leading forces in the New Village Movement. *Saemaul* leaders are responsible for providing technical skills and information to their fellow villagers and for maintaining liaison with local government officials, who provide financial assistance and basic materials (for example, cement). Government policy is that funds must be released on time, prices of farm products must be regulated, and financial assistance increased to accelerate the rate of socio-economic development. The early achievements of the New Village Movement were possible only with the full support of the government, and sometimes with substantial pressure from local government officials. Originally, villagers were not motivated to carry out the development projects, and without pressure from local govenment officials not so much happened. At first, even the officials were complacent. "The intense pressures from Seoul for quick, concrete results at the village level have jolted the local bureaucracy out of its lethargy, mobilizing officials of all government agencies to a sustained activist intervention on behalf of rural development goals" (Brandt, 1976, p. 37). But after a short time, Korean villagers began to assume responsibility for the New Village Movement, and the government's role diminished accordingly.

Male and female voluntary *Saemaul* leaders have been a major force in the movement's success to date, because of their important role in selecting and implementing development projects. Essentially, the New Village Movement amounts to a decentralization of development decisions, from the national capital in Seoul to the local level. Village leaders are largely in charge of this rural development program. And how they are connected in communication networks is an important predictor of village self-development.

Measuring Village Self-Development in Korea

Our present analysis explains village self-development with a combination of (1) conventional (non-network) village-level variables, and (2) communication network variables based on the friendship links among the volunteer members of village development committees (the councils that direct the New Village Movement in each Korean village). Our analysis procedures are similar to those we followed in the previous section. Our basic research question is: How much better can we explain village self-development by adding communication network variables to the conventional (non-network) independent variables used in past research?

We surveyed all of the village development committee (VDC) members (including the male and female New Village Movement leaders) in 24 villages purposively sampled from four townships in Cholla Bukdo Province and four townships in Choongchong Bukdo Province (Kim and Kincaid, 1979).[26] Within each of the eight townships, three villages were selected, one from each level of the official New Village Movement grading system ("basic," "self-help," and "self-sufficient"). By selecting three villages at different levels from the same township, township-level differences are held constant while the relative success of village self-development varies.

We intended to measure our dependent variable with eight scale items. But the item-to-total score correlations of these items indicated that we were measuring two different dependent variables: village self-development and development (Table 6–9). Village self-development is comprised of the first three items: (1) the official government development grade ("basic," "self-help," and "self-sufficient") for the village, (2) the number of utilities acquired or built by the village (electricity, piped water, telephone, and methane gas), and (3) the number of facilities constructed by the village (meeting halls, warehouses, public baths, etc.). Improving village facilities and utilities is a high priority of the New Village Development Movement. These three scale items each indicate *self-development*, the degree to which the members of a system carry out activities to improve its quality of life with a minimum of outside direction and assistance.

The remaining five items (Table 6–9) also indicate the village level of development, but each item is much less amenable to the rapid collective action promoted by the New Village Movement. Therefore, much of such village development is not a result of the New Village Movement, and is not a measure of a village's self-development performance. Villages

[26] It is strictly a coincidence that there are 24 Korean villages in the present analysis of self-development performance, and in our previous analysis of mothers' club performance. The two samples of 24 villages are completely different.

TABLE 6–9. **Item-Total Correlations for Village Self-Development and Development for 24 Korean Villages.***

Scale Items	Village Self-Development	Village Development
I. *Self-Development*		
1. Village grade	.87	.37
2. Utilities acquired	.71	−.02
3. Facilities built	.86	.26
II. *Development*		
1. Students per capita	.28	.63
2. Female student ratio	.35	.53
3. Electrification rate	.29	.60
4. Television sets per household	.10	.71
5. Rice production per capita	.16	.62

* The correlations in boldface indicate whether a scale item is assigned to the village self-development scale or to the village development scale.

scoring high on our village development index have higher per capita rates of students in middle school and high school, and a higher ratio of female students at these two levels of education. Electrification rate (the percentage of households with electricity), the number of households with televisions, and rice production per capita also indicate a village's level of development. The two main variables in Table 6–9 are moderately correlated with each other ($r = .39$), suggesting that they are related but different aspects of developing a higher quality village life. The former measure is mainly development that villagers do for themselves, while the latter mostly represents development activities in the village by the national government.

Communication Networks Among Village Leaders

We measured the communication network structure of each of the 24 villages without conducting a survey of all of the members of the village. We interviewed all the members of the most important group of village leaders, the village development committe, which includes the male and female New Village Movement leaders. Each of these respondents was asked to name: (1) their friends in the village with whom they interact most often, and (2) the most influential individuals in their village. An average of nine respondents per village named from 20 to 30 different friends and influentials in their village. This one-step snowball technique (chapter 3) allows us to study the communication structure of the leaders and their first-order personal communication network of friends.

We assumed reciprocity in these friendship links (that is, that the 20 to 30 individuals would also consider those who named them as friends). Then, the square binary matrix of reciprocated friendship links was submitted to correlation analysis to obtain a correlational similarity measure of dyadic proximity (chapter 3). Smallest-space analysis (chapter 4) was computed so that we could better understand the proximity of the male and female New Village Movement leaders to other village leaders in the friendship communication network of the village.

The upper diagram in Figure 6–1 shows these proximity relationships in a village with a low score on village self-development; the lower diagram shows the proximity relationships in a village with a high self-development score.[27] Identification numbers of individuals in the friendship network who were named by three or more respondents as influentials in village affairs are circled. Identification numbers of the male and female New Village Movement leaders are shown in squares.

The influentials in both villages cluster more closely to one another than to the non-influentials (whose identification numbers are neither circled nor squared). The two New Village Movement leaders are positioned differently in the low and high self-development villages. In the low self-development village, the male leader is centered among the village influentials' friendship communication network. In the high self-development village, the male leader is near the periphery, more distant from the cluster of village influentials. However, the female leader in the low self-development village is positioned at a distance from the village influentials, whereas the female leader in the high self-development village is much closer to the influentials.[28]

The average correlational proximity of male and female leaders to all the village influentials in their village across our sample of 24 villages is .14 (ranging from −.12 to .40) for male leaders, and −.15 (ranging from −.25 to .00) for female leaders in the New Village Movement.

A second measure of communication network structure is the connectedness of our respondents (the members of the village development committee plus the two New Village Movement leaders) in the friend-

---

[27] The coefficient of alienation (explained in chapter 4) of the smallest-space analysis for the low self-development village is 0.19 in two dimensions, and is 0.17 in three dimensions for the high self-development village.

[28] These general conclusions were checked with the correlational proximity measures that were inputted to the smallest-space analysis. The average correlation of each New Village Movement leader with all of his/her village influentials in the low self-development village for the male leader is .45; for the male leader in the high self-development village it is .03 (indicating much lower proximity). The corresponding average correlational proximity for the female leader in the low self-development village is −.19, compared to −.03 for the female leader in the high self-development village. These results are consistent with the visual interpretation of the correlational proximity of leaders to village influentials in the smallest-space diagram (Figure 6–1).

Figure 6–1. Smallest-Space Representation of Correlational Proximity Among Village Influentials (circles) and New Village Movement Volunteer Leaders (squares) in a Low Self-Development Village and a High Self-Development Village.

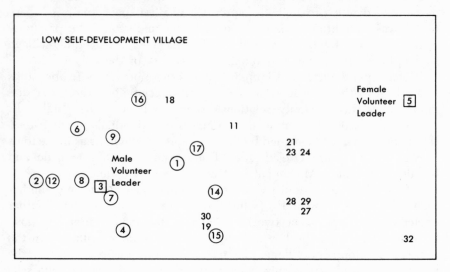

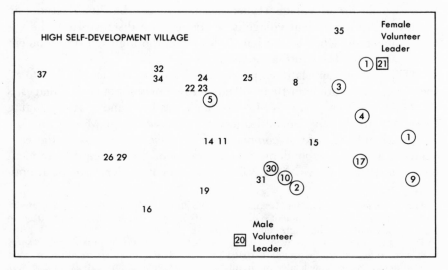

Note: The male New Village Movement leader is more proximate to the village influentials in the low self-development village, while the opposite is true for the female leader of the New Village Movement. For purposes of clarity, we have not shown the network links among these individuals in each village. The space between individuals represents correlational proximity.

ship communication network. If our respondents named friends who are not also members of the village development committee, then connectedness is lower. Connectedness was measured by the number of friendship links among members of the VDC (our average of nine respondents in each village) divided by the total possible number of dyadic links that could exist within this group. Average connectedness for our 24 villages is .46, ranging from .18 to .80. Connectedness of the VDC is positively correlated to the proximity of the male leader to the influentials $(r = .68)$, and negatively correlated with the proximity of the female leader to village influentials $(r = -.33)$. Male leader and female leader proximity to influentials is also negatively correlated $(r = -.55)$. So villages in which the male leader is closer to the influentials have female leaders who are more distant from the influentials.

Explaining Village Self-Development

The relationship of the independent variables to village (1) self-development and (2) development, is shown in Table 6–10. The best predictors of village development are (1) the amount of village farmland per household (50 percent of the variance explained), (2) the distance of the village from the nearest city (a 10 percent increase in variance explained), and (3) the population of the village per household (a 5 percent increase). These three variables together explain 66 percent of the variance of village development. Once these three variables are entered into the multiple regression, the two communication network variables do not make a significant increase in the amount of variance explained.

The best set of independent variables in explaining village self-development are (1) the male leader's proximity to village influentials (25 percent of the variance explained), (2) the average number of monthly visits by New Village Movement officials (a 17 percent increase), (3) the connectedness of the VDC (a 13 percent increase), and (4) the population of the village (a 12 percent increase). These four variables together explain 67 percent of the variance in village self-development.

Communication network variables are more important in explaining the dependent variable (self-development) most closely associated with the New Village Movement. Villages which have accomplished greater self-development performance have male leaders who are more distant from the village influentials, and VDCs whose friendship network is less connected and hence more open to other members of the village. Female leaders of more self-developed villages are also much closer to village influentials $(r = .39)$, although this relationship does not add to the overall explanation of self-development when the best four independent variables are already included in the multiple regression.

TABLE 6–10. Zero-Order Correlations and Increases in the Amount of Variance of Village Development and Self-Development Explained by Communication Network Variables in 24 Korean Villages.

Independent Variables (Communication Network variables are in boldface italics)	Type of Variable	Village Development		Village Self-Development	
		Zero-Order Correlation (r)	Increase in Variance Explained (percent) (R²)	Zero-Order Correlation (r)	Increase in Variance Explained (percent) (R²)
1. *Male leader's proximity to influentials*	Network	−.28	1	−.50*	25*
2. NVM officials' visits	Village Characteristic	.21	4	.48*	17*
3. *VDC connectedness*	Network	−.35	1	−.12*	13*
4. Population	Village Characteristic	—	—	.48*	12*
5. Population per household	Village Characteristic	−.42*	5*	—	—
6. Farmland per household	Village Characteristic	.71*	50*	.23	3
7. Distance to nearest city	Village Characteristic	−.20*	10*	.03	4
8. *Female leader's proximity to influentials*	Network	.10	—	.39	1
Multiple regression of the best set of variables (asterisked above)		R = .81 R² = 66% Adjusted R² = 61%		R = .82 R² = 67% Adjusted R² = 60%	

Perhaps effective leadership by male leaders in the New Village Movement can be hindered by too close network relationships with village influentials, thus inhibiting unpopular but constructive decision making by tying the male leader to satisfying needs of his close friends.

As in our previous investigation of mothers' club performance, *communication network variables make an important, unique contribution to explaining system performance (self-development, in the present case) that cannot be accounted for by non-network variables.*

SUMMARY AND CONCLUSIONS

In this chapter we demonstrated that group and system performance can be explained with the communication network structure of the system, as well as with more conventional, non-network variables. Little past research has focused on explaining group and/or system performance. Here, we used communication network variables to explain (1) family planning knowledge, attitudes, and adoption in 24 representative Korean villages, and (2) the degree of convergence in knowledge/attitudes and adoption among the members of each village. In a second analysis, we used certain characteristics of the communication structure of leaders in village development committees participating in Korea's New Village Movement to explain village performance in self-development (in another sample of 24 villages). In both analyses, communication structure variables added substantially to the variance explained in (1) innovation and (2) self-development, and to our general understanding of the process of social change.

Among the relatively few past researches on group/system performance, the findings of Guimarães (1972) and Korzenny and Farace (1978) are in general agreement with our present results. For example, a common finding is that a higher degree of connectedness in a system is positively related to a greater degree of behavior change.

Both the mothers' clubs and the village development committees are interventions in the communication network structure of a Korean village, by the national family planning program and the New Village Movement, respectively. Our analyses indicate that both interventions are relatively successful (although more so in certain villages than in others) in achieving their goals of higher adoption of family planning methods and greater village self-development, respectively. If the local group (the mothers' club or the village development committee) is (1) more internally connected, and (2) more connected with the rest of the village network, it has higher performance.

The convergence model of communication led us to examine village innovation and self-development from a new research perspective. Rather than limiting ourselves to the individual level of analysis most common in previous research, we measured the structure of communication behavior at the systems level of analysis, and related it to system-level innovation and self-development. Further, we measured the degree of convergence in mutual agreement and action among the members of systems and determined the relationship of these concepts with communication network structure. We can increase our understanding more by looking at the network relationships among participants in communication than by looking at what happens to them as isolated individuals, separated from the networks in which they are embedded.

Perhaps the two data-analyses described in the present chapter help illustrate one type of communication network analysis, (1) where groups and/or systems are utilized as the units of analysis, and (2) where communication structural variables are included in the analysis, along with more conventional, non-network variables. We utilized the statistical method of multiple regression in which a dependent variable (for example, system performance) is explained by various independent variables (some of which are network variables and some of which are not). We used a similar statistical approach in chapter 5, with individuals (instead of villages) as our units of analysis. The multiple regressions included certain independent variables that are indicants of communication network structure; hence, our research is one type of network analysis and it was generally guided by our thinking about communication as convergence. But our dependent variables here were not measures of communication behavior, unlike the research approach that we demonstrate in chapter 7.

7 WHOM DO NETWORKS LINK?

Whether one is seeking to explain "why" persons go to a particular place to get jobs, "why" they go to trade at a particular store, "why" they go to a particular neighborhood to commit a crime, or "why" they marry the particular spouse they choose, the factor of spatial distance is of obvious significance.

Samuel A. Stouffer (1940)

People are constantly choosing whom they will begin, continue, or cease to interact with, approaching these relations in an essentially rational manner. People seek and keep associates whom they find more rewarding than others.

Fischer and others (1977, p. 3)

Our basic unit of analysis in this chapter is the dyadic link between two individuals in a system. Here we look at the general research question of who is linked to whom. Our main conceptual variables in seeking to answer this question are certain characteristics of the network link: spatial and social proximity, network stability, and multiplexity. The conceptual apparatus to facilitate the analysis of who is linked to whom in networks has not yet been well developed. The researches completed on the issue of who is linked to whom have thus not yet been cumulated in a useful way so that a general picture emerges. Here we hope to offer some useful first steps in stringing together the loose pearls that exist in the body of completed network analyses dealing with whom networks link.

We synthesized the available evidence on how the communication structure of a network influences individual behavior change and group/system performance in chapters 5 and 6, respectively. Here we look for the antecedent determinants of communication structure.

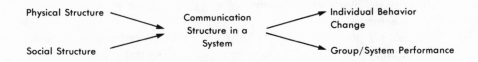

As explained previously, the vast majority of network researches have regarded network dimensions as independent variables and investigated their effects on various other types of behavior: voting, drinking, smoking marijuana, purchasing certain products, adopting innovations, and so on. In the present chapter, our synthesis of the available evidence on who is linked to whom in networks regards network variables as dependent variables.

We shall identify two main classes of determinants of who is linked to whom: (1) spatial distance, and (2) the homophily or similarity of the linked individuals in certain social characteristics. A general theme emerging from a wide variety of these investigations is that *individuals tend to be linked to others who are close to them in physical distance and who are relatively homophilous in social characteristics*. Both spatial and social proximity can be interpreted as indicators of "least-effort." Everything else equal, individuals form network links that require the least effort and that are most rewarding.[1] Homophily usually leads to more effective interpersonal communication because the linked individuals share similar views of the topics being discussed; thus homophilous communication is more rewarding (Rogers and Bhowmik, 1971).

Such homophilous contact, however, tends to be of limited value in an information-exchange sense because such network links generally are more closed and thus are "weaker" for the individual as means of reaching out into his/her environment for new information. Here we see how the social comfortability of social homophily and physical proximity leads to a more limited access to information. The relatively rare heterophile in a network is in an advantageous position to be better informed. This basic paradox has been discussed repeatedly in previous chapters in terms of Granovetter's (1973) theory of the strength of weak ties. The contradiction is that most individuals interact with others who are socially and physically closer to them (which is more facile), but who are limiting in an information-acquisition sense.

As one aspect of our synthesis of spatial and social variables as determinants of network links, we shall explore the question of which of these two is more important, and under what conditions. Very few network studies included both spatial and social variables, and so our conclusions on this score will be somewhat limited.

In chapter 4, we showed how network analysis techniques can be utilized to identify and quantitatively describe the communication structure in a system. Here we try to move beyond this approach to identify how the spatial and social structure of a system influences the communication structure.

In this chapter, we also synthesize network investigations focusing on the stability [2] of network links over time, and suggest a series of hypo-

[1] Zipf (1949) argued, more generally, that all human behavior is guided by the principle of minimizing total action in order to reach certain goals.
[2] *Network stability* is the degree to which a network link occurs at two or more points in time.

theses to guide future research. Networks do change over time. The issue of network stability is important both theoretically and practically because it is the stability of communication structure that provides regularity and predictability to behavior in a system. If there were very little stability over time, network analysis as a means of identifying the communication structure would have little utility. Instead of assuming stability (or simply ignoring the over-time issue, as many network analysts have done), we maintain that the degree of stability ought to be determined empirically. Then the time dimension can be brought more fully and explicitly into communication research, in a way that is consistent (1) with our definition of communication as a process, and (2) with Cattell's (1952) data-cube (discussed in chapter 3). The two main research questions that we pursue in our synthesis about network stability are (1) what is the degree of stability in network links? and (2) what variables determine such stability? We shall conclude that the general principle of least-effort, mentioned earlier in the context of spatial and social proximity of who is linked to whom, also influences network stability: that is, links that are relatively easier to maintain and/or relatively more rewarding, are more stable. We shall conclude that spatially proximate links, reciprocated links, more homophilous links, and ties based on ascribed relationships (like kin) are relatively more stable.

In addition to time, another dimension of the generalizability of communication structure rests on the degree to which network links are multiplex (that is, that they carry multiple contents). Multiplexity is important because it provides stability to a network. We touched on multiplexity in our description of blockmodeling in chapter 4. Here, we synthesize the available evidence about the degree to which a communication structure for one content topic also holds for one or more other topics. The main research approach to answering the question of multiplexity has consisted of determining whether a network link for one topic also carries information about another topic (or topics). Improved research approaches to determining multiplexity are suggested in the closing section of this chapter.

THE METHODOLOGY OF ASSESSING THE DETERMINANTS OF WHO IS LINKED TO WHOM

A variety of data-analytical methods can be used to determine the degree to which some variable is a determinant of who interacts with whom. All such methods, however, rest on determining the degree to which the social or spatial variable (that is expected to be a determinant of who interacts with whom) is a basis for homophily/heterophily, the degree to which two individuals who interact are similar/dissimilar. If a variable—for example, socio-economic status—is an important determinant of who interacts with whom, the two participants in a network link ought to be homophilous on this variable. If they are relatively less homophilous on some other variable such as religion (than they are on socio-economic status), we can infer that status is a more important determinant of who talks with whom in a system.

Obviously, then, in order to investigate the determinants of who is linked to whom, we must use some measure of homophily/heterophily. Several measures are possible. One is the Pearsonian correlation between the determinant variable for the pair of individuals involved in each network link; for example, r might be computed for the ages of Korean women in the 21,072 dyads in our 24 villages of study. This correlation would indicate the degree to which network links pair women who are similar or different in age, and thus the degree to which links display homophily/heterophily in regard to age. If the correlation were high, we would conclude that age is relatively important in determining who interacts with whom.

However, in order to interpret what the correlation means, we need a point of comparison. One possibility is to compare the correlational measure of age homophily/heterophily for dyads with a similarly computed correlation for all nondyad pairs.

Alba and Kadushin (1976) use eta, the correlation ratio, to measure the differences in proximity scores for links on the basis of a social characteristic variable that is measured for the two individuals who interact with each other. For instance, they find an eta of .148 for the determinant of religion among links of U.S. intellectual elites discussing the Vietnam War. Eta is only .014 for age. Thus, religion is a more important determinant of who interacts with whom than is age. Note that, instead of comparing a dichotomy of pairs of individuals who are linked versus nonlinked, Alba and Kadushin measured (with proximity scores) the degree of linkage between pairs of individuals.

Using a difference measure of homophily/heterophily in network links may be a more sound data-analysis procedure than using r, Pearsonian correlation. Bhowmik's (1972) analysis of dyadic data from Indian villagers concluded that the average absolute difference on some characteristic variable (such as age or socio-economic status) between dyadic partners is a more precise indicator of homophily/heterophily than is r.[3] This network scholar computed both r and the average absolute differ-

---

[3] As an illustration, consider a link between two Indian villagers, one aged 43 and the other 38. Their absolute difference is five years. An average absolute difference for age is thus the average of these absolute differences for all network links. In contrast, r_{xy} as a measure of homophily/heterophily on age would be computed as the covariance between the X variable (the age of the respondent in each link) and the Y variable (the age of his dyadic partner).

ence measures of homophily/heterophily for several small data-sets (artificially constructed to display both a high degree of homophily and of heterophily). The average absolute difference measure seemed to behave more closely to Bhowmik's expectations.

Nevertheless, both measures are approximate indicators of homophily/heterophily, and hence provide us with evidence about the determinants of who is linked to whom in a system.

SPATIAL DETERMINANTS OF NETWORK LINKS

The general conclusion from various researches is that space is a very important predictor of who is linked to whom. Here we review the evidence on this point.

An early, classic study of dyadic communication by Festinger and others (1950) found a strong ecological basis in sociometric links. The respondents were all of the married students living in a housing project at the Massachusetts Institute of Technology in 1946. They were asked: "What three people in Westgate [the name of the housing project] do you see most socially?" (Festinger and others, 1950, p. 37). These network data were superimposed over a map of the apartment units; physical distance was one of the major determinants of whether or not a dyadic link occurred. About two-thirds of the 426 dyads were within the same apartment building, and no link connected individuals more than four buildings (180 feet) apart. Even of the within-building choices on the same floor, physical distance greatly affected who interacted with whom: [4]

	DISTANCE (IN FEET)	PERCENT OF LINKS
1.	22	60
2.	44	25
3.	66	12
4.	88	3
5.	More than 88	0
	Total	100

These data, as well as those obtained in other investigations, such as Allen's (1977, pp. 238–239) study of the spatial aspects of network links in R & D organizations, suggest that the relationship of physical distance to interaction is not linear. Instead, the relationship is a decreasing curve; there are many links at close proximity, followed by a sharp decrease until middle distance (44 to 66 feet in the study by Festinger and others

---

[4] This relationship of space to dyadic communication existed even when the probability of potential choices among all possible dyads was controlled.

[1950]), and then a slower decrease over greater distances. This curved relationship of the distribution of network links over distance is depicted later in Figure 7–1 for two Korean villagers.

More than half (60 percent) of the choices in Westgate were to the nearest neighbor, whose door was only 22 feet away! Festinger and others (1950, p. 35) argued that one reason for the strong effect of space on who interacts with whom is that, with closer physical distance, any two individuals are more likely to contact each other accidentally, which may result in a friendship: "In hanging out clothes to dry, or putting out the garbage, or simply sitting on the porch, one is much more likely to meet next-door neighbors than people living four or five houses away." Children usually choose playmates who live very close by, and their parents may then become friends through the children's associations. Even small distances affect the rate at which individuals form network links, especially when a system is homogeneous in social characteristics (Blau, 1977, p. 90). Spatial propinquity increases the chances of accidental contact between two individuals.

Festinger and others (p. 158) suggested the concept of "functional distance" as partially distinctive from "physical distance." An example of functional distance would be a common stairway for two people living in an apartment building; this common facility increases the probability that the two individuals will meet and, perhaps, communicate. Functional distance is undoubtedly important, but investigators have not been able to measure it as a variable, and so its exact role in determining who interacts with whom has not been precisely determined.

Fischer and others (1977, p. 176), in their study of Detroit males, found "that neighborhood friends may be very intimate or not, but the farther away a friend lives (that is, the higher the cost), the more rewarding that friendship must be in order to be maintained." In other words, longer-distance network links are less stable over time, and unless other social structural variables are involved (for example, kinship), they are not maintained. The result is that at any particular point in time, shorter-distance links will predominate in a system. In a later section, we return (1) to consideration of how spatial and social variables interact in determining network links, and (2) to review the evidence on network stability, as it is affected by spatial and social distance.

The general finding from almost every network study that has included space as a variable is that *spatial distance is one of the main determinants of who talks to whom, and usually it is the main determinant.*

A similar study to that of Professor Festinger and his collaborators was conducted in a housing project in Ann Arbor, Michigan (although this community was not just for married students), by Athanasiou and Yoshioka (1973). As at MIT's Westgate Project, spatial distance from house to house was a very important determinant of who talked to whom. "Even though the housing project occupied a square which was one-fourth mile on a side and contained 427 dwelling units [homes], the median number of friendships was made within 100 feet or a distance of about five dwelling units." About 20 percent of all the network links were between next-door neighbors. Further, these close-by links were used more frequently, while longer-distance links were characterized by less frequent contact.

Space and Network Links in Korean Villages

In our Korean villages of study, we noted a general tendency for less connected individuals in the communication structure to be spatially located near the spatial periphery of their system. For example, notice that most of the isolates in Oryu Li (Figures 1–1 and 1–2) are situated on the edge of the village. A similar tendency for spatial centrality to be positively related to connectedness was evident in our other Korean villages, and in many other systems that we have studied. Which comes first, spatial centrality or individual connectedness? At least in Oryu Li, where residential location is mainly fixed, individual connectedness would seem to follow from location. An individual living near the edge of the village is less likely to have chance encounters with her neighbors; they are unlikely to pass by her house, and vice versa. But for an individual such as Mrs. Chung, the mothers' club president in Oryu Li whose home is situated near the center of Oryu Li, a stream of village women pass by, and many stop to talk.

The considerable influence of spatial location on network links is aptly illustrated in the case of Oryu Li, our miracle village of chapter 1. When the smallest-space analysis of the village's communication structure (Figure 1–2) is compared with a map showing the location of each respondent (Figure 1–1), we note a very high correspondence between the two. In fact, the smallest-space network analysis almost reproduces the household locations on the map! For instance, clique II, concentrated in the "upper village" (the upper left-hand corner of the map), is spatially located by smallest-space analysis in the upper left-hand corner of the computer printout.

Further evidence of the very high correspondence of spatial location with communication structure in Oryu Li is provided by the numerical proximity of the 69 women's identification numbers in the smallest-space analysis (Figure 1–2). We originally assigned these ID numbers when we constructed the map and conducted the personal interviews in Oryu Li in 1977. At that time, obviously, we did not know the communication structure of the village. When we did (Figure 1–2), the spatially re-lated identification numbers were close to each other in the communication structure. So in Oryu Li the spatial structure and the communication structure have a close overlap.

A careful look at the smallest-space network analysis of Oryu Li (Figure 1–2) shows that many of the links are rather long. In fact, the average length is approximately one-fourth the diameter of the village (or about one city block). Relatively few (less than 10 percent) of the links are to the most spatially proximate neighbor. In other words, space is by no means a complete explanation of who is linked to whom in Oryu Li. So what social structural variables determine network links? We explore this question in the follownng section.

Previously, we showed that the average length of a communication link in Oryu Li (Figure 1–2) is about one city block. Mrs. Chung, the heroine of the miracle of Oryu Li, occupies a unique sociometric position in the communication structure of the village. Obviously, she has many links (with about 40 percent of the 68 other women in Oryu Li). In addition, Mrs. Chung provides clique connectedness to the village through her links to women in both clique I and clique II. Because these two cliques are spatially distinct, Mrs. Chung's average length of link is much longer than that of the other links in Oryu Li in which she is not involved (about two city blocks versus one city block, respectively). In other words, Mrs. Chung provides leadership to her village through her many long links to others; the longer length of her links implies that more effort is necessary to form and maintain them, and that they must be more rewarding (or else they would not be continued over time).

We conclude, on the basis of Mrs. Chung's position in the communication structure of Oryu Li, that one function of a leader in a network is to provide connectedness to the system, and thus to link the various components (such as cliques) of the system.

We conducted a similar analysis of spatial distance in network links in village A. Figure 7–1 shows that actual links are much closer than randomly chosen pairs of individuals in the village.[5]

In interpreting the present conclusion about the importance of space in determining network links, we must keep one caveat in mind: spatial location usually indexes various social structural variables as well as physical space. For example, we found in Oryu Li that two women are more likely to interact, everything else equal, if their homes are closer rather than farther apart. Unfortunately for simplicity in interpreting this empirical result, everything else is *not* equal. Why do the two women live in adjacent homes? Perhaps their husbands are brothers, and so they are not only neighbors but also kin (by marriage). And, as is often the

[5] A similar analysis, conducted for us by Dr. Bjarne Ruby while he was at the University of Michigan, showed the importance of spatial variables in predicting who interacts with whom (1) in village B, and (2) for all 14 sociometric questions in our Korean survey (and not just family planning discussion).

Figure 7–1.   A Comparison of Actual Versus Expected Physical Distance Between Dyadic Pairs of Individuals in Village A.

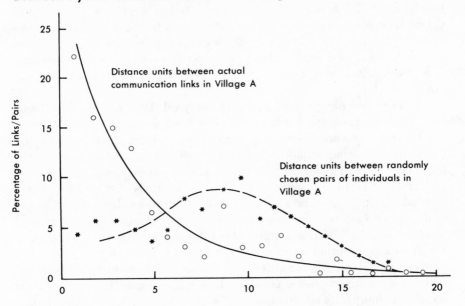

Distance Units (each of about one-tenth of a city block)

Note: Women who are linked in discussing family planning in Village A tend to live much closer together than those who are not linked. Our procedure was first to compute the linear distance between the pair of women in each link. The model distance is 3.2 "distance units" for all of the family planning links; this means that half of the linked women live within about one-third of a city block of each other. Then we measured the number of distance units between randomly chosen pairs of women; the modal distance is about 8.9 distance units (so women in half of all the *possible* links in village A are less than nine-tenths of a city block apart). Obviously, the actual links are much closer (only about one-third the distance) than randomly chosen pairs of individuals.

case in most ecological systems, two spatially contiguous individuals are likely to be similar in socio-economic status and in other characteristics. So which variable really determines who is linked to whom? Certainly the social structural determinants are entangled with the physical structural determinants. We return to this problem in a later section, to try to disengage the joint effects of both social and physical structure on who interacts with whom.

SOCIAL DETERMINANTS OF NETWORK LINKS

The process of forming network links consists of a series of tentative moves on the part of one individual toward another. So establishing a

friendship involves an offer, and its acceptance. In this sense, a link consists of two "demiarcs," one "male" and one "female" (Harary and
Havelock, 1972). A link is forged if the initiative instigated by one individual receives a positive response from the other half of the dyad. So
we view the selection of other individuals as communication partners in
a network as a decision-making process on the part of both individuals
in a network link, choice-making that is affected by social structural factors.

Fischer and others (1977, p. viii) analyzed data from a Detroit survey and from a national survey within a basic framework; "Individuals
create their networks but must build them within limits. People are
constantly choosing which of several possible relations to pursue and
how to behave in them, but they are choosing from among a small set
of socially-structured alternatives." The limits on the individual's choice
of dyadic partners may be imposed by spatial distance, by social distance,
or by other factors. The principles of least-effort and greatest-reward
result in most individuals forming network links with those close at hand.

A key proposition suggested by Fischer and others (1977, p. 7) is
that "limitation on the number of potential social relations available to
individuals leads to more communal social relations [that is, greater
social proximity]." This limitation is a pressure toward greater homophily. On what variables are the two individuals in a link most homophilous? Or, in other words, what social structural homophily variables
are the best predictors of who will interact with whom in a system? We
cannot give a complete answer from all the studies that have sought to
answer this question, but we will review several illustrative studies.

Similarity in dyadic links among New York high school students
was highest (1) on such socio-demographic variables as sex, race, age,
and grade in school, and (2) on the use of marijuana and other illegal
drugs (Kandel, 1978a and 1978b). Of 59 variables studied, homophily on
these six variables (above) was the most important determinant of who
was linked to whom in five high schools. Homophily on age and grade
in school are indirect indicators of physical proximity in a school, as
they automatically segregate the students into classes, homerooms, and
so on. Sex and race are visually evident characteristics, a class of variables
that other researchers have also found to be important determinants of
who is linked to whom. The marijuana and drug use variables presumably were important because individuals who participate in such deviant
activities especially need peer group support. Kandel (1973) found that
only 7 percent of her 8,206 respondents who perceived that none of their
friends used marijuana were marijuana users themselves; 92 percent of
those respondents who perceived all of their friends to be users were
users themselves. A great deal of learning about marijuana use took place
during high school; marijuana use increased from only 16 percent for

freshmen to 41 percent for seniors. Unfortunately, Kandel (1973) lacked longitudinal data to determine which came first among her respondents, drug use or drug-using friends.

Lionberger and others (1975, p. 64) concluded, on the basis of their investigation of agricultural diffusion networks in two Missouri communities in 1950 and in 1966–1967, that most farmers sought information from others who were generally homophilous with them in income, education, innovativeness, and so on, but who tended to be slightly higher on each of these variables.

Evidence of the important influences of oral communication ability on the network variable of individual connectedness is provided by Hurt and Preiss' (1978) study of middle-school students. These scholars measured communication apprehension as the degree to which an individual was hesitant to participate in oral communication. Apprehension scores were negatively related to individual connectedness with other students in the respondent's classroom. Only one of the apprehensive students was linked to her classroom teacher, and this student (as mentioned in chapter 5) was the only apprehensive student in the entire sample to receive a final grade of "A" (the teacher liked her because she was quiet). So Hurt and Preiss concluded that communication apprehension is negatively related to individual connectedness (which in turn is related to final grades).

Fischer and others (1977, p. 63) found that their Detroit respondents chose their friends:

1. From their occupational level about twice as often as would be expected by chance.
2. From their own educational level about twice as often as would be expected by chance.
3. From their coreligionists two to four times as often as would be expected by chance; the highest degree of religious homophily was for Jews, who chose other Jews 80 percent of the time.
4. From their age category two to four times as often as would be due to chance.

An almost universal finding of network studies is that individuals who are linked are of comparable socio-economic status (Laumann and Pappi, 1976, p. 57). Such similarity facilitates interaction by enabling reciprocal exchanges, such as visiting and dining in each other's homes (Laumann, 1973, p. 73). And to the extent that attitudes and interests are highly related to socio-economic status, such dyadic homophily on status also facilitates, indirectly, homophily on these status-linked qualities.

We conclude from the researches just reviewed, and they are but a sample of the many studies on this topic, that *social characteristics on which any two individuals are relatively homophilous, are important determinants of who interacts in a system.* The reported relationships are not high, however, suggesting that the social characteristics of dyadic pairs of individuals is far from a complete predictor of who interacts in a system. Obviously, the case is more complicated.

One caveat about our present conclusions is that in many situations, social structure has a dominant, direct effect on human behavior that is not mediated through communication structure. In these contexts, information-exchange is simply not the main determinant of behavior change. An illustration is provided by O'Sullivan's (1978) investigation of the adoption of agricultural innovations among highland Indian peasants in Guatemala. Structural factors like their small-sized farms, lack of credit, extreme poverty, and ethnic minority status so completely explained these farmers' adoption/rejection of innovations that communication structural variables were unimportant. Information about the agricultural innovations was not an important explanatory variable. The general point here is that communication scholars should not expect that communication variables are always, or even usually, the main predictors of behavior change. Instead, a research objective should be to determine the conditions under which communication structure is, and is not, important. Further, it is possible that if O'Sullivan had focused upon different aspects of the communication structure among his Guatemalan peasant respondents (such as their information relationships with development agency offiicials, for instance), he might have reached different conclusions about the unimportance of communication variables. He followed the linear model of communication in looking for effects, rather than a convergence model of searching for interpersonal network variables that might explain the adoption of agricultural innovations. Had he done so, Dr. O'Sullivan might have found that peer networks were relied upon by the Guatemalan farmers who were not being effectively contacted by government development workers.

A network analysis of communication links among medical doctors by Coleman and others (1966, p. 156) found that different social variables were important in determining who interacted with whom, on the basis of the contents of the network links. Religion and age were the main social determinants of friendship links among doctors, with hometown and medical school also of some importance. But the key determinants of who-to-whom links for the exchange of medical information for the physicians were their professional affiliations in the medical community, such as memberships in hospitals and clinics and office partnerships. These findings suggest that the contents of network links affect the exact social variables determining who interacts with whom.[6] We return

[6] Evidence supporting this point is also provided by Lincoln and Miller's (1979) network analysis in five organizations. Race and sex displayed greater influence on who was linked to whom in friendship links than in work-related links.

to this issue of multiplexity and the content topics in communication links in a later section of this chapter.

In villages A and B we investigated such variables as husband's occupation, husband's education, wife's age, and wife's education in the homophily/heterophily of networks links. Generally, we found that each of these four social characteristics were determinants of who interacts with whom, but the relationships were not very strong (perhaps because of the relatively limited variance in each of these four variables in these two villages). Clan membership was an important determinant of who was linked to whom in villages A nd B, where about one-third of all links were between women of the same clan. But when we superimposed clan membership of each household on the sociogram of Oryu Li, we could not detect any effect of clan (Kim, 1977b). In chapter 1, we explained that the Kang clan included the majority of the 69 households and seemed to be an important factor in the village social structure. Clan membership did not affect who interacts with whom in Oryu Li.

RELATIVE IMPORTANCE OF SPATIAL VERSUS SOCIAL VARIABLES

In addition to the network researches just cited, which used either spatial variables or social variables to determine who is linked to whom, several investigations included both types of independent variables in order to assess their relative importance. For example, Bochner and others (1976a) utilized the small world method (described in a previous chapter) among the 500 international graduate students in a dormitory of the East–West Center at the University of Hawaii. The main determinants of who was linked to whom were sex and culture (38 different cultures were represented among the 500 students). Physical proximity played only a very minor role, perhaps because (1) all of these graduate students lived very near to each other and typically ate together in the dormitory cafeteria, and (2) the effect of cultural homophily was so dominant. For example, a Filipino student would walk up or down several floors in the dormitory to deliver the small world message to another Filipino friend.

The small world studies described in chapter 3 also provided evidence about which factors affect who-to-whom dyads in the chains of message transmission. Geographical distance, occupational status, sex, and race are the main determinants of who is linked to whom (Bernard and Killworth, 1978c).

A similar main effect of physical distance on the likelihood of communication occurring between possible dyads has been reported in numerous other researches. For instance, Parsons (1973) identified 2,969 dyads (using 18 different sociometric questions in five personal interviews with each respondent over a 14-month period) among the 123 women in one village in the Philippines. He found that (1) physical distance (measured as the walking time from one house to another), and (2) being a relative, were the best predictors of whether dyadic communication would occur between any two respondents; homophily on socio-economic status variables was a poor predictor.

We previously mentioned the Athanasiou and Yoshioka (1973) network study in an Ann Arbor housing project; here, space was a main determinant of network links. These scholars also carried out a very careful analysis to assess whether spatial or social structural variables were more important determinants of network links. They concluded that the main determinant of short-distance links (other than the obvious determinant of space) was stage in the lifecycle, as indicated by age, years of marriage, and number of children. If two neighboring families both had small children, the children were likely to be friends, as were the parents. Differences in socio-economic status and in other social variables did not seem to affect with which of the three or four closest neighbors a household was linked.

But at longer distances, such social variables became very important as determinants of who interacts with whom. "In order for friendships to be maintained over moderate or large distances, however, additional similarities in social class must be present" (Athanasiou and Yoshioka, 1973).

An unusual opportunity to test the relative importance of space and prestige on communication links was provided by an investigation of sorority members at a midwestern university campus. Barnlund and Harland (1963) gathered sociometric data from all members of the 18 sororities, eight of which were clustered close to the campus in the "East Quad," another eight further away in the "West Quad," and the other two at a more isolated location. Space was one important factor in determining inter-sorority communication links; for example, 73 percent of the links from the eight sororities in the East Quad were within that Quad. But several anomalies suggested that spatial location was not the main determinant of sociometric patterns; for instance, the two isolated sororities had no links with each other, even though they were closest to each other spatially.

The answer to this puzzle was provided by a prestige ranking of the 18 sororities, which showed a strong tendency for high-prestige houses to be linked with other high-prestige houses, and so on. In fact, space and prestige were highly interrelated. Prestige was due in part to the date of founding of each sorority, which also affected location, as oldest houses were located in the East Quad. Sorority #18, one of the isolated houses, was mostly linked to the high-prestige sororities in the East Quad.

Despite its adverse location, Sorority #18 was moving upward rapidly in campus status. Over a two-year period, this house moved up from twelfth place among the 18 sororities, to eighth place. Barnlund and Harland concluded that the patterns of communication links represent "both a cause, and a consequence of changing prestige." Sorority #18's contacts with the higher-prestige houses increased even more as its own prestige went up.

The conventional wisdom of most U.S. sociologists until the 1960s was that the family and community were breaking up, and that the highly mobile lifestyle of the growing numbers of urbanites was leading to an individualistic, alienated existence. The lonely apartment dweller in a big city was often cited as an individual who did not even know his next-door neighor. Spatial distance was thought to have become irrelevant as a criteria for interaction; kin and neighbors were replaced by work associates as communication partners in an increasingly mass society.

This myth of growing isolation from proximate influences through network links was eventually exploded in a series of sociological investigations indicating that, even in metropolitan centers, network links to neighbors and kin were still surprisingly alive and well. For instance, Leichter and Mitchell (1967) found kin networks were very strong among Jewish families in New York City. Extensive relationships existed; the average family recognized 241 kin. Women especially maintained these kin networks; much of the interaction was by telephone. Distant spatial location was thus overcome by frequent phone calls. In this urban context of Manhattan, one would hardly expect individuals to interact with their next-door neighbors. But kin links seemed to be surviving the urban experience rather well.

Another study in Manhattan, of 270 residents in a public housing project by Nahemow and Lawton (1975), concluded that space was important in determining network links among residents in skyscraper apartment buildings: "Of all first-chosen friends, 88 percent lived in the same building as the respondent, and nearly half lived on the respondent's own floor." But social characteristics also were important determinants of network links: 60 percent of all dyads were of the same age category, and 72 percent were of the same race; 73 percent were of the same sex. Spatial and social determinants interacted in an interesting way: "When a person chose a friend of a different age, the chances were that the person lived very close to the chooser" (Nahemow and Lawton, 1975). In other words, network links between people of different ages or races were almost exclusively among pairs of individuals who lived very close to each other. The least-effort involved in the spatially contiguous links more than overcame the greater effort involved in socially heterophilous communication.

Longer links require greater effort for their maintenance, and contact is likely to be less frequent. Also, this lower communication proximity in longer links suggests that an individual's personal communication network with distant friends is less integrated; these friends are less connected to each other. So the longer (spatial) links are weaker (that is, less proximity is involved), but they are likely to be informationally stronger. Again, we encounter the basic paradox of human communication networks: more informationally valuable links require more effort to form and maintain (chapter 8). Cost and effectiveness of network links are inversely related.

What we have just said about spatially long-distance links also applies to *socially* distant links. Greater social heterophily in a link requires more effort to overcome the imbalances that are likely to result in the communication between such dissimilar individuals. The greater informational payoff must be evident to the individuals involved, or else they will not maintain such heterophilous contacts.

What can we conclude about the joint effects of spatial and social variables on who interacts with whom?

1. *Both space and social homophily are important determinants of who interacts with whom, with spatial distance more important in some situations and homophily on social characteristics more important in others.*
2. *When a system is relatively homogeneous in social characteristics, spatial distance will be the main determinant of who interacts with whom.*
3. *Among equally close neighbors, homophily on certain social characteristics is not a main determinant of who interacts with whom, but in longer distance links, social homophily is the main determinant of who is linked to whom.*

Each of these three propositions can be understood in terms of our least-effort and greatest-reward explanation of who is linked to whom by network links.

STABILITY OF NETWORK LINKS OVER TIME

Network stability is the degree to which a network link occurs at two or more points in time. Previously, we defined *communication structure* as the differentiated elements that can be recognized in the patterned communication flows in a system. We argued that this communication structure provides regularity and predictability to the patterns of behavior in a system. Here we investigate just how stable the network links in a system really are. If there were complete instability, with each link representing only a will-o'-the-wisp, here-today-gone-tomorrow quality, no communication structure would exist, other than at a fleeting slice in time. If this complete instability were characteristic of most network links, network analysis would be futile as a scientific means of understanding and predicting human behavior.

Obviously, such complete instability does not exist in most systems. Neither does complete stability. Networks change. Determining just how much stability occurs in network links is the objective of the present section. The evidence to meet this objective must come from over-time investigations of communication networks. Unfortunately for our present purposes, there are relatively few such over-time researches. So our present conclusions must necessarily be somewhat provisional and tentative.

The "timeless" nature of most past research is a serious deficiency, as noted by Stern (1979): "[Network] researchers have taken measures at only a single point in time, permitting methodological technique to dominate substantive and theoretical interpretation. They have failed to consider how the network reached the state pictured in the quantitative formulation." One shortcoming of one-shot network data is that they do not allow insight into developmental processes as they occur through time. For example, Lloyd-Kolkin (1979) investigated how a planned network of 11 R&D organizations gradually evolved into a more connected system over a nine-month period, following a federal grant to these organizations to encourage their interchange of information. This investigation network-analyzed the communication links among the 11 units, at three-month intervals, in order to trace their increasing connectedness.

Why is the longitudinal study of network stability important?

1. As we have pointed out, the communication structure identified by network analysis has little predictive value unless there is a certain degree of stability in a system.

2. Longitudinal data are necessary in order to investigate the process aspects of the convergence model of communication. Many of the main research questions that should be pursued by network analysts are process oriented in nature. An example of a very long-time network analysis (which also shows that such analysis does not have to be mathematical) is Stern's (1979) historical study of the National Collegiate Athletic Association (NCAA). This organization evolved from a loose voluntary confederation of universities in 1906 into the dominant control agency over college athletics after 1952, when member schools gave it regulatory power. Stern utilized network concepts (like multiplexity, for example) as tools to understand the rise of the NCAA, but quantification was not used (and could not be, as data about network links were not available over the 46-year-period of study). Perhaps this unusual investi-

gation shows what can be accomplished with the *philosophy* of network analysis, independent of the mathematical techniques that usually accompany (and, unfortunately, dwarf) it. Stern's (1979) study of the NCAA also shows the value of analyzing longitudinal data.

3. Over-time data are necessary to determine the effects of certain interventions in a system. At a minimum, one needs before and after data-points to evaluate an intervention's consequences. We cited an illustration in chapter 3 of the inquiry by Professors Marta Dosa and Bissy Genova at Syracuse University, in which they are determining the effects of connecting the health agencies in Syracuse with a computer-based information system. These scholars hypothesized that the intervention would lead to greater connectedness in the network of the 45 agencies, an expectation that they are testing with pre–post data on network links.

Similarly, in chapter 3, we cited the field experiment conducted by Professor Linton Freeman of the University of California, Irvine, on the Network Network, a computer-based teleconferencing intervention among the 40 top network scholars in the United States (Freeman and Freeman, 1979). Yet another example of over-time study of the effects of an intervention on network stability is Morett-Lopez' (1979) investigation in two Monterrey (Mexico) slums. This scholar gathered network data in 1976 and in 1978 from the same respondents. In one of the two squatter settlements, electricity was introduced during this time, and about half of the households purchased television sets. So this natural experiment provided understanding of the effects of television on the respondents' network links.

Methodological Complexities in Studying Stability

The general lack of attention by network analysts to the stability of networks over time has been noted in recent years by various critics: "Whatever a sociogram says about some [network] at time t_1 it says nothing about change in the [network]. Dynamic sociometric studies are rare indeed, and virtually nothing exists on *how* structures change over time" (Killworth and Bernard, 1974b). Perhaps one reason for the scarcity of researches on network stability is the methodological complexity involved in measuring such stability over time.

One concern is that the dynamic process of communication relationships among the members of a system is so fleeting that networks cannot be accurately charted, and the plotting of sociometric communication relationships within a system is but an evasive illusion. Imagine trying to capture, in quantified terms of the number of links and "arrows," your total human interaction that occurs in even one day. Impossible! you say. True. Sociometric data actually reflect only the grossest of communication behavior, the main lines of communication that are most frequently and heavily used. In studies of network stability, we must assume that a system has sufficient stability to allow for accurate measurement of network links.

Of course, indexing stability depends completely on the validity with which the links are measured; reliability (the degree to which a measuring device yields the same results at two points in time) rests on validity (the degree to which a measuring device operationalizes the concept that it is intended to measure). In chapter 3 we reviewed the methodological studies of Professors Russell Bernard and Peter Killworth that question the validity of survey sociometry questions. Until more valid measures of network links are developed, we cannot obtain a very precise understanding of the degree of stability of links.

How long is longitudinal? Just because data are collected at more than one point in time does not necessarily make a study appropriately longitudinal. For instance, if the life of a fruit fly is six weeks, data collected every six weeks will not allow an understanding of an over-time genetic process (Kimberly, 1976). In order for longitudinal data to provide an insight into a process, the length of time over which data are gathered must be appropriate to the length of the process cycle. Network links measured at two data-points are the minimum for investigating network stability. Three data-points are the minimum if one wishes to study a possible nonlinear trend. Even more appropriate are five to seven data-points so that a time-series analysis can be made of the trends in the changes in network links. Such time-series data are ideal if one wishes to investigate the effect of an intervention on the network links in a system.[7]

Another methodological problem in measuring network stability entails knowing exactly when the communication link that is reported by a respondent in answer to a sociometric question actually occurred. For instance, in our 1973 Korean village study we asked our respondents with whom they talked most frequently about family planning. *When* such discussion occurred could have been "yesterday" or ten years previously (as the national family planning program began to impact on our 24 villages of study in about 1963). More recent discussions about family planning were probably more likely to be remembered by our respondents, and reported in answer to this question. A follow-up survey in, say, 1980 would likely have captured some of the information-exchange links about family planning that occurred in the 1963–1973 period, lending a false implication of higher stability to the network data. Of course, we might have specified, in both the 1973 survey and in the 1980 follow-up survey, a particular time frame (such as by a sociometric

[7] Because one thus knows the level of some dependent variable prior to the intervention, during the process of the intervention, and afterward, as the system of study returns to a nonintervention state. In other words, the experimental system acts as its own control group in an interrupted time-series experiment.

question like, "Who have you discussed family planning with *in the past year?*" [8] In any event, measuring the stability of network links over time with any degree of accuracy depends directly on the time-reference for the communication behavior that is being studied.

Given these methodological difficulties with measuring network stability, what does the available evidence show?

Propositions about Network Stability

A variety of network research [9] results about network stability can be summarized in the following propositions:

1. *Spatially proximate links are more stable.*
2. *Reciprocated links are more stable.*
3. *Homophilous links are more stable than heterophilous links.*
4. *Links representing ascribed,*[10] *rather than achieved, interpersonal relationships (such as kinship links) are more stable.*

Here again we encounter the now familiar paradox that informationally stronger network links are more fragile (in the present case, they are less stable over time).

Most longitudinal studies measure the stability of network *links* over time. It is also possible to investigate stability at the clique level. An example is provided by Cohen (1977), who studied 49 cliques in an Illinois high school in the fall of 1958 and the spring of 1959. These cliques were highly homogeneous in a number of variables: liquor consumption, smoking, dating frequency, and so on. The cliques were much less diverse on each of these variables than was the entire high school. How does such within-clique homogeneity occur? Most of it happens through the initial selection of members—"birds of a feather" banded together. Clique diversity decreased from fall to spring; as some cliques died, and others arose, the new cliques were especially homogeneous.

---

[8] Another way to measure network stability with a specific time-reference is demonstrated in Kincaid's (1972, p. 67) network survey of Mexico City slum dwellers: respondents were asked how many years they had known each individual in their personal communication network.

[9] These researches include Morett-Lopez (1979), Moreno (1934), Kandel (1978a), and Charters (1969). One of the first studies of network stability was Moreno's (1934, p. 288) experiment in which data were gathered monthly on 16 individuals who first came together as strangers.

[10] Our review of the literature disclosed only one previous research in which the explicit use of the ascribed–achieved dimension of network links has been made: Hannerz' (1967) study of gossip networks in a Black ghetto. However, the ascribed–achieved distinction in social roles has a long history in sociology. *Ascribed* roles are those positions to which one is born, while *achieved* roles are earned; an example of the former is a son, and of the latter is a university president.

Cohen found a very slight tendency for the most disparate clique members to be eliminated from a clique over time. Some of the increased homogeneity in the cliques occurred due to the cliques pressuring their members toward conforming behavior.

Hallinan (1978) gathered data from four small sixth-grade classes (ranging in size from 18 to 30 pupils) in the rural Midwest, for seven times during a school year at six-week intervals. Each possible link in the who-to-whom matrices was classified as reciprocal, nonreciprocal, or "null" (that is, no link between the two individuals). Then Hallinan analyzed the stability and direction of change in the networks over time using a Markov chain analysis. She found:

1. That reciprocated links are more stable over time than are non-reciprocated links. The reciprocated links lasted from three to five months on the average, while the duration of the nonreciprocated links was from one to two months (less than half as long as the reciprocated links).

2. That nonreciprocated links are more likely to become null than to become reciprocated over time. The change from nonreciprocated to null was twice as high as from nonreciprocated to reciprocated. In other words, a nonreciprocated link (representing a friendship offer) was more likely to be withdrawn than to be reciprocated.

An ingenious experiment on the stablity of network links was conducted by Shapiro (1978) in a children's summer camp. During the second week of this camp, the investigator assigned the campers to teams for a series of competitive games. On the basis of results from a sociometric questionnaire, certain children were assigned to teams with their reported friends, while other children were assigned to teams to prevent opportunities for interaction with their reported friends. Sociometric measurements were repeated at the end of the four days of games, and again twelve days later. The experimental results showed that communication links were about equally likely to dissolve in either kind of team, so separation of a dyad did not affect the stability of links. The main factor affecting stability was the degree of attraction in a dyad; high-attraction ties persisted, and were even strengthened, by separation.

One of very few studies to investigate network stability intentionally is Morett-Lopez' (1979) survey in two squatter slums in Monterrey, Mexico. A squatter is an individual who has built his/her house on land without a legal right to do so. Because of their fly-by-night arrival, squatters are often called *"paracaidistas"* (literally, "parachutists") or *"precaristas"* ("those living in precarious conditions"). Monterrey contained 192 squatter settlements in the late 1970s with about 300,000 inhabitants, approximately 25 percent of the city's population. Morett-Lopez selected two of Monterrey's newer squatter communities, in which he personally

Figure 7–2.   Stability of Communication Links in a Squatter Community in Monterrey, Mexico, from 1976 to 1978.

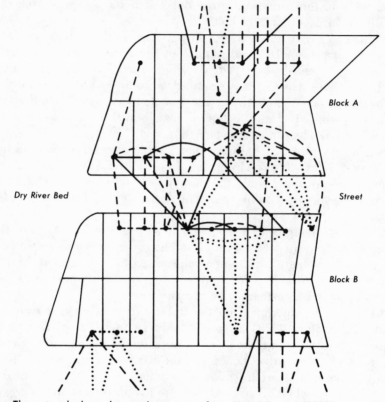

Note: The network data shown above come from Morett-Lopez' (1979) survey in 1976 and 1978 in a squatter community on the outskirts of Monterrey, Mexico. For purposes of clarity, we only show the links among the 33 respondents residing on parcels in two blocks of this community. Stable links are shown with a solid line, while unstable links are shown by dashed lines (links present only in 1976) and dotted lines (links present only in 1978). There is a great deal of change in network links; only about one-fifth were stable over the two-year period. The stable links are more likely to be spatially proximate, reciprocated, and to connect non-kin (about one-third of all links were between kin members). Note that very few of the links connect households that are back to back in the same block; Professor Morett-Lopez accordingly recommended to the community development agency serving this community that they should select local leaders to represent residents living on both sides of a street, rather than in a block.

interviewed 327 women in 1976, and 270 of them again in 1978. He found the following relationships among his measures of network stability, reciprocity, spatial propinquity, and ascription (a concept indexed by whether the two individuals in a dyadic link were connected by blood, marriage, or a religious kinship tie like godfather–godson) (Figure 7–2).

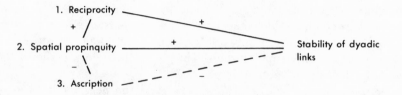

These results support propositions #1 and #2, which were mentioned at the beginning of this section. Despite Morett-Lopez' expectations, ascription (kinship) was negatively related to stability. About 30 percent of all links were between kin, and these kin links were physically more distant (as shown by the negative relationship above between ascription and spatial propinquity). Proposition #3 was not supported either; homophily on age, education, and number of children was not related to network stability. However, other investigators have reported evidence supporting this proposition that network stability is positively related to homophily: 'Where there is asymmetry in the flow over time [a lack of stability], there is very often a difference in status and power between the actors" (Boussevain, 1974, p. 34).

Stages in the Development of a Network

Several network studies suggest that there may be stages in the gradual development of a network.

In the mid-1950s, Newcomb (1961) conducted an unusual experiment at the University of Michigan. Seventeen students, previously strangers, were provided free housing in a residence in exchange for providing weekly data about their sociometric links (and other variables). This situation provided a unique opportunity to gather data about the emergence of communication relationships among the members of a system. By the end of the third week of the school year, network patterns emerged among the 17 students that thereafter changed very little. "Interpersonal relationships of attraction stabilize—at relatively early stages of acquaintance—as individuals cease to acquire new information about each other" (Newcomb, 1961, p. 207).

In a replication of his student housing study the following year, Newcomb (p. 216) assigned half of the students to room with others on the basis of similarity in answering an 85-item attitude inventory (which had been mailed to them prior to their arrival in Ann Arbor). The other students were assigned roommates who were maximally dissimilar on the attitude inventory. The researchers expected that attitudinal similarity would lead to stronger network ties, but this hypothesis was not supported, presumably because the attitudes were not very relevant to forming network links. More important factors in determining who was linked to whom were similarity in rural–urban background and age. Nevertheless, the Newcomb student housing study represents an unusual attempt to speed up the process of network formation, and to alter the communication structure of a small system. The research literature shows there have been few other such attempts.

Bernard and Killworth (1978a) observed the network links among the 40-odd crew and scientists aboard the R/V *Thomas Washington*, an oceanographic ship, for a month. These network analysts also administered a sociometric questionnaire at three times: shortly after leaving port, after two weeks at sea, and again two weeks later. At first there were two cliques (one consisting mainly of the crew, and the other composed of the scientific staff), but after two weeks at sea, the ship's network became more integrated and the cliques partly broke down. Little further change in the networks occurred after the first two weeks from port, supporting the conventional wisdom of oceanographers in this regard.

If Bernard and Killworth's findings can be generalized, at least to relatively small systems where the individuals are in intensive interaction, it seems that a network may go through a series of phases in its development. First, there is a relatively low level of interpersonal communication, as individuals do not know whom to talk to. Network links are mainly with others in a similar role; here cliques emerge consisting of homophilous individuals. At the second stage, there is a high rate of interaction as individuals begin to get acquainted. The cliques grow together to form a connected network as relatively weak ties bridge heterophilous pairs of individuals. Thereafter, at the third stage, a high degree of stability occurs in the communication structure, and the rate of interaction levels off and decreases.

Whether this particular pattern of network change and stability also occurs more generally for larger systems remains to be seen through future research on the dynamic aspects of networks.

Research questions such as the following could be answered in future analyses of network data gathered in a system at several points in time.

1. Are there indeed stages in the process of network formation, such as those just described (for example, an initial state of low-connectedness, and then higher-connectedness, followed by attrition of certain links so that more distinct cliques emerge in the communication structure)?
2. As a network "matures," is there gradually a decrease in the rate of change in the system's communication structure?
3. How are later-entering members of a system gradually interconnected into the network structure?

4. How do the size of cliques change over time? How are new cliques formed in the network?

Such directions for future inquiry could help us better understand the nature of network stability, and particularly how the communication structure in a system follows a pattern of stages as it unfolds.

MULTIPLEXITY OF NETWORK LINKS ACROSS CONTENT TOPICS

One complication involving much of the previous network analysis discussed in this book is that there may not be just a single communication network. A given individual may have a different set of communication partners for each of myriad topics. For example, one of our Korean respondents may talk to Mrs. Moon about family planning, but to Mrs. Chung about her child's health problems. Adequate means (1) of measuring *multiplexity* (the degree to which multiple contents flow through a network link between two individuals), and (2) of analyzing this dimension have not yet been fully worked out by network analysts.

The almost complete lack of attention to the content that flows through network links forces us to be cautious in interpreting the results of almost all past network analysis. An illustration of this caution is Zukerman's (1977, p. 99) finding that Nobel Prize–winning scientists in the United States are generally trained by Nobel Prize winners. What makes such a network link important? We don't know (Mullins with Mullins, 1973, p. 322). Perhaps this link carries information about future, promising directions for science. Maybe the master provides an exemplary model for the protégé. We won't know until the content of such links are determined.

In the previous section we looked at the issue of how generalizable network ties are across time. Here we center on a different aspect of generalizability: the degree to which different content topics flow through the same network link. Communication network analysis in the past has not paid enough attention to the communication content that flows through the links. Our review of literature leads to the conclusion stated by Bernard and others (1979): "As far as we are aware, content of communication is a topic universally avoided by researchers in social network theory."

One means of obtaining data about the content that flows through communication networks is illustrated by Robert Gillespie who used a small number of diary-keepers to record what they heard (and overheard) about family planning during a communicaton campaign in

Esfahan Province, Iran (Rogers and Agarwala-Rogers, 1976). He then content-analyzed these daily diaries to determine how often family planning was being discussed in interpersonal contacts, and whether these discussions were positive or negative.

The content flowing through communication networks may affect the determinants of who interacts with whom. For instance, Bhowmik (1972) found that information-seeking (about agriculture) links among Indian villagers were more heterophilous (on socio-economic status and other characteristics) than were friendship links ("whom do you talk with most?"). Again, we can interpret this research finding in terms of effort and reward: when the villagers were seeking agricultural information that was important to them in their occupation, they sought other farmers who were more educated, of higher status (such as operating larger farms), and so on. Such heterophilous links required more effort, as communication in them was more difficult, but presumably the payoff justified the greater investment.

Communication networks based on instrumental content are more stable than networks based on friendship, Kincaid (1972, p. 67) found among Mexico City slum residents. Perhaps the instrumental networks were perceived as more rewarding (by the participants in these links) than were friendship networks, thus justifying the greater effort required for their stability.

Both multiplex and stable links require greater effort, so we should expect that *multiplexity is positively related to stability in network links.* Boissevain (1974, p. 30) concluded that "there is a tendency for single-stranded [uniplex] relations to become many-stranded [multiplex] if they persist over time, and for many-stranded relations to be stronger than single-stranded ones."

Networks undoubtedly differ from innovation to innovation, and from situation to situation. For example, diffusion networks for family planning may differ from networks for abortion. Here the difference in content is one of tabooness. Taboo communication is "the category of message transfer in which the messages are perceived as extremely private and personal in nature because they deal with proscribed behavior" (Rogers, 1973). The degree of tabooness in our Korean village study was indexed on the basis of three diffusion networks ranging from least taboo to most taboo: frendship, family planning, and abortion. Abortion is a highly taboo type of communication in Korean villages, and it was illegal until a few months prior to our 1973 survey. One indicant of the degree of tabooness of family planning is the percentage of women adopting family planning methods without informing their husbands, parents-in-laws, and parents. We found that 6 percent, 55 percent, and 53 percent of our Korean respondents were practicing contraception without the knowledge of their husbands, parents-in-law, and parents, respectively.

We asked the 39 women in villages A and B, "With whom in this village do you talk most?" Village A respondents reported 164 such friendship links and village B, 191. For family planning communication, 138 and 167 communication links were reported in village A and village B, respectively. For abortion communication, only 22 and 78 communication links were reported in village A and in village B.

In both villages the number of communication links decreased from friendship to family planning, to abortion; not surprisingly the number of links decreased from the least taboo to the most taboo topic. Communication networks are more restricted for more taboo topics. In fact, there is so little abortion communication that cliques could not be identified in village A.

Our findings show that in both Korean villages *tabooness is related to less connectedness and to weaker tie strength (less communication proximity)*, as is consistent with our expectations.

Generally, the relatively few network analyses completed to date show that multiplex links often differ from uniplex links. The concept of multiplexity deserves greater research attention, in efforts to determine the relationship of this concept with stability, connectedness, diversity, and other network dimensions. Further, the content flowing through network links can be categorized into typologies like instrumental versus friendship, for example, and these content dimensions related to other network variables.

CONCLUSIONS

Past social research basically made sense of human behavior by classifying individuals according to various categories of their individual and social characteristics. Social structure was operationalized in terms of the piece of it possessed by each individual. This atomistic–mechanistic approach, criticized previously in chapter 2, contrasts with the network analysis methodology of mapping the communication structure of the system in which an individual is a participant. Explanations of human behavior are sought in the individual's communication links with other members of the system(s) in which he/she is a member. Social structural variables are brought into the analysis as they determine the nature of the communication structure.

In this chapter, our objective was to explain who is linked to whom in communication networks. We concluded that individuals tend to be linked to others (1) who are close to them in physical distance, and (2) who are relatively homophilous in social characteristics. Both spatial and social distance explain who is linked to whom because of the principle of least-effort and greatest-reward: individuals form, and maintain, network links that require the least effort, and that are most rewarding. Spatial proximity and social homophily make for easier network links, while the amount of valuable information thus obtained via these links represents the reward. A basic paradox in human communication is that more informationally valuable links require more effort to form and maintain.

Network stability is the degree to which a network link occurs at two or more points in time. Past research suggests that spatially proximate and reciprocated links are more stable, but does not support our expectations that homophilous and ascribed links are more stable.

Multiplexity is the degree to which multiple contents flow through a network link between two individuals. Because both stability and multiplexity require greater effort by participants in such links, we expect these two concepts to be related.

8 SUMMING UP

The challenge to sociologists is to turn the "network" from image to instrument, to apply the concept in ways that will inform us about the nature of society.

Claude S. Fischer and others (1977, p. 17)

The purposes of our final chapter are (1) to summarize the main conclusions of this book, (2) to critique and discuss our network/convergence paradigm in terms of its performance and potential for communication research, and (3) to describe various approaches to putting network analysis into use.

TOWARD A NEW PARADIGM FOR COMMUNICATION RESEARCH

A Brief Historical Review of Network Research Methodology

The pioneers in network analysis during the 1970s exemplified a spirit of creative originality that is remarkable in the contemporary social sciences. Out of this methodological progress has come a distinctive approach to analyzing human behavior so as to identify and understand the communication structure of systems. This capacity to measure the "big picture" of communication behavior in a system provides an alternative to the main methodologies of past social science methods, an avenue of possible escape from the limitations of atomistic–mechanistic analysis of individual behavior. Our book has argued for the exciting potential, yet unfulfilled, of using these macroscopic methods to understand the behavior of human systems, thus providing one approach to effectuating the convergence model of communication (a paradigm based rather directly on systems theory and a cybernetic view of human interaction).

The network analysis methodologists had to overcome a number of mental blocks to formulate their network analysis techniques. First, they had to create a measure (or measures) of dyadic proximity on which to base their computer procedures for identifying communication structure. Prior to the mid-1960s, network scholars had not conceived of measuring the proximity of paired individuals in a system, other than with the simplistic index of whether they were directly linked or not. Such a zero/one proximity measure is relatively crude. During the late 1960s alternative proximity measures such as linkage distance evolved, facilitated by matrix multiplication computer procedures (chapter 3). Network scholars were moving beyond the construction of Moreno-type sociograms based on the relatively subjective methods of arbitrarily arranging and rearranging individuals on a two-dimensional surface. Sociograms suffered from their limitation to rather small-sized systems, as well as from the idiosyncratic subjectivity of their construction. However, the sociograms did provide visual insight into network data.

Later, in the 1970s, network scholars formed measures of communication proximity and correlational similarity. Thus, it was possible to construct computer programs for the network analysis of larger-sized systems. These advances in network analysis technology allowed measurement of the communication structure in larger and hence more real-life systems: entire organizations, villages, invisible colleges of scientists, and other systems. The entrance of computers into the network analysis field, and their present dominance of its methods, facilitated the move to investigation of new research questions and the testing of new theories, intellectual frameworks more consistent with a convergence model of communication.

The day of the highly quantitative tool-maker in network analysis, beginning in the late 1960s, unfortunately led to a serious overmathematization of the field, making much of the literature incomprehensible to the average social scientist. We wonder if the forest of formulae in network literature is really essential. For instance, in writing the present book we found it largely unnecessary to include many mathematical formulae, preferring to sacrifice the possible precision such quantitative expression might have added, for the greater clarity to the reader of stating a similar content in prose. We feel that the special precision of mathematical notation is futile if most readers do not understand it.

The attraction of computer-competent tool-makers to the field of network analysis introduced an accompanying creative originality (mentioned previously). Many of these network pioneers were hybrid social scientists, somewhat marginal to their discipline. In several cases they represent unlikely combinations of disciplinary backgrounds and skills: a Ph.D. in sociology who also has a Ph.D. in physics, a colleagueal pair consisting of a computer-minded anthropologist and an applied nuclear physicist, a sociologist using econometric methods, a sociology Ph.D. with an undergraduate degree in chemical engineering, and a social psychologist working closely with a mathematician. The invisible college of network analysis scholars that developed during the 1970s spans a wide variety of social science disciplines; what its members hold in common is faith in a quantitative approach to macroscopic analysis of the communication structure of human systems. In the main, they reject the atomistic–mechanistic approach to data-analysis in which they were mainly trained, and search for more holistic alternatives in the methods of network analysis. Without the methodological breakthroughs by these tool-makers in the 1970s, network analysts would still be drawing little sociograms.

But perusal of contemporary literature on the methodologies of network analysis convinces one that these tool-makers did not fully realize what they had accomplished. The typical scientific journal article about network analysis described a new methodological twist in detail, usually with numerous mathematical formulae to support and explain it. Missing was a methodological synthesis of what the entire body of new tools added up to. The goal of network analysis in identifying communication structure was seldom appreciated. Network analysis programs as macroscopes for detecting communication structure were not fully understood. Missing was a theoretical frame to place the network tools in context.

Worse, as we emphasized in previous chapters, each network methodologist "did his own thing," creating new scientific procedures to elucidate communication structure but often without relating each new advance to extant network methods. The potential user of network analysis thus faced a mixed bag of presumably competing techniques, without being provided criteria for evaluating which method was best suited to particular research problems. Each network methodologist set forth the advantages of a particular tool, without much mention of its accompanying disadvantages or limitations. Past literature provides few comparisons of the use of two or more network analysis techniques with the same data-set. We tried (in chapter 4) to take the first step toward remedying this lack of comparison by using five main network analysis methods on communication data from two Korean villages.

A further, and even more serious, problem faces the potential user of network analysis techniques: the communication structural indices thus measured exhibit a cacophony of concepts that completely confuse the potential user. For instance, one of the main conceptual variables is connectedness; the network literature calls this concept (or something very much like it) by at least a half dozen other names. Many are not defined precisely. Connectedness (or "connectiveness" or "connectivity") has also been measured as if it were integration. When faced with this intellectual mess, most potential users simply walk away, shaking their heads.

In this book (chapter 4) we set forth four main concepts on which to hang our approach to communication structure: connectedness, integration, diversity, and openness. We argue that these four conceptual variables, measurable at the individual, clique, and network levels, are the main theoretical building blocks of the network/convergence paradigm.

Advantages of Network Analysis in Communication Research

Network analysis procedures, coupled with the convergence model, have several advantages as an approach to communication research.

1. Network analysis is a means of investigating behavior at a more macro level than the psychological microanalysis of individual-level variables that have been the primary (and almost complete) concern of past communication research. Once a communication scholar moves from the individual as the unit of analysis, new vistas of scientific opportunities open up. The field of communication inquiry can then move beyond its past atomistic–mechanistic "take-it-apart-and-see-how-it-works" concern with communication effects upon the individual audience member. Network analysis can display the communication structure of a system, a bigger picture of patterned flows of information-exchange in which the network link, the personal communication network, the clique, and/or the entire network are the unit of analysis. This more macro-level research is consistent with a convergence view of communication, with the long-prevailing view of communication as process. Thus the network/convergence paradigm helps remove the main contradiction of the communication research on effects that was guided by the linear models: communication was defined as a process, but studied as a push-pull-click-click kind of one-shot monologue focusing on the communication event. We feel that the broader view of communication as convergence helps move the main concern of communication research to the dialogue, to the exchange of information as the central focus.

2. Our basic paradigm helps bring social structure into communication research (chapter 7). The heavy psychological origins of the science of communication initially led it away from a concern with structure, to focus on using conceptual variables about human communication to explain the dependent variables of other social science disciplines (voting, violence, consumer purchasing, etc.). Such secondhand psychology does not hold promise for creating a discipline of human communication. More-of-the-same is not the most appropriate recipe for a theoretically integrated, cumulative body of concepts and theories about the nature of human communication. Instead, communication scholars must shift to focus on communication structural variables as their main dependent variables. Then the main conceptual dimensions from other social sciences (for example, spatial variables from geography, and structural variables from sociology, political science, anthropology, and economics) become the independent variables used to explain communication structure. *Until any scientific field begins to investigate the human behavior that is its central intellectual interest, it will not develop directly as a discipline.*

There is, however, a caveat that must be expressed concerning this about-face for communication research: we presently lack an adequate basis of communication structural concepts and theoretical propositions linking these concepts. Specifically, there are few such propositions about communication networks,[1] and even the relational concepts that must constitute the building blocks of such theories are surrounded by considerable confusion. In this book, we attempted to explicate four basic network concepts: connectedness, integration, diversity, and openness. We have reconstituted the findings from past network analyses around these four concepts. The task ahead is to expand greatly this limited repertoire of conceptual variables and to explore their utility in constructing an integrated set of theories about communication structure.

Network analysis procedures are necessary because we generally gather data at one level (usually from individuals) and need to analyze it at another (such as the clique or system level). We usually can interact with, or observe, only the lowest level of a system. Ideally, we would like to obtain information at all levels of the system, but we often have access only to the lowest level through our measurement approaches (Richards, 1974b). Network analysis procedures help convert the individual-level data to higher-level data. This transformation across levels is a crucial function of network analysis techniques. The other important function is to cope with problems of information overload (as we showed in chapter 4).

Problems with Network Analysis

In addition to the important advantages that network analysis can bring to communication research, this approach faces a number of fundamental problems.

Sampling and Generalization

Problems of statistical inference on the basis of random sampling continue to plague communication network analysis. As discussed in chapter 3, it is very difficult to select a sample of network links, the fundamental datum in network analysis. So we must draw samples of individuals (and thus of all their reported links to members of their personal networks) or of intact groups (such as Korean villages).[2] Sometimes we use snowball sampling in a research design. These special techniques

---

[1] Among past attempts to suggest a body of network propositions are Mitchell (1974), Boissevain (1974), Whitten and Wolfe (1974), Fischer and others (1977), and Danowski (1976).

[2] Intact groups can be sampled, of course, only to the extent that such intact groups have a definite boundary. Otherwise it is difficult to know where a network ends. Less connected individuals usually are found near the boundaries of a system, so when the system's boundary is drawn too tightly, the weak ties are likely to be lost, although such bridging links are especially valuable in understanding the communication structure of the system.

minimize the difficulties of sampling network links. But there is a fundamental incompatibility between random sampling (usually based on
selecting a sample of *individuals*) and network analysis. Perhaps this contradiction can only be solved ultimately by a retreat from insisting on
random sampling, and thus from the logic of statistical inference. Network analysts may eventually decide that in many researches the *social*
significance of their research results, provided by an in-depth analysis of
relational data, outweighs the use of *statistical* significance tests in generalizing from a random sample to a larger population. If a research
methodology does not fit the objectives of a certain type of investigation,
perhaps the methodology should at least be questioned. Probably it
should not be utilized. The correctness of a research methodology is
relative, not absolute, resting solely on its appropriateness to the objectives of an investigation.

Measurement

One of the main shortcomings of network analysis to date is inadequate measurement of network links. Network data in the past have
depended overwhelmingly on sociometric measurement, which we have
found wanting in certain respects. Improvements in sociometric measurement are needed, along with exploration of other types of measurement.
We advocate much greater use of multimeasurement designs in future
communication research, where various types of observations and of unobtrusive measurement are incorporated with improved sociometric study
of network links.

Network Analysis Techniques

Generally, we feel that network analysts in the past have stressed the
advancement of data-manipulation techniques over more needed progress
in network measurement. However, improvements are also needed in network analysis techniques. Unfortunately, all methods of network analysis
rest on a certain degree of arbitrariness in identifying clique boundaries,
and thus in assigning individuals to communication roles in the communication structure. Even NEGOPY, the network analysis computer program with perhaps the "least–worst" degree of arbitrariness in clique
identification, allows the setting of various computer program parameters
that can influence the communication structure resulting from the network analysis.

A Multimethod Approach

There is no single "perfect" method of network analysis for all purposes. Each of the five main methods of network analysis has certain
strengths and particular weaknesses. But when five different network
analysis techniques were used with the same data-set (chapter 4), the

five communication structures that we found were quite similar. Such results, if future study shows they indeed hold true in a variety of other systems, suggest that network analysts might use two or more of the network analysis methods with the same network data-set in order to capture certain of the advantages of each. So we advocate a multimethod, along with a multimeasurement, approach to network analysis. Eventually, scholars need a Network Package for the Social Sciences, consisting of a family of analysis techniques that can easily be utilized in a flexible, multimethod approach to identifying communication structure.

Proximity

We feel that one of the first considerations in deciding which network analysis technique to utilize ought to be the measure of proximity underlying the network analysis computer program. The importance of the proximity measure in determining exactly what aspects of communication structure are identified, and how, by a network analysis technique, has not been fully appreciated in the past. Often program descriptions of network analysis techniques say very little or nothing about their underlying proximity measure. We conclude that the most appropriate measure for purposes of communication network analysis is *communication proximity,* the degree to which two directly linked individuals in a network have personal communication networks that overlap. Our present findings (chapter 4) suggest that a measure of communication proximity is highly related to such other proximity measures as linkage distance and correlational proximity (on which certain network analysis techniques are based). But communication proximity is the most logically appropriate type of proximity to use in the network analysis of communication networks.

Despite these five methodological problems, there is heartening evidence that much of our Korean network data was of unusually solid quality and rich in depth and variety (Breiger, 1976b). For example, the results of blockmodeling with CONCOR (in chapter 4) show that each of 10 different sociometric questions measured a common communication structure. Our comparisons of the results from the five network analysis techniques (chapter 4) indicate that a strikingly similar communication structure was produced, whatever method of network analysis and whatever proximity measure were used. These empirical results generally indicate a certain robustness in what might otherwise seem to be relatively weak measurements and methods for determining communication structure in the Korean village network.

Our network analyses of the Korean village data largely looked *within* each village for explanations of the diffusion of family planning innovations. Such basic network concepts as connectedness, integration, and, to a lesser extent, diversity were emphasized more than was openness. Yet the idea of family planning had to penetrate each village system before within-village communication about it could occur. Our shortcoming is typical of many network analyses; they fail to consider fully the network's links with its environment.

Looking Back at Our Korean Network Research

We do not hold up our Korean village data-analysis as any ideal approach to network investigation. Nor is it even a very full example of the kinds of network analysis that we recommend. Obviously, we did not read this book before we designed the Korean study. Had we been able to do so, we would have done the following:

1. Asked fewer than 14 sociometric questions in our personal interviews with the 1,003 women in the 24 villages, and not limited our respondents to five choices per question. Instead, we would have measured the weaker ties (as well as the stronger ties) by means of a roster technique with one or more sociometric questions. It is possible that the rather clear-cut communication structures that we found in most of the 24 villages (and even in Oryu Li) are partly because we only measured relatively stronger ties, thus ignoring certain of the bridge links between cliques that are relatively weaker.

2. Supplemented our sociometric data with observation and unobtrusive measurements of network links in each of the villages (in addition to villages A and B, and Oryu Li). Also, we might have asked key informants in each village to provide network data, or else we could have shown them our sociograms in order to test their validity.

3. Gathered repeated measures of network links over time, so as to be able to investigate the stability/change aspect of the communication structures. In retrospect, we see how ideal it would have been to have gathered repeated measures of communication networks in sequence with the introduction of mothers' clubs in Korean villages during the period after 1968. In chapter 6, we reported our finding, based on cross-sectional correlational analysis of our 1973 survey data, that the percentage of mothers' club members in a village is positively related to the connectedness of the family planning communication network, which in turn is positively related to the percent of family planning adoption in the village. Unfortunately, we could not measure the time-order of these three village-level variables. Does a mothers' club typically contribute toward greater connectedness in a village, and thus to a higher rate of family planning adoption? We expect so. But we have no over-time evidence. Much greater understanding of the processual nature of communication could be gained with network data gathered at two or more points in time. On this score, our Korean survey is deficient.

PUTTING NETWORK ANALYSIS INTO USE

In previous chapters we described a new paradigm for communication research. We have argued, with certain important caveats, for the potential of the network/convergence paradigm for future communication *research*. In addition, the general type of network thinking that we described holds a useful potential for pragmatic application. In the following discussion, we tell briefly about several of these practical uses of our paradigm.

Feeding Back the Communication Structure from Network Analysis to the System of Study

One such pragmatic application, combining elements of communication research with its use in improving human communication structures, occurs when network analysts feed back their research results to the systems they have investigated. Our position is that no communication research should be conducted that does not provide certain direct benefits to the respondents of such studies. This position is justified by the basic logic that unless the subjects of study feel they have profited from their participation in a communication research, the researchers will be unwelcome in the future. But we caution that such feeding back of network analysis results must be conducted with important ethical considerations in mind. The results of network analysis, when understood by the system whose communication structure is so described, can break down pluralistic ignorance about this structure, with a consequence of aiding the communication effectiveness of the system and of its individual members. It can also be potentially destructive of the system and of certain of its members.

Perhaps an illustration of the negative effects of network analysis for certain members of the system of study occurred in the case of an investigation conducted by university communication scholars in one of the world's largest banks, at its New York City headquarters. These network analysts found that one of the bank's divisions had a particularly inefficient communication structure, and that it was characterized by low employee morale, high absenteeism, and other indications of unhealthy functioning. When these research findings became known to the bank's officials, they reportedly reacted by transferring the entire division to the sub-subbasement of the Manhattan skyscraper in which the bank is headquartered. The employees of this division could hardly have felt they were helped very much by the communication network analysis (although the bank officials may have been).

Network scholars have occasionally fed back the communication structures that they find to the members of the systems of study, so as to obtain a kind of validity check on their network analysis procedures. For instance, as mentioned in previous chapters, Professors Russell Bernard and Peter Killworth frequently present their network analysis results to their respondents, who then may participate in interpreting the meaning of the communication structure. As a research by-product, the system's members may be able to better understand the network of which they are part, and thus improve their functioning in this system. The eventual consequence may be planned changes in the communication structure.

A special form of such feedback may occur when the network analysis is conducted before and after an intervention in order to measure the intervention's impact on the communication structure. We described several examples of such research designs in chapter 3, such as when a new information system like teleconferencing is introduced in a system to increase the average connectedness of the network. Feedback of such data on the impact of the intervention may be useful not only to researchers and agency officials responsible for evaluating the benefits and disadvantages of the intervention for similar systems, but the feedback may have direct consequences for the particular system that was studied.

In this case, network analysis serves as a means of diagnosis and, perhaps, for the amelioration of certain problems in the communication structure that the network analysis discloses, as well as serving as a research and evaluation tool.

Unmasking Communication Structure with the Macroscope of Network Analysis

Network analysis is a kind of scientific exposé in that one of its most dramatic characteristics is the unmasking of otherwise invisible communication structures (Kadushin, 1977). An individual usually is aware of his/her adjacent network links, of course, but the communication structure of the entire system is usually unknown and invisible to the individual member in it. For instance, in an earlier chapter we reviewed the small world method; the typical reader probably had no idea that he could reach across the country with interpersonal channels in about five steps. When we know that a clique exists in a system and can see its effects but do not know exactly who belongs to it, we often refer to it as a "Mafia," implying that it is powerful but invisible. We are embedded in our systems and usually can see only the persons next to us. Perhaps with unusual vision an individual can see the person next to the person next to him/her. What network analysis does is provide us with a macroscopic view of the entire communication structure, something like the satellite photograph of the daily weather system (Kadushin, 1977). This "big picture" tells us something about our system that we cannot otherwise know.

Moreno (1934) noted the strong impact of a sociogram on the members of the group it describes. "Evidently a representation of a group in a two-dimensional Euclidian space speaks very strongly to people's feelings about themselves and their associates" (Roistacher, 1974). When the results of a network analysis are fed back to the system that has been analyzed, the system's members generally show unusual interest in the results, which are often presented in the form of a sociogram. This big picture of the communication structure is often of direct relevance to the system's members in making certain decisions. For instance, an undergraduate student at Stanford University recently gathered sociometric data from his 70 fellow members of a communal residence that makes decisions on the basis of consensus. Sociometric data were gathered and the communication structure of this residence, displayed in a sociogram, was then discussed by the members and used as a basis for their "election" of new leaders, which was guided by their desire to maximize the system's connectedness. In one sense, the network analysis fulfilled the usual function of voting; the members of the residence really were casting their votes when they reported their network links. Each individual, in a sense, was a member of the nominating committee.

In this experience with network analysis, the student residents agreed in advance to forgo the confidentiality of their network data. The names of individuals in the sociogram were identified. In other situations, confidentiality may be maintained by assigning a code number to each individual in the system. Nevertheless, feeding back the communication structure of a system to its members necessarily entails some heavy ethical considerations. For instance, what effect will learning that he/she is an isolate have on the behavior of that individual? Further, what is the effect on the isolate of knowing that all the other members of his/her system now know that this individual is an isolate? In this particular case, the decrease in pluralistic ignorance in a system about its communication structure can have destructive as well as constructive effects, depending on how such information is fed back to the system's members, and on the particular communication role (isolate, liaison, and clique member) that an individual learns he/she is filling. Frequently, a system requests feedback about its communication structure in order to change this structure in certain ways, often to increase connectedness in the entire system or in certain parts of the system.

Network Analysis and Landscaped Offices

One frequent circumstance in which the communication structure is identified and altered, occurs in a formal organization. *Bürolandschaft* is a highly controversial method of office organization begun in Germany and Sweden, and then introduced in the United States in the mid-1960s as "office landscaping" or "nonterritorial offices" (Allen, 1978). The term "office landscaping" is a direct translation of the German word "*büroland-schaft*," and derives from the low planters that are frequently used as flexible dividers between work groups in an organization (Rogers and Agarwala-Rogers, 1976, p. 102).

In most offices, physical proximity plays an important role in determining who interacts with whom. For instance, Allen (1966) found in research and development laboratories that "two people who are on the same floor, if separated by more than 25 yards, will rarely have any significant communication." Offices are usually arranged to correspond with a formal organizational chart, and this spatial arrangement usually determines, to a high degree, the communication structure.

Office landscaping provides a means of keeping the spatial structure more flexible by removing walls and other barriers, so that the communication structure, as it emerges over time, can affect the spatial structure of the arrangement of desks and other equipment. Then the organizational structure is adjusted to follow the communication structure. In a nonterritorial office, employees are allowed to rearrange their desks into physical locations that best suit their functional needs to interact with one another. Typically, network analysis procedures are followed to derive the communication structure, and such understanding provides a basis for constructing an optimum physical environment in an organization (Rogers and Agarwala-Rogers, 1976, p. 102). As work functions change over time, employees' desks can be shifted to accommodate to the new communication structure that emerges. In short, office landscaping puts the communication structure, identified by network analysis, in the driver's seat in determining spatial structure and organizational structure.

There are certain obvious disadvantages to offices without walls, such as ambient noise and the breakdown of office status symbols, but the office landscaping movement in the United States is gaining ground, and today many office buildings and schools are constructed without walls.

In an organization, administrative authorities are in a position to alter the communication structure through the transfer of individuals from one position to another, reorganization of divisions and offices, and the redesign of networks and of communication roles. Network analysis can provide a special kind of understanding of the communication structure of the organization, and thus give the organization's leaders a basis for changing the structure. In some unusually democratic organizations, all of the members may participate in redesigning their communication structure. An illustration of such self-management of the communication structure is provided by Professors Bill McKelvey and Ralph Kilman (1975) of the University of Pittsburgh. They administered a sociometric measure of communication networks to the 115 faculty members of a university business school. A factor analysis type of network analysis of these data was presented to the professors at a workshop. The faculty then decided how to arrange themselves into work groups (roughly similar to the usual university departments). These work groups were similar in about 60 percent of the cases to the cliques identified by the network analysis computer program.

Horizontal Diffusion Networks

A major function of certain government agencies in the United States, Korea, and most other nations is to diffuse technological innovations to an audience of potential adopters. These diffusion agencies mainly conceive of their function in terms of a linear model of communication, from research and development (to create the innovations), to dissemination of these technologies to the public audience, who then adopt the innovations. Typical of such top-down diffusion agencies are the extension services of the U.S. Department of Agriculture, the U.S. Department of Education, the Health Services Administration, NASA, and the U.S. Department of Transportation. Counterparts to these "mission agencies" exist in most other nations. All are patterned, more or less, after the agricultural extension model of the United States (Rogers and others, 1976b).

This predominant model of vertical diffusion has been criticized by Professor Donald Schön (1971) at MIT. He argues that the "central-periphery" model of diffusion should be replaced by a network model of horizontal diffusion. Most government diffusion programs in the past assumed that the innovation was basically perfected prior to its diffusion, and that it moved out from the "center" (for example, Washington, D.C.) via vertical spokes, to the "periphery" of local governments and the public through a carefully planned, well managed diffusion process. Schön believed that certain technological innovations involving hardware products may indeed best follow this vertical process.

But policy innovations, which often entail changing the social structure and the nature of organizations, often spread in a quite different manner. When government agencies attempt to promote such policy innovations through hierarchical diffusion, the result is often failure. Local problems and needs are so diverse in a rapidly changing and heterogeneous society, that the agency-based structure of central government cannot form standard policies to effectively meet the wide range of local needs. So the innovative policy simply cannot fit the variety of local needs. But adequate customization of the innovation is not allowed by the federal government.

Instead, Schön (1971) recommends that a more appropriate role for the federal government is to design and support horizontal networks for information-exchange about innovations. New problems could then be identified by localities, which would also begin experimentation to find policy solutions. The center should assist local governments in exchanging the resulting innovations, playing a facilitating role, rather than acting like a top-down authority. Policy initiation would thus bubble up from localities through their networks, to the federal government. Local adaptation of the policy innovations would be encouraged, in light of the heterogeneity of local conditions.

An illustration of horizontal diffusion through local networking is the Regional Medical Program of the mid-1960s, which was launched in the United States by a federal agency with grants of $100 million to 55 regions (Sarason and others, 1977, p. 175). Each was expected to form a network consisting (1) of a medical teaching and research organization (usually a university medical school), and (2) of community hospitals and practicing doctors. The needs of the regional medical networks, however, often emerged as quite different from what the federal mandate had anticipated, and these local associations began to use the federal funds to suit their own purposes. After some struggle, the center reluctantly agreed to this local autonomy. What had begun as a center-periphery type of vertical diffusion program evolved into a local network for horizontal diffusion (Schön, 1977). The Regional Medical Programs at the local level launched an informal network through which they exchanged useful experiences.[3]

During the 1970s, several additional diffusion networking approaches have been launched by the federal government. Here we briefly describe the main features of two of these: (1) the National Diffusion Network (sponsored by the U.S. Office of Education for educational innovations), and (2) the local government innovation networks (sponsored by the National Science Foundation). The NDN began in 1973 by a quirk of bureaucratic budget bungling; officials in the U.S. Office of Education were faced with the problem of "year-end money," several million dollars which had to be spent by the June 30 end of the fiscal year. In desperation, they decided to allocate the funds to local schools that had developed an innovation, so they could spread these new ideas to other local schools (Rogers and others, 1976b). These local sources of educational innovations are called "developer/demonstrators." About 150 such

---

[3] The Regional Medical Programs were phased out by the federal government in the mid-1970s, presumably because of a loss of federal appreciation of what they were accomplishing.

developer/demonstrators were funded, each to diffuse horizontally an innovation that had been approved as a "validated practice" by a committee of federal experts. The modest federal funds were used by developer/demonstrators to publish brochures and other mass media messages, to provide training for potential adopters, and to demonstrate the local innovation to other schoolteachers. Few of the initial 150 innovations were "standard" innovations like those that had been promoted previously in a decade of center-periphery diffusion by the U.S. Office of Education: team teaching, programmed instruction, teacher aides, and so on. *All* public schools were expected to adopt these new ideas, which had been invented by research and development laboratories. But the NDN innovations diffusing from the local developer/demonstrators were appropriate only to *certain* schools with particular problems. And even then, many of the developer/demonstrators' innovations were reinvented [4] by other schools when they implemented them according to their local conditions. Further, some of the innovations were relabeled with a local name by certain adopters, even when an innovation's form had not really been modified very much or at all. But the psychological effect of such renaming was to give the innovation a local identity and to encourage the pride of local ownership.

How successful is the National Diffusion Network? At the end of its first three years of operation, the 150 innovations had been accepted by several thousand adopters. The NDN was very popular with school personnel and the public. This popularity was translated into political support by the U.S. Congress, which began to give the NDN a regular budget (of $25 million in 1977). A precise measure of NDN's impact was difficult to obtain because so many different innovations were spontaneously flowing out from the developer/demonstrators, and each of these innovations took such a variety of forms. The result certainly seemed to be innovation in U.S. education, but it was not a result that could be conveniently measured.[5]

A second illustration of a contemporary horizontal diffusion networking approach began in the early 1970s, when the National Science Foundation (NSF) wished to assist local cities in the United States to utilize innovations from space technology and other federally sponsored R&D programs. The cities faced critical problems of traffic, crime, and so on. The NSF hoped that the technological innovations might be part of the answer. NSF's program of assistance to networks of local governments began in four California cities in 1971; each city was given a "tech-

---

[4] *Reinvention* is the degree to which an innovation is changed by the adopter in the process of adoption and implementation after its original development.

[5] At least as conveniently and neatly measured as in the case of a center-periphery diffusion approach, where the usual measure of impact is the rate of adoption of innovations promoted by a federal agency to local government units or to the public.

nology agent," attached to the mayor's or city manager's office, to link the city's problems with external sources of technical assistance. This program of innovation networks linking local cities was called the Urban Technology System, and was funded by NSF. This modest start soon blossomed into more than a dozen regional innovation networks of cities and three national consortia. The annual NSF budget for these networks increased from $600,000 in 1971 to $2.5 million in 1979. Much of the funding is used for partial support of the technology agents. As in the case of NDN, the National Science Foundation's urban networking program is politically popular, and hence rather well funded.

The NSF program emphasizes horizontal diffusion from city to city through loose affiliations of urban governments in networks, which are user-driven by "demand pull." Unlike federal mission agencies, these networks do not promote specific innovations; instead, solutions are sought to the perceived problems of local governments. An important function of the local networks of cities is to monitor emerging local needs and to aggregate these perceived problems in a meaningful way so that useful technological answers can be sought from private and public sources. Some of these solutions (innovations) are invented, created, or developed by a local city. This success is then publicized to other cities in the network through newsletters and conferences, with the result that other cities with a similar problem come to site-visit the innovating city. The urban officials who travel on these cross-country jaunts observe the innovation in action and question the local government leaders responsible for its implementation. Often the visitors are favorably impressed wth the potential of the innovation in meeting their local problem back home, and they return with a desire to try out the new idea under their own conditions, although often with considerable modification in the original innovation. Such reinvention means that the form of the technical innovation is often continuously changing as it diffuses spontaneously.

Thus, the horizontal networking among U.S. cities leads to a fertile disorder in diffusion patterns. Central control of these diffusion networks is difficult or impossible (to the occasional frustration of federal officials and of evaluators of such systems). The diffusion networks are not only user-driven but user-designed. The National Science Foundation provides partial funding of these networking activities, but imposes little central control over the diffusion process. In the early 1970s, local city officials such as mayors and city managers formed a new organization, based in Washington, D.C., called Public Technology, Inc. (PTI), to lend technical expertise to cities on demand. PTI serves a crucial role in the spontaneously emerging urban networks, in providing technical backup to the local technology agents and in monitoring the local needs and problems that bubble up from the local governments.

The problem facing any horizontal diffusion network is how to best bring technological expertise to bear in the process. In a vertical approach to diffusion, federal employees act as change agents in telling localities that they should adopt new ideas and in assisting them to do so. But in horizontal diffusion networks, local units are much more responsible for their own innovation decisions, and federal officials are supposed to act mainly as facilitators in helping the local units find technological solutions to their perceived problems. Most technical assistance is provided by one locality to another, by helping to give meaning to an innovation and fitting it to local conditions. So expertise is largely decentralized at the local level centered in developer/demonstrators in the case of NDN, and in technology agents in NSF's urban networks. Thus, the form of expertness is different than in the center-periphery approach to diffusion; know-how about the locally perceived problems/needs and about local conditions becomes important, as well as know-how about technological innovations.

Evaluation of horizontal diffusion networks must be different than in the case of vertical diffusion, where the rate of adoption of technological innovations is the main criterion of success. In the case of a horizontal approach, a more appropriate, but difficult to quantify, performance measure might be the degree to which localities' problems have been solved by technological innovation. More broadly, it might even be argued that the degree to which the horizontal network is connected might be the best measure of success; here the nature of the communication structure, as determined by network analysis techniques, might best show the accomplishments of networking efforts.[6]

A striking parallel to the U.S. horizontal diffusion networks is provided by a recent description of the diffusion of policy innovations in the People's Republic of China (Rogers and Chen, 1979). Innovations in China are often developed by such local units as counties, communes, and production brigades, and spread mainly via horizontal channels from "models" through "on-the-spot" conferences to other local units that reinvent the innovation as they modify it to suit their local conditions. The national government in Peking plays an important role in setting a horizontal diffusion process in motion, monitoring its progress, and providing some expertise at appropriate points. The mass media help orchestrate the entire diffusion process by informing the public about needs and problems, the existence of innovations to meet such problems that have been developed by a local model, and the results of on-the-spot conferences. Certain local models are famous for their role in horizontal

[6] Such an approach to evaluating a federally sponsored diffusion network among educational R&D laboratories in the United States is reported by Lloyd-Kolkin (1979).

diffusion; for example, Tachai Brigade in Shensi Province attracts about 350,000 visitors each year, who come to study its self-reliant approach to agricultural development.

In short, diffusion of policy innovations in China is much like the horizontal networking approach advocated by Schön (1971), and is similar to the National Diffusion Network in U.S. education and the horizontal diffusion networks of U.S. cities. All three of these approaches demonstrate how diffusion programs have outrun the classical diffusion model of center-periphery dissemination. In fact, the horizontal diffusion approaches represent a radically different, alternative model of diffusion, one that deserves careful study and analysis to determine its particular advantages and disadvantages. It should be stressed that horizontal diffusion networking is neither a complete nor a perfect solution to all problems of applying technological solutions to locally perceived problems. For example, we previously mentioned the unusual difficulties in evaluating such horizontal diffusion networks in terms of the usual criteria of successful performance, and the problems of bringing appropriate technical expertise to bear at the local level in such decentralized systems.

Further, horizontal networking may lead to greater inequality between more elite and less elite units in a system. For example, U.S. cities that are larger in size and already more innovative (like Scottsdale, Portland, and Ann Arbor) are most active in the urban innovation networks. As a result, they gain further innovativeness, at the relative expense of such smaller, less elite, and less innovative cities like Keokuk and Iron Mountain. Wider "gaps" may be one result of such spontaneously created horizontal diffusion networks.

In any event, these horizontal diffusion systems represent one contemporary illustration of the potential of applying to practical problems the network/convergence paradigm that we have described in this book.

Interventions Through Helping Networks

Another type of network thinking, mentioned previously in chapter 3 and described in detail by Sarason and others (1977), is represented by the interventions of psychiatrists and other health professionals through what are called "helping networks." This approach consists, essentially, of treating not just a sick individual, but the individual's personal communication network, and thus *indirectly* enrolling these network members to help cure the individual's illness.

Helping networks are utilized especially in certain types of mental illness, where the patient's kin and friends may have been part of the cause, and where, in any event, they can directly assist in the curing process. Reinforcement and support are provided to the individual through "network therapy," in which the patient and his/her personal network members (sometimes up to 40 persons) meet in his/her living room with the therapists. The results of using a helping network approach are encouraging as documented by numerous evaluation studies (Speck and Attneave, 1973; Speck and Rueveni, 1969).

Health professionals are seeking to change individual behavior in the direction of curing mental illness. As we might expect on the basis of our conclusions in chapter 5 about network influences on behavior change, experience in the mental health field shows that helping networks can be an important part of curing. In some cases, restructuring of the patient's personal communication network *is* the cure.

Another illustration of helping networks is provided by two contrasting models of drug treatment. The individualistic mode, representing a linear model of communication through persuasion by a credible source, is known in the drug abuse field as the "Lexington" approach (after the federal hospital in Lexington, Kentucky, where this method was first developed). It consists of three or four days of detoxification, in which the addict goes through the misery of withdrawal. Then the addict is exposed to a series of lectures about the dangerous consequences of drug dependence, about the importance of responsibility to self and to others, and so on. Within a few weeks the former addicts are released. Upon return to their former roles in drug-using networks, they relapse into their old ways in about 90 to 95 percent of the cases.

An alternative drug-curing approach, taking advantage of communication networks instead of ignoring them, was pioneered by the Synanon organization, started in California about twenty years ago. Drug addicts lived in Synanon houses, completely removed from their drug addict friends, and thus participated in new networks composed of ex-addicts. The reinforcement thus provided the addict by his complete connectedness into his residential network was the main curing method used in the Synanon approach.

In contrast to the Lexington approach, Synanon was much more successful. Recidivism rates of only 5 to 10 percent were attained. Helping networks again proved to be helpful. But unfortunately, the ex-addicts often became addicted to Synanon, and were reluctant to move out of the Synanon houses back into society.

From Know-How to Know-Who

There is a direct connection between the nature of society and the basic approach utilized by communication scientists in their research. Perhaps in recent decades "know-how" was a major factor in the effectiveness of individuals in their daily lives. But at present the information explosion, facilitated by the widespread mass media and by recent advances in communication technology (especially of an interactive sort), has created an information environment in which almost every individual possesses more know-how than he can cope with.

Such information overload is often handled by the structuring of interpersonal network links by individuals. "Know-who" thus begins to replace "know-how" as one of the main determinants of individual effectiveness. In previous chapters, we provided many examples of the richness of network links in helping individuals solve their information-handling problems. For instance, although every newspaper contains a section of employment ads and despite the existence of private and government employment services, most individuals find jobs through interpersonal networks (as we showed in the section on the strength of weak ties in chapter 2). On a similar theme, we showed in chapter 5 that most individuals do not decide to adopt an innovation on the basis of their evaluation of the technical qualities and performance of the new idea. Instead, they depend on the subjective experience with the innovation of others like themselves, conveyed through peer networks, to give meaning to the new idea. Even scientists in an invisible college depend on the communication structure of this community of scholars to cope with the uncertainty of what research topics to pursue and what scientific methods to utilize.

It seems that almost everyone depends heavily on interpersonal communication channels to obtain the information that he/she needs to make important decisions. Thus, knowing whom to obtain such information from becomes a critical quality for individual effectiveness in today's society. Essentially, this capacity consists of understanding, forming, and maintaining a personal communication structure. In this sense, network analysis is not only a scientific research procedure, it is a way of analytic and strategic thinking that can be used daily by every individual.

One subtheme of our previous chapters deals with the strength of weak ties. We have described a basic contradiction in the network relationships of most individuals: they form their most proximate network links with other individuals who are highly homophilous to them in social characteristics and who are most accessible (spatially and socially). The social *comfortability* of such ingrown links is paradoxical because they are relatively ineffective in carrying new information that the individual needs. Heterophilous links with socially and spatially distant others are "stronger" in carrying useful information.

A general principle of least-effort is usually involved in determining (1) who is linked, and (2) whether such links are stable over time (chapter 7). Such least-effort leads to the basic paradox in the nature of network links: that such links, while facile, are least functional for information-exchange. They are closed instead of open, thus limiting the individual's access to new information. This contradiction is a generalization of Professor Mark Granovetter's (1973) theory of the strength of weak ties.

How does one resolve this contradiction in one's personal communication network? Obviously, the general answer is to be a heterophile, rather than a homophile: to develop links with dissimilar others, to make friends who are not friends of friends, to seek diversity in one's information relationships. Such efforts toward heterophily require greater social costs, but they should pay greater returns in information. We expect them to be cost-effective.

So communication networks can be conceptualized theoretically, studied empirically, and managed personally.

GLOSSARY

Past literature on network analysis creates confusion about the main concepts in this field. This glossary is intended to assist the reader in understanding the standard concepts that we utilize.

Average clique connectedness is the degree to which the average member of a clique is linked to other individuals in his/her clique.

Average system connectedness is the degree to which the average member of a system is linked to other individuals in the system.

Blockmodeling is a network analysis technique for obtaining the structure for two or more networks composed of the same individuals.

Bridge is an individual who links two or more cliques in a system from his/her position as a member of one of the cliques.

Clique is a subsystem whose elements interact with each other relatively more frequently than with other members of the communication system.

Clique connectedness is the degree to which the cliques in a system are linked to each other.

Clique diversity is the degree to which cliques in a system are heterogeneous in some variable.

Clique integration is the degree to which the cliques linked to a focal clique are linked to each other.

Clique openness is the degree to which the members of a clique are linked to others external to the clique.

Communication is a process in which participants create and share information with one another in order to reach a mutual understanding.

Communication network consists of interconnected individuals who are linked by patterned flows of information.

Communication network analysis is a method of research for identifying the communication structure in a system, in which relational data about communication flows are analyzed by using some type of interpersonal relationship as the unit of analysis.

Communication proximity is the degree to which two linked individuals in a network have personal communication networks that overlap.

Communication structure is the arrangement of the differentiated elements that can be recognized in the patterned communication flows in a system.

Connectedness is the degree to which a focal unit is linked to other units.

Convergence is the tendency for two or more individuals to move toward one point or for one individual to move toward another, or for two individuals to come together and unite in a common interest or focus.

Correlational similarity is the degree to which two individuals have like patterns of links and nonlinks.

346

Divergence is the tendency for two or more individuals to move away or apart.

Diversity is the degree to which the units linked to a focal unit are heterogeneous in some variable.

Dyad is composed of two individuals connected by a communication link.

Heterophily is the degree to which pairs of individuals who interact are different in certain attributes.

Homophily is the degree to which pairs of individuals who interact are similar in certain attributes, such as beliefs, values, education, social status, and the like.

Individual connectedness is the degree to which a focal individual is linked to other individuals in a system.

Individual diversity is the degree to which the members of an individual's personal communication network are heterogeneous in some variable.

Individual integration is the degree to which the members of an individual's personal communication network are linked to each other.

Information is a difference in matter–energy which affects uncertainty in a situation where a choice exists among a set of alternatives.

Information overload is the state of an individual or a system in which excessive communication inputs cannot be processed and utilized, leading to breakdown.

Innovativeness is the degree to which an individual is relatively earlier in adopting new ideas than other members of a system.

Integration is the degree to which the units linked to a focal unit are linked to each other.

Interlocking personal network is one in which an individual interacts with a set of dyadic partners who interact with each other.

Liaison is an individual who links two or more cliques in a system, but who is not a member of any clique.

Link is a communication relationship between two units (usually individuals) in a system.

Linkage distance is the number of links or steps in the shortest path joining two individuals.

Multiplexity is the degree to which multiple contents flow through a network link between two individuals.

Network stability is the degree to which a network link occurs at two or more points in time.

Node is a unit in a network that is connected to certain other nodes by links.

Openness is the degree to which a unit exchanges information with its environment.

Participant observation is a commitment by the researcher to adopt the perspective of the respondents by sharing in their day-to-day experience.

Personal communication network is those interconnected individuals who are linked by patterned communication flows to a focal individual.

Pluralistic ignorance is the degree to which individuals hold incorrect conceptions of the behavior of other individuals in collectivities to which they belong.

Proximity is the relative nearness of a pair of individuals to each other in a communication sense.

Radial personal network is one in which an individual interacts with a set of dyadic partners who do not interact with each other.

Relational analysis is a research approach in which the unit of analysis is a relationship between two or more individuals.

Sociogram is a graphic means for displaying the patterns of communication or social choice in a system.

Sociometry is a means of obtaining quantitative data about communication patterns among the individuals in a system, by asking each respondent to whom he/she is linked.

Structure is the arrangement of the components and subsystems within a system.

Structural equivalence is the degree to which two individuals are linked to the same set of other individuals but not necessarily to each other.

System is a set of interrelated parts coordinated to accomplish a set of goals.

System effects are the influences of the structure and/or composition of a system on the behavior of the members of the system.

System openness is the degree to which the members of a system are linked to others external to the system.

Unobtrusive method is a measure that directly removes the observer from the events being studied.

REFERENCES

AGARWALA, UMESH N. (1978), "The MTMM Matrix Technique for Determining Convergent and Discriminant Validity," in B. C. Tandon (ed.), *Research Methodology in Social Science*, Allahabad, India, Chaitanya.

AGARWALA-ROGERS, REKHA, and others (1977), *Diffusion of IMPACT Innovations from 1973–1976: Interpersonal Communication Networks Among University Professors*, Stanford, California, Applied Communication Research, Report.

ALBA, RICHARD D. (1972a), "COMPLT: A Program for Analyzing Sociometric Data and Clustering Similarity Matrices," *Behavioral Science*, 17:566–567.

—— (1972b), "Some New Procedures for Sociometric Analysis," New York, Columbia University, Bureau of Applied Social Research, Unpublished paper.

—— (1973), "A Graph-Theoretic Definition of a Sociometric Clique," *Journal of Mathematical Sociology*, 3:113–126.

—— (1975), "Defining Proximity in Social Networks: A New Measure of Social Proximity in Networks," New York, Columbia University, Bureau of Applied Social Research, Unpublished paper.

—— (1978), "Ethnic Networks and Tolerant Attitudes," *Public Opinion Quarterly*, 42:1–16.

——, and MYRON P. GUTTMAN (1972), "SOCK: A Sociometric Analysis System," *Behavioral Science*, 17:326–327.

——, and CHARLES KADUSHIN (1976), "The Introduction of Social Circles: A New Measure of Social Proximity in Networks," *Sociological Methods and Research*, 5:77–102.

——, and GWEN MOORE (1978), "Elite Social Circles," *Sociological Methods and Research*, 7:167–168.

ALEXANDER, C.N. (1964), "Consensus and Mutual Attraction in Natural Cliques: A Study of Adolescent Drinkers," *American Journal of Sociology*, 69:395–403.

——, and ERNEST Q. CAMPBELL, (1968), "Balance Forces and Environmental Effects: Factors Influencing the Cohesiveness of Adolescent Drinking Groups," *Social Forces*, 46:367–374.

ALLEN, RICHARD K. (1970), *A Comparison of Communication Behaviors in Innovative and Non-Innovative Secondary Schools*, Ph.D. Thesis, East Lansing, Michigan State University.

ALLEN, THOMAS J. (1966), "Performance of Information Channels in the Transfer of Technology," *Industrial Management*, 8:87–98.

—— (1978), *Managing the Flow of Technology: Technology Transfer and the Dissemination of Technological Information within the R & D Organization*, Cambridge, Massachusetts, MIT Press.

ALT, J.E., and N. SCHOFIELD (1975), "CLIQUE: A Suite of Programs for Extracting Cliques from a Symmetric Graph," *Behavioral Science,* 20:134–135.

AMEND, EDWIN H. (1971), *Liaison Communication Roles of Professionals in a Research Dissemination Organization,* Ph.D. Thesis, East Lansing, Michigan State University.

ANDERSON, GRACE M. (1974), *Networks of Contact: The Portuguese and Toronto,* Waterloo, Canada, Wilfrid Laurier University Press.

———, and T. LAIRD CHRISTIE (1978), "Ethnic Networks: North American Perspectives," *Connections,* 2:25–34.

ANDREWS, KENNETH H., and DENISE B. KANDEL (1979), "Attitude and Behavior: A Specification of the Contingent Consistency Hypothesis," *American Sociological Review,* 44:298–310.

ANKER, RICHARD (1977), "The Effect of Group Level Variables on Fertility in a Rural Indian Sample," *Journal of Development Studies,* 14:63–76.

ARABIE, PHIPPS, and others (1978), "Constructing Blockmodels: How and Why," *Journal of Mathematical Psychology,* 17:21–63.

ARDENER, S. (1969), "The Comparative Study of Rotating Credit Associations," *Journal of the Royal Anthropological Institute,* 94.

ARNDT, JOHAN (1968), "Selective Processes in Word-of-Mouth," *Journal of Advertising Research,* 8:19–22.

ASHBY, W. ROSS (1956), *An Introduction to Cybernetics,* London, Chapman and Hall.

——— (1968), "Regulation and Control," in Walter Buckley (ed.), *Modern Systems Research for the Behavioral Scientist,* Chicago, Aldine.

ATHANASIOU, ROBERT, and GARY A. YOSHIOKA (1973), "The Spatial Character of Friendship Formation," *Environment and Behavior,* 5:43–66.

BABBIE, EARL R. (1973), *Survey Research Methods,* Belmont, California, Wadsworth.

BAGOZZI, RICHARD P. (1978), "Marketing as Exchange: A Theory of Transactions in the Marketplace," *American Behavioral Scientist,* 21:535–556.

BALES, ROBERT F. (1950), *Interaction Process Analysis: A Method for the Study of Small Groups,* Reading, Massachusetts, Addison-Wesley.

BALSWICK, JACK O., and JAMES W. BALKWELL (1977), "Self-Disclosure to Same- and Opposite-Sex Parents: An Empirical Test of Insights from Role Theory," *Sociometry,* 40:282–286.

BARNES, JOHN A. (1954), "Class and Committees in the Norwegian Island Parish," *Human Relations,* 7:39:–58.

——— (1972), *Social Networks,* Reading, Massachusetts, Addison-Wesley, Modular Publications in Anthropology 26.

BARNLUND, DEAN C., and CARROLL HARLAND (1963), "Propinquity and Prestige as Determinants of Communication Networks," *Sociometry,* 26:467–479.

BARTHOLOMEW, D.J. (1973), *Stochastic Models for Social Processes,* New York, Wiley.

BARTON, ALLEN (1968), "Bringing Society Back In: Survey Research and Macro-Methodology," *American Behavioral Scientist,* 12:1–9.

BATESON, GREGORY (1972), *Steps to an Ecology of the Mind,* New York, Ballantine.

BAUER, RAYMOND A. (1964), "The Obstinate Audience: The Influence Process from the Point of View of Social Communication," *American Psychologist,* 19:319–328.

———— (1973), "The Audience," in Ithiel de Sola Pool and others (eds.), *Handbook of Communication,* Chicago, Rand McNally, 141–152.

BAVELAS, ALEX (1950), "Communication Patterns in Task-Oriented Groups," *Acoustical Society of America Journal,* 22:727–730.

BEARDEN, JAMES, and others (1975), "The Nature and Extent of Bank Centrality in Corporate Networks," Paper presented at the American Sociological Association.

BEATON, ALBERT E. (1966), "An Inter-Battery Factor Analytic Approach to Clique Analysis," *Sociometry,* 29:135–145.

BECKER, MARSHALL H. (1970), "Sociometric Location and Innovativeness: Reformulation and Extension of the Diffusion Model," *American Sociological Review,* 35:267–282.

BELTRÁN, LUIS RAMIRO (1976), "Social Structure and Rural Development Communication in Latin America: The 'Radiophonic Schools' of Colombia," in Godwin Chu and others (eds.), *Communication for Group Transformation in Development,* Honolulu, East–West Communication Institute, Communication Monograph 2.

BENINGER, JAMES R. (1976), "Sampling Social Networks: The Subgroup Approach," *Business and Economic Statistics Proceedings.*

BERLO, DAVID K. (1960), *The Process of Communication: An Introduction to Theory and Practice,* New York, Holt, Rinehart and Winston.

———— (1977), "Communication as Process: Review and Commentary," in Brent R. Ruben (ed.), *Communication Yearbook I,* New Brunswick, New Jersey, Transaction-International Communication Association.

————, and others (1970), *Organizational Communication: A First-Line Managerial Communication System,* East Lansing, Michigan State University, Department of Communication, Mimeo Report.

————, and others (1972), *An Analysis of the Communication Structure of the Office of Civil Defense,* East Lansing, Michigan State University, Department of Communication, Mimeo Report.

BERNARD, H. RUSSELL, and PETER D. KILLWORTH (1973), "On the Social Structure of an Ocean-Going Research Vessel and Other Important Things," *Social Science Research,* 2:145–184.

————, and ———— (1977), "Informant Accuracy in Social Network Data II," *Human Communication Research,* 4:3–18.

————, and ———— (1978a), "On the Structure and Effective Sociometric Relations in a Closed Group Over Time," *Connections,* 1:44.

————, and ———— (1978b), "The Reverse Small-World Experiment," *Connections,* 1:45.

————, and ———— (1978c), "A Review of the Small World Literature," *Connections,* 2:15–24.

————, and others (1979), "Informant Accuracy in Social Network Data: A

Comparison of Clique-Level Structure in Behavioral and Cognitive Network Data," Morgantown, University of West Virginia, Department of Sociology and Anthropology, Unpublished paper.

BERTALANFFY, LUDWIG VON (1967), *Robots, Men, and Minds,* New York, Braziller.

—— (1975), "General System Theory," in Brent D. Rubin and John Y. Kim (eds.), *General Systems Theory and Human Communication,* Rochelle Park, New Jersey, Hayden.

BETTY, SAMUEL (1974), *Some Determinants of Communication Network Structure and Productivity: A Study of Clinic Staff Interaction in Two Philippine Family Planning Organizations,* Ph.D. Thesis, East Lansing, Michigan State University.

BEUM, CARLIN O., JR., and EVERETT E. BRUNDAGE (1950), "A Method for Analyzing the Sociomatrix," *Sociometry,* 13:141–145.

——, and J.J. CRISWELL (1947), "Application of Machine Tabulation Methods to Sociometric Data," *Sociometry,* 10:227–232.

BHOWMIK, DILIP K. (1972), *Differences in Heterophily and Communication Integration Between Modern and Traditional Indian Villages in Two Types of Dyadic Encounters,* Ph.D. Thesis, East Lansing, Michigan State University.

BLAU, PETER M. (1962), "Patterns of Choice in Interpersonal Relations," *American Sociological Review,* 27:42.

—— (1969), "Objectives of Sociology," in Robert Bierstedt (ed.), *A Design for Sociology: Scope, Objectives, and Methods,* Philadelphia, American Academy of Political and Social Science.

—— (1977), *Inequality and Heterogeneity: A Primitive Theory of Social Structure,* New York, Free Press.

BLOOMBAUM, MILTON (1970), "Doing Smallest-Space Analysis," *Conflict Resolution,* 14:409–416.

BLUMER, HERBERT (1969), *Symbolic Interactionism: Perspective and Method,* Englewood Cliffs, New Jersey, Prentice-Hall.

BOCHNER, S., and others (1976a), "Communication Patterns in an International Student Dormitory: Modification of the Small World Method," *Journal of Applied Social Psychology,* 6:275–290.

——, and others (1976b), "Acquaintance Links Between Residents of a High Rise Building: An Application of the 'Small World' Method," *Journal of Social Psychology,* 100:277–284.

BOCK, R. DARRELL, and SURAYA A. HUSAIN (1950), "Adaptation of Holzinger's B-Coefficients for the Analysis of Sociometric Data," *Sociometry,* 13:146–153.

BOGUE, DONALD J. (1965), "Family Planning Research: An Outline of the Field," in Bernard Berelson and others (eds.), *Family Planning and Population Programs,* Chicago, University of Chicago Press.

BOGUSLAW, ROBERT (1975), "Moreno, Sociometric Methodology, and the Redesign of Society," *Sociometry,* 38: 152–156.

BOISSEVAIN, JEREMY (1974), *Friends of Friends: Networks, Manipulators, and Coalitions,* New York, St. Martin's Press.

——, and J. CLYDE MITCHELL (eds.) (1973), *Network Analysis Studies in Human Interaction*, The Hague, Mouton.

BONACICH, PHILLIP (1972), "Factoring and Weighting Approaches to Status Scores and Clique Identification," *Journal of Mathematical Sociology*, 2:113–120.

—— (1977), "Using Boolean Algebra to Analyze Overlapping Memberships," in Karl F. Schuessler (ed.), *Sociological Methodology, 1978*, San Francisco, Jossey-Bass.

BOORMAN, SCOTT A. (1975), "A Combinatorial Optimization Model for Transmission of Job Information Through Contact Networks," *Bell Journal of Economics*, 2:216–249.

——, and HARRISON C. WHITE (1976), "Social Structure from Multiple Networks: II, Role Structures," *American Journal of Sociology*, 81:1384–1446.

BORGATTA, EDGAR F. and W. STOLZ (1963), "A Note on a Computer Program for Rearrangement of Matrices," *Sociometry*, 26:391–392.

BOTT, ELIZABETH (1955), "Urban Families: Conjugal Roles and Social Networks," *Human Relations*, 8:345–384.

—— (1957), *Family and Social Networks: Roles, Norms, and External Relationships in Ordinary Urban Families*, London, Tavistock (first edition); and (1971), New York, Free Press (second edition).

BOULDING, KENNETH (1956), "General Systems Theory: The Skeleton of Science," *Management Sciences*, 2:197–208.

BOUMAN, F.J.A., and K. HARTEVELD (1976), "The Djanggi: A Traditional Form of Savings and Credit in West Cameroon," *Sociologia Ruralis*, 16:103.

BRANDT, VINCENT S.R. (1976), "Rural Development and the New Community Movement in South Korea," *Korean Studies Forum*, 1:32–39.

BRAUN, JUAN RICARDO (1975), *Communication, Non-Formal Education, and National Development: The Colombian Radio Schools*, Ph.D. Thesis, East Lansing, Michigan State University.

—— (1976), *Comunicacíon, Educacíon Noformal y Desarollo Nacional: Las Radio Escuelas Colombianas*, Bogotá, Libreria Mundial.

BREIGER, RONALD L. (1976a), "Career Attributes and Network Structure: A Blockmodel Study of a Biomedical Research Specialty," *American Sociological Review*, 41:117–135.

—— (1976b), "Community at the Village Level: A Case of Sparse Networks," Cambridge, Massachusetts, Harvard University, Department of Sociology, Unpublished paper.

—— (1979), "Toward an Operational Theory of Community Elite Structures," *Quality and Quantity*, 13.

——, and PHILLIPPA E. PATTISON (1978), "The Joint Role Structure of Two Communities' Elites," *Sociological Methods and Research*, 7:213–226.

——, and others (1975), "An Algorithm for Clustering Relational Data, with Applications to Social Network Analysis and Comparison with Multidimensional Scaling," *Journal of Mathematical Psychology*, 12:328–383.

BRILLOUIN, LEON (1964), *Scientific Uncertainty and Information*, New York, Academic Press.

BRONOWSKI, J. (1973), *The Ascent of Man*, Boston, Little, Brown.

BRYSON, LYMAN (1948), *The Communication of Ideas*, New York, Institute for Religious and Social Studies, and Harper.

BUCKLEY, WALTER (1967), *Sociology of Modern Systems Theory*, Englewood Cliffs, New Jersey, Prentice-Hall.

BURSTEIN, PAUL (1976), "Social Networks and Voting: Some Israeli Data," *Social Forces*, 54:833–847.

BURT, RONALD S. (1975), "Corporate Society: A Time-Series Analysis of Network Structure," *Social Science Research*, 4:271–328.

———— (1977a), "Positions in Multiple Network Systems, Part I: A General Conception of Stratification and Prestige in a System of Actors Cast as a Social Typology," *Social Forces*, 56:106–131.

———— (1977b), "Positions in Multiple Network Systems, Part II: Stratification and Prestige Among Elite Decision-Makers in the Community of Altneustadt," *Social Forces*, 56:551–575.

———— (1978a), "Innovation as a Structural Interest: Rethinking the Impact of Network Position on the Diffusion of an Innovation," Paper presented at the Seminar on Communication Network Analysis, Honolulu, East-West Communication Institute.

———— (1978b), "Applied Network Analysis: An Overview," *Sociological Methods and Research*, 7:123–130.

———— (1978c), "Cohesion Versus Structural Equivalence as a Basis for Network Subgroups," *Sociological Methods and Research*, 7:189–212.

———— (1978d), "Stratification and Prestige Among Elite Experts in Methodological and Mathematical Sociology Circa 1975," *Social Networks*, 1:105–158.

————, and NAN LIN (1977), "Network Time Series from Archival Records," in David R. Heise (ed.), *Sociological Methodology, 1977*, San Francisco, Jossey-Bass.

CAMPBELL, DONALD T. and DONALD W. FISKE (1959), "Convergent and Discriminant Validation by the Multitrait–Multimethod Matrix," *Psychological Bulletin*, 56:81–104.

CAMPBELL, J.P., and M.D. DUNNETTE (1968), "Effectiveness of T-Group Experiences in Managerial Training and Development," *Psychological Bulletin*, 70:73–104.

CAPLAN, NATHAN, and STEPHEN D. NELSON (1973), "On Being Useful: The Nature and Consequences of Psychological Research on Social Problems," *American Psychologist*, 28:199–211.

CARTWRIGHT, DORWIN, and FRANK HARARY (1956), "Structural Balance: A Generalization of Heider's Theory," *Psychological Review*, 63:277–293.

————, and ALVIN ZANDER (eds.) (1962), *Group Dynamics: Research and Theory*, New York, Harper and Row.

CATTELL, R.B. (1952), "The Three Basic Factor-Analytic Research Designs: Their Interrelations and Derivatives," *Psychological Bulletin*, 49:499–520.

CHARTERS, W.W., JR. (1969), "Stability and Change in the Communication Structure of School Faculties," *Educational Administration Quarterly*, 5:15–38.

CHAVERS, PASQUAL DEAN (1976), *Social Structure and the Diffusion of Innovations: A Network Analysis*, Ph.D. Thesis, Stanford, California, Stanford University.

CHERRY, COLIN (1978), *World Communication: Threat or Promise?* New York, Wiley-Interscience.

CHO, LEE-JAY (1973), "The Demographic Situation in the Republic of Korea. Honolulu," Honolulu, East–West Population Institute, Paper 29.

CHU, GODWIN (1976), "Groups and Development," in Godwin Chu and others (eds.), *Communication for Group Transformation in Development*, Honolulu, East–West Communication Institute, Monograph 2.

—— (1977), *Radical Change Through Communication in Mao's China*, Honolulu, University of Hawaii Press.

CHUBIN, DARRYL (1979), "A Critique of Blockmodeling," *Connections*, 2.

CHURCHMAN, C. WEST (1968), *The Systems Approach*, New York, Dell.

COHEN, JERE M. (1977), "Sources of Peer Group Homogeneity," *Sociology of Education*, 50:227–241.

COLEMAN, JAMES S. (1958), "Relational Analysis: A Study of Social Organization with Survey Methods," *Human Organization*, 17:28–36.

—— (1961), *The Adolescent Society: The Social Life of the Teenager and Its Impact on Education*, New York, Free Press.

—— (1964), *Introduction to Mathematical Sociology*, New York, Free Press.

—— (1971), "Conflicting Theories of Social Change," *American Behavioral Scientist*, 14:633–650.

——, and DUNCAN MACRAE, JR. (1960), "Electronic Data Processing of Sociometric Data for Groups up to 1,000 in Size," *American Sociological Review*, 25:722–727.

——, and others (1966), *Medical Innovation: A Diffusion Study*, New York, Bobbs-Merrill.

COMSTOCK, GEORGE, and others (1978), *Television and Human Behavior*, New York, Columbia University Press.

COOLEY, CHARLES H. (1902), *Human Nature and the Social Order*, New York, Scribner.

COX, ELI P., III, and others (1975), "Relational Characteristics of the Business Literature: An Interpretive Procedure," *Journal of Business*, 48:252–265.

CRANE, DIANA (1972), *Invisible Colleges: Diffusion of Knowledge in Scientific Communities*, Chicago, University of Chicago Press.

CRONBACH, LEE J. (1977), "Remarks to the New Society," *Newsletter of the Evaluation Research Society*, 1:1–2.

CUBITT, TESSA (1973), "Network Density Among Urban Families," in Jeremy Boissevain and J. Clyde Mitchell (eds.), *Network Analysis Studies in Human Interaction*, The Hague, Mouton.

CULLER, J. (1977), "In Pursuit of Signs," *Daedalus*, 106:95–111.

DANOWSKI, JAMES A. (1975), *An Information Theory of Communication Functions: A Focus on Informational Aging*, Ph.D. Thesis, East Lansing, Michigan State University.

—— (1976), "Communication Network Analysis and Social Change: Group Structure and Family Planning in Two Korean Villages," in Godwin Chu and others (eds.), *Communication for Group Transformation in Development*, Honolulu, East–West Communication Institute, Monograph 2.

DAVIS, BURL EDWARD (1968), *System Variables and Agricultural Innovativeness in Eastern Nigeria*, Ph.D. Thesis, East Lansing, Michigan State University.

DAVIS, JAMES A. (1961), "Locals and Cosmopolitans in American Graduate Schools," *International Journal of Comparative Society*, 2:212–223.

—— (1970), "Clustering and Hierarchy in Interpersonal Relations," *American Sociological Review*, 35:843–852.

DAVIS, JAMES H. (1969), *Group Performance*, Reading, Massachusetts, Addison-Wesley.

DeCHARMS R. (1968), *Personal Causation: The Internal Affective Determinants of Behavior*, New York, Academic Press.

DELANY, JOHN L. (1978), *Network Dynamics for the Weak Tie Problem: A Simulation Study*, New Haven, Connecticut, Yale University, Department of Sociology, Harvard–Yale Preprints in Mathematical Sociology 10.

DENZIN, NORMAN K. (1976), *The Research Act: A Theoretical Introduction to Sociological Methods*, Chicago, Aldine.

DEUTSCH, KARL W. (1963), *The Nerves of Government*, New York, Free Press.

—— (1968), "Toward a Cybernetic Model of Man and Society," in Walter Buckley (ed.), *Modern Systems Research for the Behavioral Scientist*, Chicago, Aldine.

DIAZ BORDENAVE, JUAN (1972), "New Approaches to Communication Training for Developing Countries," Paper presented at the Third World Congress of Rural Sociology, Baton Rouge, Louisiana.

DIAZ-CISNEROS, HELIODORO, and DELBERT T. MYREN (1974), "The Puebla Project in Mexico," in Lyle Webster (ed.), *Integrated Communication: Bringing People and Rural Development Together*, Honolulu, East–West Communication Institute, Conference Report.

DOZIER, DAVID M. (1977), *Communication Networks and the Role of Thresholds in the Adoption of Innovations*, Ph.D. Thesis, Stanford, California, Stanford University.

DUFF, ROBERT W. and WILLIAM T. LIU (1975), "The Significance of Heterophilous Structure in Communication Flows," *Philippine Quarterly of Culture and Society* 3:159–175.

DURKHEIM, EMILE, (1950), *The Rules of Sociological Method*, New York, Free Press.

EDWARDS, JANE A., and PETER R. MONGE (1977), "The Validation of Mathematical Indices of Communication Structure," in Brent R. Ruben (ed.), *Communication Yearbook I*, New Bruswick, New Jersey, Transaction-International Communication Association.

EPSTEIN, A.L. (1961), "The Network and Urban Social Organization," *Rhodes-Livingstone Journal*, 29:29–62.

ERIKSON, B., with P.R.L. KRINGAS (1975), "The Small World of Politics or, Seeking Elites from the Bottom Up," *Canadian Review of Sociology and Anthropology*, 12:585–593.

EULAU, HEINZ (1978), "The Columbia Studies of Personal Influence in Voting and Public Affairs," Stanford, California, Stanford University, Department of Political Science, Social Network Analysis Project, Working Memorandum 3.

FARACE, RICHARD V., and others (1977), *Communicating and Organizing*, Reading, Massachusetts, Addison-Wesley.

FEINBERG, S.E., and S.K. LEE (1975), "Small World Statistics," *Psychometrika and Supplements*, 40:219–228.

FESTINGER, LEON (1949), "The Analysis of Sociograms Using Matrix Algebra," *Human Relations*, 2:153–158.

——, and others (1950), *Social Pressures in Informal Groups: A Study of Human Factors in Housing*, Stanford, California, Stanford University Press.

FIELDS, JAMES M., and HOWARD SCHUMAN (1976), "Public Beliefs About the Beliefs of the Public," *Public Opinion Quarterly*, 40:427–448.

FINIFTER, ADA W. (1974), "The Friendship Group as a Protective Environment for Political Deviants," *American Political Science Review*, 68:607–625.

FINLAYSON, ANGELA (1976), "Social Networks as Coping Resources: Lay Help and Consultation Patterns Used by Women in Husbands' Post-Infarction Career," *Social Science and Medicine*, 10:97–103.

FISHER, B. AUBREY (1978), *Perspectives on Human Communication*, New York, Macmillan.

FISCHER, CLAUDE S. (1977), *The Contexts of Personal Relations: An Exploratory Network Analysis*, Berkeley, University of California, Institute of Urban and Regional Development, Working Paper 281.

——, and others (1977), *Networks and Places: Social Relations in the Urban Setting*, New York, Free Press.

FORSYTH, ELAINE, and LEO KATZ (1946), "A Matrix Approach to the Analysis of Sociometric Data: Preliminary Report," *Sociometry*, 9:340–347.

FOSTER, BRIAN L. (1979), "Formal Network Studies and the Anthropological Perspective," *Social Networks*, 1:241–255.

——, and STEPHEN B. SEIDMAN (1978), *SONET 1: Social Network Analysis and Modeling System: Volume 1: User's Model*, Binghamton, New York, State University of New York at Binghamton, Center for Social Analysis.

FREEDMAN, RONALD (1974), *Community Level Data in Fertility Surveys*, London, World Fertility Survey, Occasional Papers 8.

FREEMAN, LINTON C. (1968), *Patterns of Local Community Leadership*, Indianapolis, Bobbs-Merrill.

—— (1976), *A Bibliography of Social Networks*, Monticello, Illinois, Council of Planning Librarians, Exchange Bibliography 1170–1171.

—— (1977a), "Computer Conferencing and Productivity in Science," *Transactional Associations*, 10:433–435,445.

—— (1977b), "A Set of Measures of Centrality Based on Betweenness," *Sociometry*, 40:35–41.

—— (1978), "Segregation in Social Networks," *Sociological Methods and Research*, 6:411–429.

—— (1979), "Centrality in Social Networks: Conceptual Clarification," *Social Networks*, 1:215–239.

FREEMAN SUE C., and LINTON C. FREEMAN (1979), "The Networker's Network: A Study of the Impact of a New Communications Medium on Sociometric Structure," Paper presented at the Seminar on Communication Network Analysis, Honolulu, East-West Communication Institute.

FRIEDKIN, NOAH E. (1978), "University Social Structure and Social Networks Among Scientists," *American Journal of Sociology*, 83:1444–1465.

FRIERE, PAULO (1973), "Extension or Communication," in *Education for Critical Consciousness*, New York, Seabury Press.

GALLIE, W.B. (1966), *Peirce and Pragmatism*, New York, Dover.

GEERTZ, CLIFFORD (1962), "The Rotating Credit Association: A 'Middle Rung' in Development," *Economic Development and Cultural Change*, 10:241–263.

GOODMAN, LEO (1961), "Snowball Sampling," *Annals of Mathematical Statistics*, 32:148–170.

GRANOVETTER, MARK S. (1970), *Changing Jobs: Channels of Mobility Information in a Suburban Community*, Ph.D. Thesis, Cambridge, Massachusetts, Harvard University.

—— (1973), "The Strength of Weak Ties," *American Journal of Sociology*, 73:1361–1380.

—— (1974), *Getting a Job: A Study of Contacts and Careers*, Cambridge, Massachusetts, Harvard University Press.

—— (1976), "Network Sampling: Some First Steps," *American Journal of Sociology*, 81:1287–1303.

—— (1977), "Reply to Morgan and Rytina," *American Journal of Sociology*, 83:727–729.

—— (1978), "Threshold Models of Collective Behavior," *American Journal of Sociology*, 83:1420–1443.

GUIMARÃES, LYTTON L. (1968), *Matrix Multiplication in the Study of Interpersonal Communication*, M.A. Thesis, East Lansing, Michigan State University.

—— (1970), *Network Analysis: An Approach to the Study of Communication Systems*, East Lansing, Michigan State University, Department of Communication, Project on the Diffusion of Innovations in Rural Societies, Technical Report 12.

—— (1972), *Communication Integration in Modern and Traditional Social Systems: A Comparative Analysis Across Twenty Communities of Minas Gerais*, Ph.D. Thesis, East Lansing, Michigan State University.

GUIOT, J.M. (1976), "A Modification of Milgram's Small World Method," *European Journal of Social Psychology*, 6:503–507.

GUTTMAN, LOUIS (1968), "A General Nonmetric Technique for Finding the Smallest Coordinate Space for a Configuration of Points," *Psychometrika*, 33:469–506.

HACKING, IAN (1975), *Why Does Language Matter to Philosophy*, London, Cambridge University Press.

HALLINAN, MAUREEN T. (1978), "The Process of Friendship Formation," *Social Networks*, 1:193–210.

HAMMER, M. (1963), "Influences of Small Social Networks as Factors on Mental Hospital Admission," *Human Organization*, 22:243–251.

HANNERZ, ULF (1967), "Gossip, Networks, and Culture in a Black American Ghetto," *Ethnos*, 1:35–60.

HARARY, FRANK (1969), *Graph Theory*, Reading, Massachusetts, Addison-Wesley.

—— (1971), "Demiarcs: An Atomistic Approach to Rational Systems and Group Dynamics," *Journal of Mathematical Sociology*, 1:195–205.

——, and RONALD HAVELOCK (1972), "Anatomy of a Communication Arc," *Human Relations*, 25:413–426.

——, and JAN C. ROSS (1957), "A Procedure for Clique Detection Using the Group Matrix," *Sociometry*, 20:205–215.

——, and others (1965), *Structural Models: An Introduction to the Theory of Directed Graphs*, New York, Wiley.

HAUSER, R.M. (1970), "Context and Consex: A Cautionary Tale," *American Journal of Sociology*, 75:645–664.

HEIDER, FRITZ (1946), "Attitudes and Cognitive Organization," *Journal of Psychology*, 21:107–112.

HEIL, GREGORY H., and HARRISON C. WHITE (1976), "An Algorithm for Finding Simultaneous Homorphic Correspondences Between Graphs and Their Image Graphs," *Behavior Science*, 21:26–35.

HILTZ, STARR ROXANNE, and MURRAY TUROFF (1979), *The Network Nation: Human Communication via Computers*, Reading, Massachusetts, Addison-Wesley.

HOLLAND, PAUL W., and SAMUEL LEINHARDT (1973), "The Structural Implications of Measurement Error in Sociometry," *Journal of Mathematical Sociology*, 3:85–111.

HOMANS, GEORGE C. (1950), *The Human Group*, New York, Harcourt, Brace and World.

HONG, SAWON (1976), *Fertility and Fertility Limitation in Korean Villages: Community and Individual-Level Effects*, Ph.D. Thesis, Honolulu, University of Hawaii.

HORWITZ, ALLAN (1977), "Social Networks and Pathways to Psychiatric Treatment," *Social Forces*, 56:86–105.

HOVLAND, CARL I., and others (1973), *Communication and Persuasion: Psychological Studies of Opinion Change*, New Haven, Connecticut, Yale University Press.

HUBBEL, CHARLES H. (1965), "An Input–Output Approach to Clique Identification," *Sociometry*, 28:377–399.

HUBERT, LAWRENCE J., and FRANK B. BAKER (1978), "Evaluating the Conformity of Sociometric Measurements," *Psychometrika*, 43:31–41.

HUGHES, EVERETT CHERRINGTON (1964), "Foreword," in Georg Simmel, *The Web of Group-Affiliations*, translated by Reinhard Bendix, New York, Free Press.

HUNTER, JOHN E., and R. LANCE SHOTLAND (1974), "Treating Data Collected by the 'Small World' Method as a Markov Process," *Social Forces*, 52:321–332.

HURT, H. THOMAS, and RAYMOND PREISS (1978), "Silence Isn't Necessarily Golden: Communication Apprehension, Desired Social Choice, and Academic Success Among Middle-School Students," *Human Communication Research*, 4:315–328.

JACOBSON, EUGENE, and STANLEY SEASHORE (1951), "Communication Patterns in Complex Organizations," *Journal of Social Issues*, 7:28–40.

JOHNSON, NORRIS R., and WILLIAM E. FEINBERG (1977), "A Computer Simulation of the Emergence of Consensus in Crowds," *American Sociological Review*, 42:505–521.

JOHNSON, STEPHEN C. (1967), "Hierarchical Clustering Schemes," *Psychometrika*, 32:241–254.

JONES, LYNNE McCALLISTER, and CLAUDE S. FISCHER (1978), *Studying Egocentric Networks by Mass Survey*, Berkeley, University of California, Institute of Urban and Regional Development, Working Paper 284.

KADUSHIN, CHARLES (1966), "The Friends and Supporters of Psychotherapy: On Social Circles in Urban Life," *American Sociological Review*, 31:786–802.

—— (1969), *Why People Go to Psychiatrists*, New York, Atherton.

—— (1976), "Networks and Circles in the Production of Culture," *American Behavioral Scientist*, 19:769–784.

—— (1977), "On the Problem of Formalizing Emergent Networks Among Innovators in Education," Washington, D.C., National Institute of Education, School Capacity for Problem-Solving Group, Unpublished paper.

KANDEL, DENISE B. (1973), "Adolescent Marijuana Use: Role of Parents and Peers," *Science*, 181:1067–1070.

—— (1978a), "Homophily, Selection, and Socialization in Adolescent Friendships," *American Journal of Sociology*, 84:427–436.

—— (1978b), "Similarity in Real Life Adolescent Pairs," *Journal of Personality and Social Psychology*, 36:306–312.

KATZ, ELIHU (1957), "The Two-Step Flow of Communication: An Up-to-Date Report on an Hypothesis," *Public Opinion Quarterly*, 21:61–78.

——, and PAUL F. LAZARSFELD (1955), *Personal Influence: The Part Played by People in the Flow of Mass Communications*, New York, Free Press.

KATZ, LEO (1947), "On the Matrix Analysis of Sociometric Data," *Sociometry*, 10:233–241.

——, and J.H. POWELL (1953), "A Proposed Index of the Conformity of One Sociometric Measurement to Another," *Psychometrika*, 18:249–256.

KELLY, GEORGE (1955), *The Psychology of Personal Constructs*, New York, Norton.

KENDALL, PATRICIA L., and PAUL F. LAZARSFELD (1950), "Problems of Survey Analysis," in Robert K. Merton and Paul F. Lazarsfeld (eds.), *Continuities in Social Research*, New York, Free Press.

KILLWORTH, PETER, and H. RUSSELL BERNARD (1974a), "CATIJ: A New Sociometric and Its Application to a Prison Living Unit," *Human Organization*, 33:335–350.

——, and —— (1974b), *The CATIJ Technique: Some Descriptive Tests of Its Adequacy*, Morgantown, West Virginia, West Virginia University, Department of Sociology and Anthropology, Report.

——, and —— (1976), "Informant Accuracy in Social Network Data," *Human Organization*, 35:269–286.

——, and —— (1978), "The Reversal Small-World Experiment," *Social Networks*, 1:159–192.

——, and —— (1979), "Informant Accuracy in Social Network Data III: A Comparison of Triadic Structure in Behavioral and Cognitive Data,"

Morgantown, University of West Virginia, Department of Sociology and Anthropology, Unpublished paper.

KIM, IL-CHUL (1977a), "A Study of the Relationship Between Leadership Behavior and Group Problem Solving in the Korean Rural Development Program," Seoul National University, Department of Sociology, Unpublished paper.

——, and D. LAWRENCE KINCAID (1979), *Leadership, Group Decision-Making, and Rural Development in Korea*, Honolulu, East–West Communication Institute, Report.

KIM, JOHN Y. (1975), "Feedback in Social Sciences: Toward Reconceptualization of Morphogeneses," in Brent D. Rubin and John Y. Kim (eds.), *General System Theory and Human Communication*, Rochelle Park, New Jersey, Hayden.

KIM, JOUNG-IM (1977b), "Family Planning Communication Structure and Residential Contiguity in a Korean Village: Oryu Li," Honolulu, University of Hawaii, Department of Sociology, Paper.

—— (1978), "Group Integrativeness in Communication Networks: A New Measure of Homogeneity," Stanford, California, Stanford University, Institute for Communication Research, Unpublished paper.

——, and JAMES A. PALMORE (1978), "Personal Networks and the Adoption of Family Planning in Rural Korea," Honolulu, East–West Population Institute, Unpublished paper.

KIMBERLY, JOHN R. (1976), "Issues in the Design of Longitudinal Research," *Sociological Methods and Research*, 4:321–347.

KINCAID, D. LAWRENCE (1972), *Communication Networks, Locus of Control, and Family Planning Among Migrants to the Periphery of Mexico City*, Ph.D. Thesis, East Lansing, Michigan State University.

—— (1976), "Patterns of Communication, Decision-Making, and Motivation for Development," in Godwin Chu and others (eds.) *Communication for Group Transformation in Development*, Honolulu, East–West Communication Institute, Communication Monograph 2.

—— (1979), "The Convergence Model of Communication," Honolulu, East–West Communication Institute, Paper 18.

——, with WILBUR SCHRAMM (1975), *Fundamental Human Communication*, Honolulu, East–West Communication Institute, Professional Development Module.

——, and JUNE OCK YUM (1976), "The Needle and the Ax: Communication and Development in a Korean Village," in Daniel Lerner and Wilbur Schramm (eds.), *Communication and Change: The Last Ten Years—and the Next*, Honolulu, University Press of Hawaii.

——, and others (1975), *Mothers' Clubs and Family Planning in Rural Korea: The Case of Oryu Li*, Honolulu, East–West Communication Institute, Case Study 2.

KLAPPER, JOSEPH T. (1960), *The Effects of Mass Communication*, New York, Free Press.

KLOVDAHL, A.S. (1978), *Social Networks: Selected References for Course Design and Research Planning*, Monticello, Illinois, Vance Bibliographies, P-79.

KORTE, CHARLES, and STANLEY MILGRAM (1970), "Acquaintance Networks Between Radical Groups: Application of the Small World Method," *Journal of Personality and Social Psychology*, 15:101–108.

KORZENNY, FELIPE, and RICHARD V. FARACE (1978), "Communication Networks and Social Change in Developing Countries," *International and Intercultural Communication Annual*, 4:69–94.

KRIPPENDORFF, KLAUS (1979), *Communication and Control in Society*, New York, Gordon and Breach.

KRUSKAL, J.B. (1964a), "Multidimensional Scaling: A Numerical Method," *Psychometrkia*, 29:1–27.

—— (1964b), "Multidimensional Scaling by Optimizing Goodness of Fit to a Nonmetric Hypothesis," *Psychometrika*, 29:115–129.

KUHN, THOMAS S. (1970), *The Structure of Scientific Revolutions*, University of Chicago Press.

KURTZ D.V. (1973), "The Rotating Credit Association: An Adaptation to Poverty," *Human Organization*, 32:49–58.

LANGLOIS, SIMON (1977), "Les Réseaux Personnels et la Diffusion des Informations sur les Emplois," *Recherches Sociographiques*, 2:213–245.

LANKFORD, PHILIP M. (1974), "Comparative Analysis of Clique Identification Methods," *Sociometry*, 37:287–305.

LASSWELL, HAROLD D. (1948), "The Structure and Function of Communication in Society," in Lyman Bryson (ed.), *The Communication of Ideas*, New York, Harper.

LAUMANN, EDWARD O. (1973), *The Bonds of Pluralism: The Form and Substance of Urban Social Networks*, New York, Wiley-Interscience.

——, and FRANZ URBAN PAPPI (1973), "New Directions in the Study of Community Elites," *American Sociological Review*, 38:212–230.

——, and —— (1976), *Network of Collective Action: A Perspective on Community Influence Systems*, New York, Academic Press.

——, and others (1974), "A Causal Modeling Approach to the Study of a Community Elite's Influence Structure," *American Sociological Review*, 39:162–174.

LAZARSFELD, PAUL F. (1970), "Sociology," in *Main Trends of Research in the Social and Human Sciences*, Paris, UNESCO.

——, and ROBERT K. MERTON (1964), "Friendship as Social Process: A Substantive and Methodological Analysis," in Monroe Berger and others (eds.), *Freedom and Control in Modern Society*, New York, Octagon.

——, and others (1948), *The People's Choice*, New York, Duell, Sloan, and Pearce.

LEE, NANCY HOWELL (1969), *The Search for an Abortionist*, Chicago, University of Chicago Press.

LEE, SEA-BAICK (1977), *System Effects on Family Planning Innovativeness in Korean Villages*, Ph.D. Thesis, Ann Arbor, University of Michigan.

LEICHTER, H.J. and W.E. MITCHELL (1967), *Kinship and Casework*, New York, Russell Sage Foundation.

LEINHARDT, SAMUEL (ed.) (1977), *Social Networks: A Developing Paradigm*, New York, Academic Press.

LERNER, DANIEL (1958), *The Passing of Traditional Society: Modernizing the Middle East,* New York, Free Press.

LESNIAK, RICHARD, and others (1977), "NETPLOT: An Original Computer Program for Interpreting NEGOPY," Paper presented at the International Communication Association, Berlin.

——, and others (1978), "NEGOPY and NETPLOT: Program Characteristics," *Connections,* 1:26–29.

LEVINE, DONALD N., and others (1976), "Simmel's Influence on American Sociology: II," *American Journal of Sociology,* 81:1112–1132.

LEVINE, JOEL H. (1972), "The Sphere of Influence," *American Sociological Review,* 37:14–27.

——, and WILLIAM S. ROY (1975), "A Study of Interlocking Directorates: Vital Concepts of Organization," Paper presented at the Mathematical Social Science Board's Research Symposium on Social Networks, Hanover, New Hampshire.

LEWIN, KURT (1948), "Feedback Problems of Social Diagnosis and Actions," *Human Relations,* 1:147–153.

—— (1951), *Field Theory in Social Science,* New York, Harper and Row.

LIGHT, JUAN H. (1972), *Ethnic Enterprise in America,* Berkeley, University of California Press.

LILIENFELD, ROBERT (1978), *The Rise of Systems Theory: An Ideological Analysis,* New York, Wiley-Interscience.

LIN, NAN (1966), *Innovation Internalization in a Formal Organization,* Ph.D. Thesis, East Lansing, Michigan State University.

—— (1968), "Innovative Methods for Studying Innovation in Education and an Illustrative Analysis of Structural Effects on Innovation Diffusion Within Schools," in James Bebermeyer (ed.), *Proceedings of the National Conference on the Diffusion of Educational Ideas,* Lansing, Michigan Department of Education.

—— (1975), "Analysis of Communication Relations," in Gerhard J. Hanneman and William J. McEwen (eds.), *Communication and Behavior,* Reading, Massachusetts, Addison-Wesley.

—— (1976), *Foundations of Social Research,* New York, McGraw-Hill.

——, and RONALD S. BURT (1975), "Differential Effects of Information Channels in the Process of Innovation Diffusion," *Social Forces,* 54:256–274.

——, and others (1977), "The Urban Communication Network and Social Stratification: A 'Small World' Experiment," in Brent D. Ruben (ed.), *Communication Yearbook I,* New Brunswick, New Jersey, Transaction–International Communication Association.

——, and others (1978), "Analyzing the Instrumental Use of Relations in the Context of Social Structure," *Sociological Methods and Research,* 7:149–166.

LINCOLN, JAMES R., and JON MILLER (1979), "Work and Friendship Ties in Organizations: A Comparative Analysis of Relational Networks," *Administrative Science Quarterly,* 24:181–199.

LINGOES, JAMES C. (1972), "A General Survey of the Guttman–Lingoes Nonmetric Program Series," in R.N. Shepard and others (eds.), *Multidimensional Scaling*, New York, Seminar Press.

——— (1973), *The Guttman–Lingoes Nonmetric Program Series*, Ann Arbor, Michigan, Mathesis Press.

LIONBERGER, HERBERT F., and others (1975), *Social Change in Communication Structure: Comparative Study of Farmers in Two Communities*, Morgantown, West Virginia University, Rural Sociological Society Monograph 3.

LITTLEJOHN, STEPHEN W. (1978), *Theories of Human Communication*, Columbus, Ohio, Merrill.

LIU, WILLIAM T., and ROBERT W. DUFF (1972), "The Strength of Weak Ties," *Public Opinion Quarterly*, 36:361–366.

LLOYD-KOLKIN, DONNA (1979), *Communication Network Analysis of an Educational Dissemination System: The Research and Development Exchange*, Ph.D. Thesis, Stanford, California, Stanford University.

LOMNITZ, LARISSA ADLER (1977), *Networks and Marginality: Life in a Mexican Shantytown*, New York, Academic Press.

LORRAIN, FRANCOIS P. (1975), *Reseaux Sociaux et Classifications Sociales*, Paris, Hermann.

———, and HARRISON C. WHITE (1971), "Structural Equivalence of Individuals in Social Networks," *Journal of Mathematical Sociology*, 1:49–80.

LUCE, R. DUNCAN, and ALBERT D. PERRY (1949), "A Method of Matrix Analysis of Group Structure," *Psychometrika*, 14:95–116.

LUNDBERG, C.C. (1975), "Patterns of Acquaintanceship in Society and Complex Organization: A Comparative Study of the Small World Problem," *Pacific Sociological Review*, 18:206–222.

MACCOBY, ELEANOR EMMONS, and CAROL NAGY JACKLIN (1974), *The Psychology of Sex Differences*, Stanford, California, Stanford University Press.

MACDONALD, DONALD (1971), *Communication Roles and Communication Contents in a Bureaucratic Setting*, Ph.D. Thesis, East Lansing, Michigan State University.

——— (1976), "Communication Roles and Communication Networks in a Formal Organization," *Human Communication Research*, 2:365–375.

MACRAE, DUNCAN, JR. (1960), "Direct Factor Analysis of Sociometric Data," *Sociometry*, 23:360–371.

MANNHEIM, KARL (1946), *Ideology and Utopia*, New York, Harcourt Brace Jovanovich.

MARCUS, ALAN S., and RAYMOND A. BAUER (1964), "Yes: There Are [sic] Generalized Opinion Leadership," *Public Opinion Quarterly*, 28:628–632.

MARSHALL, JOHN F. (1971), "Topics and Networks in Intra-Village Communication," in Steven Polgar (ed.), *Culture and Population: A Collection of Current Studies*, Chapel Hill, University of North Carolina, Carolina Population Center, Monograph 9.

——— (1972), *Culture and Contraception: Response Determinants to a Family Planning Program in a North Indian Village*, Ph.D. Thesis, Honolulu, University of Hawaii.

McCALLISTER, LYNNE, and CLAUDE S. FISCHER (1978), "A Procedure for

Surveying Personal Networks," *Sociological Methods and Research*, 7:131–148.

McKelvey, Bill, and Ralph H. Kilman (1975), "Organization Design: A Participative Multivariate Approach," *Administrative Science Quarterly*, 20:24–36.

McLaughlin, Edmund M. (1975), "The Power Network in Phoenix: An Application of Smallest-Space Analysis," *Insurgent Sociologist*, 185–195.

McLeod, Jack M., and Stephen H. Chaffee (1973), "Interpersonal Approaches to Communication Research," *American Behavioral Scientist*, 16:469–499.

McQuitty, Louis L. (1957), "Elementary Linkage Analysis for Isolating Orthogonal and Oblique Types and Typal Relevancies," *Educational and Psychological Measurement*, 28:211–238.

———, and James A. Clark (1968), "Clusters from Iterative, Intercolumnar Correlational Analysis," *Educational and Psychological Measurement*, 28:211–238.

Mead, George Herbert (1934), *Mind, Self, and Society from the Viewpoint of a Social Behaviorist*, Chicago, University of Chicago Press.

Merton, Robert K. (1968), *Social Theory and Social Structure*, New York, Free Press.

Michotte, A. (1963), *The Perceptions of Causality*, London, Methuen.

Milgram, Stanley (1967), "The Small World Problem," *Psychology Today*, 1:61–67.

——— (1969), "Inter-Disciplinary Thinking and the Small World Problem," in Muzafer Sherif and Carolyn W. Sherif (eds.), *Inter-Disciplinary Relationships in the Social Sciences*, Chicago, Aldine.

Miller, George A., and others (1960), *Plans and the Structure of Behavior*, New York, Holt, Rinehart and Winston.

———, and others (1968), "Plans and the Structure of Behavior," in Walter Buckley (ed.), *Modern Systems Research for the Behavioral Scientist*, Chicago, Aldine.

Miller, James G. (1978), *Living Systems*, New York, McGraw-Hill.

Mitchell, J. Clyde (1969), "The Concept and Use of Social Networks," in J. Clyde Mitchell (ed.), *Social Networks in Urban Situations*, Manchester, England, Manchester University Press.

——— (1974), "Social Networks," *Annual Review of Anthropology*, 3:279–299.

Moch, Michael K. (in press), *Organizational Behavior and Human Performance*.

Monod, Jacques (1971), *Chance and Necessity*, New York, Vintage.

Moreno, Jacob L. (1934), *Who Shall Survive? Foundations of Sociometry, Group Psychotherapy and Sociodrama*, Washington, D.C., Nervous and Mental Disease Monograph 58; republished in 1953, New York, Beacon House.

Morentz, James W., Jr. (1976), *The Making of an International Event: Communication and the Drought in West Africa*, Ph.D. Thesis, Philadelphia, University of Pennsylvania.

——— (1979), "Communication in the Sahelian Drought: Comparing the

Mass Media to Other Channels of Interpersonal Communication," Paper presented at the National Academy of Sciences/National Research Council Workshop on Disasters and the Mass Media, Washington, D.C.

MORETT-LOPEZ, FERNANDO J. (1979), *Communication Networks Among Marginals in a Mexican City*, Ph.D. Thesis, Stanford, California, Stanford University.

MORGAN, DAVID L., and STEVE RYTINA (1977), "Comment on 'Network Sampling: Some First Steps' by Mark Granovetter," *American Journal of Sociology*, 83:722–727.

MULLINS, NICHOLAS C., with CAROLYN J. MULLINS (1973), *Theories and Theory Groups in Contemporary American Sociology*, New York, Harper and Row.

——, and others (1977), "The Group Structures of Two Cocitation Clusters: A Comparative Study," *American Sociological Review*, 42:552–562.

NAHEMOW, LUCILLE, and M. POWELL LAWTON (1975), "Similarity and Propinquity in Friendship Formation," *Journal of Personality and Social Psychology*, 32:205–213.

NEWCOMB, THEODORE M. (1943), *Personality and Social Change: Attitude Formation in a Student Community*, New York, Holt, Rinehart, and Winston.

—— (1953), "An Approach to the Study of Communication Acts," *Psychological Review*, 60:393–404.

—— (1961), *The Acquaintance Process*, New York, Holt, Rinehart and Winston.

NIE, N.H., and others (1975), *Statistical Package for the Social Sciences*, New York, McGraw-Hill.

NOSANCHUK, TERRANCE A. (1963), "A Comparison of Several Sociometric Partitioning Techniques," *Sociometry*, 26:112–124.

OGDEN, C.K., and I.A. RICHARDS (1927), *The Meaning of Meaning*, New York, Harcout, Brace.

O'GORMAN, HUBERT J. (1975), "Pluralistic Ignorance and White Estimates of White Support for Racial Segregation," *Public Opinion Quarterly*, 39:311–330.

——, with STEPHEN L. GARRY (1976), "Pluralistic Ignorance: A Replication and Extension," *Public Opinion Quarterly*, 40:499–458.

OSGOOD, CHARLES E., and others (1957), *The Measurement of Meaning*, Urbana, University of Illinois Press.

O'SULLIVAN, JEREMIAH RYAN (1978), *The Role of Information in the Life of the Subsistence Farmer: A Study of the Guatemalan Western Central Highlands*, Ph.D. Thesis, Stanford, California, Stanford University.

PALMORE, JAMES A. (1967), "The Chicago Snowball: A Study of the Flow and Diffusion of Family Planning Information," in Donald J. Bogue (ed.), *Sociological Contributions to Family Planning Research*, Chicago, University of Chicago Press.

PARK, HYUNG JONG, and others (1974), *Mothers' Clubs and Family Planning in Korea*, Seoul, School of Public Health, Seoul National University.

——, and others (1976), "The Korean Mothers' Club Program," *Studies in Family Planning*, 7:275–283.

PARKS, MALCOLM R. (1977), "Anomia and Close Friendship Communication Networks," *Human Communication Research*, 4:48–57.

PARSONS, JOHN SANFORD (1973), *Interaction and Communication in a Philippine Barrio: A Study of Social Space and Social Distance*, Ph.D. Thesis, Honolulu, University of Hawaii.

PAYNE, ROY, and DIANA PHEYSEY (1973), "Organization Structure and Sociometric Nominations Amongst Line Managers in Three Contrasted Organizations," *European Journal of Social Psychology*, 1:261–284.

PEAY, EDMUND R. (1974), "Hierarchical Clique Structures," *Sociometry*, 37:54–65.

PERROW, CHARLES (1972), *Complex Organizations: A Critical Essay*, Glenview, Illinois, Scott, Foresman.

PITCHER, BRIAN L. and others (1978), "The Diffusion of Collective Violence," *American Sociological Review*, 43:23–35.

PITTS, FOREST R. (1979), "Bibliography: Recent Trends in Social Network Analysis," Paper presented at the Seminar on Communication Network Analysis, Honolulu, East-West Communication Institute.

POOL, ITHIEL DE SOLA (1973), "Communication Systems," in Ithiel de Sola Pool and Wilbur Schramm (eds.), *Handbook of Communication*, Chicago, Rand McNally.

——, and MANFRED KOCHEN (1978), "Contacts and Influence," *Social Networks*, 1:5–51.

Project in Structural Analysis (1977), *STRUCTURE: A Computer Program Providing Basic Data for the Analysis of Empirical Positions in a System of Actors*, Berkeley, University of California, Survey Research Center, Working Paper 5.

QUINE, W.V.O. (1960), *Word and Object*, Massachusetts, MIT Press.

RAHIM, SYED A. (1976), *Communication and Rural Development in Bangladesh*, Honolulu, East–West Communication Institute, Case Study 3.

RAPOPORT, ANATOL (1974), *Conflict in Man-Made Environment*, Middlesex, England, Penguin.

RAUM, O.F. (1969), "Self-Help Associations," *African Studies*, 28:119–141.

RICE, RON (1978a), *NEGOPY User's Manual*, Stanford, California, Stanford University, Institute for Communication Research, Report.

—— (1978b), "NEGOPY: Parameter Effects," Stanford, California, Stanford University, Institute for Communication Research, Paper.

—— (1979), "Parameter Sensitivity of the NEGOPY Network Analysis Computer Program," Paper presented at the International Communication Association, Philadelphia.

RICHARDS, WILLIAM D., JR. (1971), "An Improved Conceptually-Based Method for Analysis of Communication Structures of Large Complex Organizations," Paper presented at the International Communication Association, Phoenix.

—— (1974), "Network Analysis in Large Complex Systems: The Nature of Structure," Paper presented at the International Communication Association.

—— (1975), *A Manual for Network Analysis (Using the NEGOPY Analysis*

Program), Stanford, California, Stanford University, Institute for Communication Research, Mimeo Report.

—— (1976), *A Coherent Systems Methodology for the Analysis of Human Communication Systems,* Ph.D. Thesis, Stanford, California, Stanford University.

—— (1977), "Network Analysis Methods: Conceptual and Operational Approaches," Paper presented at the Fourth Annual Colloquium on Social Networks, Honolulu, University of Hawaii.

—— (1979), "Measurement Problems in Network Analysis: Reciprocity and Directed Relationships," Paper presented at the International Communication Association, Philadelphia.

ROBERTS, KARLENE H., and CHARLES A. O'REILLY III (1978a), "Some Correlates of Communication Roles in Organizations," *Academy of Management Journal.*

——, and —— (1978b), "Organizations as Communication Structures: An Empirical Approach," *Human Communication Research,* 4:283–293.

ROBINSON, W.S. (1950), "Ecological Correlation and the Behavior of Individuals," *American Sociological Review,* 15:351–357.

ROGERS, EVERETT M. (1962), *Diffusion of Innovations,* New York, Free Press.

—— (1973), *Communication Strategies for Family Planning,* New York, Free Press.

—— (1975), "Network Analysis of the Diffusion of Innovations," Paper presented at the Mathematical Social Science Board's Research Symposium on Social Networks, Hanover, New Hampshire; and published in Paul W. Holland and Samuel Leinhardt (eds.) (1979), *Social Networks: Surveys and Advances,* New York, Academic Press.

—— (1976a), "Where Are We in Understanding the Diffusion of Innovations?" in Wilbur Schramm and Daniel Lerner (eds.), *Communication and Change: The Last Ten Years—And the Next,* Honolulu, University Press of Hawaii.

—— (1976b), "Communication and Development: The Passing of the Dominant Paradigm," *Communication Research,* 3:121–133.

—— (1976c), "Network Analysis of the Diffusion of Innovations in Two Korean Villages," in Godwin Chu and others (eds.), *Communication for Group Transformation in Development,* Honolulu, East–West Communication Institute, Communication Monograph 2.

—— (1977), "Network Analysis of the Diffusion of Innovations: Family Planning in Korean Villages," in Daniel Lerner and Lyle M. Nelson (eds.), *Communication Research: A Half-Century Appraisal,* Honolulu, University Press of Hawaii.

—— (1979), "Network Analysis of the Diffusion of Innovations," in Paul W. Holland and Samuel Leinhardt (eds.), *Social Networks: Surveys and Advances,* New York, Academic Press.

——, and REKHA AGARWALA-ROGERS (1976a), *Communication in Organizations,* New York, Free Press.

——, and —— (1976b), *Evaluation Research on Family Planning Communication,* Paris, UNESCO, Technical Report.

——, and DILIP K. BHOWMIK (1971), "Homophily–Heterophily: Relational

Concepts for Communication Research," *Public Opinion Quarterly*, 34:523–538.

——, and Pi-Chao Chen (1979), "Diffusion of Health and Birth Planning Innovations in the People's Republic of China," in George I. Lythscott and others (eds.), *Report of the Chinese Rural Health Systems Delegation*, Washington, D.C., National Academy of Sciences, Committee on Scholarly Communication with the People's Republic of China, Report.

——, with F. Floyd Shoemaker (1971), *Communication of Innovations: A Cross-Cultural Approach*, New York, Free Press.

——, and Rahul Sood (1979), "Mass Media Communication and Disasters: A Content Analysis of Media Coverage of the Andhra Pradesh Cyclone and the Sahel Drought," Paper presented at the National Academy of Sciences/National Research Council Workshop on Disasters and the Mass Media, Washington, D.C.

——, and others (1976a), "Network Analysis of the Diffusion of Family Planning Innovations Over Time in Korean Villages: The Role of Mothers' Clubs," in Godwin C. Chu and others (eds.), *Communication for Group Transformation in Development*, Honolulu, East–West Communication Institute, Communication Monograph 2.

——, and others (1976b), *Extending the Agricultural Extension Model*, Stanford, California, Stanford University, Institute for Communication Research, Report.

Roistacher, Richard C. (1974), "A Review of Mathematical Methods in Sociometry," *Sociological Methods and Research*, 3:123–171.

Rosengren, Karl Erik (1975), "Ordered Pairs of Arcs and Demiarcs," *Journal of Mathematical Sociology*, 4:149–155.

Ross, Mark Howard, and Thomas S. Weisner (1977), "The Rural–Urban Migrant Network in Kenya," *American Ethnologist*, 4:359–375.

Ryan, Bryce, and Neal C. Gross (1943), "The Diffusion of Hybrid Seed Corn in Two Iowa Communities," *Rural Sociology*, 8:15–24.

Sailer, Lee Douglas (1978), "Structural Equivalence: Meaning and Definition, Computation and Application," *Social Networks*, 1:73–90.

Sapir, Edward (1935), "Communication," in *Encyclopedia of the Social Sciences*, New York, Macmillan.

Sarason, Seymour B., and others (1977), *Human Services and Resource Networks*, San Francisco, Jossey-Bass.

Saxena, Anant P. (1968), *System Effects on Innovativeness Among Indian Farmers*, Ph.D. Thesis, East Lansing, Michigan State University.

Schön, Donald A. (1971), *Beyond the Stable State*, New York, Random House.

—— (1977), "Network-Related Intervention," Washington, D.C., National Institute of Education, School Capacity for Problem-Solving Group, Unpublished paper.

Schramm, Wilbur (1955a), *Process and Effects of Mass Communication*, Urbana, University of Illinois Press.

—— (1955b), "Information Theory and Mass Communication," *Journalism Quarterly*, 32:131–146.

—— (1971), "The Nature of Communication Between Humans," in Wilbur

Schramm and Donald F. Roberts (eds.), *The Process and Effects of Mass Communication*, Urbana, University of Illinois Press.

—— (1973), *Men, Messages, and Media: A Look at Human Communication*, New York, Harper and Row.

SCHWARTZ, DONALD F. (1968), *Liaison Communication Roles in a Formal Organization*, Ph.D. Thesis, East Lansing, Michigan State University.

——, and EUGENE JACOBSON (1977), "Organizational Communication Network Analysis: The Liaison Communication Role," *Organizational Behavior and Human Performance*, 18:158–174.

SCHWARTZ, JOSEPH E. (1977), "An Examination of CONCOR and Related Methods for Blocking Sociometric Data," in David R. Heise (ed.), *Sociological Methodology, 1977*, San Francisco, Jossey-Bass.

SHANNON, CLAUDE E., and WARREN WEAVER (1949), *The Mathematical Theory of Communication*, Urbana, University of Illinois Press.

SHAPIRO, BEN ZION (1978), "Friends and Helpers: When Ties Dissolve," *Connections*, 1:53–54.

SHAW, M.E. (1964), "Communication Networks," in Leonard Berkowitz (ed.), *Advances in Experimental Psychology*, New York, Academic Press.

SHEINGOLD, CARL A. (1973), "Social Networks and Voting: The Resurrection of a Research Agenda," *American Sociological Review*, 38:712–720.

SHEPARD, R.N. (1962a), "The Analysis of Proximities: Multidimensional Scaling with an Unknown Distance Function, Part One," *Psychometrika*, 27:125–140.

—— (1962b), "The Analysis of Proximities: Multidimensional Scaling with an Unknown Distance Function, Part Two," *Psychometrika*, 27:219–246.

SHOEMAKER, F. FLOYD (1971), *System Variables and Educational Innovativeness in Thai Government Secondary Schools*, Ph.D. Thesis, East Lansing, Michigan State University.

SHOTLAND, R. LANCE (1976), *University Communication Networks: The Small World Method*, New York, Wiley.

SHULMAN, NORMAN (1976), "Network Analysis: A New Edition to an Old Bag of Tricks," *Acta Sociologica*, 19:307–323.

SIEBER, SAM D. (1973), "The Integration of Field Work and Survey Methods," *American Journal of Sociology*, 78:1335–1359.

SIGNORILE, VITO, and ROBERT M. O'SHEA (1965), "A Test of Significance for the Homophily Index," *American Journal of Sociology*, 70:467–470.

SIMMEL, GEORG (1964), *The Web of Group-Affiliations*, translated by Reinhard Bendix, New York, Free Press.

SMITH, DAVID H. (1972), "Communication Research and the Idea of Process," *Speech Monographs*, 39:174–182.

SMITH, RICHARD T. (1977), "Disability and the Recovery Process: Role of Social Networks," Paper presented at the American Sociological Association, Chicago.

SNYDER, D., and E. L. KICK (1979), "Structural Position in the World System and Economic Growth, 1955–1970: A Multiple Network Analysis of Transnational Interactions," *American Journal of Sociology*, 84:1096–1126.

SONQUIST J., and T. KOENIG (1975), "Interlocking Directorates in the Top U.S. Corporations: A Graph Theory Approach," *Insurgent Sociologist*, 5:196–229.

SPECK, ROSS V., and C.L. ATTNEAVE (1973), *Family Networks*, New York, Pantheon.

———, and URI RUEVENI (1969), "Network Therapy: A Developing Concept," *Family Process*, 8:182–191.

SPILERMAN, SEYMOUR (1966), "Structural Analysis and the Generation of Sociograms," *Behavioral Science*, 11:312–318.

SROLE, LEO (1956), "Social Integration and Certain Corollaries: An Exploratory Study," *American Sociological Review*, 21:706–716.

STERN, LOUIS W., and others (1976), "The Effect of Sociometric Location on the Adoption of an Innovation Within a University Faculty," *Sociology of Education*, 49:90–96.

STERN, ROBERT N. (1979), "The Development of an Interorganizational Control Network: The Case of Intercollegiate Athletics," *Administrative Science Quarterly*, 24:242–266.

STOKMAN, F.N. (1977), *Third World Group Formation in the United Nations: A Methodological Analysis*, Amsterdam, University of Amsterdam Press.

STONEHAM, A.K.M. (1977), "The Small World Problem in a Spatial Context," *Environment and Planning*, 9:185–195.

STOUFFER, SAMUEL A. (1940), "Intervening Opportunities: A Theory Relating Mobility and Distance," *American Sociological Review*, 5:845–867.

SWINEHART, JAMES W. (1968), "Voluntary Exposure to Health Communications," *American Journal of Public Health*, 58:1265–1275.

TERWILLIGER, ROBERT F. (1968), *Meaning and Mind*, New York, Oxford University Press.

THEIL, HENRI (1971), *Principles of Econometrics*, New York, Wiley.

TICHY, NOEL M., and CHARLES FROMBRUN (1978), *Network Analysis in Organizational Settings*, Research Paper 102A, New York, Columbia University, Graduate School of Business.

———, and others (1978), "A Network Approach to Organizational Assessment," in Edward Lawler and others (eds.), *Organizational Assessment: Perspectives on the Measurement of Organizational Behavior and the Quality of Working Life*, New York, Wiley-Interscience.

TINKER, JOHN N. (1977), "Social Mobility and Social Isolation: Tracing the Web of Friendship," Paper presented at the American Sociological Association, Chicago.

TOULMIN, STEPHEN (1972), *Human Understanding*, Princeton, New Jersey, Princeton University Press.

TRAVERS, JEFFREY, and STANLEY MILGRAM (1969), "An Experimental Study of the Small World Problem," *Sociometry*, 32:425–443.

TUSHMAN, MICHAEL (1977), "Special Boundary Roles in the Innovation Process," *Administrative Science Quarterly*, 22:587–605.

VALLEE, JACQUES, and others (1975), *Group Communication Through Computers: Pragmatics and Dynamics*, Menlo Park, California, Institute for the Future, Report R-35.

VANCE, STANLEY C. (1968), *The Corporate Director*, Homewood, Illinois, Dow Jones–Irwin.

VERBRUGGE, LOIS M. (1977), "The Structure of Adult Friendship Choices," *Social Forces*, 56:577–597.

WATZLAWICK, PAUL, and others (1967), *Pragmatics of Human Communica-*

tion: A Study of Interaction Patterns, Pathologies, and Paradoxes, New York, Norton.

WEBB, EUGENE J., and others (1966), Unobtrusive Measures: Nonreactive Research in the Social Sciences, Chicago, Rand McNally.

WEINER, NORBERT (1948), Cyberntics or Control and Communication in the Animal and the Machine, New York, MIT Press and Wiley.

WEISS, ROBERT S. (1956), Processes of Organization, Ann Arbor, University of Michigan, Institute for Social Research, Report.

———, and EUGENE JACOBSON (1955), "A Method for the Analysis of the Structure of Complex Organizations," American Sociological Review, 20:661–668.

WESTLY, BRUCE, and MALCOLM MacLEAN (1957), "A Conceptual Model for Communication Research," Journalism Quarterly, 34:31–38.

WHITE, HARRISON C. (1970), "Search Parameters for the Small World Problems," Social Forces, 49:259–264.

——— (1974), "Models for Interrelated Roles from Multiple Networks in Small Populations," in P.K. Knopp and G.H. Meyer (eds.), Proceedings of the Conference on the Application of Undergraduate Mathematics in the Engineering, Life, Managerial, and Social Sciences, Atlanta, Georgia, Institute of Technology.

——— (1977), "Probabilities of Homorphic Mappings from Multiple Graphs," Journal of Mathematical Psychology, 16:121–134.

———, and RONALD L. BREIGER (1975), "Patterns Across Networks," Society, 12:68–73.

———, and others (1976), "Social Structure from Multiple Networks: I. Blockmodels of Roles and Positions," American Journal of Sociology, 81:730–780.

WHITTEN, N.E., JR., and A.W. WOLFE (1974), "Network Analysis," in J.J. Honigmann (ed.), Handbook of Social and Cultural Anthropology, Chicago, Rand McNally.

WHYTE, WILLIAM F. (1943), Street Corner Society: The Social Structure of an Italian Slum, Chicago, University of Chicago Press.

WIGAND, ROLF T. (1976), "Communication and Interorganizational Relationships Among Complex Organizations in Social Service Settings," Paper presented at the International Communication Association, Portland.

——— (1977), "Some Recent Developments in Organizational Communication: Network Analysis: A Systemic Representation of Communication Relationships," Communications: International Journal of Communication Research, 181–200.

WILDER, CAROL (1979), "The Palo Alto Group: Difficulties and Directions of the Interactional View for Human Communication Research," Human Communication Research, 5:171–186.

WITTGENSTEIN, LUDWIG (1958), Philosophical Investigations, translated by G.E.M. Anscombe, Oxford, England, Blackwell.

WOELFEL, JOSEPH D., and JEFFREY E. DANES (1980), "Multidimensional Scaling Models for Communication Research," in Joseph Capella and Peter Monge (eds.), Multivariate Techniques in Communication Research, New York, Academic Press.

WOLFE, ALVIN W. (1978), "The Rise of Network Thinking in Anthropology," *Social Networks*, 1:53–64.

WRIGHT, BENJAMIN, and MARY SUE EVITTS (1961), "Direct Factor Analysis in Sociometry," *Sociometry*, 24:82–98.

YADAV, DHARAM P. (1967), *Communication Structure and Innovation Diffusion in Two Indian Villages*, Ph.D. Thesis, East Lansing, Michigan State University.

YUM, JUNE OCK, and D. LAWRENCE KINCAID (1979), "Social Networks of Korean Immigrants in Hawaii," Paper presented at the Seminar on Communication Network Analysis, Honolulu, East-West Communication Institute.

ZALTMAN, GERALD, and others (1973), *Innovations and Organizations*, New York, Wiley-Interscience.

ZIPF, GEORGE K. (1949), *Human Behavior and the Principle of Least Effort*, Cambridge, Massachusetts, Addison-Wesley.

ZUKERMAN, HARRIET (1977), *Scientific Elite: Nobel Laureates in the United States*, New York, Free Press.

AUTHOR INDEX

SUBJECT INDEX

Action, 53–57
Agenda-setting, 58–60, 73–74
Aggregate variable, 240, 257–58
Agreement, 55–56, 76
Algorithm, 145, 217
  definition, 145
Approximation, 49, 51, 64
Aristotle, 32
Atomistic approaches, 36–37, 43, 46–47
Attitude, 34, 76, 132, 231, 252
  change, 36, 258
Average clique connectedness, 139, 176,
    180–82, 183t, 207, 210
  definition, 139, 142, 218, 346
Average system connectedness, 175–76,
    182, 184t, 206, 270, 335
  definition, 140, 175, 219, 346

Balance, 131–33
Belief, 53–56
Biases of communication theory, 38–39,
    77
Blockmodeling, 156, 190–93, 202–211,
    213–15, 331
  definition, 202, 219, 346
Bridge, 29, 83, 96, 125, 130, 146, 168,
    172–73, 180, 189, 210, 213, 243,
    248, 332
  definition, 29n, 83n, 346

Cadres, 86, 251
CATIJ, 190, 194
Centrality, 178
  definition, 178n
Choi, Yang Soon, 9–10, 12, 264–65
Chung, Moon Ja, 4–6, 12–30, 178, 259,
    303–304
Clique, 29, 66, 70, 83–84, 92, 96, 99,
    110–12, 118, 124, 130, 132, 145,
    159, 177, 180, 212–14, 237–40, 243,
    303, 320, 332
  connectedness, 139
  definition, 83n, 138, 142, 160, 168,
    177, 218, 346

identification, 162–77, 185–215
structure, 93, 240
as unit of analysis, 138–39, 142, 180–
    82, 327–28
CLIQUE, 211
Clique connectedness, 180–82, 183t, 218,
    238, 304
  definition, 346
Clique diversity, 180–82, 183t, 218, 316
  definition, 346
Clique integration, 180–82, 184t, 218,
    230
  definition, 346
Clique openness, 180–82, 184t, 218
  definition, 346
Clique size, 142
Collective action, 27, 31, 35t, 39, 53, 55–
    56, 73, 250–51, 258, 283, 288–89
Collective decision making, 15–16
Communication
  act, 31, 33–35, 45
  behavior, 39, 75, 93, 111
  as convergence, 43–77
  definitions, 32, 35, 43, 63–64, 78, 346
  dyadic, 132–33, 142, 310
  as exchange, 37
  family planning, 133, 322–23
  horizontal, 337–42
  links, 91n, 96–97, 99n, 101, 127, 132–
    33, 141, 226, 230
  models, 32–38, 43–48, 49n, 238
  one-way, 31, 33, 37–39, 62
  organizational, 96, 117, 147, 162, 202
  process, 33f, 34, 37, 328
  purpose, 57, 63
  roles, 125, 138, 145–46, 159, 190, 215–
    16, 219, 235
  taboo, 133, 322
  as transaction, 37–38
  two-way, 38, 62, 68
  vertical, 38–39
Communication effects, 33–34, 37, 42,
    60n, 72–73, 75
  mass media, 74
  psychological, 39